UNLOCKING
LEGAL
LEARNING

3rd editio ... **urner**
emp

HODDER
EDUCATION
AN HACHETTE UK COMPANY

UNLOCKING THE LAW

Orders: please contact Bookpoint Ltd, 130 Milton Park, Abingdon, Oxon OX14 4SB.
Telephone: (44) 01235 827720. Fax: (44) 01235 400454. Lines are open from 9.00 - 5.00,
Monday to Saturday, with a 24 hour message answering service. You can also order through
our website www.hoddereducation.co.uk

If you have any comments to make about this, or any of our other titles, please send them to
educationenquiries@hodder.co.uk

British Library Cataloguing in Publication Data
A catalogue record for this title is available from the British Library

ISBN: 978 1 444 16786 3

First Edition Published 2005
Second Edition Published 2008
This Edition Published 2012
Impression number   10 9 8 7 6 5 4 3 2
Year   2015 2014 2013 2012

Hachette Livre UK's policy is to use papers that are natural, renewable and
recyclable products and made from wood grown in sustainable forests.
The logging and manufacturing processes are expected to conform to the
environmental regulations of the country of origin.

Cover photo © Lachlon Currip/iStockphoto
Typeset by Datapage India Pvt Ltd
Printed in Italy for Hodder Education, an Hachette UK Company,
338 Euston Road, London NW1 3BH

Contents

11 PREPARING FOR EXAMINATIONS – REVISION

12 SITTING EXAMINATIONS

v

CONTENTS

Guide to the book and website

In the Unlocking the Law books all the essential elements that make up the law are clearly defined to bring the law alive and make it memorable. In addition, the books are enhanced with learning features to reinforce learning and test your knowledge as you study. Follow this guide to make sure you get the most from reading this book.

AIMS AND OBJECTIVES

Define what you will learn in each chapter

definition
Find key legal terminology at-a-glance.

QUOTATION

Primary sources and examples to help you with legal learning.

ACTIVITY

Enables you to test yourself as you progress through the chapter.

tutor tip
Provides key ideas on how to get ahead from lecturers.

SUMMARY

Concludes each chapter to reinforce learning.

student mentor tip
Offers advice from law graduates on the best way to achieve the results you want.

Please note that some cases in this book are fictional and are provided as examples for you to learn from.

Acknowledgements

The authors would like to thank Angela Donaldson, Liaison Librarian for Law at Nottingham Trent University, for her help and enthusiasm. In particular, we would like to thank her for her hard work on Chapters 4 and 5 of this book. We hope the readers find the chapters as clear and informative as we do.

Every effort has been made to trace the copyright holders for material reproduced in this book. Copyright illustrations are: © Justis Publishing Limited for Figures 5.6, 5.12 and 5.20; © Sweet & Maxwell Ltd for Figures 5.1, 5.2, 5.4, 5.5, 5.8, 5.10, 5.11, 5.13, 5.15, 5.16, 5.17, 5.18, 5.19, 5.21, 5.27, 5.28, 5.31, 5.32, 5.33, 5.39; Figures 5.3, 5.9, 5.14, 5.22, 5.25, 5.26, 5.34, 5.35, 5.36, 5.38 reproduced by permission of Reed Elsevier (UK) Limited trading as LexisNexis Butterworths. The authors and publishers would like to thank the copyright holders who have granted permission to reproduce their material.

Parliamentary copyright material is reproduced with the permission of the Controller of Her Majesty's Stationary Office on behalf of Parliament.

The publishers apologise if inadvertently any sources remain unacknowledged and will be glad to make the necessary arrangements at the earliest opportunity.

Preface

The 'Unlocking' series is designed to make learning each subject area more accessible by focusing on learning needs, and by providing a range of different supporting materials and features.

All topic areas are broken up into 'bite size' sections with a logical progression and extensive use of headings and numerous sub-headings. Each book in the series also contains a variety of charts, diagrams and key fact summaries to reinforce the information in the body of the text. Diagrams and flow charts are particularly useful because they can provide a quick and easy understanding of the key points, especially when revising for examinations. Key facts charts not only provide a quick visual guide through the subject but are useful for revision purposes also.

The books also include much formative 'self-testing', with a variety of activities including subject specific comprehension and application of the law amongst others to help the student gain a good idea of his or her progress in the course.

This book is unlike the other titles in the 'Unlocking' series because it is not on a specific area of law. It is also probably unlike other books that you might see: it is not like a standard 'Legal Skills' book and nor is it like the usual 'Introduction to Law' type books. In fact, in some ways it might be called 'Everything that you wanted to know about a law degree but were afraid to ask'. The authors are experienced teachers and examiners with many years of experience of both between them. We have created courses and exams and developed skills programmes. Importantly each author is also very student focused and has listened to students over many years and learnt about the problems that they face when taking law courses.

The purpose of the book is to give you a taste not just of the new things that you will have to learn on a law degree or similar course involving law, but also of the kind of difficulties that you may encounter in a study of law. We hope it will give you some insight and some encouragement as you embark on your law degree or similar course. There is no reason why you should not return to it whenever you feel unsure about a particular aspect of your study.

Changes have been made from the second edition, including updating out-of-date law. Summaries and key facts charts have been added where appropriate. Sample essay and problem questions with tips on how to structure answers are included in Chapter 7. Student and tutor mentoring tips have been added as well as a glossary of terms at the end of the book. Colour coding of key features has also been added to match the series style. Chapters 7 and 8 have been completely reorganised to avoid duplication, with problem solving moving to become Chapter 7.2 and Chapter 8 now dealing with common skills appropriate to all forms of assessment. A new Chapter 7.3 on oral presentation has also been added, as well as extensive development of Chapter 10 on mooting. There is a new section on identifying key points in secondary sources in Chapter 3 and there are many new activities throughout the book.

Overall we hope that the book is now much more comprehensive in both its coverage and its features and that it is much easier to navigate for the reader. We hope finally that after reading it you will find your study of the law more relaxed, more informed and even more stimulating.

Jo Boylan-Kemp and Chris Turner

1

What Learning Law is All About

AIMS AND OBJECTIVES

After reading this chapter you should be able to:

- Understand the basic definition and character and purpose of law
- Understand the specific character of the English legal system
- Understand the various classifications of law within the English legal system
- Understand the basic sources of the law in England and Wales
- Use accepted legal terminology
- Research aspects of law by using a legal dictionary

1.1 The character and purpose of law

What do you think 'law' means? A very important legal skill is being able to define concepts and topics. To start with, you may wish to write down as many different examples or types of law that you can. Then reflect on that list and see if you can come up with a definition of 'law'.

The term 'law' is very difficult to define because it is used to mean different things in different contexts. A comprehensive definition is therefore hard to provide as it would have to be very wide.

The majority of people use the term 'law' to describe the criminal law. This may be because of the media coverage given to crimes, such as assault, murder, 'joyriding' etc. Some people use the word 'law' to describe the institutions of the legal system, such as the courts, the police, prisons and so on. Other people associate it with the rules regulating our relationships with others. Every time we purchase goods or pay for a service (like a haircut) we are entering a contract and contracts are regulated by the law. Other people would think of the processes of law, its rules and procedures, such as the steps that have to be followed when beginning a legal action under the well-advertised 'no win; no fee' schemes. Alternatively, the word law may be used to describe the rules laid down by Parliament and/or the courts that govern our behaviour and thus refers to the sources of the law.

So, which of these options, in your opinion, is right?

In fact, none of the above can be said to be 'right' to the exclusion of the others. The better way of phrasing the answer would be to say that none of them is wrong.

Consult a good English dictionary, such as *The Concise Oxford Dictionary*, and notice the numerous different ways in which the word 'law' can be defined. You may find that your understanding of these definitions changes as your knowledge increases. Clearly the word alone can have very broad meanings, which will be seen by looking for the definition of law in any dictionary. Even in a dictionary as small as the *Collins English Gem Dictionary* we found the following:

QUOTATION

'*Law.* noun. Rule binding on community; system of these rules; legal science; knowledge, administration of it; general principle deduced from facts; invariable sequence of events in nature.'

Clearly there is quite a lot of scope within these definitions and there is obviously more than a single definition included here. One definition we like because it seems to identify all of the key elements of any type of law is in the *Shorter Oxford English Dictionary*:

QUOTATION

'Any body of rules which is organised and structured and relates to a particular code of conduct.'

From this activity you will probably have realised that the word 'law' can be understood in many different ways, including those outlined above, but is very often defined in terms of rules. You are probably aware of many rules which people observe in their daily lives which regulate the way that they behave and yet these are not necessarily referred to as law. Many people also live according to moral rules and abide by religious codes and yet these are not laws either. So when is a rule regarded as part of the law? Rules are regarded as law when they originate from one of the recognised law-making institutions which you will learn about shortly. But that is not the whole story, for where does the system of law and its processes fit into the picture?

One way of defining the law so as to take account of all three aspects mentioned above, i.e. the rules of law, the legal system and its processes, is to say that law is a body of the rules of conduct formally recognised as binding or enforced by a controlling body. This definition is useful as a brief and simple way of explaining the concept of law. We could, however, say that the law is simply a way of regulating behaviour; it tells us what must be done, what may be done and what cannot be done.

ACTIVITY

Quick quiz

From your reading so far and from your general knowledge, which of the following statements are true and which are false?

- There is no difference between moral rules and legal rules.
- Procedural rules, for example how to begin a breach of contract action in court, are not part of law.
- The concept of law is not the same as the concept of justice.
- Law is an instrument of social control.

These questions should have given you some food for thought! You will probably have realised that although many of the rules which we regard as laws are based on moral codes (for example, people must not commit murder), not every moral rule is part of the law of this country. For example, envy, though forbidden by moral codes, is not forbidden by law. Therefore the first statement in the exercise above is false, as law and morality are not the same, although they may overlap.

There is a great deal more to law than this, however, and you will probably realise by now that the law also comprises many procedural rules which must be followed in order for legal issues to be dealt with by the courts. The second statement in the question above is therefore false, as these procedural rules are also part of the law.

When legal issues are considered by the courts, or when Parliament creates law, one of the aims of those involved in the process is to do justice between people who are affected by the law. Sadly, we know that this aim is not always achieved and therefore it has to be said that law and justice do not always coincide, so the third statement above is true.

The criminal law (as can be seen in Figure 1.2 on page 7) determines what behaviour is unacceptable and warrants punishment. Civil law (which again can be seen from Figure 1.2) regulates behaviour and allows individuals to make enforceable agreements or to gain compensation for wrongs caused by others. So it is true to say that law is an instrument of social control.

You should by now have a good idea of what law is and what it is not and you should also have a good working definition of the law, a suggestion of which appears in the final statement in the exercise above. This statement is true. You might wish to reflect on the following definition given by Glanville Williams in his book *Learning the Law*:

QUOTATION

'law is the cement of society and an essential medium of change'.

12th edn, London: Sweet and Maxwell, 2002, p 2.

1.1.1 Lawyers' definition of law

When we begin to study 'the law' on a law degree or other law course we need a specific definition because we are talking about law in a very specific context. Legal philosophers would say that 'the law' is quite hard to define because again it has so many aspects and must be used in so many different contexts.

A clear and straightforward one is provided by Sir John Salmond in his book *Jurisprudence*:

QUOTATION

'... the body of principles recognised and applied by the courts in the administration of justice.'

He even goes on to explain what he means:

QUOTATION

'In other words the law consists of the rules recognised and acted on by the courts of justice.'

So, when we study 'the law' we are not talking merely about any body of rules that has some type of organisation and some type of structure. Hopefully, the law is both organised and structured but what we are specifically looking for is law that can be enforced in a system of courts.

1.1.2 The character of a legal system

There are many different legal systems in the world. In the UK we obviously study the English legal system, although it is possible, usually as an elective module or option, to study comparative law or sometimes even to do degrees in the law of other jurisdictions such as American law or French law.

Whatever legal system we study there are common characteristics. Understanding what all legal systems share as common characteristics goes a long way towards helping us understand what it is we are studying and in recognising what may be expected from a particular branch of the law.

Professor Hart in *The Concept of Law* identifies five things which he suggests that all legal systems must include:

1. Rules forbidding certain behaviour on forfeit of some form of penalty or sanction for non-compliance (we would recognise this in English law as the criminal law).
2. Rules that make people compensate other people that they have wronged for the damage caused by the wrong (in English law we would refer to this as civil liability or often, in very specific circumstances, as the law of torts).
3. Rules that regulate the conduct of and that enforce agreements, arrangements and relationships between individuals (these could be contracts or wills or even involve the rights and duties within a marriage – and in a more modern context it could involve the regulation of businesses – so we could see these as contract law, the law of succession and company law respectively).
4. There must be a system of courts in which to enforce all of the above rights and obligations.
5. There must also be a legislature of some form to make new laws to fit new situations and also to get rid of or repeal outdated laws (in the UK this role is carried out by Parliament).

Hart called this body of rules to regulate conduct the 'primary rules'. He also recognised that on their own these rules are insufficient for a system of law to work effectively. There must also be 'secondary rules':

1. **Rules of recognition** – we have identified a number of separate branches of law above; crime, tort, contract, succession, matrimonial, company – each individual body of rules must have a character allowing it to be distinguished from any other body of rules.
2. **Rules of change** – we have recognised the need above for Parliament to change the law to be relevant but there must, therefore, be superior systems of conduct which will authorise alteration of the rules to accommodate social and economic changes in society but which themselves operate according to law.
3. **Rules of adjudication** – the courts are identified as the place where disputes are heard but they also must have rules regulating the methods by which those disputes are resolved, otherwise the law would be administered in an arbitrary way and may be seen as unfair.

These 'secondary rules' are equally essential and the presence of both types of rules is what separates a legal system from a more primitive code of behaviour or indeed from a dictatorship.

1.1.3 The character of the English legal system

There appear to be two main types of legal system. One is based on what we sometimes refer to as 'Roman law'. The other system, the one that we are used to in the UK, is known as a 'common law' system. The English legal system is the most well-known common law system and many other countries have followed it.

Roman law developed during the era of the Roman Empire and the many conquests made during that period. Because of the extent of the empire this type of law influenced a wide area that came under Roman rule. Examples would be found throughout western and southern Europe and indeed in North Africa. Interestingly, Britain was also under Roman rule for many centuries but still developed its own very particular type of legal system at a later stage.

The common law of England is usually traced back to the Norman Conquest and King William I. However, much of the law that developed during that period can also be traced back into Saxon society. The significant difference was that, even though the Norman and Angevin kings adopted much of the existing local law and custom following the conquest, the nature of their rule meant that it became the law that was 'common' to the whole of Britain. Previously the country was made up of many separate kingdoms and so local laws might differ. Because Britain was over a number of centuries a colonial power and there was a British Empire, the common law of England was also the law that was used in the various countries of the Empire during British rule. As a result, following independence, many of these countries have retained a common law system. These are identifiable today as the Commonwealth countries, such as Australia, Canada, India, and many African or Caribbean countries. It also includes the USA.

The basic difference between Roman and common law legal systems can be identified as follows:

- Roman law is codified:
  - codes tend to be written in very broad terms and it is then the role of the judges to interpret these broad terms in specific situations
  - many modern countries have adopted a codified law following changes to their constitutions, for instance following a revolution as in France.
- English common law, on the other hand, has developed over a long period of time:
  - it is at least in part based on precedents that emerge from an accumulation of case decisions and so the law is based on real situations and has been built up principle by principle
  - in more recent times parliamentary law, through Acts and delegated legislation, has become more important.
- The English common law is said to have had an uninterrupted and continuous growth from the time of the Norman Conquest in the eleventh century.
- Some codified systems, on the other hand, are relatively recent – France, for instance, had a revolution as recently as 1789 and French law developed from that point.
- The English legal system is preoccupied with rules of procedure. In other systems the broad spirit of the law may be more important.
- The English legal system depends mainly on an adversarial resolution of disputes:
  - this means that most law is settled in a form of contest between two parties claiming different or competing rights
  - this is true of criminal law and in most instances it is also true of civil law, although there are processes such as arbitration, conciliation and mediation now available.
- Continental systems of law, however, are sometimes more inquisitorial in character.
  - instead of the judge acting as a sort of referee between the parties in dispute he will intervene and ask his own questions and will often try to find a compromise position.
- Not all legal continental legal systems operate in the same way. The German system, for instance, is more adversarial and more like the UK system than those in France and Italy.

1.2 The various classifications of law

In order to study the law in more detail you need to be able to appreciate how it can be broken up into a number of different component parts. One method of dividing the law into different categories is to classify it as substantive law or as adjectival law.

Substantive law is the term which is used to refer to the rules which govern our rights and duties under the law, for example the cases and statutes which create criminal offences, or the cases and statutes which define contractual obligations. Adjectival law prescribes how those substantive rules can be used within the legal system, for example the rules of evidence, procedure and costs which are to be observed when bringing a case to court.

For example, the Civil Procedure Rules 1998 contain the detailed procedural steps and guidance on commencing civil proceedings (e.g. suing another party). This should therefore be classified as adjectival law. By contrast, by way of another example, s 4 of the Bail Act 1976 describes the rights and duties of those involved in criminal proceedings and this is therefore substantive law.

An alternative way of classifying the law is by reference to its subject matter. From the point of view of lawyers and those involved in the legal system, this is the most useful way of dividing the law into categories.

The broadest distinction which can be drawn is between international law and domestic law. International law is concerned with the external relationships between different States and is based on treaties and conventions. A good example here is the Treaty on European Union (also known as the Maastricht Treaty). Domestic law comprises the laws of a particular State, that is, the cases or statute law which govern relationships within that country, and can be divided into public law and private law.

Public law cases are those cases in which one of the parties to the dispute is the Crown, usually acting through a government department. Public law can be further sub-divided into the areas of criminal law and civil law.

Criminal law is concerned with conduct of which society disapproves so strongly that the State must punish the wrongdoer, for example murder, theft and driving offences. The major objective of criminal proceedings is to punish the perpetrator of the crime, not to compensate the victim. The Crown Prosecution Service, acting on behalf of the Crown, prosecutes the accused, who will be found guilty of the offence charged if the prosecutor can convince the court beyond reasonable doubt that the accused did commit that offence. Public civil law cases, by contrast, are concerned with problems in constitutional and administrative law. For example, these cases may challenge the legality of actions carried out by central or local government, or may bring test cases on individual freedoms which have been infringed by the government, such as telephone tapping.

As mentioned above, the other branch of domestic law is private law. This involves civil law and is concerned with the rights and duties which private individuals have in relation to each other. There are many different categories of civil law, for example the law of contract, the law of torts (wrongs such as negligence or slander) and the law of property. The major objective of an action which involves private civil law is to compensate the person who has suffered the wrong, usually by payment of money (damages). A civil action is commenced by the victim, that is, the claimant, who sues the defendant in order to obtain a remedy. The claimant must prove his or her case on a balance of probabilities, in other words it must be more likely than not that the defendant harmed the claimant in the manner alleged.

The following diagram illustrates the basic classifications of English law.

Substantive law	and	Adjectival law
This term refers to the actual areas of law and represents different groups of rights and obligations as we have seen above – so it could refer to contract law, tort, matrimonial law, succession, company law, property law etc.		This term refers to the rules of evidence and procedure – these determine how the case is conducted – in English law they originated from the medieval writ system but have undergone many changes.
Public law	**and**	**Private law**
This term refers to the law governing the relationship between individuals and the State – usually two types of law are included in this definition: criminal law and constitutional and administrative law.		This term refers to the law governing the relationship between individuals and includes many of the areas already identified under substantive law.
Criminal law	**and**	**Civil law**
This term concerns the rules of law concerning behaviour that the state proscribes against and will punish.		This term refers to the rules of law concerning the settlement of disputes between parties which may be individuals but may include businesses and other corporate bodies.

Figure 1.1 The basic classifications of English law

The last two, criminal law and civil law, need to be distinguished because there are many differences in the way that the law is administered and even in the language used when either type is in question. The main distinctions are classified below.

	Criminal law	Civil law
Involves	Offences against the State – behaviour which is classed as unacceptable.	Disputes between individuals.
Purpose of the action	To preserve order in the community and to deter unacceptable behaviour by punishing offenders.	To regulate relationships between individuals, to allow individuals to organise their affairs, to remedy the wrongs suffered by individuals.
Parties to the action	A prosecutor (who prosecutes the offence) and the defendant (who answers the charges).	A claimant (who sues in respect of the damage suffered) and a defendant (who answers the claim).
Burden of proof and standard of proof	The prosecutor must prove the case beyond a reasonable doubt. There is no strict obligation on the defendant to prove his or her innocence.	The claimant must prove his or her claim on a balance of probabilities.
Resolution of the action	The defendant may be convicted, if found to be guilty of the offence, or acquitted, if found to be not guilty.	A defendant will be found to be either liable or not liable for the claim.
Outcomes of the action	The defendant may be sentenced to a penalty which can range between a custodial sentence and a discharge.	The claimant may be awarded a remedy against the defendant, which can be in the form of a monetary compensation – damages – or an equitable order of the court, such as an injunction.
Courts	Magistrates' Court and Crown Court for trial. Divisional Court of the Queen's Bench Division of the High Court, Court of Appeal and Supreme Court on appeal.	Magistrates' Court, County Court and High Court for trial. Divisional Court of the High Court, Court of Appeal and Supreme Court on appeal.
Examples	Murder, theft, drink driving, applying a false trade description.	Breach of contract, negligence in tort, wills, conveyancing of property.

Figure 1.2 Classifying the differences between criminal law and civil law

ACTIVITY

Self-test questions

Answer the following questions using the information in Figure 1.2. You will find the answers in the Appendix on page 249.

1. Who usually brings an action in a criminal trial?
2. Which courts have both civil and criminal jurisdiction?
3. In a civil action what is the burden of proof on the party making the claim?
4. What happens to a person accused of a criminal offence who is found not guilty?
5. What do we call the person who is being accused in a civil action?
6. What remedies are possible in a civil action?
7. What are the major purposes of criminal actions?

This system of classifying the law according to subject matter is not watertight, however. One set of facts can have multiple legal consequences and can straddle the various categories outlined above. For example:

> *Alf is riding his bicycle on a road one morning on his way to work. Becky drives past him at very high speed and knocks Alf from his bike. She does not stop. Charles is also cycling to work. He pulls over and calls an ambulance on his mobile phone. When the ambulance arrives, Alf is taken to the hospital where he is treated for serious injuries. After a long period in hospital, Alf is recovering, but Danny, a junior doctor, gives him an antibiotic to which Alf has already shown intolerance. Danny did not read Alf's medical notes before giving him the antibiotic. Alf falls into a coma from an extreme allergic reaction to the tablets. When he eventually wakes up, he has suffered brain damage and is told he will need full-time nursing care for the rest of his life.*

Event	Consequences in criminal law	Consequences in civil law
Becky knocks Alf from his bike	Becky can be prosecuted for careless driving or possibly even for dangerous driving.	Alf (or in light of his injuries, someone on Alf's behalf) can sue Becky for personal injury. This action is part of the law of negligence. It means Becky owed Alf a duty of care and she breached it, causing personal injury to Alf.
Becky drives away	Becky can be prosecuted for failing to stop and report an accident.	
Danny gives Alf an antibiotic	Generally negligence is not actionable in the criminal law in these circumstances, but if Alf had died, Danny might have been prosecuted for manslaughter by gross negligence.	Alf or his representative could sue the doctor, the hospital or the NHS trust for negligence.

Figure 1.3 Examples of multiple legal consequences

1.3 Legal terminology – and using legal dictionaries

One of the things that you will discover almost immediately about law is that it is full of terminology with which you may be unfamiliar but that you quickly need to understand to cope with your course.

This is not just because you will find a lot of Latin phrases used such as *ratio decidendi* (meaning the legal reason for the decision in a particular case), or *obiter dicta* (meaning other things said by the way by the judge that do not affect the outcome of the case). You will almost certainly also come across the *de minimis* rule from the Latin *de minimis non curat lex* (meaning the law has no remedy for anything that is too trivial). This is an appropriate phrase in the circumstances because learning the appropriate terminology is important to you and you will be expected to know it and to use it in different forms of assessment.

It is not only Latin that will confuse you to start with. There are plenty of technical words used in textbooks and by teachers that you will also need to understand and get used to. It is important that you do understand the technical language of law. Otherwise you will struggle to follow lectures; you will struggle reading many textbooks; and you will struggle when you try to read the judgments of cases.

1.3.1 Common law

One term that you are bound to hear used repeatedly from very early on in your course, and that you will certainly see many times in textbooks, is the phrase 'common law'.

This can be a very confusing term for you because lawyers use the term in so many different contexts and for quite different meanings. It is important then for you to have an appreciation of the different meanings right from the start so that you can follow exactly what is being referred to. Usually the precise meaning is taken from the context in which the phrase is being used and from what it is being contrasted with.

In this way the phrase 'common law' can be used in the following ways:

1. Referring to the law that is common to the whole country – in contrast to the local laws and customs that existed before the eleventh century, a few of which survive in one form or another today; e.g. a by-law introduced by local councils may impose a fine for your dog fouling the footpath.
2. Referring to remedies in particular (the major one being compensation in the form of damages) – in contrast with equitable remedies such as the injunction (an order preventing someone from doing something) or specific performance (an order for a contract to be carried out – usually the transfer of land that has been purchased).
3. Referring to principles of law developed in the judgments of decided cases – in contrast with statute law, created in an Act of Parliament (some law is mainly to be found in cases such as tort – while some areas are mainly statutory, such as crime).
4. Referring to the type of system itself (one that has developed incrementally over centuries through case law as well as other sources) – in contrast with civil law systems such as that in France where the law originates in a code.

There is a very comprehensive chart explaining in detail the various meanings of 'common law' in *Unlocking the English Legal System* in the same series as this book.

1.3.2 Using legal dictionaries

As we have said, you will come across many expressions that are new to you when you start a law degree or similar course. If you are lucky your teacher will remember that he once had to learn all these expressions too and will not assume knowledge on your part that you do not have. If so, you will find that the teacher will stop and give you an explanation of these terms.

Some you will use constantly, such as the term common law above. Others though you may not come across again for some time. So it is useful for you to keep your own little 'dictionary' of the terms and expressions that you were unfamiliar with. Go through your lecture notes after the lecture and extract these terms and transfer them to a booklet that is laid out alphabetically. Then you have it for reference every time you come across the expression again but may have forgotten it.

One of the ways that you can keep up with all the new terminology you come across is to make use of a legal dictionary. There are many examples on the market, including *The Complete A-Z Law Handbook* published by Philip Allan Updates or *Mozley & Whiteley's Law Dictionary* published by Butterworths.

These legal dictionaries are never too costly – about a third of the price of the average law text that you have to buy. They have the advantage of lasting you for the whole of your course and even beyond. They are updated on a regular basis to include new expressions that come from changes to the law, but even so your copy is likely to be sufficient to last the course.

They can be very useful in helping you to keep up with things that are unfamiliar to you in lectures but left unexplained. They are probably even more useful when you are reading through law reports or through the 'weightier' textbooks, both of which tend to presume a level of knowledge which may be beyond a first-year student.

1.4 Brief overview of the sources of law and where to find them

In the first year of your course, usually in the English legal system module, you will find out very quickly that English law is not to be found in a single place or a single document. English law comes from many different sources and it is important that you remember these since it will help you in following different types of substantive law later on. It is also important for you to know quickly and easily where to look for the law in particular areas.

Below is a table with brief explanations of the main sources of law and some explanations of what can be found in them.

Source	Illumination
Custom	Not a very important source in modern times. Early law before the creation of the common law system was generally based on local custom.
	Because of the saying 'custom hardens into right' some custom survives. Public rights of way and the modern by-laws are examples of custom being incorporated into law.
Case law	Case law is the law that is developed by judges in reaching decisions in actual cases.
	The law developed by judges is important in two particular contexts (explanations of which are given in Chapter 6):
	• **The doctrine of precedent** – Judges develop the law by applying existing principles of law to the cases in front of them. If the material facts of the case differ from those from which the existing principle was found then the judges will have to produce an extension of the principle to cover those facts. If no principle can be found which might cover the facts then the judges create what is known as 'original' precedent. Judicial precedent is important in many areas of law. The law of torts for instance is mostly found in the case law. The only major statutory areas are the Occupiers' Liability Acts 1957 and 1984, the Animals Act 1971, the Defective Premises Act 1972 and Part 1 of the Consumer Protection Act 1987. So you should be prepared to learn many cases when you undertake that module. (See Section 6.2 for a detailed explanation.)
	• **Statutory interpretation** – Judges can have a major impact on the application of statute law when they are called on to interpret words contained in a specific part of an Act when the meaning of those words is in dispute in a case before them. Because the judges have so many quite different rules and aids to help them interpret the words of an Act there can be some very surprising results. (See Section 6.3 for a detailed explanation.)
	Judges also play a major role in developing or even restricting the development of law when they reach so-called 'policy' decisions. An example of this is the imposition of restrictive controls on the ability to make a claim of a 'secondary victim' who suffers 'nervous shock' (psychiatric damage) resulting from a single traumatic event caused by another person's negligence. These can be found in the leading case of *Alcock v Chief Constable of South Yorkshire* [1992] 1 AC 310.
	Judges can also have quite an impact on the law when they take a particular moral stance. For instance in the case of *Shaw v DPP* [1962] AC 220, the House of Lords (now the Supreme Court which is the highest court in the country) decided that the publisher of a contact magazine (giving contact details for prostitutes) was guilty of an offence of 'conspiracy to corrupt public morals' even though no such offence existed in law. When the judges were criticised for this they defended themselves by saying that they had a residual right to protect public morality.

Continued on next page

Source	Illumination
Equity	Equity basically means fairness. Originally equity was a separate system of law administered in separate courts and providing some relief for people who had been treated unfairly by the common law system.
	Equity is no longer a separate system of law but it is still an important concept.
	It was responsible for developing a number of remedies that were more useful to a claimant in an action than the standard damages (money compensation) allowed under common law. Examples include:
	• **Injunctions** – preventing a defendant from doing something that would interfere with the claimant's rights.
	• **Specific performance** – an order for the defendant to complete his side of a contract (usually meaning to pass over land that had been sold).
	• **Rescission** – putting contracting parties back to their precontractual position once one party had discovered defects in the contract.
	Equity was responsible for developing enforceable interests that had more flexibility than common law ones including:
	• **The trust** – a means of dividing ownership of property rights that could then be enforceable.
	• **The mortgage** – a means of lending and borrowing but with much more flexible rules and protections than the common law equivalent; the debt.
Legislation	Legislation is in two forms:
	• **Acts of Parliament** – Parliament is said to be the supreme law maker – it can make or unmake any law and the validity of Acts cannot be challenged by any court (but see the effects of membership of the EU and of the Human Rights Act 1998 below). Much modern law comes in statutory form and many areas of law are said to be mainly statutory, e.g. criminal law, company law etc.
	• **Delegated legislation** – This is subject to the control of Parliament and also can be challenged in the courts if it is *ultra vires* (beyond the powers given to the body making it) or offends the rules of natural justice. Delegated means that Parliament has given power to the body to make specific laws for specific purposes or in specific circumstances. Delegated legislation can be one of three types:
	– **Statutory instruments** – usually produced by Ministers in government departments which have more specialist expertise than Parliament itself.
	– **Orders in Council** – introduced by the Privy Council and usually only used in times of emergency, e.g. wartime.
	– **By-laws** – usually introduced by local authorities because they apply to particular local issues and the local bodies have more local knowledge.
EU law	The United Kingdom has been a Member State of the EU (originally the EC) since 1 January 1973 after signing the Treaties and passing the European Communities Act 1972, incorporating the Treaties into English law.
	On matters where EU law is relevant, the UK is bound absolutely by that law because the EU has supremacy on those issues, so the UK Parliament cannot make laws that conflict with EU law.
	Citizens can also enforce EU law in Member States through the process known as 'direct effect'.
	EU law is an important feature of English law, mostly at the moment in economic areas. It is vital to contract law, consumer law, employment law, company law and some other areas.

BRIEF OVERVIEW OF THE SOURCES OF LAW AND WHERE TO FIND THEM

Continued on next page

Source	Illumination
Human rights	The UK is also a signatory to the European Convention of Human Rights and citizens, once they have exhausted their national rights of action, can make an application to the European Court of Human Rights.
	The Convention includes many very basic rights such as the right to life and the right not to be tortured, as well as freedom of expression and freedom from discrimination.
	In 1998 the Human Rights Act gave effect to the main provisions of the Convention into English law. Now a judge in a case can consider whether or not a provision of the Convention has been infringed. Judges may also declare that new legislation is incompatible with a Convention right, although it is only Parliament that can then alter the legislation.
International treaties	Like other countries the UK frequently signs up to international treaties by which it is then bound in international law.
	Generally the United Nations oversees much international law.
	An example of such a treaty is the Geneva Convention which proscribes certain codes of conduct in warfare and prohibits the manufacture and use of certain types of weapon.

Figure 1.4 Sources of law

The concepts and issues that have been explored in this chapter form the basis of knowledge for a law student commencing a law degree. It is, therefore, important to review this information. To assist in this, try to attempt the following questions:

ACTIVITY

Multiple-choice questions

1. Select the option that has the greatest validity:
   (a) Law is an easy word to define;
   (b) Law is a word that has universal meaning;
   (c) Law is a word with a very broad meaning;
   (d) Law is a word with no meaning.
2. Select the option that has the greatest validity:
   (a) Hart suggests there are three key primary rules;
   (b) A legal system needs primary and secondary rules;
   (c) A dictatorship has primary and secondary rules;
   (d) A legal system should have no rules.
3. Select the option that has the greatest validity:
   (a) The English legal system is based on Roman law;
   (b) There is no difference between the common law and Roman law;
   (c) The English legal system is a common law system;
   (d) The common law system is unique to the English legal system.
4. Select the option that has the greatest validity:
   (a) There is no distinction between substantive and adjectival law;
   (b) The law can be classified in terms of substantive and adjectival law;
   (c) Adjectival law relates to the cases and statutes that give us our rights;
   (d) Substantive law focuses on issues like rules of evidence.
5. From the statement below identify which are civil matters and which are criminal:

Beyond all reasonable doubt	Liable for a claim
Prosecutor	Balance of probabilities
Theft	Damages

6. Identify which of the following is not a source of law:
   (a) Legislation
   (b) EU law
   (c) Case law
   (d) Media.

Answers can be found in the Appendix on page 249.

SUMMARY

- A general definition of law is 'any body of rules which is organised and structured and relates to a particular code of conduct' – whereas law in the lawyers' sense means 'the body of principles recognised and applied by the courts in the administration of justice' so we are concerned very much with enforceability.
- Any legal system incorporates rules of recognition (e.g. the individual branches of law), rules of change (e.g. the ability of Parliament to introduce new law) and rules of adjudication (e.g. the rules of procedure and evidence).
- The English legal system is a common law system – it has developed from and incorporates law from custom, from the judgments of decided cases, as well as from Acts of Parliament and subordinate legislation, and the laws resulting from membership of the European Union.
- English law can be classified in different ways: substantive law (the body of rules regulating rights and responsibilities) and adjectival law (the rules regulating legal processes); public law (regulating the relationship between citizen and state) and private law (regulating the relationship between individuals); and also divides into criminal law (a system for punishing unacceptable behaviour) and civil law (a method of regulating disputes between individuals).
- Law involves precise language and terminology – so legal dictionaries are a useful aid.
- The major sources of English law are: custom, case law, equity, legislation, EU law, Human Rights law, and international treaties.

2

Lectures and Seminars

AIMS AND OBJECTIVES

After reading this chapter you should be able to:

- Understand how to listen effectively
- Understand the factors that might prevent you from listening effectively
- Understand the most effective ways of preparing for lectures
- Understand how and when to take notes in lectures
- Understand how to prepare effectively for seminars
- Understand what to do in seminars
- Prepare effectively for lectures
- Listen effectively and make useful notes in lectures
- Prepare effectively for seminars
- Participate effectively in seminars

2.1 Learning to listen

2.1.1 Listening

One of the key delivery methods used by universities is the lecture. A lecture involves the dissemination of a body of legal knowledge. Its aim is to give an overview of the major themes and cases related to a particular legal issue e.g. offer and acceptance. Lectures may last for one, two or possibly even three hours, and each will involve you listening to the delivery of set subject content. Your techniques in listening will have a dramatic effect on the amount that you will get out of lectures. If you are unable to master the techniques of listening effectively then it will affect your understanding of the issues under discussion and the quality of your lecture notes, which are a significant part of your later success in exams or in coursework.

It is important that you learn to listen and not just simply to hear. Effective listening will build your understanding while merely hearing may well cause misunderstanding.

2.1.2 Barriers to effective listening

Distraction

You need to have maximum concentration in a lecture. A few seconds of lost concentration could have a dramatic effect on your ability to absorb information. Common distractions include mobile phones, friends, day-dreaming and a lack of resources, e.g. stationery.

Lecturers inevitably get upset with disturbances and will try to put a stop to them so they can go on with the lecture. However, this in itself breaks the flow and breaks your concentration. So you should always be punctual for lectures and seminars, take the correct equipment with you (never go out without a pen), turn your mobile phone off before you go in, do not rustle sweet papers etc. More importantly, show that you have ownership of your own education by encouraging your friends to follow these simple rules; although if you are going to take them to task over disturbances that they have created, make sure that you do it outside of the classroom and after the lecture.

Tiredness and hunger

Make sure you are fully refreshed for your lectures. Take a bottle of water and make sure you have eaten if you are not allowed to take a snack into the lecture theatre with you. This will boost your energy and your attentiveness.

Concentrating on note-taking

If your focus is to try and write everything down, you will soon start to miss out key issues and concepts.

Lack of preparation

Law has a number of technical terms and some difficult concepts. If you go into lectures unprepared then these issues will confuse and distract you.

2.1.3 Improving listening

Prior preparation

Skim read the lecture material beforehand. This will give you an awareness of the concepts and allow the lecture to build upon your awareness – hence assisting the development of knowledge.

Develop a note-taking system

Use text language or a version of shorthand. This allows you more time to listen as opposed to writing. However, remember not to use sloppy language or shorthand of any type in your assessments. Your lecturers will tell you any accepted legal abbreviations that you may use.

Actively listen

Sit in a good position to listen. Some lecture halls have poor acoustics. Avoid areas that make listening difficult. Write follow-up questions on areas of misunderstanding and ask lecturers or friends to explain. Also, if it is permitted, ask questions.

Practise

Listening is a skill. Like most skills it develops through practice.

2.2 Preparing for lectures

There are common features of law lectures:

2.2.1 Length and style of delivery

Law lectures normally involve one lecturer disseminating and explaining a legal area. Lectures can vary in length but could be as long as three hours. Different lecturers have different delivery styles. Some will give handouts at the beginning of the module or beginning of the lecture. Some may use information technology and refer to web or intranet areas. Others will give handouts at the end. Some will allow questions. Others will not tolerate interruptions. Knowing the individual styles of your lecturers will help you in your preparation.

2.2.2 Focus on the delivery of subject content

There will be an introduction by the lecturer to outline the subject content of each lecture. This may be done verbally or on, for example, PowerPoint at the start of the class. Be on time so you can identify the topic area for focus. The lecture will not be a complete overview of a legal issue. It will be an insight into the major cases and concepts related to a particular legal issue. Make a note on the key areas for further reading that the lecturer recommends.

2.2.3 The common mistakes

Lectures are perceived by many students to be a vehicle to gain a complete set of notes on a topic. This may be because there are a number of competing demands placed on the student in a lecture:

- listen to subject content
- take notes
- understand subject matter
- relate this to tutorial tasks.

Many students make note-taking the highest priority believing that by reviewing the notes they will be able to complete all of the other tasks above after the lecture. The danger with this is that they may fail to understand the legal issues being outlined and find the notes they have taken have gaps, which result in a difficulty in understanding the subject content. Never rely merely on lecture notes when preparing for tutorials because your knowledge and understanding will be incomplete.

If you think about the stages of learning that you have to go through to attain high marks, gathering the basic knowledge of a topic is the first rung on the ladder. After the essential knowledge is attained, the student then has to ensure he or she understands the area. This is called the comprehension stage. Following that, the learner must be able to apply the understanding to new scenarios and analyse it in relation to a factual problem. Next comes evaluation – making judgments on the strengths and weaknesses of the topic. Finally comes synthesis. This is where the student hypothesises on the area: he or she asks questions of the topic, and ponders 'what if we changed it to ...?'.

Each of these stages involves an activity, as shown in the grid below:

Stages to develop high levels of learning	Activity
Knowledge	Pre-reading Lectures
Comprehension	Lectures Research
Application	Research Tutorials
Analysis	Tutorials Reflection
Evaluation	Reflection Revision
Synthesis	Revision Assessment

Figure 2.1 Stages of learning

As you can see, the lecture is a vital part of the process. It is where you will build your foundation knowledge from which your higher learning stems. You therefore need to make the best use of the lecture.

2.2.4 Getting the most out of lectures

- **Select an appropriate place to sit** – Do not sit in a position where you cannot see visual aids or have difficulty hearing. This may necessitate you turning up slightly early to get a good position.
- **Pre-reading and note-gathering** – Some lecturers give handouts or place their lecture notes 'online' or on the university intranet. Law courses are information rich; the lecture will cover many cases and issues for discussion. By skim-reading the handouts or pre-available material you will gain an awareness of the issues for discussion and will improve your learning. It will also prevent you wasting time taking notes on topics that are covered in detail on the handouts or elsewhere. If materials are available take them into the lecture and supplement them with your own comments in a way suitable to your understanding.
- **Connections** – In the lecture focus on how the issues relate to each other e.g. what cases are linked and how they developed. This not only improves understanding but also aids listening. You may find it useful to keep a separate page of A4 to one side of you and draw a flowchart of how the lecturer progresses from one stage to the next. This will help you to build up a logical structure to your own notes.
- **Focus on listening** – Pre-reading will assist in gaining a broad awareness of the issues/topics which will allow you to focus on the lecture as opposed the note-taking. As previously mentioned, you need to listen actively using the strategies given to improve your listening focus.
- **Use the lectures as guidance for your further study** – The lecture should provide a guide as to how much depth and what importance individual legal issues have. The lecture, therefore, is a guide to direct your subsequent research and also to highlight the importance of areas in terms of assessment.
- **After the lecture** – If you have listened actively you need to make further notes to support your understanding. It is important to do this as soon as possible after the lecture has taken place. You will quickly forget the issues discussed in the lecture. Within 48 hours, 80 per cent of the information that was presented to you will be forgotten unless reviewed within that period.

2.3 Taking notes in lectures

2.3.1 The reasons for taking notes

For many of you your degree course will be the first time that you have ever studied law. Even if you have studied and have been successful at A-Level Law, you will have studied two or maybe three subjects at most (English legal system plus one or two areas of substantive law such as contract law, criminal law or tort).

A major difference that you will find, or may have already found, from other subjects is the volume of information that you will need to understand and be able to remember. You will also discover a great many new terms and expressions that you have never come across before. In many ways studying law is almost like studying a new language. Besides this, studying law demands that you develop a wide range of skills. You will not only need to learn huge quantities of information. You will also need to develop practical skills of applying the law to factual situations, and to develop critical awareness and be able to see how the law operates in context.

For these reasons it is important that you have a good set of notes that are easily understandable and can form the basis of your revision.

You have a number of resources available to you to help you to learn and indeed to help you when you come to revision. Your teacher or lecturer may have given you prepared handouts, but your own notes are best because you will understand them. You can take notes in class and when you read textbooks. Getting into the habit of reading and note-taking will ensure that you are building up information to help your learning. The more you do it, the more familiar you become with the information and the more you get used to writing about law, so that you feel comfortable doing so in the exam. Note-taking promotes active learning and aids memory.

2.3.2 When to take notes

There are four different times when you are likely to need to take notes:

- when you are in lectures from what the tutor is saying or writing on the board or from discussion or even from watching videos
- when you are following up information given by your tutor
- when you have been asked to prepare for a seminar/tutorial
- when you are preparing the outline for assignment work.

The last three obviously apply to Chapter 3, but you should see the connection between building up your bank of learning resources in lectures and in your outside reading and research.

2.3.3 Note-taking in lectures

As discussed, it is better to listen actively and not focus on trying to write everything the lecturer is stating. There are a number of different approaches to how notes should be taken. Although each approach has advantages and disadvantages, it is about finding the method that not only suits you, but also matches the lecturer's delivery style. Whatever approach is taken it is important that you do the following:

- date all notes
- paginate
- file as soon as possible
- title the work
- use highlighters to focus on cases and important issues
- question-mark the parts of the subject content you do not fully understand
- make sure all notes are legible.

2.3.4 Note-taking methods

The traditional approach

This involves you trying to copy out what the lecturer is saying as he or she is delivering the subject matter. If you adopt this technique only use three quarters of a page as this allows you to add your own comment and analysis, either during the lecture or just after when reviewing the notes. (See Figure 2.2 below.)

Omissions	Add your own comment here. This could be to highlight its importance to the exam or the tutorial or simply to aid in the understanding.
Definition:	
An omission is a failure to act.	
In criminal law there is no liability for a failure to act. However there are exceptions.	
1) Statutory exceptions	
These are normally strict liability offences, e.g. failure to provide a police officer with a breath sample ...	

Figure 2.2 Traditional approach to note-taking

Advantages

■ strong comfort factor because you believe you are walking away with a complete picture
■ easy to do
■ can be recorded quickly with shorthand writing techniques or abbreviations for words, e.g. \ = therefore.

Disadvantages

■ assumes you can write quickly and that the lecturer has an even/slow delivery speed
■ you become a passive listener
■ you can easily miss important concepts.

Taped lectures

This involves the use of a Dictaphone or digital recorder to record the lecture.

Advantages

■ you can concentrate on listening
■ negates the need for extensive note-taking
■ can be used in revision and is particularly good for auditory learners
■ if written up, repetition enforces grasp of the information heard in the lecture.

Disadvantages

■ getting a good recording can be difficult
■ not allowed by all lecturers
■ can be expensive in relation to the volume of resources needed, e.g. tapes or VCDs
■ time-consuming to write up.

Summary sheets

This involves focusing on the main themes and issues in the lecture and making a brief note of them and using these as a springboard to make notes post lecture.

For example, see Figure 2.3 Example of a summary sheet on the next page.

Advantages

■ reinforces active listening
■ provides a framework for further note-taking
■ focus is on the core important issues.

Disadvantages

■ requires pre-lecture reading familiarisation with subject matter to be discussed
■ requires post-lecture time for more detailed note-taking
■ requires selection skills in breaking down what is important during the lecture.

Concept maps or spider diagrams

See Chapter 11 page 224 for an example.

Advantages

■ gives a logical flow of the lecture from the perspective of the writer
■ focus is on active listening
■ gives a logical linkage and the inter-connections relating to a subject
■ excellent for visual-based learners
■ can be used as a revision aid.

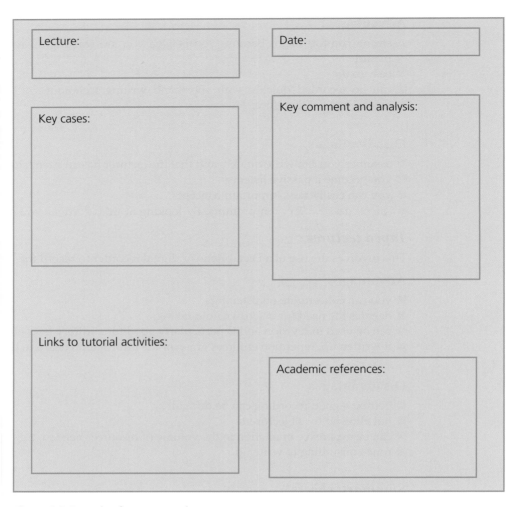

Lecture:

Date:

Key cases:

Key comment and analysis:

Links to tutorial activities:

Academic references:

Figure 2.3 Example of a summary sheet

Disadvantages
- requires practice to produce effective diagrams
- needs follow-up work to produce detailed notes.

Cornell note system

This involves dividing your note-taking page into two columns. The second and bigger of the two columns is used to make traditional notes or diagrams etc. The smaller column is there to write self-test questions regarding the notes. The areas should be interrelated in that each section of notes should have questions or comment attached. (See Figure 2.4 below.)

	Arrest
What powers of arrest does (the amended) s 24 PACE allow a police officer?	Section 24 lays down general conditions of arrest without a warrant for any offence. A police officer may arrest:
	Anyone who is about to commit an offence, who is in the act of committing an offence, or whom he has reasonable grounds to suspect is about to commit an offence, is committing an offence, or if he has reasonable grounds to suspect that an offence has been committed anyone he has reasonable grounds to suspect of being guilty of it, or where an offence has been committed, anyone who is guilty of the offence or who he has reasonable grounds to suspect is guilty of the offence.

Continued on next page

Continued

What powers of arrest do citizens have?	(The amended) section 24 states that a citizen can only arrest where an indictable offence is being committed or he has reasonable grounds to suspect that the person is committing the offence or where an indictable offence has been committed and he has reasonable grounds to suspect the person is guilty of it, but only then when it is impracticable for a police officer to make the arrest and where the arrest is necessary.

Figure 2.4 The Cornell note system

Advantages

- an excellent technique for auditory learners
- can be used as revision prompts. By looking at the questions you should be able to explain the related notes
- encourages active learning.

Disadvantages

- can be difficult to keep pace
- questions may need to be done after the lecture
- some students find it difficult to relate the notes to a question.

ACTIVITY

Exercise

Below is a sample of traditional notes on precedent that could have been taken in a lecture. Alter these notes to the following note-taking methods:

- Summary sheet
- Cornell note system
- Spider diagram.

The Supreme Court (formerly the House of Lords)

This is the most senior domestic court. When matters do not involve Europe it has the final decision on the case. This court binds all courts below it. The House of Lords did not bind itself due to the Practice Statement 1966.

House of Lords & the Practice Statement
Originally the House of Lords had flexibility and could change its mind about its own past decisions but in 1898 the court decided that certainty in the law was more important than flexibility so in *London Street Tramways v London County Council* the court decided that the House of Lords was bound by its own previous decisions.

This created a rigid system as seen in DPP v Smith
A man murdered a police officer. The House of Lords made a mistake by giving a poor definition as to the mental test for murder. Due to this mistake Parliament passed the Criminal Justice Act 1967 to replace the mistake.

1966: Lord Gardiner issues a Practice Statement. This allows the judges in the House of Lords to depart from past decisions when it is right to do so.

It was first used in *Conway v Rimmer*. This was not seen as a major use as it only involved a technical matter.

In 2009 the Supreme Court was created to replace the House of Lords. Changes of the law have to be requested in applications to the court and the court will change past precedents where there is a good reason to do so.

Examples Civil

Herrington v British Railways Board overruled *Addie v Dumbreck*
These cases concerned what duty of care was owed to a child trespasser. In *Addie* it was decided that there was only a duty when injuries to a child were caused deliberately or

recklessly. *Herrington* overruled this due to the changes in social conditions and made the duty owed stronger. *Herrington* was the first major use of the Practice Statement.

Pepper v Hart overruled *Davis v Johnson*

These cases concerned the use of Hansard. In *Davis* the use of Hansard by a judge as an aid to statutory interpretation was not allowed. *Pepper v Hart* removed this limit.

Example Criminal

R v Shivpuri overruled *Anderton v Ryan*

These cases concerned the criminal nature of attempting the impossible. *Anderton* decided that you could not have criminal liability if what you were doing was impossible. This was contrary to an Act of Parliament. *Shivpuri* therefore overruled *Anderton*. It can now be a crime if you attempt the impossible. This was the first criminal case to use the Practice Statement.

Answers can be found in the Appendix on pages 249–251.

2.4 Preparing for seminars/tutorials

The seminar/tutorial system in university education is very common. It involves independent research on a directed legal area followed by a timetabled group session to discuss your findings. The group size is normally small. The research task will take the form of a tutorial brief with a series of questions and activities for address/completion. Some tutorials may require presentations. A lecturer may lead the tutorial session and use the activities as a method of discussing the subject matter. The tutorial will involve answering the questions or adding to a debate leading from them.

The lecture and seminar/tutorial system may be different from your previous educational experience where prior investigation or research has not been required as most learning occurred in the classroom. Developing knowledge and understanding should occur before a tutorial. Application and analysis should be practised before the tutorial and enhanced during it. An effective tutorial should build evaluative skills.

Whether you are familiar with the tutorial system or not, there are key strategies that can be adopted to make the experience more successful.

Law students are commonly given a tutorial guide book that contains the activities and guidance for the tutorials which they will have. A typical layout might look something like Figure 2.5 below.

TORTS TUTORIAL 4:

Special Duty Situations: Psychiatric Damage (nervous shock)

Essential reading: *Unlocking Torts*, Chapter 7.1

                         Cases and Commentary on Tort, Harvey & Marston, Chapter 2

Essential cases that you must know

Victorian Railway Commissioners v Coultas (1888) 13 App Cas 222

Dulieu v White & Sons [1901] 2 KB 669

Hambrook v Stokes [1925] 1 KB 141

Bourhill v Young [1943] AC 92

Chadwick v British Railways Board [1967] 1 WLR 912

McLoughlin v O'Brian & Others [1982] 2 All ER 298

Alcock & Others v Chief Constable of the South Yorkshire Police [1992] 1 AC 310

Attia v British Gas Plc [1988] QB 304

Taylor v Somerset Health Authority [1993] PIQR 262

McFarlane v EE Caledonia Ltd [1994] 2 All ER 1

Page v Smith [1996] 1 AC 155, [1995] 2 WLR 644 (HL)

White v Chief Constable of the South Yorkshire Police [1999] 1 All ER 1

Continued on next page

Continued

North Glamorgan NHS Trust v Walters [2002] EWCA Civ 1792
Vernon & Bosely (No. 1) [1997] 1 All ER 577
Sion v Hampstead Health Authority [1994] 5 Med LR 170
McLoughlin v Jones [2002] 2 WLR 1279
Greatorex v Greatorex [2000] 1 WLR 1970 QBD
W v Essex CC [2000] 2 WLR 601

Be prepared to answer the following questions

1. What is meant by the phrase 'nervous shock'? Is 'psychiatric damage' a preferable phrase?
2. What was the principle laid down in *Dulieu v White*?
3. How was the law developed in *Hambrook v Stokes*?
4. What was the test of liability laid down by Lord Wilberforce in *McLoughlin*?
5. What is meant by the phrase 'immediate aftermath'?
6. What are the essential requirements of liability for psychiatric damage in relation to secondary victims in *Alcock & Others v Chief Constable of the South Yorkshire Police*?
7. What is meant by the use of the word 'bystander'?
8. Following the decision of the House of Lords in *White v Chief Constable of the South Yorkshire Police*, what types of claimant are now treated as 'primary victims'?
9. What distinctions between primary and secondary victims are shown in the case of *Page v Smith*?
10. How does the Law Commission propose this area of the law should be reformed?

Problem-solving exercise

Because of the negligence of his employers, SLS Construction Ltd, Ron is badly injured when a large section of crane falls and lands on him as he is working below. He is taken to hospital and dies two hours later in hospital from multiple injuries.

Consider the possibility of each of the following succeeding if they claim for psychiatric injury (nervous shock) against SLS Construction Ltd:

(a) Gurdeep, Ron's close workmate, who is on the site at the time of the accident, and although he is in no danger from the falling crane, witnesses the accident from nearby, and suffers severe depression as a result.
(b) Bill, a firefighter who was called to the scene and freed Ron from the debris. Bill suffers post-traumatic stress disorder after seeing the extent of Ron's injuries. While Bill was freeing Ron there was always a danger that more metal from the crane might become dislodged and fall.
(c) Elizabeth, Ron's mother, is telephoned by Ron's manager immediately and gets to the hospital in time to see Ron as he is being carried out of the ambulance. Elizabeth suffers from grief and insomnia (cannot sleep) after the accident.

Figure 2.5 An example from a tutorial guide book

2.4.1 Start planning the tutorial before the lecture

The first step to successful tutorials is to attend lectures. Lecture content is normally highly related to tutorials which follow, and lecturers often direct you to the subject matter for discussion in the tutorials. Therefore, look at the tasks that are given for tutorials and relate them to specific lectures. For example, an EU law lecture on the institutions of the European Union will normally be followed by a tutorial related to that topic. By looking at the materials and tasks before the lecture you will gain an understanding of the key issues that are being directed in terms of your learning. During the lecture, these issues will be discussed and you can make notes next to the tasks, which will start helping you complete some of the activities. This process will also focus your attention during the lecture, improving your listening ability.

2.4.2 Use your lecture notes as a starting point

The next stage of the tutorial process is to utilise the lecture notes and the annotations that were made on the tutorial sheet. The lecture will provide answers to some of the tutorial activities. Use these notes to help complete as many tasks as possible. Reviewing the lecture notes will also improve and refresh your understanding of the issues that will be discussed in the tutorial.

2.4.3 Research

The next stage is to explore the recommended reading. You may need to explore further afield for these resources, e.g. the library for law journals, law reports etc. Law courses involve a significant amount of research and you will be required to research specific legal issues independently. It is therefore important to be organised – the key to a successful tutorial is the preparation. It is also important for you to manage your time effectively. There will be more than one tutorial each week and law courses traditionally involve significant research and reading.

Some students find it embarrassing when they have failed to prepare for the tutorial. An unprepared student cannot answer any of the questions and can offer nothing in the discussions that take place. It is impossible to understand the legal issues if you have not done the preparation beforehand. It may be useful to produce an action plan for the materials needed and to stick to it. For example:

Topics	Resource	Priority	Completed?
ELS/M	Walker & Walker Chapter 4.	Priority 1	Yes/no
Tort	*Unlocking Torts* C. Turner & S. Hodge, Chapter 7.1, pages 184–202 *Cases and Commentary on Tort* Harvey & Marston, Chapter 2	Priority 2	Yes/no
Crime	Smith & Hogan pages 56–88. D. Lanser, 'Intention and Recklessness', *The Legal Executive Journal*, 1995, Nov. S. Cooper, 'Summing up Intention', *New Law Journal*, 18 August 2000.	Priority 3	Yes/no

Figure 2.6 An action plan to help prepare for tutorials

This list is quick to prepare and is a methodical way to gain the materials for upcoming tutorials and makes library visits and research effective. There is nothing worse than trying to complete directed activities and realising that you have forgotten to get an article.

Once you have gathered the material you should be able to begin successfully completing the tasks assigned in your tutorials.

2.5 Getting the most out of seminars/tutorials

2.5.1 Study buddy

Tutorial research does not have to be a solitary activity. You can split the task of finding law reports, journals and relevant articles with a fellow student. This can be an invaluable method of saving time. Time can then be spent on digesting the information and completing the directed tasks. There is, however, a note of caution – the person you choose should be reliable and there needs to be a clear indication of who is gathering what, when it will be done by and when you will swap information. Without clear parameters like this, you or your study buddy may become frustrated through different priorities (e.g. your land law seminar may not be until the end of the following week. For you it is a low priority, but for your research partner the required resources will be a high priority if it is their first tutorial of the week).

2.5.2 Using text books

To gather the research you will either need to make photocopies from the sources, take notes or highlight relevant texts. You do not need to take copies of everything that many of the texts discuss, because they will include many of the same cases, although the analysis and comment may differ. Your priority after reviewing your lecture notes is to complete the essential reading. It is a waste of time making complete notes from this because you should already have gained a core of knowledge from your lecture notes. So, when making notes from the essential reading look for the following:

■ different cases
■ academic comment and analysis
■ differences in interpretations of the law from your lecture notes
■ materials that focus on the tutorial topics.

This process will allow you to build a stock of knowledge that not only allows you to complete a tutorial successfully but also gives you a complete set of materials that can be used for exam preparation.

2.5.3 The activities

Through study carried out during the lecture and research cycle you will have probably completed the majority of the tasks set. There may be activities that still require completing because they require your judgment; e.g. you are asked to assess the validity of a case which requires your own interpretation. These should be quickly achieved due to having all the requested materials. It may be that the answer is not clearly gained from the research. In this case make a list of the issues you do not understand and try to adopt one or more of the following tactics.

Explaining the difficulties that you are having in the tutorial

This approach is sometimes not favoured because of a sense of failure and self-consciousness in front of others. Some may decide to go along to the tutorial and hope the discussion gives elaboration, but there is danger with this approach because you may be asked to give a response to the topic causing difficulty.

The tutorial may not discuss in detail issues of uncertainty and if left until the time of the examination, this could be fatal. It may be useful to catch the tutorial leader before the commencement of the tutorial to explain that you had difficulty with a particular activity and that you are hoping the tutorial will aid you in your understanding.

Seeking your tutorial leader's support before the session

This will allow you to talk through specific difficulties and improve your understanding of the task. It may not always be possible to gain the precise support that you need at this point because the availability of lecturers varies due to their individual commitments. In most instances you will still be able to arrange a suitable time to see your lecturer to discuss your issues. Besides this there are extensive student support services available in all universities which can offer you varying forms of advice and guidance.

Peers

As mentioned previously, some students may find it beneficial to discuss issues with other students. This not only allows them to help each other with areas of difficulty but can also be used to confirm conclusions to other activities, which builds confidence.

2.5.4 The tutorial/seminar

If you have followed the tactics, the tutorial itself should be a rewarding experience as you will be able to share and discuss the concepts you have prepared. But remember:

- **Be considerate** – It is natural to be proud of your understanding but give others the opportunity to have an input.
- **Make notes** – There will be issues raised that you may not have considered. These may offer a different approach.
- **Ask questions** – If issues are raised with which you need help, seek clarification.
- **Positive body language** – Make use of positive body language. Make eye contact with the person talking, lean forward in your seat when you want to contribute.
- **Do not be afraid** – At first you may be unsure about the validity of your responses. Someone may offer a different interpretation of the law to what you have perceived. The law has many conflicting opinions and there is a vast amount of case law that can cause conflict. It is therefore usual, considering the range of activities set for tutorial, that there will be no right answer as the questions are there to form the basis for the discussion. You will find that the more you contribute the more confidence you will gain and the easier the tutorial experience will become.

student mentor tip

It sometimes seems quite daunting to ask a question or to make a contribution but you will be surprised how many people will be grateful that you asked it because they were afraid to.

2.5.5 After the tutorial

It is important to consolidate after each tutorial:

- put notes in order and file them
- research areas of poor understanding
- ensure all notes are legible and comprehensible. During a lecture you may have written a specific comment next to a task, but will you understand it in three months' time when beginning your revision?

SUMMARY

- Effective listening is vital to gain the most from lectures.
- Barriers to effective listening include: distractions, tiredness, hunger, lack of concentration, excessive note-taking and lack of preparation.
- Listening can be improved by prior preparation, using an effective note-taking system, active listening and practising of all of these.
- Lectures vary in length and style but the lecturer will explain the focus of the lecture.
- Lectures are only one stage in the process of learning.
- To get the most out of lectures it is important to know when to take notes and how to make notes effectively.
- There are various approaches: verbatim note-taking, taping lectures and then producing notes, using summary sheets and supplementing these after the lecture, using concept maps or spider charts, and the Cornell system using two columns – one for key points and the other for expansion.
- Preparing for seminars is also vital as this is the opportunity for active learning and ensuring that knowledge is complete – so research is necessary.
- Preparation can involve using study buddies and textbooks.
- It is important to take part in the tutorial to assess knowledge and gaps in knowledge and understanding.
- After the tutorial gaps in knowledge and understanding should be filled.

3

Reading

AIMS AND OBJECTIVES

After reading this chapter you should be able to:

▦ Understand the purpose of reading legal materials
▦ Understand how to read effectively
▦ Understand how to use the supports to reading effectively – i.e. the contents table and index
▦ Read effectively
▦ 'Scan' read
▦ Make effective notes from reading

3.1 The purpose of reading

In Chapter 2 we focused on lectures and seminars and this personal interaction with your lecturers is one source of information available to you on your course. Lectures are an overview on a topic and seminars/tutorials are essentially practical sessions where you are called on to demonstrate your knowledge and understanding, whether through discussion, problem solving or simply answering short questions.

Reading is another and different source of information. A lecture on a particular topic area may last only two or three hours; you only have to look at the shelf in your library/learning centre to discover that there will be sufficient books on that particular subject to keep you reading for a very long time. This inevitably means that there is a great deal more information and understanding to be gained on the subject than can be gained in the lecture.

Reading helps you to build on the understanding that you have been given already. It may also help to clear up areas of confusion and is a vital means to follow up information that your tutor did not have time to tell you. The tutor in any case may want you to discover particular information for yourself and direct you to specific reading. This may be a way of building your skills, or he or she may want you to find that there are complications that could only be touched on in a tutorial, or indeed may want you to read ahead so that you are able to gain more benefit from a particular session.

There are a number of reasons why you should read and it is vital that you get into the habit of reading extensively and reading regularly.

3.1.1 Different legal materials

There is a wide range of reading materials available to read when you study law. These include:

- textbooks
- case books
- articles in academic journals
- the law reports themselves
- statutes and statute books
- periodicals and daily newspapers
- e-books.

3.1.2 Where to find reading materials

You will find that there are many stimuli to reading and aids that will direct you to specific or relevant material:

- Your module guide will usually suggest specific textbooks and, if the guides are detailed enough, they will even provide you with a breakdown of the chapters or pages that you need to read on relevant topics.
- Your lecturer may well refer to specific supplementary reading in lectures and give you appropriate references so that you can locate the material.
- Textbooks very often have references for further reading in footnotes or suggested extra reading indicated at the end of chapters or sections and many will carry bibliographies where other useful works are listed.
- Journal articles will usually make reference to source materials.
- If you look into law reports at the start of these there is always a list of cases that were suggested as being relevant.
- Increasingly sources such as textbooks and e-books have dedicated online resources that you can access for further guided reading.

So there are many places that you can look to find extra sources of relevant reading.

3.1.3 Assessing your existing skills

Reading is a skill that any student would naturally assume they are good at. But it is important you take stock of your reading skills. It is important to focus on two key skills – your reading rate and your recall rate. Your reading rate relates to how long it takes for you to read a set number of pages and your recall rate focuses on your ability to understand and retain the core information contained in the material.

ACTIVITY

Exercise

Select a reading task from a seminar topic. Make a note of how many pages it asks you to read. Start reading the material, but time yourself on how long this takes. Once completed you should have an awareness of your reading time; e.g. if you are directed to read 15 pages and it takes you 15 minutes you are reading on average one page per minute.

Why is reading speed important?

- **It allows you to plan** – understanding your reading time will give you a good idea of how long reading tasks for tutorials and other reading tasks will take.
- **It allows you to monitor improvements** – law is a subject which requires the reading of significant amounts of material. For you to be an effective student your reading rate needs to be as strong as possible. By adopting the techniques and suggestions in this chapter you should notice an improvement in your reading rate. It is important to check this rate regularly, e.g. once every couple of months.

You also need to understand the key issues you are reading about. There is no point in having a fantastic reading rate if you cannot recollect any of the cases and concepts you have read. It is, therefore, also important to reflect on your recall rate and again, by adopting the techniques in this chapter, your recall rate should improve.

3.1.4 Reading effectively

Being able to read is not the same thing as being able to read *well*.

The important point is that you should read effectively. Law texts and other legal reading material are not like novels that you can read from cover to cover. In fact you should not be reading them from cover to cover because your reading must be both specific and relevant to what you are studying at the time. In any case you do not have time to read textbooks on your subjects from start to finish.

What you must do is to read those things that are relevant to you at the time. In order to achieve this you must develop certain skills:

■ **Signposting**
  – Build a familiarity with the common layouts of the textbooks and other materials that you use so that you do not spend hours and hours reading the irrelevant sections.
  – Get used to using the contents page to find the specific area that you want to read, and the index for the relevant aspects.
  – Get used to using the brief information at the start of each law report, known as the head note or case abstract, so that you do not read one unnecessarily. This is particularly important as many law reports are very lengthy, sometimes 100 or more pages!
  – See Section 3.2 for further details on signposting.

■ **Extraction of relevant information**
  – You must learn how to find the maximum amount of information in the shortest possible time.
  – You need to learn the skill of scan reading so that you can look through books quickly to locate appropriate information.
  – You can develop the skill by learning to focus on key words as you 'scan' down the page. For example, if you were reading a law report on a negligence case you might focus on the words 'duty of care' or 'breach of duty' or 'cause' – these are the classic elements of a negligence action and whenever you see them you can be sure that the judge is talking about something important to you.
  – See Section 3.3 for further details on scan reading.

■ **Context and comprehension**
  – You must be able to distinguish between reading to locate information and reading in depth.
  – Get used to reading a little before and even a little after the point where aids, such as the index, direct you as then you won't miss an important lead up to the point you are focusing on or where it developed from.
  – When you are reading to try to understand something that you are not clear on then you must read more slowly and comprehensively and at these times in particular you should always make notes on what you have read.

■ **Re-reading**
  – You must be able to make use of the information that you have gained from your reading – so you must always have a way of going back to the specific points without having to read at length all over again.
  – Get used also to making notes while you read.
  – If note-taking is proving to be too time-consuming then you must learn the skill of effective highlighting.
  – See Sections 3.4 and 3.5 for further details on note-taking and highlighting.

3.1.5 How you can benefit from effective reading

There are a number of positive benefits to be gained from regular reading:

- It increases your knowledge and understanding of the subject.
- It exposes you to a different perspective than you might get in your lectures.
- It develops critical awareness as you may find a wider range of analytical material in textbooks and articles than you may get from a lecture.
- It will improve your vocabulary and your appreciation of technical terms.
- It will develop your knowledge of how to structure your work in a logical and fluent way.
- It will benefit your coursework as you are not just giving your lecturer back what he or she has already given you.
- It will increase your performance in exams by giving you a wider spread of knowledge and understanding from which to draw.

3.2 Using the shortcuts – the contents page and the index

If you want to make the most of reading textbooks then you need to be able to locate the precise piece of information quickly, rather than having to read half the book to find it.

For this reason you need to be familiar with finding your way round a legal textbook. One of the best ways to make your reading effective is to get used to using as many shortcuts to the information as are available to you. Key in these are the contents page and the index. If you know how to use them then they can save a lot of time and effort.

3.2.1 The contents page

contents pages
a list detailing chapters/topics/ subject matters and the page that they start on

Contents pages are located at the front of texts and are many and varied in style and format. What they hopefully do is to present you with a way of finding your way easily round the book so that you can get straight to the point that you want.

Below is an example of a contents page taken from the front of a standard textbook on tort and covering the area of 'Trespass to the person'.

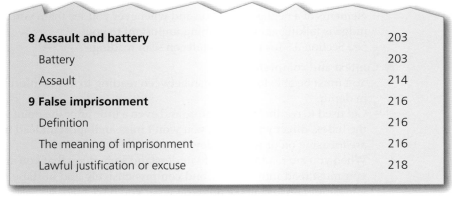

8 Assault and battery	203
Battery	203
Assault	214
9 False imprisonment	216
Definition	216
The meaning of imprisonment	216
Lawful justification or excuse	218

Figure 3.1 An excerpt from a contents page

You will see that this contents page does not actually give a lot away. You can easily locate the section on battery, if that is what you are looking for; however, that subject covers 11 pages of the text. If you wanted to look more precisely at one of the defences available in an action for battery, say necessity, then the contents page is little help and you are going to have to read through those 11 pages until you find it.

Below is a more detailed contents page from a different textbook on tort.

Chapter 2 Trespass to the person: 28

2.1 The origins and character of trespass 28

2.1.1 Historical origins 28

2.1.2 Direct 28

2.1.3 Forcible 29

2.1.4 Injury 29

2.1.5 The tort 30

2.2 Assault 31

2.2.1 Definition 31

2.2.2 Ingredients of the tort 32

2.3 Battery 35

2.3.1 Definitions 35

2.3.2 Ingredients of the tort 35

2.4 Defences to assault and battery 39

2.4.1 Lawful authority 39

2.4.2 Consent 40

2.4.3 Necessity 45

2.4.4 Parental authority 45

2.4.5 Self-defence 46

2.5 False imprisonment 48

2.5.1 Definition 48

2.5.2 Ingredients of the tort 48

2.5.3 Defences 50

2.6 Intentional direct harm and protection from harassment 52

2.6.1 Acts intended to cause harm 53

2.6.2 Protection from Harassment Act 1997 55

2.6.3 A developing tort of harassment? 55

Figure 3.2 An excerpt from a more detailed contents page

This contents page is much more detailed and it breaks the subject down into many more specific aspects. This time if you wanted to read about the defence of 'necessity' in battery you would find it straightaway under the subsection on defences and it even has its own subsection which you can find at page 45, according to Figure 3.2.

The difference between the two different contents pages above also probably tells you something different about the styles of the two books. The second tries to give the student as much information as possible right from the start of the book so that areas of interest can be instantly found, whereas the first only provides the bare minimum of detail at the outset and assumes an expectation of some prior knowledge of the subject matter from the reader.

When selecting a text book it may be worth looking at how detailed or not the contents page is as the more detailed it is the easier it will be for you to find your way round the book and to the specific information you need at the time.

index
an alphabetised list of subjects that provides details of the page or pages on which each subject is mentioned so as to facilitate reference

3.2.2 The index

A detailed **index** is just as important as the contents page. However, it serves a different purpose:

- The contents page should lead you quickly to the particular area that you are interested in at the time.
- The index should lead you inside that area to even more specific points of interest.

Professionals usually prepare indexes. They read through books and find key words that keep repeating themselves and put these in the index with a reference to all the pages where the word appears.

Some authors like to produce their own index, usually because they have an idea from their teaching of the words that students are likely to look up. Very often, the words are cross-referenced, and as well as appearing on their own they also appear under broader and more logical headings.

The difference between the two may well mean that you have to learn how to use the index by thinking more laterally. So sometimes instead of looking up the word that you are actually concerned with you will have to think of a broader heading and look there and see if it is included in a sub-list under that broader word.

Look at the extract from an index below taken from a book on the law of torts. Various words are highlighted to show how to use the index.

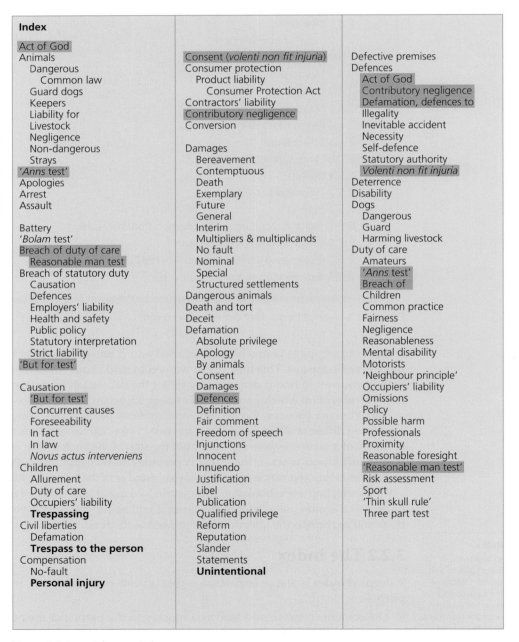

Index

Act of God
Animals
    Dangerous
        Common law
    Guard dogs
    Keepers
    Liability for
    Livestock
    Negligence
    Non-dangerous
    Strays
'*Anns* test'
Apologies
Arrest
Assault

Battery
'*Bolam* test'
Breach of duty of care
    Reasonable man test
Breach of statutory duty
    Causation
    Defences
    Employers' liability
    Health and safety
    Public policy
    Statutory interpretation
    Strict liability
'But for test'

Causation
    'But for test'
    Concurrent causes
    Foreseeability
    In fact
    In law
    Novus actus interveniens
Children
    Allurement
    Duty of care
    Occupiers' liability
    Trespassing
Civil liberties
    Defamation
    Trespass to the person
Compensation
    No-fault
    Personal injury

Consent (*volenti non fit injuria*)
Consumer protection
    Product liability
        Consumer Protection Act
Contractors' liability
Contributory negligence
Conversion

Damages
    Bereavement
    Contemptuous
    Death
    Exemplary
    Future
    General
    Interim
    Multipliers & multiplicands
    No fault
    Nominal
    Special
    Structured settlements
Dangerous animals
Death and tort
Deceit
Defamation
    Absolute privilege
    Apology
    By animals
    Consent
    Damages
    Defences
    Definition
    Fair comment
    Freedom of speech
    Injunctions
    Innocent
    Innuendo
    Justification
    Libel
    Publication
    Qualified privilege
    Reform
    Reputation
    Slander
    Statements
    Unintentional

Defective premises
Defences
    Act of God
    Contributory negligence
    Defamation, defences to
    Illegality
    Inevitable accident
    Necessity
    Self-defence
    Statutory authority
    Volenti non fit injuria
Deterrence
Disability
Dogs
    Dangerous
    Guard
    Harming livestock
Duty of care
    Amateurs
    '*Anns* test'
    Breach of
    Children
    Common practice
    Fairness
    Negligence
    Reasonableness
    Mental disability
    Motorists
    'Neighbour principle'
    Occupiers' liability
    Omissions
    Policy
    Possible harm
    Professionals
    Proximity
    Reasonable foresight
    'Reasonable man test'
    Risk assessment
    Sport
    'Thin skull rule'
    Three part test

Figure 3.3 Excerpt from an index

This is a good index. It is well cross-referenced and the indexer has anticipated the words you may look for. For instance:

- The 'Anns test' appears both as an individual entry and under the 'Duty of care' reference (if more of the index was reproduced here then you would also find 'Duty of care' under a reference for 'Negligence').
- Many other words repeat the same point – 'Act of God' is also entered under 'Defences'; 'Breach of duty of care' appears on its own and also under 'Duty of care'; 'Reasonable man test' appears under 'Breach of duty' and also under 'Duty of care' and so on.
- You will also see that most of the words to the left side of the index have lists of other words underneath them and indented because they are important aspects of the broader word.

student mentor tip

I always look at the index in a book before deciding to buy it as if it's quite limited it tells me something about how easy the book will be to use.

Do not be put off if you cannot go straight to the word that you want in the index. Use a bit of lateral thinking, and you could use the words in the headings in the contents page as a guide. If you cannot find the word itself you may find it under a different heading.

One final point worth making is that you may use the index to find aspects of the particular area that you are researching in chapters other than the ones that are more obvious from the contents list.

ACTIVITY

Exercise

Imagine that you have looked at the whole of the index (the extract of which is provided above at Figure 3.3) but cannot find the words that you want. Use lateral thinking and see if you can do the following:

1. You want to find the difference between 'special damages' and 'general damages' and you have no idea at all what 'exemplary damages' are but none of them is listed in the index under those phrases – see if you can find them in the excerpt.
2. You need to do some research on 'guard dogs' but there is no entry under 'guard dog' – see if you can find them in the extract and spot more than one reference.
3. You have been told that a person will not be liable in tort if the damage has resulted from an 'inevitable accident'; again there is no entry under those words – see if you can think under what broad heading you might find it.

A bit of practice at the start of your course in looking through indexes will save you time as you become more efficient at your reading. The quicker you can get directly to the information you need, the more time you have for reading and the more widely you can read.

3.3 Scan reading

As we have already identified, you will soon run out of time if you try to read everything word by word, particularly where you are reading initially for research. There are times when you need to read in depth, but you must learn to focus on key aspects of your reading and be able to get very quickly to the particular information that you need.

One of the ways in which you can increase the speed of your reading is to scan read. Scan reading is about focusing in on key words in whatever you are reading so that you can concentrate on those parts that are particularly relevant and not get bogged down with those parts that are not.

You may think that it is quite a hard skill to master how to read something by actually missing out large parts of it, but in fact it is not because your brain already does it for you all the time. For instance, read the following:

Aoccdrnig to rsaeerch, it deos not mttaer in waht oredr the ltteers in a wrod are, the olny iprmoatnt tihng is taht the frist and lsat ltteer are in the rghit pclae. The rset can be in a toatl mses and you can sitll raed it wouthit porbelm. Tihs is bcuseae the huamn mnid deos not raed ervey ltteer by istlef, but the wrod as a wlohe.

There! Did you get the message? Recognition of language is about appreciating the whole just as it is with visual imagery. Our brain records things to make sense for us, even if they are jumbled or out of order, and often even when bits are missing. You will have been doing this unconsciously for almost all of your life.

You will not have to make a conscious effort when you are looking something up in a book and scanning down the page to miss out the introductory words and the connecting words. Although they may prove important at times, you do not initially need to register all the words such as 'the', 'and', 'but' etc. If you register just the 'nouns' (such as 'duty of care') and the verbs (the active words such as 'breaching the duty') then you are simplifying and speeding up your reading. Concentrating on words that have specific importance will allow you to spot the relevant while glossing over everything else. However, adopting this method of scan reading does not mean that you will miss other important points, as once you have located the key words you can then focus your more in-depth reading on the text around these key words so that you understand the context of what is written.

One of the benefits of using an e-book and/or e-reader is that most of these devices and formats come with a search function allowing you to search for a specific word or phrase throughout the entirety of the text. Once you have been taken to the location of the key word you are interested in then you can read the sections before and after it so as to understand the context in which it is being referred to. If you struggle to find what you're looking for in an e-book then you may have to think laterally about under what other heading the topic might be listed so as to identify other key words to use. Most e-books also have a contents page and index, again both normally with search facilities.

So trhee you are i'nst taht azanmig!

3.4 Highlighting

3.4.1 Identifying key points in primary source materials

Bar
the strand or organisation of the legal profession to which barristers belong

brief
the legal documents or case file relating to a particular case

student mentor tip

I use different coloured highlighters to mark different things; I use pink for cases, green for specific words and blue for other things of interest. The trick is to not highlight everything and only colour in the bits that are really important.

Students often tend to read a chapter of a book, or an article, or a judgment in a law report from start to finish. So it appears from our experience that students are not always fully aware of how to focus their reading, or how to scan through to capture the most significant points of information.

The fact that students have yet to learn the skill of scan reading is confirmed when we look at what students choose to highlight from books or articles or judgments. This is often pretty much everything, producing a page full of yellow highlight. It is shown up even more in a small session tutorial when we ask the student to list the critical points that he or she has discovered from their reading. The consequence is that teachers have to coax the points out of the students by giving clues as to what might have been gathered from what a particular judge said in a particular part of a judgment. Students then have to spend some time looking through their extensive highlighting to try to find what the tutor is suggesting and the tutorial becomes more like a lecture in style.

With law, possibly even more than in other subjects, you need to develop the arts of scan reading and highlighting because you have lots of often quite complex information to assimilate, and only fairly limited time in which to do it. Besides this, if you go on to professional practice, the skill will be even more important, particularly if you choose to join the **Bar**. It is not unusual for barristers to have to get to know the **brief** on the day of the case itself and in court they may need to refer to documents and find what they need very quickly in order to react effectively to what is going on.

Highlighting relevant phrases and words (especially when initially scan reading a document) will allow you to easily revisit these particular points in the prose at a later stage as the highlighting will enable you to be able to identify the relevant passages quickly and without having to re-read everything that you have already read.

It is also important to develop the skill of reading the information and breaking it down into the basic points that you understand. You can then apply this process to your coursework and, just as importantly, the revision skills that you will find in Chapter 11 when you need to translate your knowledge and understanding into the more pressurised environment of the examination.

ACTIVITY

Exercise

You may be asked by your tutors to use case books as a quicker way of gaining familiarity with case judgments than going to the law reports themselves. Case books do not usually give all of the judgment. The author has selected wisely the parts that he or she feels tell the reader most about the principles that emerge from the case and also use these edited extracts to identify the difficulties that can arise from a particular case. As a result you will often find some critical commentary which should prove useful.

Using adapted extracts from judgments, or indeed sections from articles or books, is one way of helping students to gain the required skills before practising on the real thing. Below is an adapted case extract taken from the judgment in *Church* [1966] 1 QB 59 – an important case on involuntary manslaughter in criminal law.

The judgment has already been reduced to make the exercise more manageable. In learning what the case has to say about unlawful act manslaughter you can break it down still further into critical points. When you have mastered the skill of reading and highlighting the important points you can do the same with law reports themselves, by trying to build up the skill of taking in what is important. This is identified below.

To show how the process should work in your own reading, various parts of the judgment have been highlighted. The amount of highlighting should be a pointer for you when you are doing this yourself because there is a lot more in this little extract than you would usually expect to find. In addition to the highlights, a simpler version of the point made, or some other commentary is included in the right-hand box. Underneath the extract a list of bulleted points is included of the type that you could make as notes and feed into coursework or into key cards for revision (see Chapter 11).

R v Church (1966) 1 QB 59	
Facts	
Church was mocked about his impotence by his female victim. He knocked her unconscious and, not being able to revive her, he panicked thinking she was dead, and threw her into a river where she drowned. He was acquitted of murder but convicted of manslaughter. He appealed unsuccessfully on the direction of the trial judge on the requirements of manslaughter.	*Significant fact is that he thought she was dead when he threw her in the river.*
Judgment EDMUND-DAVIES LJ:	
Two passages in the summing up are material here. They are these: (1) 'If by an unlawful act of violence done deliberately to the person of another, that other is killed, the killing is manslaughter even though the accused never intended death or grievous bodily harm to result. If this woman was alive, as she was, when he threw her into the river, what he did was the deliberate act of throwing a living body into the river. That is an	*Trial judge has said that manslaughter is based on unlawful act – and no need for intent to kill or cause serious harm.*

Continued on next page

unlawful killing and it does not matter whether he believed she was dead or not, and that is my direction to you,' and (2) 'I would suggest to you, though it is of course for you to approach your task as you think fit, that a convenient way of approaching it would be to say: What do we think about this defence that he honestly believed the woman to be dead? If you think that it is true, why then, as I have told you, your proper verdict would be one of manslaughter, not murder.' Such a direction is not lacking in authority ... Nevertheless, in the judgment of this court it was misdirection. It amounted to telling the jury that, whenever any unlawful act is committed in relation to a human being which resulted in death there must be, at least, a conviction for manslaughter. This might at one time have been regarded as good law ... it appears to this court that the passage of years has achieved a transformation in this branch of the law and, even in relation to manslaughter, a degree of *mens rea* has become recognised as essential. To define it is a difficult task, and in *Andrews v DPP* Lord Atkin spoke of the 'element of "unlawfulness" which is the elusive factor'. Stressing that we are here leaving entirely out of account those ingredients of homicide which might justify a verdict of manslaughter on the grounds of (a) criminal negligence, or (b) provocation, or (c) diminished responsibility, the conclusion of this court is that an unlawful act causing the death of another cannot, simply because it is an unlawful act, render a manslaughter verdict inevitable. For such a verdict inexorably to follow, the unlawful act must be such as all sober and reasonable people would inevitably recognise must subject the other person to, at least, the risk of some harm resulting therefrom, albeit not serious harm. If such be the test, as we judge it to be, then it follows that in our view it was a misdirection to tell the jury simpliciter that it mattered nothing for manslaughter whether or not the appellant believed Mrs Nott to be dead when he threw her in the river ... in the circumstances, such a misdirection does not, in our judgment, involve that the conviction for manslaughter must or should be quashed.

Trial judge said that if accused believed woman was dead then must be manslaughter not murder.

Appeal judge says that the above was a misdirection – because trial judge is suggesting that whenever an unlawful act results in death it must be a manslaughter.

Appeal judge suggests that there must be some mens rea.

Appeal judge says that an unlawful act on its own is not sufficient.

The act also has to be dangerous – judged against the standards of a 'sober and reasonable man'.

Trial judge's direction was a misdirection – but no need for conviction to be quashed.

Figure 3.4 Extract adapted from the judgment in *R v Church* [1966] 1 QB 59

So, having gone through the exercise above, highlighting the appropriate parts of the judgment, and making your own brief commentary on what the judge is saying, you can then reduce it still further into a set of small notes. You may find that using bullet points is a good way of remembering what you need to. One of the reasons for this is that in later testing yourself you are likely to remember the number of bullets that you have to remember for the case in question.

KEY FACTS

Key points from *Church*:

The extract from the judgment above seems to contain seven critical points:

- Unlawful act manslaughter does not depend on the existence of an intention to kill or to cause serious harm.
- It does depend on a death resulting from the defendant's unlawful act.
- But the act on its own is insufficient for a conviction for manslaughter.

Continued on next page

Continued

- There must also be the *mens rea* for the unlawful act.
- The act must be dangerous.
- What is dangerous is that which all sober and reasonable people would recognise would put the victim at risk of harm.
- This harm need not be serious harm.

ACTIVITY

Exercise

Read the following very brief example of a judgment and, in the same way as in the example in Figure 3.4 above, highlight what you think is important in the extract, make brief explanatory notes in the right-hand margin; then add your own brief Key Facts chart. (A suggested answer can be found in the Appendix at page 253.)

Hyde v Wrench	
Rolls Court [1840] 3 Beav 334; Jur 1106; 49 ER 132	
June 6. The defendant wrote to the plaintiff offering to sell his farm for £1,000. The plaintiff's agent immediately called on the defendant and made an offer of £950, which the defendant wished to have a few days to consider.	
June 27. The defendant wrote to say that he would not accept this offer.	
June 29. The plaintiff wrote accepting the offer of June 6.	
The plaintiff bought an action for specific performance.	
The defendant filed a general demurrer.	
THE MASTER OF THE ROLLS (LORD LANGDALE): Under the circumstances stated in this bill, I think there exists no valid binding contract between the parties for the purchase of the property. The defendant offered to sell it for £1,000, and if that had at once been unconditionally accepted, there would undoubtedly have been a perfect binding contract; instead of that, the plaintiff made an offer of his own, to purchase the property for £950, and he thereby rejected the offer previously made by the defendant. I think that it was not afterwards competent for him to revive the proposal of the defendant, by tendering an acceptance of it; and that, therefore, there exists no obligation of any sort between the parties; the demurrer must be allowed.	

Once you have mastered the art of paraphrasing judgments or even articles and books in this way you will then be able to make much more effective use of your time. You will then end up with a much clearer understanding than if you try to associate pages and pages of writing with what you have read in total.

When you look at what has been done in the highlighting exercise above, it really only reflects the points made in Section 3.3 on scan reading. The one feeds into the other.

3.4.2 Identifying the key points from secondary sources

As we have already identified in Section 3.4.1 it is vital that you become able to read effectively and extract from your reading the key points from all the different less important detail.

In judgments from decided cases you will find the principles of law as identified by the judges. There is often some critical analysis. However, it is from secondary sources, textbooks, but particularly from articles in refereed journals that you will find debate about the law and on suggestions as to what may be wrong with it or how it could be reformed or improved. For this reason your reading of secondary sources is vital to building up your critical awareness of the law, particularly in preparation for essay questions.

The basic rules on focusing on and highlighting that we discussed in Section 3.4.1 are just as applicable. The difference is that you will be building up the basis of arguments rather than just extracting points of law, factual information, and the reasoning behind them.

Below is an adapted extract from a journal article considered in the same way that we looked at an extract from a judgment in Figure 3.4. Again key points are highlighted and again a more simplified commentary is provided in the right-hand column. You should focus on the level of highlighting in both Figures 3.4 above and 3.5 below and bear the extent of the highlighting in mind when you read Section 3.5. The extract concerns a case on occupiers' liability in torts. The author of the article makes some very interesting critical comments about liability under that area of law in the circumstances of the case, which is evidenced by the title of the article. It also provides some interesting critical insight for an essay-style question on the area.

Extract adapted from 'An outbreak of common sense'. Jeremy Pendlebury. Barrister. *New Law Journal*. 27 April 2007.	
On a fine spring evening, a woman walked across an ostensibly well kempt village green to the adjacent pub … She placed her foot into a hole, hidden by the grass, and broke her leg so badly that six years on she still suffered considerable pain and disability. The hole was a purpose-built maypole hole which had become exposed.	*Basic facts*
Before the Court of Appeal decision in *Cole v Davis-Gilbert* and the *Royal British Legion* [2007] All ER (D) 20, a lawyer might have held the view that she had a decent case … under the Occupiers' Liability Acts of 1957 or 1984 against either the maker of the hole or the person responsible for the village green.	*Speculation on how the law might have been seen before the case*
The press (and subsequent public) reaction to this decision was perhaps a surprise … 85 comments appear on the *Daily Mail's* website under the headline, *An Outbreak of Common Sense*. So why is this?	
The answer may be that this case has demonstrated how the perceived compensation culture has arguably created a lawyer's subculture of assumption of liability, when on a proper analysis and an application of basic principles, there is none. As Lord Justice Scott Baker observed, in giving his judgment in *Cole*, sometimes accidents are just pure accidents.	*Strong phrase* *The author believes that lawyers are making assumptions not based on law* *Mirrors the defence of inevitable accident*
Cole's case against the owner [of the village green] was that, as occupier, he had a duty to ensure that visitors were reasonably safe; and her case against the [Royal British] legion was that it had failed in its neighbour's duty of care properly to fill in the maypole hole after the fete of 1999 or 2000.	*Basis of the claimant's argument*

Continued on next page

Continued

<table>
<tr><td>

Cole's case against the owner was that there was a duty to inspect the green; and the existence of the hole demonstrated a failure of that duty. President Sir Igor Judge asked:

- how often should the owner inspect the green – every day, every week or every month; and
- assuming a failure to inspect, would proper inspection have revealed the hole?

Those questions effectively sealed the fate of Cole's appeal against the owner, for there was no answer. Even a daily inspection would not ensure the absence of holes; this was a village green used by many for all sorts of purposes; children or animals might dig holes or leave piles of debris – both tripping hazards. Thus a morning inspection which had established reasonable safety might be rendered redundant by teatime.

Cole's argument [against the Royal British Legion] was that [it] had a duty to ensure that the making good [of the maypole hole] was such that it could not become exposed for the foreseeable future; it had become exposed, thus the legion was liable. The court asked whether that duty should last one, five, 10, 20 or 100 years or more.

This question sealed the fate of Cole's appeal against the legion, for again there was no answer. Had the hole been dug out by someone or something the day after it was filled in, provided the legion had properly filled it in – thus fulfilling its neighbour's duty – there was no liability.

</td><td>

Key questions – showing us how exacting the duty would be

Again shows how impossible it would be to impose a duty

Again points out how difficult it would be to impose a duty in the circumstances

</td></tr>
</table>

Figure 3.5 Extract adapted from 'An outbreak of common sense'. Jeremy Pendlebury. Barrister. *New Law Journal.* 27 April 2007

The extract has been adapted so that most of it is relevant to the point being made. Even though the case was lost you can extract some telling points about the law on occupiers' liability:

- an occupier does owe a duty to keep lawful visitors safe for the purposes of their visit
- there can be dual occupation of land
- but the duty is not unlimited and indefinite and precautions have to be practicable (which actually only reflects factors taken into account when assessing if a breach has occurred)
- and, as the judge identified in the case, sometimes accidents are just that – accidents (which again could reflect the defence of inevitable accident).

The author is also clearly excited by the case and makes some wonderful critical comment, not about the state of the law, but about how he feels lawyers would apparently like it to be administered.

- he refers to the 'compensation culture' – clearly a critical label
- he criticises lawyers for persuading people that it is too easy to sue
- and also for encouraging people to sue
- and he states that the press and public reaction was a surprise – presumably a comment that the 'compensation culture' was entrenched
- The *Daily Mail*'s headline is also a very strong critical comment in its own right – 'An outbreak of common sense'.

3.5 Making notes from reading

Not everybody makes notes in the same way. There is any number of different ways of putting down information. Note-taking is a very personal process and the most important thing about your notes is that they should mean something to you, so that you are able to use them easily and effectively, and that they make perfect sense to you.

Many of the hints on structuring your notes and different styles of note-taking in Chapter 2 are useful to you here, but of course making notes from your reading is slightly different:

- because you have more time to do it
- because you are not following the directions of your teachers
- because you are taking notes from an entirely different source
- because you are able to determine the structure of your notes and in what order you make them, rather than having it dictated for you.

In any case what you have to do at some point is to make a version of your notes that includes both the basis of your lectures and the extra information that you find from other sources. This is why it is so important to understand how to produce a good structure to your notes that makes sense to you. This is obviously vital when you are preparing for your exams because, if you do not have a set of notes that you clearly understand or if you have to move between a variety of different pieces of paper for the same point or the same area, then you are likely to miss important details and your revision will be less effective.

You do have certain aids already for creating a good structure for your notes if you think about it carefully:

- If your lecturer has indicated headings or sub-headings or any natural breaks in a topic area during your lectures then you can take this as a reasonable breakdown of the subject area and use them yourself.
- Your teacher may have given you handouts. These will almost certainly be broken down by headings and sub-headings and at the very least by different paragraphs. Again this is a useful indication of how the topic area breaks down and how you might structure your own notes.
- If you are taking notes from textbooks these will almost certainly have some headings and possibly sub-headings which again can feed into your own structure and the contents list (that we have already looked at) is another hint on how to structure notes.
- Even law reports, if you look at the letters down the side next to paragraphs, can give you some idea of structure.

There are also many other practical points about taking notes that you can follow to make your notes a more effective aid:

- Scan the material first. This allows you to build up an awareness of the material. It presents you with the big picture so you can appreciate what is important in the text. It will provide you with more effective notes and it will take less time.
- Try to make your notes clear but also try hard to be concise when taking notes. If you merely copy down everything from a book you will have a lot of irrelevant detail and what you have will be no different and no shorter (and could even be longer) than that section of the book.
- You can and should make good use of headings and sub-headings. This will give a structure not only to your notes but also to your learning as well as to your revision for exams. You have many sources, as indicated above, from which to work out how to divide up your notes by section. (You can test your ability to section off your notes under headings by choosing an area that you are currently studying. Divide the topic into what you think are the most the important headings and then look in a textbook and see how your headings and even sub-headings compare.)
- You can also make very effective use of bullet points. While you may want a lot of detail in your notes, they are for your later use when writing coursework assignments or revising for exams, so they do not need to be written like a book.
- Your notes are also very personal. So there is no reason why you should not make extensive use of abbreviations as long as you use them consistently and you do not

forget what they are. There are some very obvious ones like D = defendant, C = claimant. Your teachers may in any case inform you of recognised abbreviations such as CA = Court of Appeal, SC = Supreme Court and HL = House of Lords.

■ Because you are studying law your teachers will always want you to give authority for the points that you make in coursework assignments or in exams. So you should make sure that you do this in your notes too and use cases or statutory sources in your notes.

■ One other thing that you need to remember is that essay questions in coursework and examinations will require you to make critical comments. You need to include such comment from books and articles in your notes. You also might want to extract particular quotes in your notes or even copy down useful statistical information. With so many different features in your notes (basic information, key principles, cases, sections of Acts, as well as key comments or quotes) it may also be useful to have a set of key symbols. By doing this, when reading subsequently you can head straight to the particular feature you require. An alternative is to colour code.

■ When you are reading from lots of different sources it is also useful to leave spaces so that you can add in other information from the different sources later.

■ Visual stimuli are particularly useful learning aids. So if you are good at drawing diagrams add them or if you find pictures or diagrams in things that you read you might choose to photocopy them and cut and paste them into your notes.

student mentor tip

So that I don't clutter up my notes about legal principles with lots of case facts I keep a separate set of notes listing all the different case facts which I can refer to when I need to.

3.6 Making use of your notes

It is important to remember that your notes can, and probably should, be the most central core of your learning. They represent the information that you have gathered from all of the different sources available to you: from your lessons, from the textbooks, from articles, from judgments or statutes, and from other sources that supplement and add extra detail to your class notes.

If your notes are effective then, as well as being used to help with the overall development of your understanding, they can also be very useful when you are preparing coursework assignments and indeed when you want to make reduced notes or revision aids during your revision preparation for the exams (see Chapter 11).

There is one very important point that applies both to the notes that you have taken in your lectures and those that you have made in your reading, whether from paper sources like textbooks or from electronic sources, and that is that you should always read through your notes soon after you have made them to ensure you understand them. It is one thing developing the art of taking good notes but notes are only good if they make sense to you. Finding out that you do not understand your notes when you are in the middle of revision is probably worse than taking no notes at all because then you have little time left to do anything about it and you will probably panic.

Your notes are vital to you in various respects:

tutor tip

For your notes to be of maximum value to you remember that they must:

• be complete
• be up to date
• be organised and in order
• be compact but also comprehensive
• make use of all of your sources (lecture notes and from reading).

■ First, your lecture notes are one of the best guides that you have for making notes from other sources.

■ Second, notes made from reading are the best way of clarifying, illuminating and expanding the notes that you take in lectures.

■ Your completed notes are the basis of your coursework answers or the guide to other sources that you will use at that time.

■ They also form the basis for whatever type of revision aids you devise in preparation for exams.

3.7 Keeping references

As we have said, it is important that your notes are organised and in order. This is vital at times of writing coursework assignments or revising for exams, so you can move methodically through the information without having to spend hours reading to find the bit that you want.

As you read to supplement your notes or for research you may come across and identify cases or even articles from journals that you think are worth referring to and include a reference to them in your notes.

You may find that you save a lot of time by highlighting passages from books or law reports that you have copied, instead of making notes from all the directed sources. You may feel that it is sufficient to return to these when needed rather than laboriously rewriting them in your notes.

In either case you need to be able to refer to these sources again and not waste time looking for them.

If you have collected materials, such as articles, photocopies of pages from large text books in the library or from specific law reports, make sure that you create files of these with some form of code to identify where they are kept and insert a reference to your code in your notes so that once again you can easily go back to them and find them quickly.

Students are increasingly reliant on electronic sources for research purposes and so if you favour using this form of information ensure that you keep an electronic list of all online or e-book sources that you access and use so that you do not have to undertake new searches every time you want to re-find a particular site or article.

3.8 Making sense of difficult material

Law texts are full of technical terms and difficult concepts. When you read material, you may fail to understand the issues you are reading about. If this is the case, try to adopt the following methods:

- **Summary or chapter overviews** – Many texts have introductory overviews or summaries. Read these to provide a context to the material. These sections are normally guides to the information that is presented.
- **Read critically** – By reading set material passively you will gain a poor understanding. Try to read the material actively. Make annotations next to areas on misunderstanding; try to link the subject matter to tutorial or coursework tasks in order to give it a context. Question the validity of the viewpoints. Make a note of the technical terms you do not understand and then look them up in a legal thesaurus.
- **Read the whole passage** – Do not give up if you find the material difficult. Many texts are not written in terms of ease of understanding. There may be greater explanation on issues that are causing you concern later on in the reading material.
- **Break the material into manageable chunks** – Look at the section headings. Read one section at a time and review it. Make a note of its key themes. Repeat this for the rest of the text.
- **Seek support** – Focus on the issues you do understand and then make a list of the issues that you do not. Seek tutor or peer support – they may be able to explain the issues in a way you will understand.

tutor tip

Make a habit of providing a reference to all materials used when making your notes. Then if you want to go back and look at a particular case in a law report you will be able to because you will have the full citation in your notes by the side of the case name or in the margin.

ACTIVITY

Exercise

1. On the next page you will find an extract from the case of *Woolmington v DPP* [1935] AC 462 where Viscount Sankey LC sets out one of the most important legal principles found within the English legal system.
2. Try to read the passage actively, thinking about what you are reading and the questions that occur to you. Make notes to aid your understanding of what Viscount Sankey LC is saying, question how it links in with other areas of law and say why you think it is such an important legal speech.
3. You will find short annotations in the right-hand box which you can use to compare your own notes and questions with.

Continued on next page

Woolmington v DPP [1935] AC 462

Facts

Woolmington's wife (the victim) had left him. In an effort to convince her to return to the matrimonial home he took a shotgun and went to where she was staying with the alleged intention to shoot himself if she did not return to him. The gun went off and the wife was killed. Woolmington was convicted of his wife's wilful murder after failing to prove that he did not intend to kill her. He appealed unsuccessfully to the Court of Appeal, which then refused leave to appeal to the House of Lords.

Judgment

Viscount Sankey LC:

Throughout the web of the English criminal law one golden thread is always to be seen, that it is the duty of the prosecution to prove the prisoner's guilt subject to what I have already said as to the defence of insanity and subject also to any statutory exception. If, at the end of and on the whole of the case, there is a reasonable doubt, created by the evidence given by either the prosecution or the prisoner, as to whether the prisoner killed the deceased with a malicious intention, the prosecution has not made out the case and the prisoner is entitled to an acquittal.

Question: What does the law say about the defence of insanity, and what statutory exceptions are there? Why is there this difference?

Link: To the study of Criminal law.

No matter what the charge or where the trial, the principle that the prosecution must prove the guilt of the prisoner is part of the common law of England and no attempt to whittle it down can be entertained. When dealing with a murder case the Crown must prove (a) death as the result of a voluntary act of the accused and (b) malice of the accused. It may prove malice either expressly or by implication. For malice may be implied where death occurs as the result of a voluntary act of the accused, which is (i) intentional and (ii) unprovoked. When evidence of death and malice has been given (this is a question for the jury) the accused is entitled to show, by evidence or by examination of the circumstances adduced by the Crown that the act on his part, which caused death, was either unintentional or provoked.

Question: What does 'malicious intention' mean?

Key theme: What needs to be proved in relation to a murder charge.

Key theme: Who has to prove what in a criminal case.

If the jury are either satisfied with his explanation or, upon a review of all the evidence, are left in reasonable doubt whether, even if his explanation be not accepted, the act was unintentional or provoked, the prisoner is entitled to be acquitted. It is not the law of England to say, as was said in the summing-up in the present case: 'if the Crown satisfy you that this woman died at the prisoner's hands then he has to show that there are circumstances to be found in the evidence which has been given from the witness-box in this case which alleviate the crime so that it is only manslaughter or which excuse the homicide altogether by showing it was a pure accident'. If the proposition laid down by Sir Michael or in the summing-up in *Rex v Greenacre* 8 C & P 35, 42 means this, those authorities are wrong.

Link: To the study of the English legal system.

Question: What did the case of Rex v Greenacre *say? Was it wrong? Why?*

We were then asked to follow the Court of Criminal Appeal and to apply the proviso of s 4 of the Criminal Appeal Act 1907, which says: 'the Court may, notwithstanding that they are of opinion that the point raised in the appeal might be decided in favour of the appellant, dismiss the appeal if they consider that no substantial miscarriage of justice has actually occurred'. There is no doubt that there is ample jurisdiction to apply that proviso in a case of murder.

Question: What is a 'capital case'?

Question: What does this conclusion mean? What is the ratio decidendi of this case?

Continued on next page

The Act makes no distinction between a capital case and any other case, but we think it impossible to apply it in the present case. We cannot say that if the jury had been properly directed they would have inevitably come to the same conclusion. In the result we decline to apply the proviso and, as already stated, we order that the appeal should be allowed and the conviction quashed.	*Question: What does the word 'quashed' mean?* *Questions: What effect does allowing the appeal have* *(i) on the case;* *(ii) on the law in general?*

Figure 3.6 An extract from the case of *Woolmington v DPP* [1935] AC 462]

4. After reading the extract above you may find that you have asked the same (or similar questions) as found in the right-hand box, or you may even have asked different questions or identified other links and key themes. It matters not whether your annotations match those above but the important point is that you are forming your own questions and making your own links to other areas of your studies and that you are reading actively.

SUMMARY

- Reading is an effective way to develop and widen your understanding of a particular subject or topic.
- Legal material and information can be found in a variety of different sources, such as cases, journals, textbooks and online etc.
- To gain the most benefit from your reading you need to ensure that you are reading effectively and extracting relevant information in a timely fashion.
- Use the shortcuts provided, such as the contents pages and index, to help you identify quickly the location of what you are looking for.
- If you cannot find what you want when using these shortcuts then remember to think laterally about what you are looking for.
- Scan reading is a crucial skill to learn as it allows you to quickly scan a long piece of prose and identify the specific parts you need to read in detail.
- Make sure you use highlighting effectively and target only the words and phrases you are interested in; don't just highlight everything.
- Make short organised notes that bullet or list the important principles you are researching.
- Make sure you can understand your notes.
- Keep a comprehensive record of source references as it will save you time in the long run.
- Ensure that you read actively. Question what you are reading and relate it back to what you have learnt so far.

Further reading

Adler, M. J. & Van Doren, C., *How to Read a Book: The Classic Guide to Intelligent Reading* (1st edn, a Touchstone book, 2011) [Kindle edition].

4

Explaining Primary Sources and Secondary Sources

AIMS AND OBJECTIVES

After reading this chapter you should be able to:

- Understand the difference between primary sources and secondary sources
- Understand the methods of citation for bills, statutes, statutory instruments and case law
- Understand the relevance of legal encyclopaedias, journal articles and textbooks
- Understand the basic sources of the law in England and Wales
- Use citations to research law
- Use legal encyclopaedias, journal articles and textbooks to research law
- Understand the difference between official and non-official sources of legislation
- Understand the range and importance of secondary sources of legal information

During the course of your legal studies you will be expected to use primary sources and secondary sources in your coursework. This chapter aims to explain what is meant by these terms and to give you an idea of when you should consult a primary source and when to consult a secondary one. The text of this chapter is correct at the time of writing, October 2011.

What are primary sources?

legislation
broadly defined as law made by Parliament

case law
broadly defined as law made from the published decisions of judges in courts of law

Primary sources fall into two categories: **legislation** and **case law**. What defines these as primary sources is the fact that they contain the actual text of the law – i.e. the text of an Act of Parliament or the judgment of the court. You may find reading primary sources heavy going at first as the language used can be very legalistic, but you should persevere as there is no real substitute for reading the primary source. A case summary or an article about an Act may present a particular point of view, but only by reading the primary sources can you get the full picture and begin to form your own opinions.

What are secondary sources?

Secondary sources provide background information to supplement the primary sources and include journal articles, legal encyclopaedias and textbooks. In conjunction with primary sources, secondary sources can help you become better informed about a topic.

4.1 Legislation

Legislation is defined as 'the whole or any part of a country's written law' (Martin, 2009). In the United Kingdom the term is most commonly used to mean law which is made by, or on behalf of, Parliament (as opposed to case law, which is made by judges). Legislation comes in two different kinds – **primary legislation** and **secondary legislation**.

4.2 Primary legislation

Primary legislation is the name applied to Acts of Parliament or Statutes.

Acts of Parliament can be divided into two categories – Public General Acts and Local and Personal Acts.

Type of Act	Characteristics	Example
Public General Acts	• Cover matters of public policy • Apply to the whole country	• Human Rights Act 1998
Local and Personal Acts	• Limited application • Only apply to either a specific area, a specific individual or estate	• Nottingham City Council Act 2003 • Valerie Mary Hill and Alan Monk (Marriage Enabling) Act 1985

Figure 4.1 Types of Acts of Parliament

4.2.1 How to refer to primary legislation

Acts of Parliament can be referred to in a number of ways (see Figure 4.2 below):

▪ by short title
▪ by long title
▪ by official citation (year and chapter number).

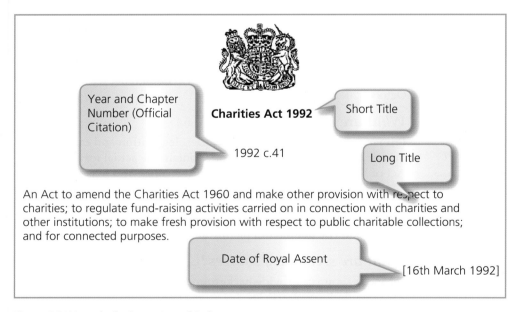

Figure 4.2 Ways of referring to Acts of Parliament

An Act is divided into a series of numbered sections, each with a descriptive title. The word 'section' is often abbreviated to 's' or 'ss' in the plural. Sections of an Act may be divided into subsections ('subs'); subsections may be divided into paragraphs ('para'); and paragraphs may be further divided into subparagraphs ('subpara').

4.2.2 Official Citations

The Official Citation for Acts of Parliament is made up of the year (in which the Act received Royal Assent) and the Chapter number (a running number throughout each calendar year). Chapter can also be abbreviated to c., cap. or chap.

1992 Chapter 41	1992 c. 41	1992 cap. 41	1992 chap. 41
All refer to The Charities Act, which was the 41st Act to receive Royal Assent in 1992.			

Figure 4.3 Citations for The Charities Act

4.2.3 Regnal years

The Regnal year refers to the number of the year of the sovereign's reign (e.g. whether it is the first, second or third year of the sovereign's reign) and was used in Official Citations until 1963.

Colonial Courts of Admiralty Act
53 & 54 Vict c. 27
This was the 27th Act to be passed during the Parliamentary Session which commenced in the 53rd year of Queen Victoria's reign (1889) and ended in the 54th year of her reign (1890).

Figure 4.4 Regnal years

4.2.4 The difference between official sources and non-official sources

The official version of primary legislation is a series of annual volumes called Public General Acts and General Synod Measures, published by Her Majesty's Stationery Office (HMSO). This official source was first published in 1831, although from 1831 until 1870 the series was known as Public General Statutes.

HMSO also publish Public General Acts individually as they receive Royal Assent and the official website – www.legislation.gov.uk – contains the full text of many Public General Acts which, at the time of writing, are available from 1988 onwards.

Non-official sources of Acts of Parliament are those produced by commercial publishers. In order to encourage people to buy them, the commercial publishers add value to their products in a number of ways, such as including amendments to legislation or extensive notes. Figure 4.5 below lists the main non-official sources of Acts of Parliament and outlines the extra features of each.

Title	Publisher	Format	Features	Updated or historical text
Halsbury's Statutes of England and Wales	LexisNexis	Print and online	Annotations to the text – includes details of amendments and repeals.	Updated
Current Law Statutes	Sweet & Maxwell	Print	Reference service covering public and private legislation. Notes are provided for all Acts with major Acts receiving more detailed comment. Includes references to Hansard debates.	Historical
Westlaw	Sweet & Maxwell	Online	Annotations to the text – includes details of amendments and repeals.	Updated

Figure 4.5 The main non-official sources of Acts of Parliament

4.2.5 Finding older Statutes

If you are looking for the original text of an Act from before 1831 (the date when the Public General Acts series began to be published) then you could consult either of the following two series:

Statutes of the Realm

Statutes of the Realm covers Statutes from 1235 until 1713. Private Acts from before 1539 are also included. You can find the Act you want by consulting either the alphabetical, chronological or subject indexes.

Statutes at Large

The *Statutes at Large* series contains reprints of Statutes from the thirteenth century through to the eighteenth and nineteenth centuries.

4.2.6 Historical versions versus updated versions of an Act

Ultimately, the decision as to which version of an Act you should consult comes down to you and will depend very much on your essay question or coursework topic. For much of your studies, you will need to refer to legislation currently in force and so you should use updated versions of Acts of Parliament. However, there will be occasions when you need to look at the original text of an Act, perhaps to compare how it was originally with how it is in force currently, and then you will need to consult historical sources.

4.3 Secondary legislation

Secondary legislation is the term used to describe Statutory Instruments (also known by the abbreviation SIs). The term Statutory Instrument came into usage in 1946. Before this date, secondary legislation was known by the name Statutory Rules and Orders.

Whereas an Act of Parliament tends to give a broad outline of the law in a particular area, it is the Statutory Instruments which provide the detail. Statutory Instruments are drawn up under powers delegated by specific Acts of Parliament and a single Act can give rise to many individual Statutory Instruments. The actual drafting of Statutory Instruments can be done by individuals or bodies, to whom Parliament has delegated the authority.

Statutory Instruments can also be divided into two categories – local and general. Local Statutory Instruments apply only to a specific area of the country, while general Statutory Instruments cover matters of public policy.

tutor tip

Secondary legislation may also be referred to as subordinate legislation or delegated legislation.

tutor tip

There are many more Statutory Instruments published each year than there are Acts. In 2006, 55 Acts of Parliament received Royal Assent and 3,511 Statutory Instruments were made.

student mentor tip

A handy hint for spotting Statutory Instruments is that they often contain one of these words in their title: Rules, Regulations or Order.

4.3.1 How to refer to Statutory Instruments

The Official Citation for Statutory Instruments is by year (the year in which the Statutory Instrument was made) and then a running number (allocated to all Statutory Instruments in a year), e.g. 2003, No. 118 or 2003/118.

Statutory Instruments can also be referred to by their short title, e.g.:

> The Intercountry Adoption (Hague Convention) Regulations 2003
> The County Court (Forms) (Amendment No. 2) Rules 1997

Figure 4.6 An example of a Statutory Instrument

A Statutory Instrument is divided into a series of numbered divisions, which may be further subdivided. The name given to the divisions is determined by the title given to the SI:

- If the SI title contains the word 'Order', then the numbered parts are known as articles
- If the SI title contains the word 'Regulations', then the numbered parts are known as regulations
- If the SI title contains the word 'Rules', then the numbered parts are known as rules.

4.3.2 The difference between official sources and non-official sources

The official source for Statutory Instruments is an annual printed series published by HMSO, known simply as Statutory Instruments. This series reprints only those Statutory Instruments still in force at the end of the calendar year in which they were made. HMSO also publishes Statutory Instruments individually, shortly after they come into force and the official website – www.legislation.gov.uk – contains the full text of Statutory Instruments from the beginning of 1987 onwards (at the time of writing).

The main non-official sources for Statutory Instruments are outlined in Figure 4.7 below.

Title	Publisher	Format	Features	Updated or historical text
Halsbury's Statutory Instruments	LexisNexis	Print and online	Full text online. In print, full text of some SIs, summaries of many more.	Updated
Westlaw	Sweet & Maxwell	Online	Full text	Updated

Figure 4.7 Non-official sources for Statutory Instruments

4.3.3 Historical versions versus updated versions of a Statutory Instrument

As with Acts of Parliament, whether you choose the original text or the updated text of a Statutory Instrument will depend on the nature of your coursework topic. Use updated sources when you need to quote current law and historical sources when you need to quote the original text.

4.4 Parliamentary Bills

4.4.1 What is a Bill?

Bills are draft versions of proposed legislation. Although not actually legislation, they are still important and you may often be required to read a Bill or track its progress through Parliament.

4.4.2 The different types of Bill

The three main types of Bills are Public, Private and Hybrid. Figure 4.8 below outlines these:

Bills
prospective legislation under consideration by Parliament which, if passed, will become Acts

tutor tip

All Acts of Parliament began life as Bills, but not all Bills end up as Acts.

Type		Introduced by	On gaining Royal Assent, becomes
Public – relating to matters of public policy	Government Bill	Government Ministers	Public General Act
	Private Members' Bill	Private Members of Parliament (e.g. an MP or a peer)	
Private – relating to individuals, companies or local authorities		Outside bodies (e.g. local authorities or companies)	Local or Personal Act
Hybrid – has characteristics of both a public and a private Bill		Government Ministers or private MPs	Public General Act

Figure 4.8 Different types of Bill

4.4.3 How Bills are structured

Figure 4.9 shows the structure of a Bill.

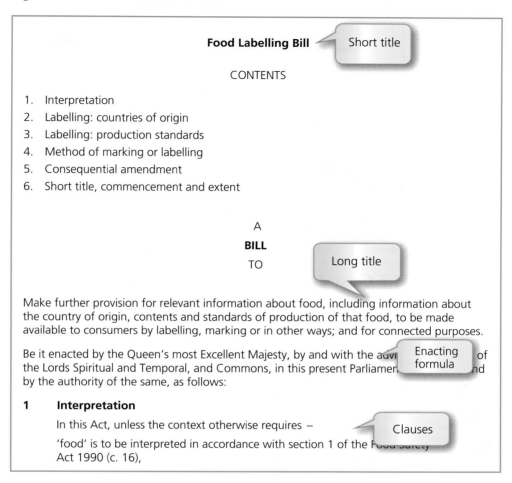

Figure 4.9 The structure of a Bill

A Bill is divided into a series of numbered clauses, each with a descriptive title. The word 'clause' can be abbreviated to 'cl.'. Clauses may be divided into subsections; subsections may be subdivided into paragraphs; and paragraphs may be further divided into subparagraphs.

4.4.4 How Bills are cited

Each Public Bill is given a serial number. This number will change if a Bill is reprinted at any stage. Public Bills should be cited as follows:

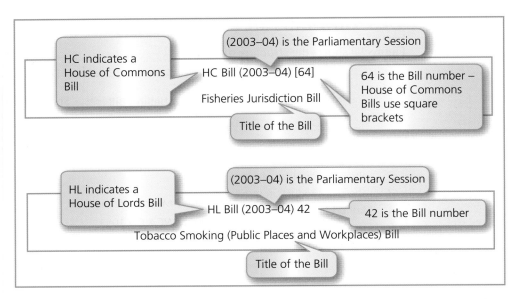

Figure 4.10 How Bills are cited

4.5 Case law

4.5.1 What is case law?

Case law is based on published reports of decisions and judgments of the courts on points of law.

4.5.2 What is a law report?

law reports
named series of published judgments which can be cited as legal precedent in arguing and deciding cases. Examples include the Weekly Law Reports and the All England Law Reports

The published reports are known collectively as **law reports**. There are lots of different series of law reports, each with its own title and referred to by its own legal abbreviation. Most law reports are available in print and many are also available in electronic format.

4.5.3 The difference between a law report and a transcript

Law reports are published by commercial publishers who will add extra features such as catchwords, headnotes and subject indexing, to make the law report easier to trace and use. They will make decisions about which cases to include in their series, based on their own particular criteria (see Section 4.5.5).

Law reports series can be divided into three categories in terms of the types of cases they include. Figure 4.11 gives you an idea of the types of law reports series available:

Type	Coverage	Examples	Citation
General series	Major cases from all subject areas	Weekly Law Reports	WLR
Subject specific series	Major cases relevant to their subject coverage	Housing Law Reports Medical Law Reports	HLR Med LR
Historical series	Reprints of historical cases, usually from before 1865	English Reports Revised Reports	ER RR

Figure 4.11 Types of law reports series available

Transcripts will contain the judgment, but they won't contain any of the added extras that come with a published law report. Online sources and databases now mean that it has become much easier to track down case transcripts, but there will still be many which do not appear on these sites. Individual transcripts may be available by contacting the relevant court, but there is likely to be a cost involved in getting hold of them in this way.

4.5.4 Catchwords and headnotes

Figure 4.12 below illustrates the catchwords and headnote within a law report.

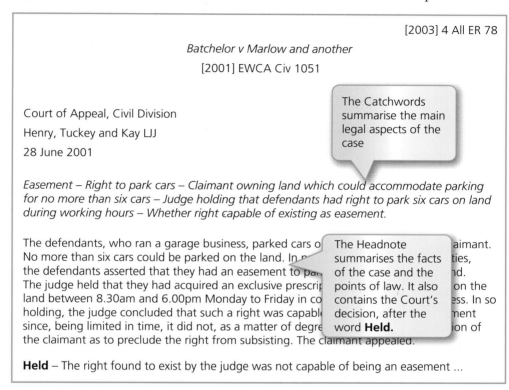

Figure 4.12 Catchwords and headnote within a law report

4.5.5 How cases get reported

You might think that every case heard in court gets reported in a law reports series, but that is not so. In fact, only a small percentage of the cases heard each year actually make it into a law reports series.

So what selection criteria do publishers use when deciding which cases should be included in their law reports series? In general, cases should fall into one of the following categories:

- cases that make new law because they deal with a new situation
- cases that make new law because they extend the application of new principles
- cases that give a modern judicial restatement of existing principles
- cases that clarify conflicting decisions of lower courts
- cases that interpret legislation which is likely to have wide application
- cases that clarify an important point of practice or procedure.

In general, reported cases have been heard in the High Court, the Court of Appeal or the House of Lords. This is because cases have to be of some significance in order to be referred on to the senior courts. Cases heard in the lower courts, e.g. local magistrates' courts, rarely get reported in law reports series.

Also you should note that '*legal interest*' is not the same as '*media interest*'. Cases which receive a lot of media coverage will not automatically be reported in law reports series. Murder cases, for example, often get a lot of coverage on television and in the newspapers, but are not often reported in law reports, as they rarely meet the criteria listed above.

You might also think that each case is only reported in one law reports series, but again this isn't true. The same case can be reported in a number of different law reports series and the version you use will depend on the law reports available to you and the hierarchy of law reporting (see Section 4.5.6 below).

4.5.6 Knowing which version of a case to choose

If a case has been reported in five or six different law reports, does it matter which one you choose? The answer is yes, it does matter, as within the legal profession some law reports take precedence over others. Barristers will follow this hierarchy in court and you should also follow it in your coursework or moot trials. Figure 4.13 will explain the hierarchy:

	Title	Citation	Publisher	Comments
1.	The Law Reports (*includes the Appeal Cases, the Chancery Division, the Family Division and the King's/Queen's Bench Division*)	AC Ch Fam KB/QB	Incorporated Council of Law Reporting for England and Wales	The most authoritative series available. The only reports that are checked by the judges and counsels involved before publication. Can take some time to appear in print.
2.	Weekly Law Reports	WLR	Incorporated Council of Law Reporting for England and Wales	These appear more quickly than the above series. Many of the cases in the Weekly Law Reports will eventually appear in The Law Reports.
3.	All England Law Reports	All ER	LexisNexis	A general series, covering cases on all subjects.
4.	Individual law reports series	If your case has not been reported in any of the above three series, then you can cite whichever individual law report series you choose.		

Figure 4.13 Hierarchy of law reports

You should follow the hierarchy at all times, particularly for a moot or a piece of coursework.

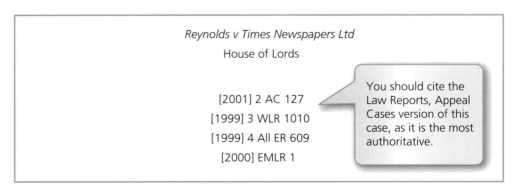

Reynolds v Times Newspapers Ltd

House of Lords

[2001] 2 AC 127
[1999] 3 WLR 1010
[1999] 4 All ER 609
[2000] EMLR 1

You should cite the Law Reports, Appeal Cases version of this case, as it is the most authoritative.

Figure 4.14 Applying the hierarchy

ACTIVITY

Exercise

For each of the three cases below, say which law reports version you would cite in your essay. If you're feeling adventurous, you can also identify what each of the abbreviations stand for (see Section 4.5.12).

Grobbelaar v News Group Newspapers Ltd
House of Lords
[2002] 4 All ER 732
[2002] 1 WLR 3024
[2003] EMLR 1

Rees v Darlington Memorial Hospital Trust
House of Lords
[2004] 1 FLR 234
[2003] 3 WLR 1091
[2004] 1 AC 309

MCC Proceeds Inc v Lehman
Court of Appeal
[1998] 4 All ER 675
[1998] 2 BCLC 659
(1998) 142 SJLB 40

Answers can be found in the Appendix on page 254.

4.5.7 'The Law Reports'

You might have noticed from some of the examples above that there appears to be a series of law reports called *The Law Reports*. We know this sounds confusing but here is the explanation. The Incorporated Council of Law Reporting for England and Wales publish a series known as *The Law Reports*, illustrated in Figure 4.15. This series is the most authoritative version of a law report as it is the only series where the text of the report is checked before publication by the judges and counsel involved in the case.

It is probably better to describe this series as a family of reports because they produce a report that corresponds with each of the higher divisions of Her Majesty's Court Service:

Title	Citation
Law Reports, Appeal Cases	AC
Law Reports, Chancery Division	Ch
Law Reports, Family Division	Fam
Law Reports, King's/Queen's Bench Division	KB/QB

Note: The title of this report changes depending on the gender of the monarch at the time.

Figure 4.15 The Law Reports

case citations
shorthand references to locating full text versions of case judgments. Case citations usually include the year of reporting, volume number, abbreviation for the law report series and the page number

4.5.8 Understanding case citations

Case citations tell you where you can find a complete report of a case. Although they may look confusing at first glance, once you learn how to break them down and understand them, they are really quite easy. Case citations contain the following parts:

- year
- volume number (where appropriate – not every law reports series has more than one volume in a year)

▦ abbreviation for the law reports series
▦ page number on which the law report starts.

Figure 4.16 below gives a number of different citations for the same case and illustrates how to break each one down:

Airedale NHS Trust v Bland			
[1993] AC 789			
[1993] 2 WLR 316			
[1993] 1 All ER 821			
[1993] The year in which the case was reported	**AC** The abbreviation for the law reports series (Law Reports, Appeal Cases)		**789** The page number on which the law report starts
[1993] The year in which the case was reported	**2** The volume number	**WLR** The abbreviation for the law reports series (Weekly Law Reports)	**316** The page number on which the report starts
[1993] The year in which the case was reported	**1** The volume number	**All ER** The abbreviation for the law reports series (All England Law Reports)	**821** The page number on which the law report starts

Figure 4.16 Breaking down case citations

4.5.9 Neutral citations

Neutral citations were introduced by the House of Lords, the Court of Appeal and the Administrative Court in 2001. In 2002, this system was extended to all High Court judgments and now also includes the Supreme Court. While they look very similar to a law report citation, neutral citations have two main differences:

▦ the abbreviation refers to the court rather than to a law reports series
▦ the number refers to the judgment number instead of a page number.

See Figure 4.17 below for an example of a neutral citation. Neutral citations should not be used when a law report citation exists for the case and can be used instead.

| Gorringe v Calderdale Metropolitan Borough Council | | |
[2004] UKHL 15		
[2004] The year in which the case was heard	**UKHL** The court in which the case was heard – United Kingdom, House of Lords	**15** The judgment number – in this example, this was the 15th judgment to be delivered in the House of Lords in 2004

Figure 4.17 A neutral citation

4.5.10 Other citations that might catch you out

There are some other citations which might confuse you. In 2002, Sweet & Maxwell (one of the largest law reports publishers in the United Kingdom) adopted a citation system similar to that of neutral citations. In citations to Sweet & Maxwell law reports, the final number now refers to the case number rather than to the page number. See Figure 4.18 for an example.

Smith v Spaul [2003] HLR 38		
[2003]	**HLR**	**38**
The year in which the case was reported	The abbreviation for the law reports series – Housing Law Reports	The 38th case to be reported in the Housing Law Reports in 2003, (the report actually starts on page 540)

Figure 4.18 Example of Sweet & Maxwell's citation system

4.5.11 The square brackets [ ] and round brackets ( ) rule

The type of brackets used in a citation is significant because it indicates the importance of the date in finding the case.

Square brackets mean that the year is essential in finding the case. For example, in the case *Campbell v Mirror Group Newspapers Ltd* [2003] 1 All ER 224, the year is very important. Because the All England Law Reports produce a Volume 1 every year, you wouldn't be able to find this case very easily if the only information you had was 1 All ER 224.

Round brackets mean that the volume number is more important than the year in locating the case. In these series, each volume may contain cases heard in a number of different years, which is why you must rely on the volume number. For example, although the following three cases were heard in different years, they are all reported in the same volume (15) of the *Butterworths Medico-Legal Reports*:

> *AB v Glasgow and West of Scotland Blood Transfusion Service* (1989) 15 BMLR 91
>
> *Cotgreave v Cheshire County Council* (1992) 15 BMLR 50
>
> *Digby v Essex County Council* (1993) 15 BMLR 34

Figure 4.19 Understanding round brackets

4.5.12 Finding out what the abbreviations stand for

Printed case citators and journal indexes will contain a list of the abbreviations used within them – simply look up the abbreviation to find out the name of the law report.

Electronic legal databases usually provide details of what the abbreviation stands for – see the help pages within the individual database or ask your law librarian for more information.

One of the most comprehensive online abbreviation websites is the Cardiff Index to Legal Abbreviations, www.legalabbrevs.cardiff.ac.uk, developed by Peter Clinch and his team at Cardiff University. It is easy to use, regularly updated and allows you to search either by abbreviation or by title.

For older and foreign legal citations, you may find this book useful:

▦ Raistrick, Donald, *Index to Legal Citations and Abbreviations* (3rd edn, London: Sweet & Maxwell, 2008).

ACTIVITY

Quick quiz

Go to the Cardiff Index to Legal Abbreviations and answer the following:

- What does EMLR stand for?
- What does BWCC stand for?
- What is the correct abbreviation for the Criminal Appeal Reports (Sentencing)?
- What is the correct abbreviation for the Criminal Law Review?

Answers can be found in the Appendix on page 254.

tutor tip

Transcripts will contain the judgment, but they won't have the added extras that come with a published law report, such as headnotes, catchwords and subject indexing.

student mentor tip

Think carefully when using unreported cases in your work. If the case has not been deemed important enough to be reported in any of the law reports series, then are you really sure you should be relying on it?

4.5.13 Unreported and not yet reported cases

Unreported cases are all those cases which don't make it into any of the law reports series. It used to be quite difficult to find information about unreported cases, but the internet has changed all that. There are lots of electronic databases which contain transcripts of unreported cases, such as LexisLibrary, Westlaw, Lawtel and CaseTrack. Find out from your library if you can access any of these databases.

Not yet reported cases refer to very recent cases where a published law report is not yet available. Again, the internet makes it much easier to find information about these cases. Many of the databases mentioned in the previous paragraph provide transcripts or summaries of cases on a next-day basis. The Supreme Court makes its judgments available on its website the day after the judgment is handed down.

4.5.14 Old cases (pre-1865)

There is an important date in the history of law reporting and that date is 1865. In 1865 the Incorporated Council of Law Reporting for England and Wales was formed, to standardise the law reporting system. Before 1865, it appeared as though anybody could set themselves up as a law reporter and produce their own law reports series, which made it quite difficult for people to locate cases.

If you are looking for a case dated earlier than 1865, then there are three main reprinted series of law reports which you should consult – *The English Reports*, *The Revised Reports* and *The All England Law Reports Reprint*. These series reproduce historical law reports and between them they contain most of the major cases from before 1865. Note that the text is simply reprinted from the original series, which means that in some early law reports the text may be in Norman French or Latin.

4.5.15 Finding out if a case is still good law or has been referred to by a later case

If you're going to quote a case in an essay or a moot, you need to make sure that the case is still regarded as 'good law' and has not been overruled at a later date. Case law is constantly evolving and the original decision in any case may be overruled by another judge in a later case. Similarly, you may want to find out if the decision in a particular case has been followed or applied in any subsequent case, so you need to consider the case's complete history.

The direct history of a case refers to other court hearings for the same case (there could be earlier or later hearings, in lower or higher courts). Figure 4.20 shows the history of a case from the High Court through to the House of Lords.

1. *Campbell v Mirror Group Newspapers Ltd*
    High Court, Queen's Bench Division
    27 March 2002
The decision of the High Court was reversed by the Court of Appeal in:
2. *Campbell v Mirror Group Newspapers Ltd*
    Court of Appeal, Civil Division
    14 October 2002
The decision of the Court of Appeal was reversed by the House of Lords in:
3. *Campbell v Mirror Group Newspapers Ltd*
    House of Lords
    6 May 2004

Figure 4.20 The history of a case

The indirect history of a case refers to other cases which have, in some way, judicially considered the judgment in your original case. Figure 4.21 gives an example of an indirect history:

<table>
<tr><td colspan="2" align="center">*Reynolds v Times Newspapers Ltd*</td></tr>
<tr><td colspan="2" align="center">House of Lords</td></tr>
<tr><td colspan="2" align="center">28 October 1999</td></tr>
<tr><td colspan="2">Applied by: *Grobbelaar v News Group Newspapers Ltd* [2001] EWCA Civ 33</td></tr>
<tr><td colspan="2">The decision in *Reynolds v Times Newspapers Ltd* was applied in the case *Grobbelaar v News Group Newspapers Ltd*.</td></tr>
<tr><td colspan="2">Followed by: *Loutchansky v Times Newspapers Ltd* (No. 2) [2001] EWCA Civ 1805</td></tr>
<tr><td colspan="2">The decision in *Reynolds v Times Newspapers Ltd* was followed in the case *Loutchansky v Times Newspapers Ltd* (No. 2).</td></tr>
<tr><td colspan="2">Considered by: *Al-Misnad v Azzaman Ltd* [2003] EWHC 1783</td></tr>
<tr><td colspan="2">The decision in *Reynolds v Times Newspapers Ltd* was considered in the case *Al-Misnad v Azzaman Ltd*.</td></tr>
</table>

Figure 4.21 The indirect history of a case

tutor tip

The *annotating* case is the later case and the *annotated* case is the earlier case. In the example in Figure 4.21, *Reynolds v Times Newspapers Ltd* is the annotated case and *Grobbelaar v News Group Newspapers Ltd*, *Loutchansky v Times Newspapers Ltd* and *Al-Misnad v Azzaman Ltd* are the annotating cases.

Many electronic legal databases, like Westlaw, JustCite and LexisLibrary, will tell you if a case has subsequently been overruled, applied, followed, considered or distinguished. If you don't have access to electronic resources, then a printed case citator will provide the same information. For a more detailed explanation of case citators, please see Section 5.4.1.

It's all very well to say that one case may have applied or overruled the decision in another case, but what exactly do these terms mean? LexisNexis provides a useful explanation of all the terms used to denote how cases have been judicially considered, available on its website – www.butterworths.com/userguides/pdf/CaseSearch.pdf – and presented in Figure 4.22 below.

Applied	Used where the court in the annotating case (which is of a superior jurisdiction) has applied the principle of law enunciated in the annotated case by a court of inferior jurisdiction to a new set of facts
Approved	Used where the court in the annotating case has approved the decision of an inferior court in unrelated proceedings in the annotated case although the decision is not necessary for the disposition of the annotating case
Considered	Used where the court in the annotating case has discussed the decision in the annotated case but has not actually followed, applied, distinguished, etc.
Doubted	Used where the court in the annotating case has disagreed with the decision in the annotated case but either it was not necessary to overrule the decision or the court had no power to do so
Disapproved	Similar to where doubted is used, except that the court has clearly stated that the reasoning in the annotated case is wrong
Distinguished	Used where the court in the annotating case has decided that it need not follow the decision in the annotated case, by which it would otherwise be bound, because of some salient difference between the annotated case and the annotating one
Explained	Used where the court in the annotating case has interpreted the decision in the annotated case and stated what it means

Continued on next page

Continued

Extended	Used in similar circumstances to 'applied'
Followed	Used where the court in the annotating case has expressed itself as bound by the decision in the annotated case which is by a court of a co-ordinate or superior jurisdiction
Not followed	Used where the court in the annotating case has declined to follow the decision in the annotated case which is by a court of co-ordinate jurisdiction
Overruled	Used where the court in the annotating case has decided that the decision in the annotated case, which was given by a court of inferior jurisdiction in unrelated proceedings, is wrong
Referred	Used where the court in the annotating case has dealt with the point of law in the annotated case without comment of any definite character on the latter

Figure 4.22 Explanation of case terms

For more on checking the history of a case, see Section 5.4.5.

4.6 Secondary sources

So far, we have concentrated on primary sources of law, but there are some secondary sources of legal information which you should be aware of and know how to use. If primary sources give you the text of the law (either as legislation or case law), then secondary sources give you additional background material. Examples of secondary sources include legal encyclopaedias, journal articles and textbooks. Secondary sources can help you to more fully understand a piece of legislation or why a judge made a particular decision in a case.

4.6.1 Legal encyclopaedias

Legal encyclopaedias give definitions of the law and often focus on a particular subject area, such as environmental law or health and safety law. They can be an excellent starting point for research as they will refer you to relevant legislation and case law.

Halsbury's Laws of England and Wales

Halsbury's Laws is an exception to other legal encyclopaedias in that it does not simply focus on one specific subject area. Instead it aims to provide a 'restatement of the whole of the laws of England and Wales'. It is produced by LexisLibrary and is available in hard copy or online – check in your own library to see if you have access to the print version, electronic version or both. Section 5.5.1 provides more information on how to use *Halsbury's Laws*.

Subject specific legal encyclopaedias

There are a number of legal encyclopaedias available covering a variety of different subject areas. These may be available in hard copy, usually in a loose-leaf format, or electronically. The loose-leaf approach means that old pages can be removed and new pages inserted as the law changes, ensuring that the information is as up to date as possible. The advantages of these encyclopaedias are that they bring together all the relevant materials on a particular subject and they are regularly updated.

Woodfall's *Law of Landlord and Tenant*, published by Sweet & Maxwell, is an example of a legal encyclopaedia. In hard copy, this is available in a multi-volume loose-leaf format. Woodfall's *Law of Landlord and Tenant* is also available electronically via the Westlaw database. In the electronic version, the text is updated online, so again you can be confident that the information is current and accurate.

Check your library's catalogue, browse the shelves or speak to your librarian to find out what legal encyclopaedias you have access to.

4.6.2 Journal articles

Journal articles are an excellent secondary source of legal information and you should get into the habit of reading them. Section 5.5.3 will discuss in detail how to locate relevant journal articles, but in this section you will learn about legal journals themselves.

Legal journals can be roughly divided into two categories – professional titles and academic titles. Professional titles are those journals which are primarily aimed at practising lawyers, while academic titles are those aimed at scholars and people studying and researching the law. Figure 4.23 outlines some of the main differences between the two types of journal:

Type	Primary audience	Some examples	Defining characteristics
Professional	Practising solicitors or barristers	*Law Society's Gazette*; *The Lawyer*	Short articles; newsy approach; usually weekly
Academic	Scholars, academics, researchers, students	*Modern Law Review; Cambridge Law Journal*	Lengthier, in-depth articles; bibliographies and references; usually quarterly or bi-monthly

Figure 4.23 Differences between professional and academic journals

One specific advantage that journal articles have is that they take a lot less time to be published than books, which makes them a particularly good source for current topics. If you are looking for opinions on a recent case or you want background information about a Bill currently before Parliament, it is unlikely that there will be a book on your topic but quite likely that journal articles will have been written on it.

4.6.3 Textbooks

Textbooks are another very useful secondary source of information. The reading lists you are given by your tutors will recommend titles to you and you should use these as your starting point. If any items on your reading list are identified as essential purchases then you should buy a copy. After all, if a particular book is going to be used every week in tutorials, then it makes sense to have your own copy. But never forget that the library will have many more books on a subject than just those titles on your reading list and that by reading widely on a particular topic you will be better informed and more able to form your own opinion on a subject.

SUMMARY

- Primary sources of law contain the text of the law – the two types of primary source are legislation and case law.
- Legislation is available as primary legislation (Acts) and secondary legislation (Statutory Instruments).
- Legislation is available in its original (historical) version and its amended (updated or current) version.
- Statutory Instruments generally contain one of these words in their title – Rules, Regulations or Order.
- Case law is law based on the published reports of judgments of the courts.
- Not all cases are reported in law reports series – only those which are deemed 'legally interesting'.
- Reported cases are given case citations to help you identify where the case has been published.
- Secondary sources of law supplement the primary sources, and can include textbooks, journal articles and encyclopaedias.
- Secondary sources of law should not be relied on as a substitute for reading the primary sources.

5
Using Primary and Secondary Sources and Some Other General Tips

AIMS AND OBJECTIVES

After reading this chapter you should be able to:

- Understand how to find primary and secondary legislation and case law through using secondary sources
- Understand how to check if an Act of Parliament or a Statutory Instrument is still in force
- Understand how to track the progress of a Bill through Parliament
- Understand how to find primary and secondary legislation and case law through using appropriate citations
- Understand how to use both paper and electronic resources to find law
- Understand how a Law Library works
- Use secondary sources and citations to research law
- Find out if law is still in force
- Understand how to check the history of a case
- Understand how to find legal journal articles

In Chapter 4 we looked at the difference between primary and secondary sources. Now that you are familiar with them, we are going to look in more detail at how to use these sources. To end this chapter, you will learn a few library secrets which will help you to make more effective and efficient use of your time.

Before we start, however, there is a small matter of a disclaimer to be addressed. You will soon find out, if you do not know already, how quickly websites and databases can change, often without warning. You might use a database one day, then access it the following day and find that it looks totally different and the way you search it has completely changed. Because of this, we are careful to point out that the images used in this chapter and the references made to individual databases and websites (including URLs) are correct at the time of writing, October 2011. So, what should you do if you access one of these databases and find it looks nothing like our examples? The most important thing is not to panic. Most databases have their own help pages, so you could use these to get started and then ask your Law Librarian for further advice. Remember, there are no problems, only challenges!

5.1 Primary legislation

5.1.1 Finding an Act of Parliament

Printed sources

Halsbury's Statutes of England and Wales

In its printed form, *Halsbury's Statutes of England and Wales* is a multi-volume work arranged in broad subject groups. It is kept up to date by means of an annual *Cumulative Supplement*, a regular loose-leaf *Noter-Up Service* and the periodic reissuing of the main volumes. Each main volume will have its individual date of publication printed on the spine and is only likely to be reprinted when substantial amounts of the text have been changed. There are also a number of loose-leaf *Service Binders* where recent Acts will be filed until such time as they are incorporated into a reissued main volume.

How you locate an Act within *Halsbury's Statutes* depends very much on the information you have about the Act. The Consolidated Index contains alphabetical and chronological lists of Statutes printed in the volumes, so if you know the Act's name you should look it up in the Alphabetical List of Statutes, which will tell you the volume and page number where it is reprinted. Use the Chronological List of Statutes when you know the year and chapter number (e.g. 1992 c. 10), but not the title. If you have none of this information, then you should use the Consolidated Subject Index to find Acts relating to your subject.

Once you have located your Act in the main volume, you need to consult the *Cumulative Supplement* and *Noter-Up Service* to check if there have been any changes to this Act since the date of publication of the main volume. The *Cumulative Supplement* updates the main volume to a particular date during the previous calendar year. Look up the same volume and page number from the main volume in the *Cumulative Supplement* and any changes that have occurred will be listed here. You will then need to consult the loose-leaf *Noter-Up Service* to bring yourself right up to date. The *Noter-Up Service* is issued six times a year and contains details of any amendments which have occurred since the publication of the *Cumulative Supplement*.

tutor tip

The *Consolidated Index to Halsbury's Statutes* is published annually. Main volumes may be reissued after the publication of the Index which means that the Index will no longer correspond with those particular volumes. In this situation you should consult the index within the individual volume.

Current Law Statutes

Current Law Statutes is arranged by year, often with three or four volumes produced each year. The Acts are printed in chapter number order but there is also an alphabetical index for each year which you can use if you only know the Act's title. Each year of *Current Law Statutes* contains a numerical table of Statutory Instruments for that year, an alphabetical table of Statutes from 1700 onwards and a subject/title index to Acts passed within that year.

Public General Acts

These annual volumes are produced by Her Majesty's Stationery Office (HMSO), and contain the year's Acts in chapter number order. There is also an alphabetical index to Acts for each year.

Statutes at Large

This is a multi-volume printed work containing Acts from 1225–1865. The volumes are in chronological order and within each volume the Statutes are in chapter number order. Each volume also has an alphabetical list of Acts covered. *Statutes at Large* uses regnal years for its dates – see Section 4.2.3.

Loose-leaf encyclopaedias

Loose-leaf encyclopaedias are another useful source for the amended text of Acts. Find out if there is a loose-leaf encyclopaedia covering the subject area you are interested in – you could do this by checking the library catalogue, by browsing the library shelves at the relevant class number or by asking your Law Librarian. As well as the updated text, loose-leaf encyclopaedias often provide additional annotations and commentary related to the subject.

Textbooks

Lots of textbooks also reprint whole or significant sections of Acts. 'Cases and Materials' books (e.g. *Cases and Materials on the English Legal System* by Michael Zander, or *Cases and Materials on Criminal Law* by Janet Dine and James Gobert) provide just that – key cases and legislation related to a particular subject.

Many legal publishers also produce their own books of Statutes in different subject areas, (e.g. *Blackstone's Statutes on Intellectual Property* edited by Andrew Christie and Stephen Gare), which bring together the main pieces of legislation on each topic.

Electronic sources

LexisLibrary

LexisLibrary is a subscription-based database produced by LexisNexis. The legislation section provides electronic access to the amended text of Statutes. You can search by Act name or subject, or alternatively you can browse an alphabetical list of Acts. Most amendments are incorporated into the main body of the text but you should always click on the 'Stop Press' icon, if displayed, as this is where very recent amendments will be listed before being amalgamated into the main text.

The legislation.gov.uk website (www.legislation.gov.uk)

This freely available website contains the original (historical) text, alongside the current revised text of Acts from 1988 onwards. Most pre-1988 primary legislation is available on this site, although in some cases only the original published (historical) version will be available. You can search the site at a basic or advanced level.

Westlaw

Westlaw is a subscription-based database produced by Thomson Reuters/Sweet & Maxwell. The legislation section within *Westlaw* contains amended, full text Statutes. You can search it at a basic or advanced level, using any combination of title, section number or keyword, or you can browse an alphabetical list of Acts to find the one you want. The advanced search option also allows you to search historic law, e.g. if you want to know what the text of an Act was on any given date.

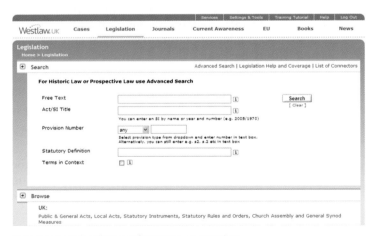

Figure 5.1 UK legislation information on *Westlaw*

Lawtel

Lawtel is a subscription-based database produced by Thomson Reuters/Sweet & Maxwell. To access Acts on *Lawtel* you should select the Statutory Law option. You can search by title or keyword. The text provided on *Lawtel* is the original (historic) version of the legislation, but if your library also subscribes to the *Westlaw* database, it is possible to link from *Lawtel* to the current version on *Westlaw*.

JustCite

JustCite is a subscription-based database produced by Justis Publishing Ltd. *JustCite* will not provide you with the full text of an Act, but will instead point you in the direction of other databases and sources which contain the full text. It is up to you to find out which of these sources to use. You can search *JustCite* using the title or official citation of an Act.

BAILII British & Irish Legal Information Institute (www.bailii.org)

BAILII is a freely available website which provides selected full text UK Statutes from the 1200s onwards. The text is taken from the legislation.gov.uk website, so it can offer the original and updated versions, depending on the date of the Act.

ACTIVITY

Quick quiz

Using any of the sources available to you (printed or electronic), answer the following questions:
- What is the chapter number of the Access to Justice Act 1999?
- What is the title of the Act with the official citation 1995 Chapter 50?
- On what date did the Education Act 2002 receive Royal Assent?

Answers can be found in the Appendix on page 254.

5.1.2 Checking if an Act is still in force

Legislation is constantly evolving and changing. Whole Acts or individual sections of an Act may be repealed; other sections may be amended; and new sections may be inserted into an Act. If you need to quote current law, for example in a moot court case, then you must make sure that you use up-to-date legislation. The following sources will all provide the current status of primary legislation.

Printed sources

Halsbury's Statutes of England and Wales

This service provides the amended text of primary legislation currently in force in England and Wales. It keeps itself up to date through a combination of reissued main volumes, *Current Service Binders*, an annual *Cumulative Supplement* and a monthly *Noter-Up Service*. Where changes to the original Act occur, references to the amending or repealing legislation are included.

Is it in Force?

Is it in Force? is published by LexisNexis and is a guide to the commencement dates of Acts in England and Wales passed since 1960. It is published twice a year, so each new volume includes recent statutes, as well as any recent amendments to the other Acts that *Is it in Force?* covers.

Current Law Legislation Citator

The *Current Law Legislation Citator* is a member of Sweet & Maxwell's Current Law family of publications. In print, it will provide the current status of an Act of Parliament. Acts are listed in chronological order. It also gives details of commencement orders, Statutory Instruments made under the Act and gives references to cases where the Act was judicially considered. Figure 5.2 below provides an example of the citator's layout. Updates to the latest version of the citator can be found in the *Current Law Statutes* loose-leaf service binder.

---

tutor tip

Don't fall into the trap of automatically thinking that if an Act doesn't appear in *Is it in Force?* then it can't be in force. Remember that *Is it in Force?* tells you the commencement date of Acts from 1960 onwards only. There are lots of Acts from before this date which are still in force but which won't be covered by *Is it in Force?* because of its specific date range.

Statute Citator
12. Example Act 1993.   – Chapter number, name of Act and year
Royal Assent, May 5, 1993   – Date of Royal Assent
Commencement Orders SI 94/1234 SI 95/78   – Commencement orders bringing provisions into force
s.1, enabling, SI 94/1234; SI 95/78   – Statutory Instruments made under the powers of s.1 of the Act
s.2, see *R. v Brown* [1995] Crim.L.R: 43   – Case judicially considering s.2
s.3, amended: 1996 c.3 s.2   – s.3 amended by Act (s.2 of chapter 3 of 1996) and two SIs
s.3, enabling: SI 93/82; SI 96/70
s.4, repealed: 1996 c.3. Sch. 4   – s.4 repealed by Schedule 4 of chapter 3 of 1996
s.4A added: SI 94/42   – s.4A added by SI Number 42 of 1994
Sch. 8, C. 1994 c. 1 s. 89   – Schedule 8 consolidated by s.89 of chapter 1 of 1994

Figure 5.2 *Current Law Legislation Citator*

Halsbury's Statutes Citator

The *Statutes Citator* comes out twice a year and is published as part of the *Halsbury's Statutes of England and Wales* series. Part 1 is a comprehensive alphabetical list of over 7,600 statutes which have been published in *Halsbury's Statutes*. Part 2 records any changes to the statutes included in the alphabetical list.

Loose-leaf encyclopaedias

Because of the ease with which these sources can be updated, they can usually be relied on for an up-to-date version of an Act. Check any loose-leaf encyclopaedias in your library related to your topic.

Electronic sources

LexisLibrary

LexisLibrary provides the amended text of primary legislation of general application in England and Wales. It is updated daily and so is an excellent source for the current text of an Act. Where changes to the original Act occur, references to the amending or repealing legislation are included – see Figure 5.3 below.

Within the legislation section, you can access a Status Snapshot document, which gives details of commencement information and subsequent changes, combining the information contained in the printed volumes *Is it in Force?* and the *Statutes Citator*.

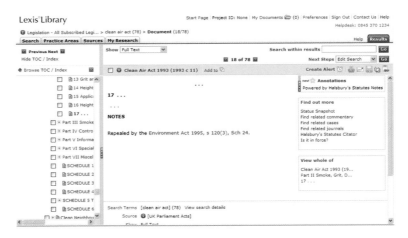

Figure 5.3 UK legislation information on *LexisLibrary*

Westlaw

The legislation basic search screen only searches legislation currently in force and includes references to any amending or repealing legislation – see Figure 5.4 below.

Figure 5.4 UK legislation information on *Westlaw*

Lawtel

Lawtel's Statutory Law database has coverage from 1984 onwards. For each Act it provides a Statutory Status Table, which lists the current status of each section of the Act, with references to any amending or repealing legislation – see Figure 5.5 below. If your library also subscribes to the *Westlaw* database, then you will be able to follow links from acts on *Lawtel* to the current text on *Westlaw*.

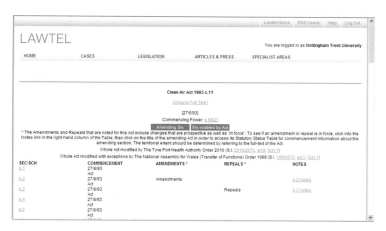

Figure 5.5 Statutory Law database from *Lawtel*

JustCite

JustCite provides an overview and status report for primary legislation and gives references to any amending or repealing legislation – see Figure 5.6 on page 68. Although *JustCite* will not provide the full text, it will refer you to other sources where the full text is available.

Figure 5.6 *JustCite*

Legislation.gov.uk (www.legislation.gov.uk)

Legislation.gov.uk is the official place of publication for newly enacted legislation. The aim is to publish legislation on legislation.gov.uk simultaneously or at least within 24 hours of its publication in printed form. See Figure 5.7 below.

Figure 5.7 UK legislation information on legislation.gov.uk

ACTIVITY

Quick quiz

1. What is the title of the 5th Act to receive Royal Assent in 2011?
2. What is the title of Section 13 of the Human Rights Act 1998? Which source did you use to find out?

Answers can be found in the Appendix on pages 254–255.

5.2 Secondary legislation

5.2.1 Finding Statutory Instruments

Printed sources

Statutory Instruments

HMSO has been publishing these volumes annually since 1949. They contain all those Statutory Instruments made during the year which are still in force at the end of the same year. The text provided is as it was on the date when the Statutory Instrument came into force, so it will not include any amendments or repeals. Statutory Instruments are listed in numerical order and each volume contains a subject index.

Statutory Rules and Orders and Statutory Instruments Revised to December 1948

This series consists of 25 volumes arranged in broad subject order, giving the text of all general Statutory Instruments, Rules and Orders in force on 31 December 1948.

Halsbury's Statutory Instruments

Halsbury's Statutory Instruments is a multi-volume work arranged in broad subject areas, listing all general Statutory Instruments currently in force in England and Wales. Some are included in full text with annotations; others are summarised; but the majority are simply listed. *Halsbury's Statutory Instruments* is kept up to date through a combination of reissued main volumes and a regular updating service.

Current Law Monthly Digest/Current Law Year Book

The Current Law series will provide a brief summary of many Statutory Instruments. The *Current Law Monthly Digest* contains an alphabetical table of Statutory Instruments. The *Current Law Year Book* has an alphabetical table and a numerical table of Statutory Instruments.

Halsbury's Laws of England and Wales Monthly Review

Halsbury's Laws of England and Wales Monthly Review provides brief summaries of many Statutory Instruments together with an alphabetical Table of Statutory Instruments. At the end of the year, this information is cumulated into the *Halsbury's Laws Annual Abridgment*.

Loose-leaf encyclopaedias

These bring together different types of legal material on a particular topic and will include relevant Statutory Instruments. They are especially useful because they are regularly updated and many of them also include annotations and commentary related to the subject.

Textbooks

Textbooks can be a useful way to locate Statutory Instruments on a particular topic. Even if they don't reprint the Statutory Instrument in full, 'cases and materials' books may give summaries of the key pieces of secondary legislation.

Electronic sources

LexisLibrary

The legislation section of *LexisLibrary* contains the updated text of Statutory Instruments currently in force. You can search by keyword, title or SI number or you can browse a chronological list.

Westlaw

The legislation section within *Westlaw* contains amended full text Statutory Instruments and can be searched at a basic or advanced level, by title or keyword. You can also browse an alphabetical or a chronological list of Statutory Instruments to find the one you want.

The legislation.gov.uk website

This freely available website contains the original (historical) text of Statutory Instruments from 1987 onwards with selected SIs available in full text between 1948–86. Statutory Instruments can be browsed by year and number and you can also search the site at a basic or advanced level.

Lawtel

To access Statutory Instruments via *Lawtel*, select the Statutory Instruments option. You can search by title or keyword. *Lawtel* will provide the full original text of SIs, from 1984 onwards, with links available to *Westlaw* for the current text of the SI.

JustCite

JustCite will not provide you with the full text of a Statutory Instrument, but will instead point you in the direction of other databases and sources which contain the full text. It is up to you to find out which of the sources you use. Within *JustCite* you should select the 'Legislation' section as this also covers Statutory Instruments. You can search *JustCite* using the title or Statutory Instrument number.

BAILII (www.bailii.org)

BAILII provides full text UK Statutory Instruments from 2002 onwards, with selected SIs. The text is taken from the legislation.gov.uk website, so should be used as an historical source. You can search by title or keyword.

5.2.2 Checking if a Statutory Instrument is still in force

The following list details printed and electronic sources which will tell you the current status of a Statutory Instrument.

Printed sources

Halsbury's Statutory Instruments

Use the main volumes in conjunction with the loose-leaf service binder to get the up-to-date status of Statutory Instruments. Alternatively, you could check the *Halsbury's Statutory Instrument Citator*, which is an annual citator published as part of the *Halsbury's Statutory Instruments* series. It provides a guide to the current status of Statutory Instruments and is quick and easy to use.

Current Law Legislation Citator

The printed *Current Law Legislation Citator* (part of the Current Law family) provides the current status of a Statutory Instrument and also gives details of any cases where the Statutory Instrument has been judicially considered. Statutory Instruments are listed in chronological order. See Figure 5.8 below for an example of the citator's layout.

Updates to the latest volume of the citator can be found in the *Current Law Statutes* loose-leaf service binder.

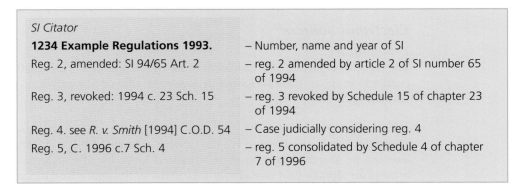

SI Citator	
1234 Example Regulations 1993.	– Number, name and year of SI
Reg. 2, amended: SI 94/65 Art. 2	– reg. 2 amended by article 2 of SI number 65 of 1994
Reg. 3, revoked: 1994 c. 23 Sch. 15	– reg. 3 revoked by Schedule 15 of chapter 23 of 1994
Reg. 4. see *R. v. Smith* [1994] C.O.D. 54	– Case judicially considering reg. 4
Reg. 5, C. 1996 c.7 Sch. 4	– reg. 5 consolidated by Schedule 4 of chapter 7 of 1996

Figure 5.8 *Current Law Legislation Citator* – Statutory Instruments

Loose-leaf encyclopaedias

The ease with which these sources can be updated makes them an excellent source for the current status of Statutory Instruments. Check in your library for any loose-leaf encyclopaedias related to your topic.

Electronic sources

LexisLibrary

The legislation section is updated daily and contains the full amended text of UK Statutory Instruments – see Figure 5.9 below.

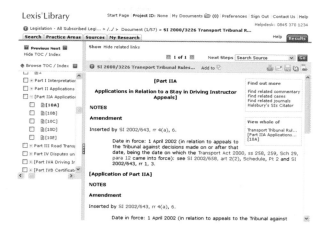

Figure 5.9 *LexisLibrary* – Statutory Instruments

You can access an online version of the *Halsbury's Statutory Instruments Citator*. You can search by keyword, or you can browse a chronological list of Statutory Instruments.

Westlaw

The basic legislation search screen only searches legislation currently in force and includes references to any amending or repealing legislation – see Figure 5.10 below.

Lawtel

Lawtel's Statutory Instruments index gives the current status of Statutory Instruments from 1984 onwards and provides references and links to any amending or repealing legislation – see Figure 5.11 below. *Lawtel* also provides links to the current text on *Westlaw*, so if your library subscribes to both you can follow the links.

JustCite

JustCite will tell you the current status of a Statutory Instrument. Select the 'Legislation' option as this covers both primary and secondary legislation – see Figure 5.12 on page 72. *JustCite* will not provide the full text of a Statutory Instrument, but will direct you to other electronic resources where the full text is available.

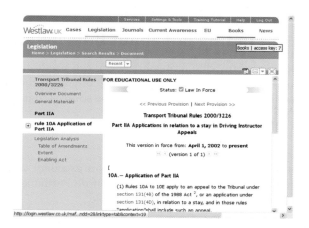

Figure 5.10 UK Statutory Instruments on *Westlaw*

Figure 5.11 *Lawtel*'s Statutory Instruments

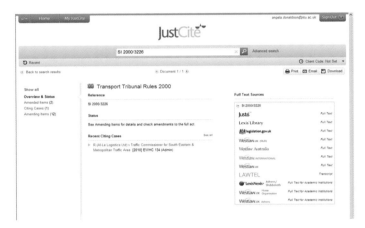

Figure 5.12 *JustCite*'s Statutory Instruments

ACTIVITY

Quick quiz

What is the title of the 99th Statutory Instrument to be made in 2011?
The answer can be found in the Appendix on page 255.

5.3 Parliamentary Bills

5.3.1 Finding out about Bills before Parliament

There are many different sources you can use to find the text of Bills and to track their progress before Parliament. This list contains some of the major ones, so check in your own library to find out which of these sources/databases you can access.

Printed sources

Current Law Monthly Digest

The *Current Law Monthly Digest* is an excellent current awareness tool. It contains a 'Progress of Bills' section for Bills before Parliament during the current parliamentary session. See Figure 5.13 for an example.

Halsbury's Laws of England and Wales Monthly Review

Another current awareness service, this records the progress of Bills through Parliament in its Parliament section. It also includes summaries of new Bills.

Bill	Parliamentary Progress
PROGRESS OF BILLS	
The following Bills are those of the 2003–04 session. This statement is complete to **May 10, 2004**. Government Bills are in bold. *Lords* or *Commons* denotes the House in which the bill originated (Stages and dates in italics are provisional only.)	
Bill	**Parliamentary Progress**
Age-Related Payments (*Commons*).	Commons, first reading, April 22, 2004. (*Second reading, May 12, 2004*).
Air Traffic Emissions Reduction (*Lords*).	Lords, passed. Commons first reading, No date. (*Second reading, no date*).
Armed Forces (Pensions and Compensation) (*Commons*).	Commons, Remaining Stages, May 6, 2004.
Arms Trade (*Commons*).	Commons, first reading, May 5, 2004. (*Second reading, July 16, 2004*).
Assisted Dying for the Terminally Ill (*Lords*).	Lords, Second reading, March 10, 2004. (*Committee, July 7, 2004*).
Asylum and Immigration (Treatment of Claimants, etc) (*Commons*).	Commons, passed. Lords, Committee Stage, April 26, 27 & 28 & May 4, 2004. (*Report Stage, May 18, 2004*).
Balance Charitable Foundation for Unclaimed Assets (Allocation) (*Commons*).	Commons, first reading, May 6, 2004. (*Second reading, June 18, 2004*).
Cardiac Risk in the Young (Screening) (*Commons*).	Commons, Bill withdrawn.
Carers (Equal Opportunities) (*Commons*).	Commons, Committee, March 10, 2004. (*Report Stage, May 14, 2004*).
Child Trust Funds (*Commons*).	Commons, passed. Lords, third reading. May 4, 2004.
Children (*Lords*).	Lords, Committee Stage, May 4 & 6, 2004. (*Committee, May 20, 2004*).
Christmas Day (Trading) (*Commons*).	Commons, Second reading, March 26, 2004. (*Committee, No date*).
Civil Contingencies (*Commons*).	Commons, Committee, January 27 & 29 & February 3, 5 & 10, 2004. (*Report Stage, no date*).
Civil Partnership (*Lords*).	Lords, second reading, April 22, 2004. (*Committee, May 10, 12, & 17, 2004*).
Civil Service (*Commons*).	Commons, first reading, January 12, 2004. (*Second reading, May 14, 2004*).
Civil Service (No 2) (*Lords*).	Lords, Committee, March 26, 2004. (*Report Stage, May 13, 2004*).
Companies (Audit, Investigations and Community Enterprise) (*Lords*).	Lords, passed. Motion for approval, March 22, 2004. (*Report Stage, No date*).
Constitution for the European Union (Referendum) (*Commons*).	Commons, first reading, January 7, 2004. (*Second reading, June 18, 2004*).
Constitutional Reform (*Lords*).	Lords, Committee, April 1, 20, 22, 27 & 29, 2004.
Corporate Killing (*Commons*).	Commons, first reading, March 30, 2004. (*Second reading, May 21, 2004*).
Criminal Justice (Justifiable Conduct) (*Commons*).	Commons, first reading, January 12, 2004. (*Second reading, May 14, 2004*).
Crown Employment (Nationality) (*Commons*).	Commons, first reading, January 20, 2004. (*Second reading, May 14, 2004*).
Dolphins and other Cetaceans Protection (*Commons*).	Commons, first reading, March 31, 2004. (*Second reading, October 15, 2004*).
Domestic Energy Efficiency (*Commons*).	Commons, first reading, May 4, 2004. (*Second reading, July 16, 2004*).

Figure 5.13 Progress of Bills from *Current Law Monthly Digest*

PARLIAMENT	

04/1535   Bills in Progress

The following is a list of Public Bills for England and Wales before Parliament this session. The list shows the state of progress as at 26 June 2004. Private Members' Bills are marked * and are not included until read a second time. A brief summary of each new Bill appears below.

Title of Bill	Stage
Age-related Payments	Passed the Commons, Lords, first reading, 9.6.2004
*Air Traffic Emissions Reduction (see REVIEW para 04/575)	Lords, third reading, 29.3.2004
*Assisted Dying for the Terminally Ill (see REVIEW para 04/870)	Lords, second reading, 10.3.2004
Armed Forces (Pensions and Compensation)	Passed the Commons, Lords, second reading, 10.6.2004

Figure 5.14 Bills in Progress from *Halsbury's Laws of England Monthly Review*

The Stationery Office Daily List – www.tsoshop.co.uk

This publication contains information about the progress of Bills before Parliament. *The Stationery Office Daily List* is available in print (often cumulated into a weekly publication) and is also summarised via The Stationery Office's online bookshop.

Electronic sources

LexisLibrary

Within the legislation section of *LexisLibrary*, is a subsection called Bill Tracker. You can search for a Bill here and the database will tell you which stages it has cleared so far, with the dates.

Lawtel

The *Lawtel* database has a section on parliamentary Bills which lists the progress of Bills so far. A useful feature of *Lawtel* is that it provides links to the UK Parliament website, so you can link straight to the text of the Bill or to discussions at the various committee stages.

UK Parliament website – www.parliament.uk/business/bills-and-legislation/

The UK Parliament website has a page dedicated to Bills before Parliament, covering Bills of all types. From this page, you can link to the Bill Index database (bills.parliament.uk/AC.asp) which lists all the various stages reached by a Bill so far and provides links to *Hansard* debates and other relevant reports and documents.

5.4 Case law

In Chapter 4 we looked at how case law is made and how a case citation is constructed. Now let's move on to look at how to locate a law report for a particular case, or how to find out which law reports series have reported the case you want.

There are both printed and electronic sources which you can use to look up case citations and we will look at both kinds. It is important that you know about both kinds of sources because, even if you prefer to use electronic sources wherever possible, there may be times when your favourite database is unavailable and you need to refer to printed sources instead.

When you are searching for cases, you need to consider what information you have about the case you are looking for (do you know the names of the parties involved or do you just know what the case was about?), as this could affect the resource you use to locate it, particularly when using printed sources.

The next section will suggest some of the major sources for locating case law and highlight any particular strengths or weaknesses. Remember to check within your own library to see which printed sources it stocks and which electronic databases you are able to access.

5.4.1 Finding cases by name

tutor tip

The appellant is the first of the two parties and was formerly referred to as the plaintiff. In the case of *Donoghue v Stevenson*, Donoghue is the appellant. The second party, Stevenson, is known as the respondent, formerly known as the defendant.

If you know the names of both parties involved in the case (e.g. *Donoghue v Stevenson*) then you should consult one of the following sources.

Printed sources

Current Law Case Citator

The *Current Law Case Citator* series is published by Sweet & Maxwell and is best described as an alphabetical index of cases by appellant.

The *Current Law Case Citator* is available as a series of volumes which date from 1947 onwards. If you know the date of your case, as well as the party names, then you simply need to select the index containing that date and look up the case. When you don't know the year in which your case was reported then you will need to check all the citators starting with 1947, until you find it.

Figure 5.15 below gives you an example of a *Current Law Case Citator* reference.

Crest Homes Plc *v.* Marks [1987] A.C. 829; [1987] 3 W.L.R. 293; [1987] 2 All E.R. 1074;
    [1988] R.P.C. 21; (1987) 84 L.S.G. 2362; (1987) 137 N.L.J. 662; (1987) 131 S.J.
    1003, HL; affirming [1987] 3 W.L.R. 48; [1987] F.S.R. 305; (1987) 84 L.S.G. 2048;
    (1987) 137 N.L.J. 318, CA.. *Digested*, 87/**2885**:
                Applied, 88/2837, 91/2858, 93/3212, 93/4265, 96/5659, 98/471, 01/554:
                        Considered; 88/2833, 92/3475, 93/3211, 96/762:
                Distinguished, 96/689; 00/309: *Followed*, 97/465, 99/321

Figure 5.15 A *Current Law Case Citator* reference

Let's use the *Crest Homes v Marks* case from Figure 5.15 as an example. As you'll remember from our earlier look at case law, it is common for cases to be reported in more than one series. *Crest Homes Plc v Marks* is a good example of this as it has been reported in the *Law Reports Appeal Cases*, the *Weekly Law Reports*, the *All England Law Reports*, the *Solicitors Journal*, and many others besides.

Your Law Library should stock at least one of these series, so check your own library catalogue to find out which ones are available to you. If your library stocks more than one of the series, then remember the hierarchy of cases as described in 4.5.6 in the previous chapter. In the *Crest Homes* example, the *Law Reports Appeal Cases* version ([1987] AC 829) is the most authoritative report.

Strengths	The printed *Current Law Case Citators* are very quick and easy to use. A table of abbreviations is included at the beginning of each volume.
Weaknesses	As it lists cases in order of appellant, you need to know this name to be able to use it. If you only know the respondent's name then you will need to consult one of the electronic sources.

Current Law Monthly Digest

The *Current Law Monthly Digest* is another member of the Sweet & Maxwell Current Law family. As its name suggests, it provides a monthly summary of legal happenings and is a very useful tool to use to keep yourself up to date with current events. If you are looking for a recent case (i.e. within the current year) then you will need to check the *Current Law Monthly Digest*. It will provide the same information as the *Current Law Case Citator* and eventually the cases will be cumulated into the *Current Law Case Citator*.

CUMULATIVE TABLE OF CASES

Malekshad v. Howard de Walden Estates Ltd (No.1) [2002] UKHL 49. [2003] 1 A.C. 1013, [2003] 1 C.L. 375 .... **Mar** 413
MALEWSKI v. EALING LBC [2003] EWHC 763, 89 Con. L.R. 1 .... **May** 409
Malik v. Bank of Credit and Commerce International SA (In Liquidation) [1998] A.C. 20, [1997] C.L.Y. 2192 .... **Feb** 181, 311
MALLIA v. ISLINGTON LBC *[Ex rel.]* .... **Jan** 40
Malloch v. Aberdeen Corp (No.1) [1971] 1 W.L.R. 1578, [1971] C.L.Y. 12835 .... **Feb** 60
MALLONE v. BPB INDUSTRIES PLC *see* MALLONE v. BPB INDUSTRIES LTD
MALLUSK COLD STORAGE LTD v. DEPARTMENT OF FINANCE AND PERSONNEL; *sub nom.* ANGLO BEEF PROCESSORS LTD v. DEPARTMENT OF FINANCE AND PERSONNEL [2003] R.A. 370 .... **Apr** 388
MAN NUTZFAHRZEUGE AG v. ERNST & YOUNG [2003] EWHC 2245, [2004] P.N.L.R. 19 .... **May** 53
Mannai Investment Co Ltd v. Eagle Star Life Assurance Co Ltd [1997] A.C. 749, [1997] C.L.Y. 3256 .... **Apr** 311
Mannai Investment Co Ltd v. Eagle Star Life Assurance Co Ltd [1997] A.C. 749, [1997] C.L.Y. 3256 .... **Feb** 339; **Mar** 292
MANX ELECTRICITY AUTHORITY v. JP MORGAN CHASE BANK [2003] B.L.R. 477 .... **May** 87
MAPAH v. SECRETARY OF STATE FOR THE HOME DEPARTMENT *see* R. (ON THE APPLICATION OF MAPAH) v. SECRETARY OF STATE FOR THE HOME DEPARTMENT
MARCIC v. THAMES WATER UTILITIES LTD [2003] UKHL 66, [2003] 3 W.L.R. 1603 .... **Mar** 364
MARIE BRIZARD ET ROGER INTERNATIONAL SA v. WILLIAM GRANT & SONS LTD (NO.2); MARIE BRIZZARD ET ROGER INTERNATIONAL SA, PETITIONER (NO.2) *see* MARIE BRIZZARD ET ROGER INTERNATIONAL SA v. WILLIAM GRANT & SONS LTD (NO.2)
Markass Car Hire Ltd v. Cyprus (51591/99) (Unreported, November 6, 2002) .... **May** 118
MARKEM CORP v. ZIPHER LTD (NO.1) [2004] R.P.C. 10 .... **May** 335
MARKEM CORP v. ZIPHER LTD (NO.2) [2004] R.P.C. 11 .... **May** 52
Marley v. Mutual Security Merchant Bank & Trust Co Ltd [1991] 3 All E.R. 198, [1991] C.L.Y. 1730 .... **Feb** 522
Marsden's Estate, Re (1889) L.R. 40 Ch. D. 475 .... **Mar** 44
MARSH v. SOFAER [2003] EWHC 3334 .... **Apr** 317
Marshall (Inspector of Taxes) v. Kerr [1995] 1 A.C. 148, [1994] C.L.Y. 359 .... **Feb** 382
Marshall v. NM Financial Management Ltd [1997] 1 W.L.R. 1527 .... **Feb** 182
MARSHALL v. RENNOCKS *[Ex rel.]* .... **May** 402
MARTIN (ANTHONY EDWARD), RE; MARTIN (ANTHONY EDWARD), RE; R. (ON THE APPLICATION OF MARTIN) v. PAROLE BOARD *see* R. (ON THE APPLICATION OF MARTIN) v. SECRETARY OF STATE FOR THE HOME DEPARTMENT
MARTIN v. MCINNES *see* MARTIN v. MCGUINESS
MARTIN v. N (A CHILD) 2004 S.L.T. 249 .... **Apr** 562
MARTIN v. SOUTH BANK UNIVERSITY (C4/01) [2004] 1 C.M.L.R. 15 .... **May** 191
MARTIN v. UNITED KINGDOM (63608/00) *The Times*, February 26, 2004 .... **Apr** 251
MARTYN ROSE LTD v. AKG GROUP LTD *see* WAKE + WALKER v. AKG GROUP LTD
MARUBENI HONG KONG AND SOUTH CHINA LTD v. MINISTRY OF FINANCE OF MONGOLIA *see* MARUBENI HONG KONG AND SOUTH CHINA LTD v. MONGOLIA (JURISDICTION)
Maryland Estates Ltd v. Joseph [1999] 1 W.L.R. 83, [1998] C.L.Y. 3634 .... **Apr** 312
MASON v. TOTALFINAELF UK LTD [2003] EWHC 1604, [2003] 3 E.G.L.R. 91 .... **May** 365
Massey v. Boulden [2002] EWCA Civ 1634, [2003] 1 W.L.R. 1792, [2003] 1 C.L. 477 .... **May** 480
MATHER SEAL/FRESH GROUND FOR OPPOSITION (T131/01) [2003] E.P.O.R. 50 .... **Mar** 302
MATTILA v. COUNCIL OF THE EUROPEAN UNION (C353/01 P) [2004] 1 C.M.L.R. 32 .... **Apr** 150
MAUD v. CASTLE POINT BC *see* R. (ON THE APPLICATION OF MAUD) v. CASTLE POINT BC
Max.Mobil Telekommunikation Service GmbH v. Commission of the European Communities (T54/99) [2002] E.C.R. II-313, [2002] C.L.Y. 1540 .... **Feb** 67
Mayne v. Ministry of Agriculture, Fisheries and Food [2001] E.H.L.R. 5, [2000] C.L.Y. 2338 .... **Feb** 208
MCAULEY v. MULHOLLAND *see* MCAULEY v. BROWN
MCAULEY, PETITIONER *see* MCAULEY v. HIGHLAND COUNCIL
McCall's Entertainments (Ayr) Ltd v. South Ayrshire Council (No.1) 1998 S.L.T. 1403, [1999] C.L.Y. 6324 .... **Feb** 638
McCann v. United Kingdom (A/324) [1996] 21 E.H.R.R. 97, [1995] C.L.Y. 2665 .... **Apr** 5
McCathey v. Patriotic Investment Society Ltd (In Liquidation) 1910 1 S.L.T. 121 .... **Apr** 544
McColl v. Listing Officer [2001] EWHC Admin 712, [2001] R.A. 342, [2002] C.L.Y. 3156 .... **Jan** 262
McCONDICHIE v. MAINS MEDICAL CENTRE 2004 Rep. L.R. 4 .... **May** 760
McConnell v. McConnell 1997 Fam. L.R. 108 .... **Mar** 583
MCCORMACK v. DPP *see* R. (ON THE APPLICATION OF MCCORMACK) v. DPP
McCORMACK v. TOPHAM *[Ex rel.]* .... **Jan** 291
MCDONALD v. PROCURATOR FISCAL, ELGIN *see* MCDONALD v. DICKSON
McDONNELL v. CONGREGATION OF CHRISTIAN BROTHERS TRUSTEES (FORMERLY IRISH CHRISTIAN BROTHERS) [2003] UKHL 63, [2003] 3 W.L.R. 1627 .... **Feb** 45
MCDOUGALL v. SPEIRS *see* MCDOUGALL v. SPIERS
McDyer v. Celtic Football & Athletic Co Ltd (No.1) 2000 S.C. 379, [2000] C.L.Y. 6599 .... **Feb** 658
McFarlane v. Tayside Health Board [2000] 2 A.C. 59, [2000] C.L.Y. 6162 .... **Mar** 132
McGhee v. National Coal Board [1973] 1 W.L.R. 1, [1972] C.L.Y. 2356 .... **May** 404
McGINTY v. CORNWELL PARKER PLC *[Ex rel.]* .... **Mar** 395
McGlennon v. Chief Constable of Cumbria [2002] I.C.R. 1156, [2002] C.L.Y. 1415 .... **Jan** 316

For full case references see the *Current Law Case Citator*

Current Law May Digest 2004

Figure 5.16 *Current Law Monthly Digest* from Sweet & Maxwell

Strengths	Excellent printed source for recent cases.
Weaknesses	Cases are listed by appellant, so you won't be able to use it if you only know the name of the respondent.

Indexes to individual law reports series

Many law reports series produce their own indexes to the cases that they contain. An alphabetical table of cases covered will tell you where to find a full version of your case.

Strengths	Quick and easy to use.
Weaknesses	Only cover cases reported in that particular law reports series, so you may need to consult more than one index if your case is not included in that particular series. In alphabetical order by appellant, so you need to know the names of both parties involved.

Halsbury's Laws of England and Wales

Halsbury's Laws of England and Wales has a Consolidated Table of Cases volume which refers to cases mentioned in the main volumes of *Halsbury's Laws*. Although the main volumes will not provide the full text of these cases, they should provide you with citations so you can track down a full version using another source.

Strengths	Also covers Commonwealth cases and older cases.
Weaknesses	Cases are listed by appellant, so you won't be able to use it if you only know the name of the respondent.

Electronic sources

Westlaw

To locate cases on *Westlaw*, select the Cases tab from the menu at the top of the screen. The basic search facility allows you to search by word or phrase, by party name or by citation (see Figure 5.17). The advanced search facility offers a more structured search screen which allows you to search using any combination of subject, legislation cited, case cited, court or date (see Figure 5.18). Alternatively, you can browse lists of case analysis documents, law reports and transcripts.

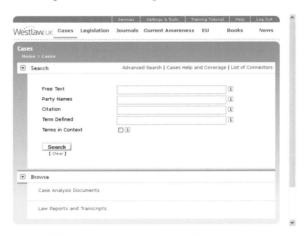

Figure 5.17 Basic case searching on *Westlaw*

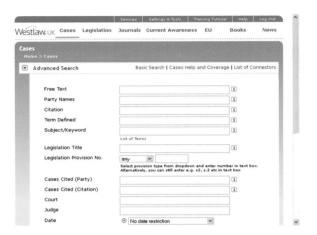

Figure 5.18 Advanced case searching on *Westlaw*

Your search results will be presented to you in brief, with a link to the Case Analysis document (an overview of the case and its history) and, where available on *Westlaw*, a link to the full text law report. See Figure 5.19.

Figure 5.19 Case analysis result from *Westlaw*

Strengths	You don't need to know both parties involved, so if you only know the respondent you can still find your case. The history of the case is all presented on the same screen. You may be able to access the database from off campus. If the case is available on *Westlaw* in full text, you will be given a link to take you straight to it.
Weaknesses	Will be subject to 'normal' network/internet problems, so there may be times when access is unavailable.

JustCite

JustCite acts as a traditional case citator, providing citations and judicial history information and, in addition, it also tells you which electronic services offer the full text. You can then choose a database that you have access to and view the full text. See Figure 5.20.

Figure 5.20 Case search on *JustCite*

Strengths	You can search by either party name, appellant or respondent. You may be able to access the database from off campus.
Weaknesses	Doesn't provide the full text (but does provide links to platforms that hold the full text). Will be subject to 'normal' network/internet problems so there may be times when access is unavailable.

Lawtel

Lawtel is made up of a number of different sections, one of which is case law. In the case law section, you can search by party name, court, judge or citation – see Figure 5.21 below.

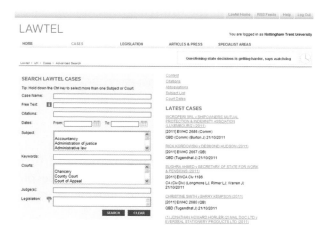

Figure 5.21 Case law section on *Lawtel*

Strengths	You can search by either party name, appellant or respondent. *Lawtel* provides extensive summaries of cases and in many instances it also provides a link to the case transcript. You may be able to access the database from off campus.
Weaknesses	Doesn't provide law reports in full text.

LexisLibrary

The Cases section within *LexisLibrary* contains case history documents and full text law reports and transcripts. You can search by any combination of keyword, headnote and catchwords, party name, citation, court or judge. Alternatively you can browse individual law reports series. See Figure 5.22.

Strengths	Can be searched by either party name, keyword or citation. Some links to full text are available. May be accessed from off campus.
Weaknesses	Will be subject to 'normal network/internet problems so there may be times when access is unavailable.

Figure 5.22 Case search options on *LexisLibrary*

BAILII (British & Irish Legal Information Institute) www.bailii.org

BAILII is a freely available website which contains case transcripts from courts in England and Wales and the United Kingdom. The idea behind the website is to bring together legal information in the public domain and make it available in one place. *BAILII* is based on a similar site which has been running successfully in Australia for many years (*AUSTLII*, www.austlii.edu.au – the Australasian Legal Information Institute).

Strengths	Unrestricted access. Search by either party name, keyword or neutral citation.
Weaknesses	Not comprehensive in coverage so not every case will be available. There can be delays in cases being added to the *BAILII* database so recent cases may not appear until sometime after the judgment has been given.

The House of Lords Judgments Archive (www.publications.parliament.uk/pa/ld/ldjudgmt.htm)

This page lists HTML versions of all House of Lords judgments delivered from 14 November 1996 to 30 July 2009. Judgments are divided into years, and are then listed in alphabetical order.

Strengths	Freely available service.
Weaknesses	Poor search facility. Better options are either to scroll through the page to find the case you want or to use the 'Edit' and 'Find' commands on the internet browser to search for your case name.

The Supreme Court website (www.supremecourt.gov.uk)

The Supreme Court makes its judgments available on its website the day after they have been delivered. The list of Decided Cases can be sorted by neutral citation, by hand-down date or by case name. A press summary document, summarising the case, is usually provided to accompany the judgment.

Strengths	Speed with which judgments are published. Freely available service.
Weaknesses	Poor search facility.

Casetrack

Casetrack is a subscription-based database provided by WordWave International. *Casetrack* provides transcripts from the Supreme Court, the Court of Appeal, the High Court, the Administrative Court, the Employment Appeals Tribunal and the VAT Tribunal.

Strengths	Searchable by either party name, keyword or neutral citation. Off-campus access may be available. Browsable index of recent judgments.
Weaknesses	Can sometimes be a bit slow.

ACTIVITY

Exercise

Look up the case '*Whiston v Whiston*, Court of Appeal, Civil Division, 23 March 1995'. What is this case about? Which database or printed source did you use to find out?

Answers can be found in the Appendix on page 255.

5.4.2 Finding cases by subject

You may not always be lucky enough to have the name of the case you are looking for but instead you may be looking for any cases to do with a particular subject. This section will recommend printed and electronic sources that can be used to find cases in this way. Where a source has already been described in detail in the previous section, the description will not be repeated.

Printed sources

The Digest

Published by LexisNexis, *The Digest* contains summaries of over 500,000 cases, as well as citations to direct you to a full text version. *The Digest* is a multi-volume work arranged in subject order, which comes with an extensive subject index to help you find what you're looking for – see Figure 5.23 below. There is a *Consolidated Table of Cases*, so you can also use this source to find cases by name. The series is kept up to date by means of reissued main volumes – see Figure 5.24 below – and a *Cumulative Supplement*.

> **ANNEXATION**
> *See* seizure
> effect of
> conquered country
> articles of pace inviolable **8(2)** *Comwlth* 1563
> conquered state
> contractual liabilities of, to individuals **8(2)** *Comwlth* 1565–1567
> financial liabilities of **8(2)** *Comwlth* 1564
> proclamation, necessity for **8(2)** *Comwlth* 1560, 1561
> **ANNOTATED EDITION**
> literary work **13** *Coprt* 654
> **ANNOYANCE 36(2)** *Nuis* 728, 739
> **ANNOYANCE, COVENANT RESTRAINING**
> advertisement across shop front **31(2)** *L&T* 7812
> conversion of dwelling-house into flats **31(2)** *L&T* 7816
> dog show **31(2)** *L&T* 7811
> hospital **31(2)** *L&T* 7809, 7810
> inconvenience **31(2)** *L&T* 7813

Continued on next page

Continued

interference with reasonable enjoyment of adjoining
premises **31(2)** *L&T* 7808
interference with reasonable peace of mind **31(2)** *L&T*
7806, 7807
letting wall to bill-posting company **31(2)** *L&T* 7814
use of blind for business **31(2)** *L&T* 7813
ANNUAL ALLOWANCE
car for private and business purposes **28(1)** *Inc T* 998;
28(2) *Inc T* 2489
industrial buildings, whether dwelling-houses qualify
28(2) *Inc T* 3673

Figure 5.23 Subject index from *The Digest*

Strengths	Detailed subject index. Covers not only English cases but also cases from Scotland, Ireland, Canada, Australia, New Zealand, the Commonwealth and the EU. Its coverage goes back to medieval times so it is also a useful source for historical cases.
Weaknesses	Only a summary is provided so once you have identified a case you will need to consult another source to find the full text.

6 Provision of recreational facilities
LAW See Halsbury's Laws (4th edn) vol 5 para 544–547
STATUTE See RECREATIONAL CHARITIES ACT, 1958 (c 17); 5
Halsbury's Statutes (4th edn) 689
7 Other cases
CROSS REFERENCES See no 2664 ante (bell-ringing to
celebrate the Restoration); nos 2694 et seq ante
(publication of books)
**2916 Reduction of National Debt – Charitable
use**
Ashton v Langdale (Lord) (1851) 4 De G & Sm 402;
20 LJ Ch 234; 17 LTOS 175; 15 Jur 868; 64 ER 888
ANNOTATIONS **Expld** Thornton v Kempson (1854) Kay
592 **Apprvd & Folld** Alexander v Brame (1861) 30
Beav 153 **Consd** Imperial Mercantile Credit Assocn
v Newry & Armagh Ry (1868) 16 WR 1070; Attree v
Hawe (1878) 9 Ch D 337; Jervis v Lawrence (1882)
22 Ch D 202 **Dbtd** Re Christmas, Martin v Lacon
(1885) 30 Ch D 544
**2917 Chancellor of Exchequer – Benefit of
country – Valid**
Nightingale v Goulbourn (1848) 2 Ph 594; [1843–
60] All ER Rep 420; 17 LJ Ch 296; 11 LTOS 169; 12
Jur 317; 41 ER 1072, LC
ANNOTATIONS **Consd** Whicker v Hume (1858) 7 HL Cas
124; Re Tetley, National Provincial & Union Bank of
England v Tetley [1923] 1 Ch 258 **Apld** Re Smith,
Public Trustee v Smith [1932] 1 Ch 153
2918 Lifeboat – Good as to personalty
Johnston v Swann (1818) 3 Madd 457; 56 ER 573
ANNOTATIONS **Consd** Giblett v Hobson (1834) 5 Sim
651; Ellis v Selby (1836) 1 My & Cr 286 **Apld**
Hartshorne v Nicholson (1858) 26 Beav 58 **Expld**
Re Holburne, Coates v Mackillop (1885) 53 LT 212
Dbtd Re Piercy, Whitwham v Piercy [1898] 1 Ch 565

Figure 5.24 *The Digest*

Halsbury's Laws of England and Wales

Within its footnotes on a particular subject, *Halsbury's Laws of England and Wales* often refers to relevant cases, with citations to full text versions. *Halsbury's Laws* has a detailed subject index which will help you locate cases on any topic – see Figures 5.25 and 5.26 on page 84.

see Figures 5.25 and 5.26 on page 84.

BANKRUPT – *continued*
    distress for rent – *continued*
        loss of right, **3(2)**, 686
        persons able to distrain, **3(2)**, 693
        preferential debts, charge for, **3(2)**, 690
        restrictions, **3(2)**, 687; **13**, 729
        right of, **3(2)**, 686
        sheriff, claim against, **3(2)**, 689
    documents. *See* books and records *above*
    duties towards trustee, **3(2)**, 345
    dwelling house–
        meaning, **3(2)**, 401n[1]
        application for possession, **3(2)**, 651
        disclaimer of, **3(2)**, 482
        rights of occupation, **3(2)**, 650
        spouse's matrimonial home rights, **3(2)**, 648
    equity of redemption, **32**, 515
    estate of. *See* BANKRUPT'S ESTATE
    examination–
        private. *See* PRIVATE EXAMINATION
           (BANKRUPTCY)
        public. *See* PUBLIC EXAMINATION
           (BANKRUPTCY)
    executor, as, **17(2)**, 20
    false statement by, **3(2)**, 716
    falsification of books etc, **3(2)**, 714
    family: meaning, **3(2)**, 216n[8]
    farmer, **3(2)**, 416
    fraudulent dealing with property obtained on credit, **3(2)**, 719, 720
    fraudulent disposal of property, **3(2)**, 717
    gambling by, **3(2)**, 723
    gift by, **20(1)**, 14, 62
    gift to or from spouse, passing of, **3(2)**, 427
    goodwill of business–
        passing to trustee, **3(2)**, 424
        sale by trustee, **3(2)**, 458
    income payments order. *See* INCOME PAYMENTS ORDER
    insolvency practitioner prohibition, **3(2)**, 701
    insurable interest, **25**, 609
    intellectual property, passing to trustee, **3(2)**, 425

Figure 5.25 Subject index from *Halsbury's Laws*

Strengths	Detailed subject index. Regularly updated, so can be used to find recent cases. Also useful for tracking down older pre-1865 cases.
Weaknesses	Provides a citation rather than the full text so you will still need to go elsewhere to find the full text.

717. Fraudulent disposal of property. The bankrupt is guilty of an offence if:

(1) he makes or causes[1] to be made, or has in the period of five years ending with the commencement of the bankruptcy[2] made or caused to be made, any gift or transfer of, or any charge on, his property[3]; or

(2) he conceals or removes, or has at any time before commencement of the bankruptcy concealed or removed, any part of his property after, or within two months before, the date on which a judgment or order for the payment of money has been obtained against him, being a judgment or order which was not satisfied before the commencement of the bankruptcy[4].

A person who commits such an offence is liable on conviction on indictment to imprisonment for a term not exceeding two years or a fine, or to both, or on summary conviction to imprisonment for a term not exceeding six months or a fine not exceeding the statutory maximum, or to both[5].

A person is not, however, guilty of such an offence if he proves that, at the time of the conduct constituting the offence, he had no intent to defraud[6] or to conceal the state of his affairs[7].

1 For the meaning of 'cause' see para 713 note 4 ante.

2 As to the commencement of bankruptcy see para 213 ante.

3 For the meaning of references to property comprised in the bankrupt's estate see para 708 note 2 ante. For these purposes, the reference to making a transfer of or charge on any property includes causing or conniving at the levying of any execution against that property: Insolvency Act 1986 s 357(2). 'Conniving' imports knowledge together with acquiescence in the facts constituting the offence. Suspicion may, however, be enough, although mere negligence is not: *Rogers v Rogers* (1830) 3 Hag Ecc 57.

4 Insolvency Act 1986 s 357(1), (3).

5 Ibid ss 350(6), 357(1), (3), 430, Sch 10. For the meaning of 'the statutory maximum' see para 4 ante.

6 See para 708 note 6 ante.

7 Insolvency Act 1986 ss 352, 357(1), (3).

Figure 5.26 Footnotes from *Halsbury's Laws*

Indexes to individual law reports series

Many individual law reports series produce their own subject indexes. Simply look up the subject you're interested in and you'll be referred to relevant cases that have been published within that particular series.

Strengths	Quick and easy to use.
Weaknesses	Only covers cases reported in a particular law reports series, so you may not always find what you are looking for. If you don't get any results then this does not necessarily mean that there aren't any cases on your subject, but just that there aren't any cases on it reported in that particular series – so try another one.

Textbooks

Don't overlook textbooks as a means of tracking down cases on a particular subject. A textbook on land law, for example, is going to refer to key cases which illustrate specific aspects of land law. A textbook is unlikely to reprint the whole case, normally just summarising the main points or including a key paragraph or two, but you should find the case name and citation to enable you to locate a full text version.

Strengths	The author of the textbook has done much of the hard work for you.
Weaknesses	You'll still need to go elsewhere to find the full text of the law report.

Current Law Monthly Digest

The *Current Law Monthly Digest* has a subject index to recent cases. A summary is provided and, where possible, a citation.

Strengths	Good source for locating recent cases.
Weaknesses	Summary only, so you'll need another source to find the full text.

Electronic sources

Westlaw

Strengths	Comprehensive database of case summaries. *Westlaw* allows you to search by keyword, subject or phrase. Links to the full text, where available within *Westlaw*, are provided. Off-campus access may be available.
Weaknesses	Not all cases will be available in full text within the *Westlaw* database, so you may have to consult other sources.

LexisLibrary

Strengths	Comprehensive database of case summaries. Search by keyword or phrase. Full text links may be available to other sections of the database. Off-campus access may be available.
Weaknesses	Not all cases will be available in full text within LexisLibrary, so you may have to consult other sources.

Lawtel

Strengths	Search by keyword or phrase. Extensive summary with citations. Links to transcripts provided where available.
Weaknesses	You will need to consult another source to access a law report of the case, rather than just the transcript.

JustCite

Strengths	Search by keyword or phrase. Indicates where a full text version is available electronically.
Weaknesses	You will need to consult another source to access the full text.

BAILII

Strengths	Transcripts are available.
Weaknesses	The search engine is not as sophisticated as those on subscription-based databases. You can search for a phrase, but you can't specify where that phrase appears, e.g. in the subject field.

Casetrack

Strengths	Subject, keyword and phrase searching is permitted. You can search for more than one keyword or phrase at a time.
Weaknesses	Will be subject to 'normal' network/internet problems, so there may be times when access is unavailable. Can sometimes be a bit slow.

5.4.3 Finding cases by legislation cited

Printed sources

Current Law Legislation Citator
The *Current Law Legislation Citator* will refer to cases brought under particular sections of an Act. When you look up the Act you are interested in, you will find relevant cases listed by section – see Figure 5.27 on page 86.

Halsbury's Statutes
The notes sections accompanying the text of an act in *Halsbury's Statutes*, will give citations for leading cases which have been brought citing the Act, or specific sections of the Act.

CAP.   CAP.

1994—cont.   *1994—cont.*

26. Trade Marks Act 1994—*cont.*

s.1—*cont.*

see *BACH and BACH FLOWER REMEDIES Trade Marks* (1999) 96(42) L. S. G. 42 (CA), Morritt, L.J., see *Philips Electronics NV v Remington Consumer Products Ltd* [1998] R.P.C. 283 (Pat Ct), Jacob, J.; see *Swizzels Matlow Ltd's Trade Mark Application, Re* [1998] R.P.C. 244 (TMR), RA Jones

s.3, see *AD2000 Trade Mark, Re* [1997] R.P.C. 168 C, Geoffrey Hobbs Q.C.; see *BACH and BACH FLOWER REMEDIES Trade Marks* [1999] R.P.C 1 (Ch D), Neuberger, J.; see *BACH and BACH FLOWER REMEDIES Trade Marks* (1999) 96(42) L.S.G. 42 (CA), Morritt, L.J.; see *Dualit Ltd's Trade Mark Application (No.2023846)* Times, July 19, 1999 (Ch D), Lloyd, J.; see *FROOT LOOPS Trade Mark, Re* [1998] R.P.C. 240, Simon Thorley Q.C.; see *Philips Electronics NV v Remington Consumer Products Ltd* [1998] R.P.C. 283 (Pat Ct), Jacob, J.; see *POST-PERFECT Trade Mark, Re* [1998] R.P.C. 255, Geoffrey Hobbs Q.C.; see *Procter & Gamble's Trade Mark Application* [1999] E.T.M.R. 375 (CA), Robert Walker, L.J.; see *Swizzels Matlow Ltd's Trade Mark Application, Re* [1998] R.P.C. 244 (TMR), RA Jones; see *Waterford Wedgwood Plc v David Nagli Ltd* [1998] F.S.R. 92 (Ch D), Sir Richard Scott V.C.

s.4, See *AUTOMOTIVE NETWORK EXCHANGE Trade Mark* [1998] R.P.C. 885 C, Geoffrey Hobbs, Q.C.

s.5, see *AUDI-MED Trade Mark* [1999] E.T.M.R. 1010 (TMR), Allan James; see *Oasis Stores Ltd's Trade Mark Application* [1998] R.P.C. 631 (TMR), Allan James; see *POSTPERFECT Trade Mark, Re* [1998] R.P.C. 255, Geoffrey Hobbs Q.C.

s.6, amended: SI 1999/1899 Reg.13

s.9, see *Beautimatic International Ltd v Mitchell International Pharmaceuticals Ltd* [1999] E.T.M.R. 912 (Ch D), Neuberger, J.

s.9, applied: SI 1996/714 Art.4

s.10, see *AUTOMOTIVE NETWORK EXCHANGE Trade Mark* [1998] R.P.C. 885 C, Geoffrey Hobbs, Q.C.; see *Avnet Inc v Isoact Ltd* [1998] F.S.R. 16 (Ch D), Jacob, J.; see *Barclays Bank Plc v RBS Advanta* [1996] R.P.C. 307 (Ch D), Laddie, J.; see *Beautimatic International Ltd v Mitchell International Pharmaceuticals Ltd* [1999] E.T.M.R. 912 (Ch D), Neuberger, J.; see *British Sugar Plc v James Robertson and Sons* [1996] R.P.C. 281 (Ch D), Jacob, J.; see *British Telecommunications Plc v One in a Million Ltd* [1999] 1 W.L.R. 903 (CA), Aldous, L.J.; see *Cable & Wireless Plc v British Telecommunications Plc* [1998] F.S.R. 383 (Ch D), Jacob, J.; see *Emaco Ltd v Dyson Appliances Ltd* [1999] E.T.M.R. 903 (Ch D), Jonathan Parker, J.; see *European Ltd v Economist Newspapers Ltd* [1998] F.S.R. 283 (CA), Millett, L.J.; see *Marks & Spencer Plc v One in a Million Ltd* Times, July 29, 1998 (CA), Aldous, L.J.; see *Vodafone Group Plc v Orange Personal Communications Services Ltd* [1997] F.S.R. 34 (Ch D), Jacob, J.; see *Waterford Wedgwood Plc v David Nagli Ltd* [1998] F.S.R. 92 (Ch D), Sir Richard Scott V.C.

s.10, applied: SI 1996/714 Art.4

26. Trade Marks Act 1994—*cont.*

s.11, see *Allied Domecq Spirits and Wine Ltd v Murray McDavid Ltd* 1998 S.C. 354 (OH), Lord MacFadyen; see *Bravado Merchandising Services Ltd v Mainstream Publishing (Edinburgh) Ltd* [1996] F.S.R. 205 (OH), Lord McCluskey; see *NAD Electronics Inc v NAD Computer Systems Ltd* [1997] F.S.R. 380 (Ch D), Ferris, J.; see *Scandecor Development AB v Scandecor Marketing Ltd* [1998] F.S.R. 500 (Ch D), Lloyd, J.

s.11, applied: SI 1996/714 Art.4

s.12, see *Microsoft Corp v Computer Future Distribution Ltd* [1998] I.T.C.L.R. 88 (Ch D), Rimer, J.

s.12, applied: SI 1996/714 Art.4

s.14, applied: SI 1996/714 Art.4

s.15, applied: SI 1996/714 Art.4

s.16, applied: SI 1996/714 Art.4, SI 1999/929 r.3.5.2

s.17, applied: SI 1996/714 Art.4

s.18, amended: SI 1996/729 Art.2, Sch para.2

s.18, applied: SI 1996/714 Art.4

s.19, amended: SI 1996/729 Art.2, Sch para.3

s.19, applied: SI 1996/714 Art.4, SI 1999/929 r.3.5.2, r.3.5.3

s.19, enabling: SI 1999/929

s.20, applied: SI 1996/714 Art.4

s.20, repealed: SI 1996/729 Art.2, Sch para.4

s.21, see *Prince Plc v Prince Sports Group Inc* [1998] F.S.R. 21 (Ch D), Neuberger, J.

s.21, applied: SI 1996/714 Art.4, SI 1996/1908 Reg.4

s.22, applied: SI 1996/714 Art.5

s.23, applied: SI 1996/714 Art.5

s.24, applied: SI 1996/714 Art.5

s.28, applied: SI 1996/714 Art.7

s.29, applied: SI 1996/714 Art.7

s.30, amended: SI 1996/714 Art.6

s.30, applied: SI 1996/714 Art.7

s.31, amended: SI 1996/714 Art.6

s.31, applied: SI 1996/714 Art.7

s.32, amended: SI 1996/714 Art.3

s.33, amended: SI 1996/714 Art.3

s.34, amended: SI 1996/714 Art.3

s.34, enabling: SI 1998/925

s.35, applied: SI 1996/714 Art.8

s.37, see *AUDI-MED Trade Mark* [1999] E.T.M.R. 1010 (TMR), Allan James; see *POSTPERFECT Trade Mark, Re* [1998] R.P.C. 255, Geoffrey Hobbs Q.C.

s.37, applied: SI 1996/714 Art.20

s.38, see *AUDI-MED Trade Mark* [1999] E.T.M.R. 1010 (TMR), Allan James

s.38, applied: SI 1996/714 Art.20

s.38, enabling: SI 1998/925

s.39, enabling: SI 1998/925

s.41, see *Interlego AG's Trade Mark Applications, Re* [1998] R.P.C. 69 (Ch D), Neuberger, J.

s.41, enabling: SI 1998/925

s.43, applied: SI 1996/1908 Reg.3

s.43, enabling: SI 1998/925

s.45, applied: SI 1996/1908 Reg.3

s.46, see *United Biscuits (UK) Ltd v Asda Stores Ltd* (1997) R.P.C. 513 (Ch D), Robert Walker, J.

s.46, applied: SI 1996/714 Art.13, SI 1996/1908 Reg.3

s.47, see *DUCATI Trade Mark* [1998] R.P.C. 227 (TMR), SJ Probert

Figure 5.27 *Current Law Statute Citator*

Electronic sources

Westlaw

If you want to search for cases by legislation cited using *Westlaw*, you need to select cases from the menu at the top of the screen and then select the advanced search option. You can then enter your terms in the 'Legislation Title' search box. You can even add a particular provision in the 'Legislation Provision No.' box, if you want to make your search even more specific – see Figure 5.28 below.

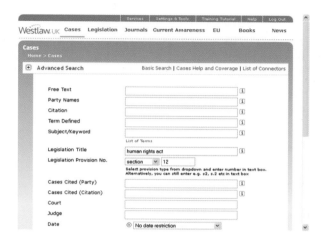

Figure 5.28 Finding cases by legislation cited on *Westlaw*

5.4.4 Finding old cases (pre-1865)

Printed sources

English Reports

To find an *English Reports* version of a case, you should look up the name of the case in the *Index of Cases*. In Figure 5.29 on page 88, you will see that the index contains the case name, the original (pre-1865) citation and then the volume and page number within the *English Reports* where you will find a reprint of the case – see Figure 5.30 on page 88.

Revised Reports

The *Revised Reports* has accompanying index volumes which contain an alphabetical table of cases and a subject index.

All England Law Reports Reprint

The *All England Law Reports Reprint* has an accompanying index volume containing an alphabetical list of cases and a subject index.

Figure 5.29 Index of cases from *The English Reports*

Reed v. Spurr, Administrator.   Exch. of Pleas.   1836.—A plea of plene administravit does not require to be signed by counsel.

[S. C. 2 Gale, 230; 6 L. J. Ex. 15.]

To an action of assumpsit, the defendant pleaded plene administravit, but the plea was not signed by counsel, and the plaintiff signed judgment.

Mansel now moved to set that judgment aside for irregularity. He referred to Tidd's Practice, 9th edit. 671, to shew, that, according to the practice of the Court of **[77]** King's Bench, this was a common plea, which need not be signed by counsel. The rule of Hilary Term, 2 Will. 4, No. 107, only refers to pleadings which conclude to the country, and does not apply to this case. Mr. Tidd enumerates many instances of pleas which conclude with a verification, as not being necessary to be signed by counsel; as, this plea of plene administravit, solvit ad diem, and comperuit ad diem.

Sewell shewed cause in the first instance. This plea ought to have been signed. Where a plea traverses matter alleged in the declaration, and concludes to the country, it need not be signed by counsel. But, where the plea introduces new matter, it must conclude with a verification, and requires the signature of counsel. This plea concludes with a verification. In *Macher* v. *Billing* (1 C. M. & R. 577), it was held that a plea of the statute of limitations required to be signed by counsel. According to the practice of the Court of Common Pleas, it ought to be so signed. [Parke, B. This ought to have been provided for by the new rules.]

Lord Abinger, C. B. We must follow the practice stated by the Master, which is, that this plea does not require counsel's signature.

Parke, B. This Court follows the practice of the King's Bench. The judgment is irregular, and must be set aside with costs.

Rule absolute with costs.

Figure 5.30 Reprint of a case from *The English Reports*

Halsbury's Laws of England and Wales

If you know the name of the case, then you can use *Halsbury's Laws* to find a citation. Look up the name of the case in the *Consolidated Table of Cases* and this will refer you to the relevant volume and paragraph of *Halsbury's Laws*. In the footnotes, you will find the name of your case, followed by the citation. You may find a brief description of the case itself but you will need to consult another source to find the full text law report.

The Digest

Like *Halsbury's Laws*, *The Digest* is another useful way to find citations for cases, particularly older ones. Look up the name of the case in the *Consolidated Table of Cases* and then go to the relevant section of *The Digest*, where you will find a summary of the case and a citation to the full text.

Electronic sources

The English Reports

The English Reports are available online via a number of different providers, including *HeinOnline*, *Justis*, *LexisLibrary* and *Westlaw*. Check to see which of these your library provides access to. The electronic versions offer a variety of different search options, allowing you to search by party name, keyword or citation – either by the original pre-1865 citation or by its *English Reports* citation.

LexisLibrary

You can find citations for older cases by using the electronic version of *Halsbury's Laws of England and Wales*, accessible via the Commentary tab. Enter your case name in the search terms box and the results list will take you to the relevant sections of *Halsbury's Laws* where that case name appears. *Halsbury's Laws* will provide basic information only so you will need to follow up the citation in another source to get a full text version.

The *All England Law Reports Reprint* series is available online via *LexisLibrary*. Choose the Cases tab, and then select *All England Law Reports Reprint* from the list of sources. You can search on any combination of term, catchword or headnote, case name or citation.

5.4.5 Checking the history of a case

Printed sources

Current Law Case Citator

As well as telling you where you can find a full version of a case, the *Current Law Case Citator* can also give you other information about cases. In Figure 5.15 on page 75 we saw that there were some words and numbers after the citations – 'Digested, 87/2885: Applied, 88/2837: Considered, 88/2833' – so let's look at what they refer to and what they mean.

First, you need to be aware that references of this type within the *Current Law Case Citators* are always pointing you to its sister publication, the *Current Law Year Book*. (The *Current Law Year Book* is also published by Sweet & Maxwell and is another member of the 'Current Law' family of publications.) Once you know this, it becomes much easier to work them out.

Leaving aside the words for a moment, let's concentrate on deciphering the numbers. All you need to remember is that the first number (before the slash) represents the year and the second number (after the slash) represents the paragraph number. So to find the reference 87/2885 you need to consult paragraph number 2885 of the 1987 *Current Law Year Book* and for 88/2837 you should go to paragraph 2837 within the 1988 *Current Law Year Book*. Easy, isn't it!

Let's move on to the words now, so you understand their importance. We'll start with 'Digested' as this is the simplest to explain. Digested simply means summarised, so if you want a concise summary of the *Crest Homes v Marks* case, go to paragraph 2885 of the *Current Law Year Book* for 1987. Most cases in the *Current Law Case Citators* are digested within the *Current Law Year Book*.

> **2885.** **Anton Piller order – use of documents – discovery of documents in second Anton Piller relevant to first such order – whether usable in contempt proceedings.**
>
> [Supreme Court Act 1981 (c.54), s.72.]
>
> In exceptional circumstances the court can modify or release a plaintiff from his undertakings in relation to documents discovered in an action.
>
> The plaintiff in a first action obtained an Anton Piller order in respect of certain documents. A year later they commenced another action and obtained a second order in respect of that action. On execution a number of documents were discovered that allegedly broke undertakings given in the first action and which should then have been disclosed. The plaintiffs applied for leave to use those documents in taking contempt proceedings in respect of the first order. The judge refused the application, the appeal was allowed.
>
> *Held*, dismissing the defendants' appeal, that quite exceptionally the court could modify or release a plaintiff from the usual implied undertakings given on discovery, and the defendants here would suffer no injustice (*Berkhor (A.J.) & Co. v. Bilton* [1981] C.L.Y. 2159 considered).
>
> CREST HOMES *v.* MARKS [1987] 3 W.L.R. 293, H.L.

Figure 5.31 Excerpt from the *Current Law Year Book 1987*

The other references are slightly more complicated because they refer to later cases in which the decision in your original case (*Crest Homes v Marks*) has played a part, either positively or negatively. In Chapter 4 we saw how important it is to check if a case had been referred to in any subsequent case. It's terms like 'Applied', 'Considered' and 'Followed', and the *Current Law Year Book* references which will provide you with that information. Let's look at an example and see if it makes it any clearer.

Following the instructions detailed above, if we look up the reference 'Applied, 88/2837', it will lead us to this paragraph in the 1988 *Current Law Year Book*:

> **2837. Discovery – use of documents – Anton Piller order – committal proceedings**
>
> [Civil Evidence Act 1968 (c.64), s.14]
>
> S.14 of the 1968 Act does not extend to proceeding for committal for contempt of court.
>
> G. sued two companies for wrongful dismissal, arrears of salary and an account of profits. She obtained a Mareva injunction, and later an Anton Piller order covering documents which might be used in proceedings for committal for contempt of the Mareva injunction. The Anton Piller order was obtained subject to a requirement that leave be obtained before s⌐⌐⌐⌐⌐⌐⌐ ⌐⌐⌐⌐ed ain an application for committal.
>
> *Held*, on G's application ⌐⌐⌐⌐⌐⌐⌐⌐ould be granted, since s.14 of the Civil Evidence
>
> Act did not apply to proceed⌐gs for c⌐⌐⌐⌐⌐⌐⌐⌐ (⌐⌐⌐⌐⌐⌐ ⌐ ⌐⌐⌐⌐⌐⌐⌐⌐ (1⌐⌐⌐) 1⌐ Ch D. 435 and *Crest Homes v Marks* [1987] ⌐⌐⌐⌐⌐⌐⌐⌐⌐⌐⌐⌐⌐⌐⌐⌐⌐⌐⌐⌐ ng M.R. in Comet Products U.K. v Hawkex Plastics [1971] C.L.Y. 9083 appl⌐⌐⌐).
>
> GARVIN *v.* DOMUS PUBLISHING [1988] 3 W.L.R. 344, Walton, J.

The reference to our original case

The name of the case which has applied the decision from Crest Home v Marks

Figure 5.32 Excerpt from the *Current Law Year Book 1988*

tutor tip

In the example in Figure 5.32, the annotating case is *Garvin v Domus Publishing* and the annotated case is *Crest Homes v Marks*.

Put simply, applied means that the court has applied the principle of law of an earlier case (*Crest Homes v Marks*) in a subsequent case (*Garvin v Domus Publishing*).

Electronic sources

Westlaw

Westlaw's Case Analysis documents include sections called 'Key Cases Citing' and 'All Cases Citing'. The 'Key Cases Citing' section will list leading cases which have referred in some way to your original case. The 'All Cases Citing' section will tell you about every single subsequent case which has referred to your original case.

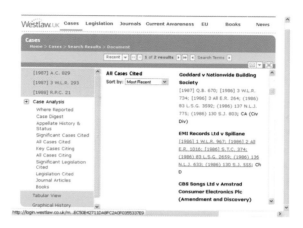

Figure 5.33 Cases cited on *Westlaw*

LexisLibrary

LexisLibrary's Case Search documents include a section called 'Cases referring to this case'. This section will tell you about later cases which have referred in some way to your original case.

Figure 5.34 Cases referring to this case on *LexisLibrary*

5.5 Using secondary sources

5.5.1 Using *Halsbury's Laws of England* in print

Halsbury's Laws of England is a loose-leaf legal encyclopaedia that aims to provide a 'restatement of the whole of the laws of England and Wales'. It is available in print and online versions and how you search it depends on which version you are using.

The main volumes of *Halsbury's Laws* are arranged alphabetically by broad subject areas such as agriculture, animals or children and young persons. The legal definitions are provided in numbered paragraphs and every statement is backed up with a footnote which provides the authority for that statement, such as a Statute, Statutory Instrument or law report.

131. Offences. Any person who knowingly contravenes any prohibition or fails to comply with any duty or requirement imposed by or under the provisions relating to travel restrictions[1] is guilty of an offence and liable on summary conviction to imprisonment for a term not exceeding three months or a fine not exceeding level 4 on the standard scale, or to both[2].

1 ie the provisions contained in the Prevention of Terrorism (Temporary Provisions) Act 1989 s 16(1), Sch 5: see paras 121–130 ante.

2 Ibid Sch 5 para 11. For the meaning of 'the standard scale' see para 808 post.

F. TERRORIST INVESTIGATIONS

132. Search for material other than excluded or special procedure material. On an application made by a constable, a justice of the peace may issue a warrant if satisfied that a terrorist investigation[1] is being carried out and that there are reasonable grounds for believing:

(1) that there is material on premises[2] specified in the application which is likely to be of substantial value, whether by itself or together with other material, to the investigation;

(2) that the material does not consist of or include items subject to legal privilege[3], excluded material[4] or special procedure material[5]; and

(3) that any of the specified conditions are fulfilled[6].

The specified conditions are:

(a) that it is not practicable to communicate with any person entitled to grant entry to the premises;

(b) that it is practicable to communicate with such a person but it is not practicable to communicate with any person entitled to grant access to the material;

(c) that entry to the premises will not be granted unless a warrant is produced;

(d) that the purpose of a search may be frustrated or seriously prejudiced unless a constable arriving at the premises can secure immediate entry to them[7].

A warrant so issued authorises a constable to enter the premises specified and to search the premises and any person found there and to seize and retain anything found there or on any such person, other than items subject to legal privilege, if he has reasonable grounds for believing:

(i) that it is likely to be of substantial value, whether by itself or together with other material, to the investigation; and

(ii) that it is necessary to seize it in order to prevent it being concealed, lost, damaged, altered or destroyed[8].

1 'Terrorist investigation' means any investigation to which the Prevention of Terrorism (Temporary Provisions) Act 1989 s 17(1) applies: s 17(1), Sch 7 para 1.

For the purposes of s 17, 'terrorist investigation' means (1) an investigation into (a) the commission, preparation or instigation of acts of terrorism to which s 14, applies (see para 118 ante); or (b) any other act which appears to have been done in furtherance of, or in connection with, such acts of terrorism, including any act which appears to constitute an offence under s 2 (see para 111 ante), s 9 (see para 115 ante), s 10 (see para 114 ante) or s 11 (see para 116 ante) or the Northern Ireland (Emergency Provisions) Act 1978 s 21; or (c) without prejudice to head (b) supra, the resources of a proscribed organisation within the meaning of the Prevention of Terrorism (Temporary Provisions) Act 1989 s 1 (see para 111 note 1 ante) or a proscribed organisation for the purposes of the Northern Ireland (Emergency Provisions) Act 1978 s 21 (see para 114 note 2 ante); and (2) an investigation into whether there are grounds justifying the making of an order under the Prevention of Terrorism (Temporary Provisions) Act 1989 s 1(2)(a) or the Northern Ireland (Emergency Provisions) Act 1978 s 21(4): Prevention of Terrorism (Temporary Provisions) Act 1989 s 17(1).

Figure 5.35 Excerpt from *Halsbury's Laws of England*

Each main volume has a date on the title page, which indicates when it was issued. If you look at lots of different volumes of *Halsbury's Laws*, you will see that these dates can differ greatly – some may be one or two years old, others may be five years old or more. Individual volumes are only reprinted when a substantial amount of the text has changed, so in the interim *Halsbury's Laws* updates itself by means of an annual *Cumulative Supplement* and monthly *Noter-Up Service*.

Use one of the index volumes to find the volume and paragraph number that you want, then go to the *Cumulative Supplement* and look up the same volume and paragraph number. The *Cumulative Supplement* updates each main volume to a particular date – check in the introduction to Part 1 of the *Cumulative Supplement*, to find out when that date is.

Looking up our topic from Figure 5.35 in the *2004 Cumulative Supplement*, we see that there have been some amendments to this area of the law in the intervening period between the date of issue of the main volume and the date of issue of the *Cumulative Supplement*.

132–138 Terrorist Investigations

For the purposes of a terrorist investigation, an area may be designated, under the Terrorism Act 2000 s 33, in accordance with s 34 (amended by the Anti-terrorism, Crime and Security Act 2001 Sch 7 para 30), during the period specified by the Terrorism Act 2000 s 35, as a cordoned area. 'Terrorist investigation' means an investigation of (1) the commission, preparation or instigation of acts of terrorism, (2) an act which appears to have been done for the purposes of terrorism, (3) the resources of a proscribed organisation, (4) the possibility of making an order proscribing an organisation under s 3(3) (see para 111 ante) or (5) the commission, preparation or instigation of an offence under the Terrorism Act 2000: s 32. For the meaning of 'terrorism' see s 1; and para 102 ante.

As to police powers in relation to a cordoned area see s 36. As to the obtaining of information for the purposes of a terrorist investigation see s 37, Sch 5 Pt I; and as to the obtaining of financial information for the purposes of such an investigation see s 38, Sch 6 (Sch 6 as amended). See also s 38A, Sch 6A (account monitoring orders) (s 38A added by the Anti-terrorism, Crime and Security Act 2001 Sch 2 para 1(2); Terrorism Act 2000 Sch 6A added by the Anti-terrorism, Crime and Security Act 2001 Sch 2 para 1(3)).

The disclosure of anything which is likely to prejudice a terrorist investigation or the interference with material which is likely to be relevant to the investigation is prohibited: see Terrorism Act 2000 s 39. Section 39 has been applied to certain persons in the public service of the Crown: see s 119; and the Terrorism Act 2000 (Crown Servants and Regulations) Regulations 2001, SI 2001/192 (amended by SI 2001/3649, SI 2002/1555).

Certain existing disclosure powers, listed in the Anti-terrorism, Crime and Security Act 2001 Sch 4, are extended: s 17. The Secretary of Stage may give a direction prohibiting the disclosure of information for the purposes of overseas proceedings and any contravention of such a direction is an offence: s 18. There is no obligation of secrecy, except by virtue of the Data Protection Act 1998, in relation to information held by or on behalf of the Commissioners of Inland Revenue or the Commissioners of Customs and Excise where disclosure is made for the purposes of facilitating the carrying out by any of the intelligence services of any of that service's functions, for the purposes of any criminal investigation being carried out or for the purposes of any criminal proceedings whatever, whether in the United kingdom or elsewhere; for the purposes of the initiation or bringing to an end of any such investigation or proceedings or for facilitating a determination as to whether any such investigation or proceedings should be initiated or brought to an end: Anti-terrorism, Crime and Security Act 2001 s 19.

A failure to disclose information which may help prevent another person carrying out an act of terrorism or may help in bringing a terrorist to justice in the United Kingdom is an offence: Terrorism Act 2000 s 38B (added by the Anti-terrorism, Crime and Security Act 2001 s 117(2)).

Figure 5.36 Excerpt from *Halsbury's Laws 2004 Cumulative Supplement*

But let's imagine that it is now the summer of 2004, some months after the *2004 Cumulative Supplement* was published. What if there have been changes to the law since then? To be absolutely sure that the text is as up to date as it can possibly be (it is of course very important to quote accurate and up-to-date sources) we need to check the *Noter-Up Service*. The *Noter-Up Service* is updated monthly and, put simply, does for the *Cumulative Supplement* what the *Cumulative Supplement* does for the main volumes. It works in the same way – you look up the volume and paragraph number and if there have been any amendments they will be presented there – see Figure 5.37 on page 94.

> ### Volumes 11(1), (2) (Reissue)
> ## CRIMINAL LAW, EVIDENCE AND PROCEDURE
>
> In the monthly reviews material updating this title appears under three titles: CRIMINAL EVIDENCE AND PROCEDURE, CRIMINAL LAW AND SENTENCING.
>
> ### Volume 11(1) (Reissue)
>
> **23   Consent to assault**
>
> NOTES 5, 6 – See *R v Dica* [2004] EWCA Crim 1103, (2004) Times, 11 May.
>
> NOTE 8 – 1985 Act replaced: Female Genital Mutilation Act 2003.
>
> **132–138   Terrorist Investigations**
>
> 2001 Act Sch 4 amended: Enterprise Act 2002 Sch 26; Communications Act 2003 Sch 19(1); Health and Social Care (Community Health and Standards) Act 2003 Sch 4 para 120.
>
> **153   Harassment, alarm or distress**
>
> NOTE 4 – See *DPP v Hammond* (2004) Times, 13 January, CA.
>
> **166   Obstruction of court officers executing process against unauthorised occupiers**
>
> TEXT AND NOTES – Criminal Law Act 1977 s 10 further amended: Courts Act 2003 Sch 8 para 189.
>
> **168   Having article with blade or point in public place**
>
> NOTE 1 – *Roberts*, cited, reported at [2004] 1 WLR 181.
>
> NOTE 5 – See *R v Cheong Wang* [2003] EWCA Crim 3228, (2004) 168 JP 224.
>
> **197   Meaning of 'firearm'**
>
> NOTE 7 – *Bentham*, cited, reported at [2003] EWCA Crim 3751, (2003) 168 JP 278.
>
> **199   Meaning of 'air weapon'**
>
> NOTES – See *DPP v Street* (2004) Times, 23 January, DC.
>
> **223   Control of movement of firearms and ammunition**
>
> NOTE 7 – SI 1990/2621 revoked: SI 2003/3228.

Figure 5.37 The *Noter-Up Service*

Halsbury's Laws has a number of different indexes to help you find what you're looking for. As well as a comprehensive subject index, running to two volumes, there is also a *Consolidated Table of Cases* and a *Consolidated Table of Statutes/Statutory Instruments*.

Checking in three different sections of *Halsbury's Laws* just to find one piece of information may seem a daunting prospect and certainly you will need plenty of space to spread the different parts of *Halsbury's* out in front of you, so you may be wondering if there isn't an easier way to do it. Well, yes there is – if your library subscribes to the *LexisLibrary* database then you can access the same information online.

5.5.2 Using the online version of *Halsbury's Laws of England*

As well as the normal benefits that electronic access has over hard copy, such as 24-hour access and not physically having to be in the library, the online version of *Halsbury's Laws* has the added benefit of presenting all the relevant information on one screen. You can see at a glance which text is taken from the main volume and which comes from the *Cumulative Supplement* or *Noter-Up Service*, without having to juggle three separate volumes – see Figure 5.38 on page 95. The numbering system for the online *Halsbury's Laws* is the same as for the printed version, so the same subject volume and paragraph numbers are used. This means that you can refer to a section of *Halsbury's Laws* in an essay by volume and paragraph number and your tutor will be able to find it using either the printed or electronic versions.

You can search the database by keyword or you can browse the individual subject volumes.

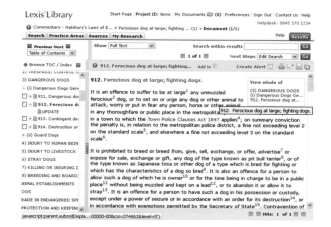

Figure 5.38 *Halsbury's Laws* online

ACTIVITY

Quick quiz

Using *Halsbury's Laws* (either in print or online via *LexisLibrary*), find out what the punishment is for possessing a live badger.

The answer can be found in the Appendix on page 255.

5.5.3 Finding journal articles

In Section 4.6.2 we looked at why journal articles are valuable, so now let's look at how to track them down. Most library catalogues will tell you which journals are in stock within the library but they are unlikely to tell you which articles have appeared in the individual issues. To find that level of information you need to consult an abstracting and indexing service or database.

Finding a reference to a journal article by using an indexing service or database that your library subscribes to does not necessarily mean that your library will also stock the relevant journal. These services are commercially produced and cover many relevant journals in their particular field, so they will tell you what has been written about a topic, regardless of whether those journals are available in your library. When you have identified relevant articles in this way you must then search your own library catalogue to see if your library subscribes to the individual journals, either in print or electronic format.

Legal Journals Index

The *Legal Journals Index*, published by Sweet & Maxwell, is the most comprehensive index to UK law journals. It covers over 400 law journal titles and also incorporates the *European Legal Journals Index* to give more extensive coverage. It is available in print and also in electronic format via the *Westlaw* database.

Using the printed version

The printed version of the *Legal Journals Index* has a subject index, author index, case index, legislation index and book review index. Information provided in the *Legal Journals Index* consists of the titles of relevant articles, the author(s), the bibliographic details (i.e. the year, volume, issue and page numbers) and a brief summary. It will not provide the full text of an article but it will direct you to where the full text is available.

Using the electronic version via *Westlaw*

The *Legal Journals Index* is also available through the *Westlaw* database and the electronic version has many advantages. It is quick and easy to use and can be searched at a basic or advanced level, but its major advantage over the printed index is that it provides links to full text articles also on *Westlaw*. *Westlaw* contains a number of law journal titles in full text, so hypertext links are provided to these from the *Legal Journals Index* – see Figure 5.39 below.

ACTIVITY

Quick quiz

Using the *Legal Journals Index* (either in print or online via *Westlaw*), find out how many articles have been written about the case '*Savage v Fairclough*'.

The answer can be found in the Appendix on page 255.

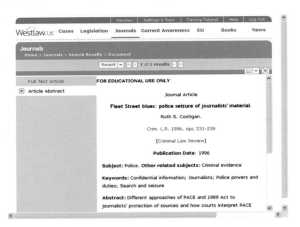

Figure 5.39 The *Legal Journals Index* on *Westlaw*

Lawtel

The *Lawtel* database contains an Articles Index. This index is not as extensive as the *Legal Journals Index*, covering around 75 titles at the time of writing, but it does have some points to recommend it. Lawtel also includes a News & Press index, which indexes broadsheet newspaper articles and press releases.

Index to Legal Periodicals & Books

Published by HW Wilson, this is a particularly useful source for locating US and international law journal articles, while still covering a significant number of UK titles. The *Index to Legal Periodicals & Books* is available in both print and electronic formats and searching is by author, subject, case name or legislation. If you are able to access the electronic version of this index, then you can take advantage of the 325 law journal titles available on it in full text.

Current Law Monthly Digest

The *Current Law Monthly Digest* contains information about recently published articles, so can be useful for current research. Articles are indexed according to their subject.

Halsbury's Laws of England Monthly Review

Similar to the *Current Law Monthly Digest*, *Halsbury's Laws Monthly Review* contains details of very recently published UK articles.

Index to Periodical Articles Related to Law

Published by Glanville Publishers Inc, this index covers articles that are about legal topics, but which have appeared in non-law journals. If you have access to this index then you may find it a useful one to consult to get a wider perspective on a particular topic. This index is also available online via the *HeinOnline* database.

Index to Foreign Legal Periodicals

Published by The University of California Press, this service indexes articles from over 500 legal periodicals. Foreign is defined as not the UK, USA, Canada or Australia, so if you are researching the legal system in France or Germany then this would be a useful source to choose. It should be pointed out, however, that although the index is published in English, many of the articles referred to will be published in their original languages.

Current Law Index

Published by The Gale Group, the *Current Law Index* is another extensive index covering journals from the USA, UK, Ireland, Canada, New Zealand and Australia. In total, it indexes over 900 titles and is available in print and electronic formats. The printed version has a subject index, an author/title index, a Table of Cases and a Table of Statutes, while the electronic version will allow basic and more advanced searches to be constructed.

British Humanities Index (BHI)

The *British Humanities Index* covers the humanities subject fields in a very broad sense. It includes a number of UK law journals within its coverage, as well as the broadsheet newspapers. In its printed format, you can search by subject and by author. The *British Humanities Index* is also available electronically, which allows searching at a basic and more advanced level.

Applied Social Sciences Index & Abstracts (ASSIA)

ASSIA is similar to the *British Humanities Index* in that it covers the social sciences very broadly, including criminology and legal issues. *ASSIA* is an online database, which offers greater flexibility in searching than a printed index.

Other subject databases

As we've seen from the *British Humanities Index* and *ASSIA* examples above, a non-law index or database can have some legal content within it, so it is worth considering other non-law databases when researching particular subjects. As an example, business and management databases may also include articles on different aspects of business law, such as insolvency or directors' duties, so it would be wise to search these too. The best advice to offer here about non-law databases is to have a chat with your Law Librarian. Explain to them that you have a piece of work to do about environmental law or business law (or whatever it may be) and ask them if they can recommend any other resources (apart from the law ones) that you could use.

5.6 Some tips for effective library use

5.6.1 Getting the most out of your library

You may think that you know perfectly well how to use a library – you walk in, choose the book you need from the shelves and borrow it; what could be simpler? In an ideal world this would be the case but, unfortunately, in the real world it doesn't always work like that. Think about how many other students there are in your year, doing your course and how all of you are likely to be competing to get hold of the same library materials. Sadly, few libraries have book budgets large enough to enable them to buy a copy of each reading list item per student (not to mention the library shelf space that would be needed to shelve them all). But before you get too despondent and start thinking that there's obviously no point in even going to the library, read on, and you will discover some tips to help you get the most out of your library and your Law Librarian.

5.6.2 Visit the library as early as possible

This doesn't necessarily mean that you should be standing outside the library's door first thing in the morning, waiting for it to open (although that's not such a bad idea – you may find that your library is much quieter and less busy early in the morning). Instead, it means that once you've been set a piece of coursework or other task, you should go to the library as soon as possible.

Lots of students will all want to look at the same books as you do, so it makes sense to get to the library and borrow them as soon as you can. Whatever you do, please don't commit the cardinal sin of leaving things until a few days (or hours!) before your deadline and expecting all the books you need to be right there on the library shelves. They won't be there, because the more organised students, who manage their time well, will have borrowed them weeks ago.

5.6.3 Make use of any reservations or booking facilities

Most libraries offer a reservation facility, so if someone else has beaten you to one of the key texts, you should make use of this service. In many instances, the person who has the book out on loan can be asked to return it at an earlier date, so you may find that you get access to the item sooner than you originally thought.

5.6.4 Use short loan collections

A short loan collection is a common feature within most academic libraries, although the length of the loan period may vary. Check within your own library to find out if you have such a collection and how it operates.

The items kept in the short loan collection are usually key texts on your reading lists and the shorter loan period means that more people have an opportunity to use them. Although not long enough to read the whole book, the loan period (whether it be an hour, a morning or a day), is usually long enough for you to make any necessary photocopies (abiding by the copyright guidance given out by your institution of course!) or to do the required preparatory reading before a lecture or a tutorial.

Some libraries offer a booking service for short loan material, so you may be able to order a particular item for a specific time when you know you'll be able to use it. Again, check within your own library to find out exactly what services they offer.

5.6.5 Consult other books with the same class number

There will be times when the key texts on your reading list are all out on loan and you haven't got time to wait for a reserved copy, so what should you do in these situations? A good tip is to look for other books with the same class number as the book you originally wanted to use. In library terms the class number represents the subject content of the book, which means that all books about criminal law should have the same class number, as should all books about family law or employment law. It doesn't matter which classification scheme your library uses (or even which version of the classification scheme), you will find that books about the same subject have the same class number.

If, for example, you need to read up on a particular aspect of company law before your next tutorial, you will find that topic covered in many more books than just those ones referred to on your reading list. OK, so you haven't read the chapter from the recommended textbook, but at least you have read something. Your lecturer is far more likely to be impressed by the fact that you've used your initiative than if you had just turned up to the tutorial saying, 'I haven't done any reading because the book on the reading list was out.' Remember – no reading you do is ever wasted.

5.6.6 Use your library staff

One of the greatest resources in any library is its staff (and I'm not just saying that because I'm a librarian). Think about it – they work in the building; they know about the loan procedures and the collections; they use the electronic databases and other material – so who better to answer your library questions?

Most academic library staff are friendly and helpful people who are used to working with students, so don't be afraid to approach them if you have any questions, however stupid you think you might appear. Chances are you won't be asking anything the library staff haven't been asked before. Also, the staff would much prefer that you leave the library satisfied, instead of wandering aimlessly around the shelves hoping to find what you need, getting gradually more frustrated before deciding that the library is hopeless and you'll never come back. As was said before, most academic library staff are friendly and helpful, but they're not psychic. If you need help, ask – and you should find that you receive it.

If you are lucky enough to have a dedicated Law Librarian (a professionally qualified librarian who specialises in the subject of law), then you would be well advised to get to know this person. The Law Librarian will have an in-depth knowledge of the law resources within your library. They can help you locate material, understand citations and references and can recommend sources to you for particular coursework. A word of caution, however – Law Librarians are not lecturers and generally won't be able to pass comment on your work. Academic librarians are in the business of encouraging students to develop the skills necessary to research more effectively and efficiently. When it comes to advice about whether or not the case you've selected accurately illustrates the point you're trying to make, then these questions are better directed at your tutors.

5.6.7 Take advantage of any training offered

If you have the opportunity to attend any training sessions run by the Law Librarian or other library staff, then you would be strongly advised to do so. Most Law Librarians offer training sessions not because they like the sound of their own voice, but because they want to help students get the most out of the library resources. As you've probably realised by now, law can be a confusing and challenging subject with lots of different resources (in print and electronic formats) to consult. Knowing which resource to choose is a skill in itself, as is knowing how to get to the information you're looking for when you've chosen your resource. Any library training sessions that will help you navigate your way through this vast array of information should be seized with both hands.

Library training sessions are often run on a voluntary rather than compulsory basis (that is to say they are not a timetabled lecture or tutorial slot) but this doesn't mean that they are any less valuable. By attending these sessions, you'll be investing in your future success and equipping yourself with the skills you need to become an independent learner.

SUMMARY

- Check within your own institution to find out which printed and electronic sources you have access to.
- Always consider your own particular research needs when deciding which source to use – for example, whether you need to quote the current status of the law or how the law was in the past.
- Take advantage of any training events on legal resources which are offered by your Law Librarian or library staff.
- Use any reservations or bookings facilities in your library to ensure you get access to the books you need.
- Start your library research as soon as possible after you have been set your assignments.

6

Understanding Legal Skills And Using Legal Reasoning

AIMS AND OBJECTIVES

After reading this chapter you should be able to:

- Understand the basic rules of precedent
- Understand the basic rules of statutory interpretation
- Use legal reasoning
- Apply the rules of precedent to factual situations
- Apply the rules of statutory interpretation to factual situations

6.1 The process of deductive logic

Law depends completely on the process of deductive logic. When judges make decisions in cases they have to do so on the basis of legal reasoning. They cannot simply make their own minds up on what they want to decide; they must have a reason based on law. This can come from law found in statutes (Acts of Parliament) or it can come from a principle of law found in decided cases. This is the so-called *ratio decidendi* of a case, which simply means the reason for the decision.

Wherever the law comes from the process in court is the same:

- both sides introduce the facts on which the dispute hinges
- the lawyers then introduce the law that is appropriate to those particular facts
- the law is applied to the facts by the judge
- a decision is reached.

6.2 The use of precedent

6.2.1 A brief overview of the rules of precedent

As you will learn in your English legal system course on your degree, the doctrine of precedent is one of the most important features of English law. This is because judges are not allowed to decide the law as they see fit but must base their decisions on existing law.

There are a few key areas that you need to remember about precedent:

- where the law comes from
- the nature of binding precedent
- other things that are influential on judges when deciding cases
- the hierarchy of the courts
- the ways of avoiding binding precedent.

You will learn about precedent in much more detail in your English legal system course and from those textbooks recommended to you by your teachers. Below are some brief notes of the key areas to give you a general idea and for you to be able to complete the exercises in Section 6.2.3.

Where the law comes from

Precedents to be followed in later cases come from principles of law that are found in existing cases.

- The part of the judgment where the law is found and that provides precedent for later judges to follow is called the *ratio decidendi*. This simply means the reason for the decision, the principle of law that decided the case. A *ratio* may simply extend or develop the previous law or it may be 'original', which means in effect that there was no previous law on the particular issue. It is of course possible to find more than one *ratio* in a case and, as you will find, it is not always easy to find the *ratio*.
- Judges will make other statements in a case, for instance saying what the law might be if the facts of the case were slightly different. These statements are referred to as *obiter dicta*. This simply means 'things said by the way', or in other words things that have no relevance to the outcome of the actual case. These can still be influential on later judges, particularly if they are made by high-ranking judges such as those in the House of Lords.

Binding precedent

The doctrine of *stare decisis* (simply meaning 'stand by what has already been decided') is followed quite rigidly in English law. This means that whenever a judge is deciding a case if there is a principle of law from a previous case that applies to the facts of the present case then this principle should be followed in the present case.

In fact a binding precedent is a principle of law that must be followed by the court in a later case, if the facts in the case are analogous, even if the judges do not agree with the principle in it.

Binding precedent comes from only one place, the *ratio decidendi* of the past analogous case. It will only apply in the present case if the facts of this case are sufficiently similar to those in the case in which the precedent is found and also only if the precedent was made in a court capable of binding the court hearing the later case. Normally, this would be a court on a level with or higher up the hierarchy of courts, although the Human Rights Act 1998 has had an effect on when courts are bound by a higher court's decision made before the Act came into force on a decision made after that date.

Persuasive precedent

Persuasive precedent will not bind a future court so it does not have to be followed. However, the judges in a future case may well be influenced by the principle and wish to apply it in later cases. This will be the case particularly when in the present case there is no obvious binding precedent to follow.

Persuasive precedent can come from a variety of different sources, including:

- *Obiter dicta* from a decided case. For example the *obiter* comments in *Rondel v Worsley* [1969] 1 AC 191 were later applied by the court in *Saif Ali v Sidney Mitchell & Co* [1978] 3 WLR 849.
- Dissenting judgments (these are statements made by judges in an appeal case who disagree with the principles stated by the majority judges and want to state what they think the law should be). They may well be followed in the future if sufficiently senior judges make them. For example the House of Lords eventually followed Lord Denning's dissenting judgment from *Candler v Crane Christmas & Co* [1951] 2 KB 164 in *Hedley Byrne v Heller & Partners* [1964] AC 465.

- Minority judgments (these are additional comments made by the judges in a case who do not give the leading judgment).
- Judgments made in the Privy Council and in other Commonwealth courts. For example the definition of remoteness of damage for negligence from *The Wagon Mound (No. 1)* [1961] AC 388, of foreseeable damage is now the standard test.
- The works of leading academics. For example the House of Lords in *Dunlop v Selfridge* [1915] AC 847 approved Sir Frederick Pollock's definition of consideration contained in his 'Principles of Contract' that '... *an act of forbearance or the promise thereof is the price for which the promise of the other is bought, and the promise thus given for value is enforceable ...*'.

The hierarchy of courts

- **The European Court of Justice** – EU law applies mostly to economic areas and does not affect every area of English law. However, if a case is affected by a point of EU law then from 1 January 1973 the European Court of Justice (ECJ) is the highest court. Decisions made in this court are binding on all courts in England and Wales, although not on itself.
- **The Supreme Court (formerly The House of Lords)** – This is the highest domestic court. Decisions made here bind all lower courts. Traditionally the House of Lords was bound by its own past decisions following *London Street Tramways v London County Council* [1898] AC 375. It could avoid its past decisions through using the 1966 *Practice Statement* [1966] 3 All ER 77.
- **The Court of Appeal** – The Court of Appeal is made up of two divisions: the Civil Division and the Criminal Division. Each division is bound to follow decisions of the Supreme Court and the ECJ. The divisions also bind the respective civil and criminal courts below them. It is generally bound to follow its own past decisions except in certain circumstances.
- **The Divisional Courts** – The term Divisional Court is used when one of the three divisions of the High Court (Family, Chancery and Queen's Bench) acts as an appeal court or in a supervisory capacity. The Divisional Courts are bound by all courts above them, and bind all lower courts. They are generally bound by their own past decisions but with some flexibility similar to the Court of Appeal.
- **The High Court** – The High Court is bound by all higher courts and in turn binds lower courts. Judges are not bound by the decisions of other High Court judges but usually follow them.
- **The inferior courts** – The Crown Court, the County Court, and the Magistrates' Court are bound by the decisions of the higher courts. They do not themselves create any precedent. Technically, however, a point of law made by a judge in the Crown Court binds the Magistrates' Court.

Ways of avoiding precedent

There are a few limited ways that enable certain courts to avoid binding precedent:

- **overruling** – this is where one of the appeal courts finds in a later case that the precedent from the case was wrong
- **reversing** – this is where during the appeal in a case a higher court changes the decision from the court below
- **distinguishing** – this is available to all courts and is where the court finds that the material facts of the present case are essentially different from the precedent it is being asked to apply e.g. the principle in *Balfour v Balfour* [1919] 2 KB 571 was not applied in *Merritt v Merritt* [1970] 1 WLR 1211.

The House of Lords could also use the *Practice Statement* [1966] 3 All ER 77 to change its past decisions and depart from a previous decision when 'it appears right to do so'.

This only applied in two situations:

- to avoid injustice in the present case, and
- to allow for the proper development of the law.

However, the House of Lords judges rarely used it, even when they thought that the law may lead to injustice; e.g. in *Jones v Secretary of State for Social Services* [1972] AC 944 they would not overrule the decision in *Re Dowling* [1967] 1 AC 725 even though they all felt this would lead to injustice and some felt the case had been wrongly decided:

- It was first used in *Conway v Rimmer* [1968] AC 910 but only on a technical point.
- The first major use was in *B R Board v Herrington* [1972] AC 877, overruling *Addie v Dumbreck* [1929] AC 358 on the duty of care owed to a trespasser.
- The first use in criminal law was *R v Shivpuri* [1986] 2 WLR 988, overruling *Anderton v Ryan* [1985] AC 567 on impossible attempts and this was only to correct their own error.
- In any case the *Practice Statement* itself identified the need for certainty in the law, particularly in the case of contracts, tax arrangements and in the criminal law.
- The Court of Appeal is usually bound by its own past precedent but there are exceptions in *Young v Bristol Aeroplane Co* [1944] KB 718
  - where there are two conflicting past Court of Appeal decisions it may choose one and reject the other
  - where a Court of Appeal decision, though not overruled, is inconsistent with a later decision of the House of Lords, then it must follow the House of Lords decision
  - where a Court of Appeal decision was made *per incuriam* (or without reference to all the appropriate authorities) then it may ignore that decision.
- The Criminal Division of the Court of Appeal can also avoid its own decisions if the law has been 'misapplied or misunderstood' because of the possible loss of liberty as in *R v Taylor* [1950] 2 KB 368 and *R v Gould* [1968] 2 QB 65.
- More recent exceptions include the Court of Appeal being able to ignore House of Lords precedent when
  - a House of Lords decision has been overruled by the European Court of Justice or
  - a House of Lords decision is incompatible with the European Convention on Human Rights.
- Now the Supreme Court may overrule if it is right to do so.

ACTIVITY

Self-test questions

Now test your understanding of the basic elements of precedent above by answering the following questions:

1. What is the difference between the *ratio decidendi* of a case and *obiter dicta*?
2. What is the difference between 'binding' precedent and 'persuasive' precedent?
3. What is a dissenting judgment and what effect can it have on precedent?
4. Which court is higher in the hierarchy of courts – the High Court or the Court of Appeal (Civil Division)?
5. Which courts do not create precedent?
6. Which courts are able to use the practice of 'distinguishing' in order to avoid past precedent?
7. When does the *Practice Statement* suggest that judges should be careful to avoid changing the law?
8. What are the three exceptions in *Young* when the Court of Appeal is able to avoid its own past precedent?
9. What precisely does *per incuriam* mean?
10. In what circumstances does the Court of Appeal (Criminal Division) have extra power to avoid its past precedent?

An alternative version of precedent in a diagram form similar to those that you will find in Chapter 11 is given below.

Basic principles	Ways of avoiding precedent
Stare decisis (stand by decisions of past cases) is the basis of the doctrine of precedent. All courts are bound to follow decisions (*ratio decidendi*) made by courts above them in the hierarchy – this is **binding precedent**. Only the principles of law which are essential to the decision are the *ratio decidendi*. Statements of principles of law which are not relevant to the decision are *obiter dicta* and do not need to be followed. **Persuasive precedent** is when a court does not have to follow the principle but may do so. It comes from a variety of different sources: • *Obiter dicta* statements by a higher ranking court • a dissenting judgment • *ratios* from decisions by courts lower in the hierarchy • decisions by courts outside the English legal system.	**Distinguishing** If the material facts of the present case are sufficiently different from an earlier case, the case may be distinguishing so that the earlier decision is not followed: *Shepherd* (1987) and *Sharp* (1987). **Overruling** Where a court changes a past precedent of its own (e.g. House of Lords under the Practice Statement). **Reversing** Where a higher court changes the ruling of a lower court in the same case.
Court of Appeal	**The Supreme Court**
Must follow decisions of the Supreme Court **Exceptions** to this rule are where a House of Lords decision • has been overruled by the European Court of Justice or • is incompatible with the European Convention on Human Rights. The Court of Appeal must follow its own past decisions. *Young's case* (1944). **Except** • where there are conflicting decisions, the Court of Appeal can choose which to follow • where a decision has been impliedly overruled by Supreme Court, the Court of Appeal must follow the Supreme Court's decision and not its own • where a decision has been made *per incuriam*. The Criminal Division of the Court of Appeal will also not follow where law has been misapplied or misunderstood. *Gould* (1968).	The Supreme Court was created to replace the House of Lords in 2009. There is no Practice Statement but changes of the law have to be requested in applications to the court. The court will only change past precedents where there is a good reason to do so. 1966 *Practice Statement* gave the House of Lords power to depart from past decisions. The Statement said that former decisions would normally be treated as binding but the Lords could 'depart from a previous decision when it appears right to do so'. • 'to avoid injustice in the present case' or • 'to allow for proper development of the law'. But the Statement stressed the need for certainty, *especially in the criminal law*, and the danger of disturbing retrospectively the basis on which contracts, settlements of property and fiscal arrangements had been entered into. The first civil use was in *Herrington v BRB* (1972); and the first criminal use was in *Shivpuri* (1986).

Figure 6.1 Alternative version of precedent in diagram form

The basic rules on precedent and the ways that courts may avoid past precedents, as indicated above are reasonably straightforward. While precedent is often stated to be rigidly applied in the English legal system, this is in fact not always the case – a factor that can often prove confusing to students of substantive law areas. This is illustrated below in an article written for the *A-Level Law Review* (published by Philip Allan Updates) by one of the authors of this book, Chris Turner.

> As law students you are taught that, while there are complex rules regarding when courts can avoid their own past precedent, one aspect of the doctrine of precedent is quite simple. A court in England and Wales is strictly bound to follow decisions of a court equal to it or higher than it in the hierarchy of courts, subject to those well defined exceptions.

Continued on next page

Students are also taught that decisions of the Judicial Committee of the Privy Council, while it includes the most senior judges, can be persuasive only, because the Court is not strictly part of the hierarchy of courts.

The basic rule is very straightforward and even the exceptions are once you know them. However, once you begin to study [areas of substantive law] you will realise that the reality is not so straightforward.

In an important recent case, *R v Holley* [2005], the Privy Council, hearing an appeal from Jersey, decided that the House of Lords was wrong in *R v Smith (Morgan James)* [2000] on the issue of loss of self control in the defence of provocation in murder. *Smith* has been unpopular with both judges and academics. However, as we know *Holley* is at best persuasive. In fact the Privy Council had already decided in previous cases that, where a case in front of it was in effect bound by English law, then it should follow it. On this basis, the result of *Holley* should have been clear, the Privy Council should have followed *Smith*.

In an even more recent case, *R v James, R v Karimi* [2006], the Court of Appeal (Criminal Division) had to consider whether to apply *Smith* or whether it had in fact been overruled by the Privy Council in *Holley*. The Court of Appeal chose the latter view and held that, in very exceptional circumstances, a decision of the Privy Council can take precedence over a decision of the House of Lords. It justified this on the grounds that the Privy Council in *Holley* was made up of 9 of the 12 judges from the House of Lords and, as it was decided 6:3, the majority of the House of Lords wished the rule in *Smith* to be changed. What the Court of Appeal did in *James* and *Karimi* in effect was to overrule the precedent of a higher court.

It is not unusual for courts to overrule their previous decisions. In *Davis v Johnson* [1978] Lord Denning ignored two recently decided Court of Appeal cases on domestic violence. Nevertheless, he was severely criticised by the House of Lords for doing so. Without being subjected to the same criticisms but with equally important effect, the Court of Appeal in *Doughty v Turner Manufacturing* [1964] chose to ignore its own well established test on remoteness of damage in negligence from *Re Polemis and Furness, Withy & Co* [1921] and applied instead a different test established by the Privy Council in an Australian appeal, *The Wagon Mound (No 1)* [1961], which is now the established law.

Of greater significance is where a court ignores the precedent of a higher court. The Court of Appeal was again strongly criticised by the House of Lords in *Miliangos v George Frank Textiles Ltd* [1976] for applying its own precedent in *Schorsch Meier GmbH v Henning* [1975], in which it in effect overruled a House of Lords decision from *Re Havana Railways* [1961] on the ground that the reason for the rule had gone so the rule should go too. The House of Lords reminded the Court of Appeal that only the House itself could overrule its past decisions.

In *Great Peace Shipping Ltd v Tsavliris Salvage (International) Ltd* [2002] the Court of Appeal held that equity did not apply to common mistake in contract law and that in effect its previous decision in *Solle v Butcher* [1950] was wrong. It is interesting to analyse this decision applying the rule in *Young v Bristol Aeroplane*. The Court of Appeal can avoid its own past precedents:

- Where the case (here it would be *Solle v Butcher*) is inconsistent with a later decision of the House of Lords – here there is no later House of Lords decision which is inconsistent.
- Where there are two conflicting decisions of the Court of Appeal – this could not apply in *Great Peace* since the two main decisions, *Solle v Butcher* and *Magee v Pennine Insurance Co Ltd* [1969], were consistent.
- Where the decision was decided *per incuriam* (without reference to relevant statute or case law) – in *Solle v Butcher* there was no appropriate law that had not been referred to.

Applying the rule in *Young*, the Court of Appeal in *Great Peace* had no justification for overruling its previous precedent.

Continued on next page

Continued

All judges can also avoid past precedent by distinguishing where the material facts of the two cases are sufficiently different. Distinguishing has been criticised because judges may split hairs and suggest illogical distinctions just to avoid law they do not like. In *Williams v Roffey Brothers & Nichols* [1990] the House of Lords distinguished from *Stilk v Myrick* [1809]. In that case the court had decided that a person could not use something that they were already bound to do under an existing contract as consideration for an entirely new arrangement. In *Chappell v Nestle Co* [1960] the court explained that consideration must be something real, tangible and of (economic) value. In *Williams* the claimant was trying to enforce a second agreement where he would gain more money merely for doing what he was already bound to do under his existing contract. As the other party would suffer financially if the contract was not performed, the House of Lords decided that there was consideration in the 'extra benefit' gained by that party. It is possible to see the economic benefit here but it could never be seen as either real or tangible. So in essence the court was bending the rules to reach the decision that it wanted.

Sometimes judges even just make up the law. The House of Lords in *Shaw v DPP* [1962] created the offence of 'conspiring to corrupt public morality', even though there was no precedent for it and no statutory offence. It was heavily criticised but justified its decision, arguing that judges are the moral guardians of the public. Nevertheless, it promised not to do it again. However, in *Knuller v DPP* [1973] it declared that there was a crime of 'outraging public decency', which was later accepted and applied by the Court of Appeal in *R v Gibson* [1991].

Adapted from *Precedent. A-Level Law Review,* Volume 2, Number 1, pp 10–12.

6.2.2 Understanding how precedent works

In your first year studying law at degree level you will usually undertake a course called English Legal System. The actual title of the course may vary; for instance at my own university the course is called English and European Legal Systems, but also incorporates a course on Legal Skills. If you have already taken A Level Law you will have already studied English Legal System but the assessments that you encounter in the subject may be very different from those that you have already completed. In this course you will inevitably be taught about the doctrine of precedent.

The doctrine sometimes seems complex and certainly you will come across many aspects of it that seem to be contradictory once you start looking at what judges have said or done in decided cases. Despite this, the basic operation of the doctrine makes perfect sense if you have a practical understanding of what is going on and how the various peculiar phrases that you come across apply.

The brief extract below is taken from a fairly simple case in contract law that you may also study in the first year of your course. It is taken from a casebook so it has already been reduced in size.

The purpose of using the extract is to show you the different aspects of the judgment and how a principle of law, a precedent, develops from the case. The extract from the judgment is in the left-hand box; a simple commentary identifying the key aspects of the judgment is in the right-hand box; and explanations of these are given below.

CASE EXAMPLE

Hyde v Wrench

Rolls Court [1840] 3 Beav 334; Jur 1106; 49 E.R. 132. ◄——— | The case citation

June 6.   The defendant wrote to the plaintiff offering to sell his farm for £1,000. The plaintiff's agent immediately called on the defendant and made an offer of £950 which the ◄—— | Brief summary of the facts of the case
defendant wished to have a few days to consider.

June 27.   The defendant wrote to say that he would not accept this offer.

June 29.   The plaintiff wrote accepting the offer of June 6.

The plaintiff brought an action for specific performance.

The defendant filed a general demurrer.

THE MASTER OF THE ROLES (LORD LANGDALE): ◄—— | The judgment |

Under the circumstances stated in this bill, I think there exists no valid binding contract between the parties for the purchase of the ◄—— | Brief statement of the existing law |
property. The defendant offered to sell it for £1,000, and if that had at once been unconditionally accepted, there would undoubtedly have been a perfect binding contract; instead of that, the plaintiff made an offer of his own, to purchase the property for £950, and he ◄—— | The *ratio decidendi* of the present case |
thereby rejected the offer previously made by the defendant. I think that it was not afterwards competent for him to revive the proposal of the defendant, by tendering an acceptance of it; and that, there- ◄—— | The decision |
fore, there exists no obligation of any sort between the parties; the demurrer must be allowed.

The citation

Your lecturers, and no doubt the Law Librarian, will tell you how important it is for you to learn the abbreviations for the various law reports so that you can find the cases for yourself once you have found the citation in the particular textbook you are using. The crucial parts of the citation for finding the case are the names of the parties, the year and the abbreviation indicating the particular law report. In this extract it is 49 ER 132 that is important to you. This is an old report that came before the Incorporated Council for Law Reporting was created and therefore we would usually be looking in what are called the *English Reports*. An index is available to go with these.

Brief summary of facts

Professor Michael Zander defined the principle of law coming from a case (the *ratio decidendi*) as 'a proposition of law which decides the case, in the light or in the context of the material facts'. Therefore, the facts of each case are important because, when compared with the facts of previous cases, it can be seen whether the past precedent applies, or whether a new or modified principle has to be developed.

In our example here the facts can be briefly stated in bullet form:

- one party made an offer to sell at a set price
- the other party wanted to buy at a lower price
- the party making the offer rejected the alternative price
- the party to whom the offer had been made then tried to accept the offer at the original price by which time the other party had sold the farm
- the party receiving the original offer then tried to sue for breach of contract.

These facts would have to be compared with the material facts of earlier cases to see whether or not a contract was actually formed.

Brief statement of existing law

Precedent is a process of applying past principles of law to existing cases. If the principles are appropriate because the facts fall within them then the answer is relatively straight-forward; the past precedent must be applied; and the case decided in this way. If the facts of the present case do not allow this then the difference between the cases must be established to see what the developed principle in the present case would be.

In our case above Lord Langdale states the past law very clearly in the first passage underlined. It can be stated simply by saying that if an offer is unconditionally accepted then a contract is formed.

The facts in the case above of course are slightly different. Hyde did not unconditionally accept the offer of the farm for £1,000. Instead he suggested that he wanted to pay only £950.

The ratio decidendi *of the case*

This is the principle of law, the precedent, to emerge from the case, and one which will bind future judges if the material facts are analogous.

In this instance the *ratio* provided by Lord Langdon has two key components:

▨ changing the terms of the offer is the same as rejecting the offer
▨ rejecting the offer means that it can no longer be open to the party to whom it was made, and so they can no longer accept it.

The decision

The decision in a case is only the result of the principle of law being applied to the facts in question.

Here the defendant in the case was asking for a 'demurrer'. This is an old-fashioned word, but what it basically means is that he was suggesting that the claimant, in effect, did not have any reason for bringing an action, that there was no legal substance to the claim that he was making.

In the circumstances, by applying the principle of law to the facts, Lord Langdale was agreeing with this argument in his decision.

6.2.3 Exercises using precedent and deductive reasoning

As in the example above both lawyers and the judges in a case must use both the existing precedents (the principles of law found in earlier cases) and the processes of deductive logic that they have been trained to adopt. They will do so in order to reach conclusions about how they should interpret the facts in front of them and apply the appropriate law. Deductive logic or reasoning simple means that the judges reach a decision by looking at past law and seeing how it fits or applies to the facts of the present case.

To do this they will look back at the law reports as we have already seen and it is the responsibility of the lawyers to introduce into the case all of the appropriate cases that may influence the outcome of the current case. It is with the benefit of the law coming from these cases (the *rationes decidendi* – or legal principles) that deductive reasoning can be used, applying the appropriate law to the facts of the current case in order to reach a conclusion.

Below are a series of exercises on precedent. The exercises involve the judgments from five different completely fictitious cases reported upon in entirely fictitious law reports, the *Hodder Weekly Reports* (HWR). Following the judgment in each case is a series of questions. The expected solutions to the questions are given to you for the first set of questions together with some explanation for the answers. Using these and the information given in the later four judgments you should try to answer the questions that follow each case. The answers are given in the Appendix at the end of the book, except for the first exercise where the answers are reproduced to give you an idea of what is expected.

In answering the questions you should ignore any precedents of which you are aware and concentrate entirely on the law to be found in the judgments themselves. In fact the judgments concern areas of law that would ordinarily be found in the law of torts and more particularly negligence. However, you should treat the cases here as though the first judgment, *Berry v Branch*, is an original precedent and the first time that the particular issues have been considered and, therefore, the first time that the legal principles arising have been stated. In the exercises then you should use only the law given to you in the various extracts to decide the answers to the questions that follow them.

ACTIVITY

Exercise 1: Fictitious case example

The judgment in *Berry v Branch*
Hodder Weekly Reports **[2002] 2 HWR 1142**
Berry v Branch

QUEEN'S BENCH DIVISION

Rough-Justice J

1 April. 1 May 2002

a   *Civil liability – tree growing into neighbour's garden – leaves eaten by neighbour's dog – leaves poisonous – dog dies – whether owner of tree liable.*

b   The defendant planted a yew tree in his garden which, over many years, grew across the fence between the defendant's garden and the claimant's. The claimant's dog ate some of the leaves which fell into the claimant's garden and, as a result, died. The claimant claimed damages from the defendant for the loss of his dog.

c   **Held** – civil liability attaches to any damage done by anything which a person throws off his property or allows to escape from his property.

Cases referred to in judgment

R v Woodstain [1992] 3 HWR 198

Action

d   The claimant, Arnold Berry, brought an action against the defendant, Henry Branch, for agreed damages of £350 for the death of the claimant's dog, Ginger, which was agreed to have been caused by the dog's eating the leaves of a yew tree which grew in the defendant's garden and overlooked the claimant's garden. The facts are set out in the judgment.

Herbert Leafmould for the claimant

Alicia Twig for the defendant

1 May. The following judgment was delivered.   *Cur adv vult*

e   **ROUGH-JUSTICE J** This is an action for damages arising out of the distressing and entirely unnecessary death of a noble specimen of man's best friend. The setting for this sad tragedy is Westiddling Avenue, one of Allwhiting's loveliest streets.

f   The houses on Westiddling Avenue are substantial and all have very large gardens. Most of the properties are owned by professional people, including doctors, lawyers and accountants. In this case, however, the defendant is an American car salesman and the claimant is a university lecturer.

g   At No 29, the defendant planted a yew tree in his back garden. The defendant was a wholly novice gardener – he had always lived in high-rise apartments in New York prior to moving to England. He chose the yew tree solely because he had seen wooden bowls made out of yew logs and thought that any tree which had such pretty wood must be a good one to have in his garden.

h   Now it has always been well known in England that yew trees, apart from being lugubrious looking objects, reminiscent of old churchyards and quite unsuitable for suburban gardens, are poisonous in all their parts. That is, of course, why they are planted in churchyards – to keep cattle out.

i   In the course of time this particular yew tree grew, as even yew trees will, albeit slowly, as is their nature. It grew so that it towered over the claimant's garden at No 27.

j   The claimant was away, working abroad, for five years before the incident which this claim concerns. When he returned home he brought with him a very valuable pet golden retriever. He shipped the dog to England six months prior to his own return so that it would come out of quarantine only a few days after he arrived back in England.

k   As a result of the excitement of seeing its master once again, this lovely animal, of which I have been shown numerous fetching photographs, was off its food for the first two

Continued on next page

days after it arrived home. It is a well known fact that when they have some gastric upset, dogs will often eat grass or leaves. When this hapless animal was turned out into the back garden for a run, it ate some of the leaves of the yew tree which had dropped into the claimant's garden. It was unfortunate that in his first few days at home, the claimant had given higher priority to other jobs than clearing away the accumulation of yew leaves and other debris which he found had built up during his absence. The inevitable result of the dog consuming the yew leaves was that the poor dog died. The claimant naturally expects damages for his loss.

l   Ms Twig, for the defendant, argues that the fault for the demise of the dog lies with the claimant who failed to keep his lawn clean of what he, as a botanist, must have known were poisonous leaves. Ms Twig says that the defendant cannot be held responsible for where the wind, willy-nilly, deposits the leaves which fall from his tree.

m   Since our laws have not previously dealt with this point – there is neither a decided case nor a Statute to assist me – I am thrown back upon first principles. This is despite the Herculean efforts of Ms Twig to convince me that I should be guided by the case of *R v Woodstain* [1992] 3 Hod Cr Rep 198. [Hodder Criminal Reports] I am afraid that I am unable to see the relevance of this case, which first was heard in our criminal courts and second concerned the destruction of a common garden fence, despite Ms Twig nagging on about it for quite some time.

n   It seems to me to be a matter of ordinary fairness that if someone embarks on any activity which is dangerous, then they should take the consequences. So, if someone plants a poisonous tree, they must be liable for the damage it does and this is true whether the damage occurs on the planter's property or off it.

o   Is this situation not akin to one where a man throws acid into his neighbour's property or fires a shotgun over the fence? In such cases the neighbour is entirely innocent and should not suffer a loss. It is entirely obvious in such cases that the neighbour may well suffer damage and the miscreant takes the risk, not the neighbour. People who live cheek by jowl with each other in cramped suburbia must pay due regard to those who live next to them.

p   Accordingly, I award damages of £350 to the claimant.
   Solicitors: *Cherry, Lime, Walnut and Co.*, Allwhiting (for the claimant); *Roots and Roots*, Allwhiting (for the defendant)

Rafael Valentine-Collins *Barrister*

Having read *Berry v Branch* you now have an idea of how a law report looks and the various elements from which it is made up. Rough-Justice J is obviously a very interesting judge, with very particular attitudes. He clearly has very particular views about the facts of the case also. Before you look at the questions below look back at the judgment. Underline the key points that Rough-Justice J makes.

The answers to the questions are printed on the following pages, but before you look at the answers see if you can answer the questions without their guidance.

Questions on the judgment in *Berry v Branch*

1.   When looking at the judgment of Rough-Justice J what legal propositions can you identify?
2.   Legal principles can be both narrow (meaning that they will only apply in very few and specific factual circumstances) and broad (meaning that the principle could be used in lots of different factual circumstances). Try to place the legal principles that you have found in the case for question 1 in order, with the narrowest principle first moving to the broadest principle last.
3.   Decide on which of these principles Rough-Justice J actually based his decision – (i.e. using the proper legal terminology, decide what you think is the '*ratio decidendi*' of the case).
4.   Looking back at the principles of law you have found, consider whether there are any *obiter dicta* statements in the judgment. (In other words does Rough-Justice J make any comments on what he thinks the law would have been if the facts had been different? Look for any statements that have no bearing on the outcome of the case itself but could be useful to judges in later cases.)

Continued on next page

Answers to Exercise 1

You will have noticed that Rough-Justice J spends a good deal of his judgment setting out and commenting on the facts of the case. So it is only really in the last few paragraphs of his judgment that he discusses what he thinks are the legal issues.

1. In respect of question 1 you might have been able to discover the following 'legal princi-ples' set out in Rough-Justice J's judgment:

    *   '... if someone embarks on any activity which is dangerous, then they should take the consequences.' (He states this in lines 1 and 2 of n.)
    *   '... if someone plants a poisonous tree, they must be liable for the damage it does and this is true whether the damage occurs on the planter's property or off it.' (He states this in lines 2, 3 and 4 of n.)
    *   In cases where acid is thrown into a neighbour's property or a shotgun is fired over a neighbour's fence, the neighbour, being innocent, should not suffer a loss; 'the miscreant takes the risk.' (This is a paraphrase of the statement that he makes in lines 1–4 of o.)
    *   'People who live cheek by jowl with each other in cramped suburbia must pay due regard to those who live next to them.' (Finally he states this in lines 4–5 of o.)

2. The next question demanded that you should be able to set these in a particular order, so you needed to be thinking about the potential application of the principles to other factual situations. Rearranged in order, with the narrowest application first and the broadest last you should have arranged them as follows.

    *   '... if someone plants a poisonous tree, they must be liable for the damage it does and this is true whether the damage occurs on the planter's property or off it.' (*This is quite a narrow principle. It applies only to poisonous trees causing damage. It could of course be even narrower for example if it only applied to a particular type of tree or it could apply to damage done on only one property rather than both planter and neighbour.*)
    *   In cases where acid is thrown into a neighbour's property or a shotgun is fired over a neighbour's fence, the neighbour, being innocent, should not suffer a loss; and if he does, 'the miscreant takes the risk.' (*This principle is still quite narrow but unlike the one above it applies to two things, 'acid thrown into a neighbour's property' and 'a shotgun fired over a neighbour's fence'. So it is not as narrow as the first which only applies to one thing: 'poisonous trees that cause damage'.*)
    *   'People who live cheek by jowl with each other in cramped suburbia must pay due regard to those who live next to them.' (*This of course is quite a broad principle as it applies in a general sense to neighbours living in suburbia who it is clear from Rough-Justice J's statement owe a duty to each other.*)
    *   '... if someone embarks on any activity which is dangerous, then they should take the consequences.' (*This, however, is clearly the broadest judgment of all with the widest application to different factual circumstances since it imposes liability on anyone who is responsible for a dangerous activity and presumably for any kind of damage caused by that activity.*)

3. You may well have found it difficult to highlight which of the principles set out above is the actual *ratio* of the case. You should not worry about this. It is a quite common difficulty when reading judgments. This is why the barrister writing the report identifies what he or she thinks the *ratio* is in the section headed Held in section c of the judgment, and this is checked with the judge. Nevertheless, on reading the judgment it is easy to say that Rough-Justice J did not actually indicate any preference for one legal principle over another or say precisely on what basis he decided the case. Clearly the facts of the case would also support any of the principles that have been laid out, except of course for the one that refers to acid and shotguns. We are able, therefore, to eliminate this principle and decide definitely that this is not the *ratio*. However, it would be for a future judge referring to the case to determine which of the remaining principles would be the *ratio*. If the facts of the future case were to match exactly this one then it is likely that the narrowest of the principles would be applied. The more the facts in the future case

Continued on next page

Continued

differed from *Berry v Branch*, then the wider of the principles coming from the case is likely to be applied by the future judge.

4. You may by now have worked this one out and it is really quite easy. *Obiter dicta* are statements of legal principle that concern circumstances that cannot be found in the case itself. In this case it is the statement about acid and shotguns in lines 1–4 of o.

   It is also true to say that, if you have a fairly clear idea what the *ratio* is, then the other statements of principle must be *obiter*. In other words any statements of legal principle made by the judge which prove not to be decisive in the case will be *obiter*: i.e. if the case was decided on the narrowest principle (planting of poisonous trees), then the wider principles (responsibility for their dangerous acts) will be *obiter*. It is of course also possible for there to be more than one *ratio* in a case.

Whatever we take as being the *ratio* of the case, it is clear that *Berry v Branch* has developed original law, since we stated at the beginning that none of the issues involved had been discussed before. Once a decision was reached in *Berry v Branch* the next question inevitably would be for later judges to decide whether a new form of liability had entered into the law. If it had, it would be for judges in later cases to decide how wide ranging this liability was in respect of injuries to other persons or property.

Let us now imagine that the legal significance of the case was tested in a later case in the same year and in the same court, the case of *Bunny v Browning* [2002] 4 HWR 62 which again was heard in the Queen's Bench Division of the High Court. Once again you should read the report, remembering what you have discovered from the judgment in *Berry v Branch*, and now, applying the law from that case, answer the questions that follow. This time the answers are at the back of the book in the Appendix and you should try to answer the questions without referring to the answers, but of course check that you are right after you have completed Exercise 2.

ACTIVITY

Exercise 2: Fictitious case example

The judgment in *Bunny v Browning*
***Hodder Weekly Reports* [2002] 4 HWR 62**
Bunny v Browning

QUEEN'S BENCH DIVISION

Jittery J

1 October. 1 November 2002

a *Civil liability – rabbit loose in garden – neighbour shoots air rifle pellet at target on fence – pellet penetrates target and goes through knothole hitting rabbit – rabbit dies – whether neighbour firing air rifle liable.*

b The defendant fired an air rifle from his back garden at a target on a fence. The pellet passed through the target and through a knothole in the fence into the claimant's garden killing the claimant's pet rabbit.

c **Held** – civil liability attaches to any damage done by anything which a person throws off his property or allows to escape from his property.

Cases referred to in judgment

Berry v Branch [2002] 2 HWR 1142

Action

d The claimant, Hermione Bunny, brought an action against the defendant, Bradley Browning, for agreed damages of £100 for the death of the claimant's rabbit, Floppy, which was agreed to have been caused by the rabbit having been shot by the defendant while it was in the claimant's garden. The facts are set out in the judgment.

Continued on next page

Continued

Julian Bobtail for the claimant

Daphne Trigger for the defendant

1 November. The following judgment was delivered.   *Cur adv vult*

e **JITTERY J** The death of a loved one is at times distressing for the bereaved, even if that loved one is a mere pet – in this case a rabbit named Floppy. Floppy had indeed occupied a highly esteemed place in the Bunny household for more than four years since he was first purchased. He was in fact a constant companion of Mrs Hermione Bunny. It was Mrs Bunny's habit to turn Floppy out into her back garden for several hours each day so that he might graze in the grass there. While the rabbit was thus occupied one day in October of 2001, the 22nd to be precise, his life was brought to a sudden and most untimely end when young Bradley Browning, who lived in the next house along the terrace, at No 87, shot him with an air rifle.

f Mr and Mrs Browning and their two children had moved into No 87 only one month previously. Bradley was given the air rifle as a present on his 18th birthday, which was on that very day, 22nd October 2001. His immediate reaction on receiving the gift was to rush outside to try it out. He pinned a paper target on the fence which separated the gardens of the two houses and fired the gun at the target. Even without practice Bradley was a good shot. The pellet penetrated the target, and then, remarkably enough, it passed straight through a knothole in the fence behind the target and it struck poor Floppy a fatal blow.

g Mr Bobtail, who is acting as counsel for Mrs Bunny, has said that the claimant freely accepts Bradley Browning's assertion that he had no intention at all of causing harm to the poor deceased animal – and I am bound to agree on a study of the facts presented to this court that this is indeed the case. But, says Mr Bobtail, a mere absence of intention does not negate young Mr Browning's liability to compensate Mrs Bunny for her loss. He has urged upon me the views of the eminent jurist Rough-Justice J as he expounded them in the recent case *Berry v Branch*: '… if someone embarks on any activity which is dangerous, then they should take the consequences,' and also 'People who live cheek by jowl with each other in cramped suburbia must pay due regard to those who live next to them.' Mr Bobtail points out that firing a gun over the fence into a neighbour's garden is one of the situations which Rough-Justice J actually instanced as creating such a liability.

h Miss Trigger, counsel for the defendant, argues that *Berry v Branch* should be distinguished on the ground that the essential facts of the current case are too dissimilar from those in *Berry v Branch*. She argues that there is no inherent, natural hazard here as there was in the earlier case. Floppy's demise, though unfortunate, could never have been foreseen, she says; while in the case of the much loved pooch whose death brought about the action in *Berry v Branch*, his tragic end may have been unlikely, but given the proximity of the deadly yew tree to his owner's garden, and the natural proclivity of dogs to consume vegetation as a remedy for stomach-ache, it could be foreseen that eventually the dog might be poisoned. Nor, says Miss Trigger, can Mr Justice Rough-Justice's remarks regarding the mutual duty of care owed to each other by neighbours living in 'cramped suburbia' be regarded as binding me to decide this case in favour of the claimant. Given the spaciousness of the properties on Westiddling Avenue, Rough-Justice J's remarks concerning the duty of neighbours living in cramped suburbia must be considered to be no more than *obiter dicta*. In connection with the distinguished judge's comments regarding a general liability to others of those who undertake dangerous activities, Miss Trigger argues that if such views were regarded to be the law of the land it would result in a revolutionary extension of legal responsibility. Miss Trigger asserts and I find myself bound to agree, that such a principle is not a part of the law. The day may come when it may be found to be, but, in my opinion, that time has not yet arrived.

i Despite the fervour with which Miss Trigger has pressed me to treat this case as being without precedent, I feel that the decision in *Berry v Branch* leaves me little choice but to honour convention and to find in favour of the claimant. I do so willingly for I find Rough-Justice J's statement regarding the duties owed each other by city-dwellers to be

Continued on next page

Continued

highly persuasive. Life in Westiddling Avenue may be a wholly more spacious affair than that enjoyed by Mrs Bunny and the Browning family, but compared to country living they are both cut from the same cloth.

j   Therefore, I award damages in the amount of £100 to Mrs Bunny.

Solicitors: *Hare, Brer and Co.*, Bighampton (for the claimant); *Load and Lock*, Bighampton (for the defendant)

Rafael Valentine-Collins *Barrister*

Questions on the judgment in *Bunny v Browning*

1. Jittery J in his judgment indicates that he is bound by the decision of Rough-Justice J in *Berry v Branch*. Consider what you think Jittery J believes to be the *ratio decidendi* of *Berry v Branch*. (Remember that it is only the *ratio decidendi* of a previous decision which can bind a judge in a later case.)
2. Consider whether in his judgment Jittery J has in fact widened the application of the principle from *Berry v Branch*.
3. Identify the *ratio decidendi* of *Bunny v Browning*.
4. Assuming that *Berry v Branch* is sufficiently analogous to *Bunny v Browning* to serve as a precedent in the case, consider whether it is a persuasive precedent or a binding precedent.

Answers can be found in the Appendix on pages 255 – 256.

Now let us imagine that these basic principles in the law continue to develop. So on the same day that *Bunny v Browning* is decided let us suppose that there is a contemporaneous case being heard by another judge in the QBD where again the judgment in *Berry v Branch* is being referred to and considered.

Below is the judgment of the case, *Dove v Digger*, heard by Careless J. This time you are not given any of the introductory matter in the law report but only the appropriate extract from the judgment of Careless J. Again, read the judgment, note the judge's comments on *Berry v Branch* and consider the questions that follow the extract. The answers to the questions are also in the Appendix at the end of the book.

ACTIVITY

Exercise 3: Fictitious case example

The judgment in *Dove v Digger*
Hodder Weekly Reports [2002] 4 HWR 131
Dove v Digger

QUEEN'S BENCH DIVISION

Careless J

1 April. 1 May 2002

CARELESS J The facts of this case are eminently straightforward. The defendant, Lancelot Dove, a retired gentleman, wished to take up a sporting activity to pass his time in fruitful and engaging activity. He therefore installed a device in his garden at 53 Booze Street, Woolhampton. Such a device is known as a trap. A device of such type operates by a powerful spring which throws pieces of clay, somewhat approximating the size of a dinner plate, into the air. The sportsman then tries to shoot down these 'clay pigeons' with a shotgun. This is a noble and excellent sport and is widely practised by many people, including, it is worth noting, the very highest in the land. Mr Dove's property includes a small garden, typical of those found in 19th Century terraces. He set up his trap in the garden and shot at the clays from his back bedroom window, from where he had a better field of view and of fire. On the first occasion when he tried this activity, Mr Dove, with some misfortune, missed the clay. The clay soared over the immediately neighbouring properties eventually falling through the glass of a greenhouse located in the garden of 73 Booze Street, the home of Mr Albert Digger. Unfortunately, when the shattered glass fell into the greenhouse it decapitated Mr Digger's best carnation.

Continued on next page

Continued

This misfortune deprived him, not only of an almost certain first prize at the International Carnation Show, which was to be held in Woolhampton the next day (Mr Digger had won first prize for his carnations for the past seventeen years), but also cost him the kudos and indeed the financial rewards which would have flowed from victory at the show.

Mr Digger applied to Mr Dove for compensation for the loss he had sustained. Mr Dove rejected Mr Digger's claim, asserting that it was everyone's patriotic duty to learn to shoot accurately. Mr Digger dismissed this statement as no more than 'sentimental tosh' and commenced this action.

Surprisingly, in argument, counsel for *both* the claimant and defendant have relied heavily on the decision in *Berry v Branch* to make their case.

Although there is but a fine difference between the persuasiveness of these two able and astute counsel, I find Mr Whiskey's argument on behalf of the defendant the more compelling. This claim is dismissed.

Questions on the judgment in *Dove v Digger*

1. Consider what you think could be said in favour of using *Berry v Branch* as precedent to be followed in this case.
2. Consider the reasons that might be used in the case to distinguish it from *Berry v Branch*.

Answers can be found in the Appendix on pages 256–257.

Unfortunately we are now left in a situation where the decisions of the last two cases, *Bunny v Browning* and *Dove v Digger* are conflicting. We also have little real idea from his judgment what was the real reasoning behind Careless J's decision. This inevitably would lead to a situation of confusion for lawyers as to when compensation could or could not be claimed in such situations. Let us imagine that in the following year a case is heard in the Court of Appeal in which the judges try to clarify the rules. This is identified in the judgment of Highman LJ who delivered the leading opinion in a unanimous decision of the court.

Once again, remembering what you have learnt so far from the judgments in the three High Court cases and looking carefully at the judgment of Highman LJ, try to answer the questions that follow applying the principles of precedent. The answers are again in the Appendix on page 257.

ACTIVITY

Exercise 4: Fictitious case example

The judgment in *Blaster v Burns*
***Hodder Weekly Reports* [2003] 1 HWR 1 CA**
Blaster v Burns

COURT OF APPEAL

Highman LJ

Lofty LJ

Haughty LJ

1 May 2003

HIGHMAN LJ The respondent in this case, Mr Burns, is claiming compensation from the appellant, Mr Blaster, in regard to damage which was caused to his home when a shed in the appellant's garden exploded, showering flaming timbers onto the roof of the respondent's home causing it to catch fire and burn to the ground. The cause of the explosion and fire in Mr Blaster's shed was an experiment which went wrong. Mr Blaster had become obsessed with the need to develop more efficient batteries during the years that he had spent as a milk roundsman with a local dairy. On numerous occasions the batteries used to propel his milk float had become exhausted before he had actually completed his milk round as a result of which he had been forced to wait for a tow or had been required to push the heavy vehicle back to the depot. When he retired from his employment at the beginning of 2001 he decided that he would attempt to develop a much more efficient battery. This was indeed a

Continued on next page

most laudable and admirable ambition. Nevertheless, it was also, if anything, slightly unrealistic given that Mr Blaster had neither academic knowledge nor a practical understanding of basic chemistry. It was in any event in the single minded pursuit of his goal that Mr Blaster created the chemical mixture that was to prove so destructive. Mr Blaster indeed was fortunate to escape with his life following the explosion. Mr Burns was somewhat less fortunate in that he lost his home and his possessions in the ensuing fire.

In finding for the respondent the trial judge in this case, Jittery J, relied on the principle laid down in the landmark case, *Berry v Branch*, a precedent which he had in fact used once before in deciding *Bunny v Browning*, where he said:

> 'Despite the fervour with which Miss Trigger has pressed me to treat this case as being without precedent, I feel that the decision in *Berry v Branch* leaves me little choice but to honour convention and to find in favour of the claimant. I do so willingly for I find Rough-Justice J's statement regarding the duties owed each other by city-dwellers to be highly persuasive.'

Counsel for Mr Blaster, Mr Spark, has argued that this interpretation amounts to a misreading of the *ratio decidendi* of *Berry v Branch*. He has urged upon us the view taken in *Dove v Digger*: a view which confines the relevance of *Berry v Branch* to its own facts. *Berry v Branch* involved the death of a pet which ate poisonous leaves. This case involves the destruction of a house following upon the explosion of a neighbouring shed. Mr Spark has emphasised that in the former case there is no redeeming social objective which might have justified the undertaking of the dangerous activity of rearing a yew tree in a suburban neighbourhood. The owner was seeking no more than decoration for his garden. Mr Blaster, on the other hand, was in pursuit of a scientific breakthrough which would have been of inestimable benefit to society and the environment. Surely, says Mr Spark, this disparity in objectives is enough on its own to rule out any consideration of *Berry v Branch* in this case.

Counsel for the respondent, Mr Ash QC, has pointed out in his usual cogent fashion that even though the cause of the damage in this case was different from that in *Berry v Branch*, it is clear that such an undertaking, involving the mixture of highly unstable and volatile chemicals, was inherently dangerous, even if Mr Blaster's knowledge of chemistry was insufficient for him to know this. And as Rough-Justice J stated in *Berry v Branch*: 'if someone embarks on any activity which is dangerous, then they should take the consequences.' Therefore, says counsel for the respondent, Mr Blaster must bear the burden of making good any loss suffered by his neighbour as a result of these experiments. Especially so when one considers that such experiments were, wholly foolishly, being conducted in the back garden of a house located in the middle of a congested inner city council estate. This hardly shows what Rough-Justice J called 'the due regard' neighbours must give each other in such living conditions. But even if they had been carried out in open country, Mr Ash insists, and I must say that I agree with him, Mr Blaster would have been liable for the damage they caused.
I believe this appeal should be dismissed.

Questions on the judgment in *Blaster v Burns*

1. Identify the *ratio decidendi* of the Court of Appeal in *Blaster v Burns*.
2. On the basis of Highman LJ's judgment what do you consider the *ratio* in *Berry v Branch* now to be?
3. Identify anything in Highman LJ's judgment that you consider to be *obiter dicta*.
4. Assuming that the essential facts of the cases are sufficiently similar, consider whether Highman LJ is in fact bound to follow the decision in *Berry v Branch*.

The issue was in effect settled when the case was appealed to the House of Lords (now the Supreme Court). Their Lordships, in a unanimous opinion given in a brief judgment, declined to explore in any greater depth the leading speech of Highman LJ but upheld the ruling of the Court of Appeal in the case.

The final stage in our fictitious series of cases can now be seen in one final case heard the following year, again in the High Court. This decision, *Fly v Porker*, is outlined below.

Continued on next page

Continued

Once again use your understanding of the cases so far, remembering that *Blaster v Burns* is a Court of Appeal decision and answer the questions that follow.
Again the answers are given in the Appendix on page 258.

ACTIVITY

Exercise 5: Fictitious case example

The judgment in *Fly v Porker*
Hodder Weekly Reports [2004] 1 HWR 77
Fly v Porker

HIGH COURT

CLEARLY J

1 April 1 May 2004

CLEARLY J This action for damages arises as a result of the most unfortunate destruction of one of the finest stretches of river for trout fishing in the countryside surrounding Bighampton. Mr Porker is a pig farmer and the effluent from his pig houses he stores in a large tank that is situated at the top of a hill near to the boundary between his own land and that of Mr Fly. As the result of a most unhappy sequence of events, and indeed without fault on the part of Mr Porker, the effluent container was breached with the result that 200,000 gallons of the effluent flowed down the hill and onto Mr Fly's land, eventually finding its way into the river which traversed his estate. The effect of the effluent on the trout in the stream was to say the least catastrophic. Virtually every one was killed and the stream itself was rendered quite worthless as an attraction for anglers, who up to the time of the unfortunate event had been prepared to pay hundreds of pounds for a day's fishing. Mr Fly now seeks compensation for the loss of his valuable enterprise.

The question which I am now called on to answer is whether or not there is any precedent that might guide me in reaching an appropriate decision. Counsel for the claimant, Miss Gill, in an eloquent and convincing speech, has asserted that I am bound by the recent decision of the Court of Appeal in *Blaster v Burns* to decide in favour of her client, the claimant. She has drawn my attention to certain words in the judgment of Highman LJ in that case:

> 'even though the cause of the damage in this case was different from that in *Berry v Branch*, it is clear that such an undertaking, involving the mixture of highly unstable and volatile chemicals, was inherently dangerous, even if Mr Blaster's knowledge of chemistry was insufficient for him to know this. And as Rough-Justice J stated in *Berry v Branch*: "if someone embarks on any activity which is dangerous, then they should take the consequences".'

Highman LJ then went on to say that this was especially so when one considers that Mr Blaster's experiments were, wholly foolishly, being conducted in the back garden of a house located in the middle of a congested inner city council estate. And he then agreed with the claimant's counsel that even if the experiments had been carried out in open country, Mr Blaster would have been liable for the damage they caused.

According to Miss Gill, this statement leaves me no choice but to find in favour of her client, especially as the Court of Appeal's decision in *Blaster v Burns* has been affirmed unanimously by the Judicial Committee of the House of Lords.

Mr Trotter, Mr Porker's eminent advocate, argues that *Blaster v Burns* provides no authority for a decision favouring the claimant. *Blaster v Burns* was a case concerning neighbours living in the close confines of a large city. In such situations it seems only sensible to impose a strict duty of care not to cause damage to your neighbours. And that is exactly what Highman LJ did. But, Mr Trotter says, since the facts of *Blaster v Burns* were wholly to do with life in the city I must treat Highman LJ's statement quoted above as an *obiter dictum*. He says I am not bound to follow. Nor should I be persuaded by the Lord Justice's *dictum* to open up such a huge new potential area of litigation as would arise if the law were considered to give people in any circumstances of living the right to hold their neighbours liable for any injury they suffer as a result of the neighbours' inattention or carelessness.

Continued on next page

Continued

Now what is the balance that should be struck between these two arguments? An academic might be prepared to contend that the opinion expressed by Highman LJ as to the liability of Mr Blaster had this incident taken place in the country amounts to no more than *obiter dictum*. After all, it is true that nothing in *Blaster v Burns* had to do with activities outside the cramped circumstances of urban life. But I believe that to regard Highman LJ's opinion as having no more than persuasive authority is not only unrealistic, given the unanimous support of the Judicial Committee of the House of Lords (now the Supreme Court) for the Court of Appeal's judgment in *Blaster v Burns*, but that it would also amount to discourtesy to a judge of a court of authority superior to this one. And I am not prepared to be discourteous to a jurist of the eminence and sagacity of Highman LJ.

Therefore I am willing to take it that it is now good law that if a person undertakes a dangerous activity, whether in the context of urban confines or in the countryside, he or she must bear responsibility for the consequences. But that is not to say that I also find for the claimant in this case. For what is required is a 'dangerous activity' and I do not believe that the storing of pig effluent is dangerous. It is not the same thing at all as, for example, the storage of explosives or volatile substances. Pig muck may be offensive but there is no necessary equivalence between offensiveness and danger. Danger requires that some inherent risk of injury to persons or to their property is present. Risk which arises merely out of an unfortunate combination of circumstances will not suffice.

Therefore I would reject this claim and find for the defendant.

Questions on the judgment in *Fly v Porker*

1. Identify the *ratio decidendi* of the case.
2. Is the law on responsibility of neighbours now settled and in what way could it be developed or changed?
3. Consider whether any of Clearly J's comments in the case amount to *obiter dicta*.
4. Consider in what way the case is a development from the decision in *Berry v Branch*.

Answers can be found in the Appendix on page 258.

If you managed to answer most of the questions in the above exercise successfully than you should now have a pretty good understanding of the way in which the law develops through precedent. This will be useful to you not only in your English legal system course but in all areas of substantive law also.

6.3 The interpretation of statutes

6.3.1 The purpose of statutory interpretation

As we have already identified at the start of this chapter in any case before a judge he or she will be called on to reach a decision by applying the existing law to the facts of the case. This as we have said is because judges are prevented from making up the law as they go along. Parliament is the supreme law maker and statute law takes precedence over case law. The so-called 'declaratory theory of law' assumes that judges discover the law in a given factual situation from existing law.

Judges then, as we have seen, play an important role in developing and applying the law through the doctrine of precedent. They also though have a major role in relation to statute law. This is because, whereas the common law is based on individual principles arising from specific factual circumstances, statute law is essentially theoretical. Parliament states what the law is, but not necessarily how to apply it in factual circumstances. Even where statutes state the law in fairly explicit terms the law still needs to be understood before it can be applied. Since drafters of Acts are likely to engage in some fairly technical legal language the whole process of interpretation comes into play where the law in a particular case comes from statute.

Lawyers will inevitably, in representing their clients, question the actual meanings of words. Judges in these circumstances are bound to decide what is meant in the Act and to give effect to what Parliament was trying to do in passing the Act. This is the process known as statutory interpretation.

You may think that the meanings of words should be straightforward and not need questioning. Sometimes this is the case. For instance if you were studying Occupiers' Liability in Tort this is a statutory area of negligence represented in the Occupiers' Liability Act 1957 (which covers problems suffered by lawful visitors caused by the state of the occupiers' premises) and the Occupiers' Liability Act 1984 (which does exactly the same but for visitors who are not classed as lawful – most importantly for trespassers). You would be surprised to find few cases on the tort other than those that existed before the Acts when the law was still part of the common law of negligence. There are probably two main reasons for this:

■ The 1957 Act in particular is usually accepted as being a very straightforward and well-drafted Act.
■ The principles involved are already well established in the law of negligence and are generally well understood.

However, you will soon find out when you study criminal law that statutory interpretation can be very important and that the meanings of words are not necessarily at all straightforward when it comes to law. If you want a good example of this you will find it when you study the concepts of 'dishonesty' and 'appropriation' in the Theft Act 1968. If you want an even better example you will find it in the wording of the various non-fatal offences under the Offences Against the Person Act 1861.

Generally then you will find that there is no particular need for statutory interpretation unless the words in an Act or other instrument are in dispute. There are, however, many reasons why lawyers might dispute the meaning of words or why judges feel that they need to interpret statutory interpretation. Figure 6.2 below is a table of just some of them.

Problem	Example
Bad drafting It may be as simple as the parliamentary draftsmen getting the provisions in the Act wrong in some way	A classic example of this that you are likely to learn about fairly early in your law course either in English legal system or in contract law is the case of *Fisher v Bell* [1961] 1 QB 394 where the draftsman used a word usually given another meaning in law. As a result Parliament had to pass another Act.
Ambiguous words The word may have more than one meaning	In *R v Allen* [1965] 2 QB 295 applying the meaning 'being validly married' to the words 'shall marry' would have made the offence of bigamy unworkable. 'Going through a marriage ceremony' was preferred.
Technical meanings and particular legal meanings Some words have specific technical meanings	*Royal College of Nursing v DHSS* [1982] AC 800 is a good example of this: the words 'registered medical practitioner' can only really be applied to a doctor. This was the difficulty identified by the Court of Appeal.
Social or technological developments Many things change over time and were not envisaged at the time of the legislation	*Royal College of Nursing v DHSS* [1982] AC 800 is also a good example of this. This involved interpreting the words 'registered medical practitioner' under the Abortion Act 1967. By the time of the case it was nurses rather than doctors who were carrying out the procedures.
Terms phrased too broadly	An example of this is *Brock v DPP, The Times*, 23 July 1993 where the words 'type of dog' were used and the problem was whether this referred only to breed or had a wider meaning.

Figure 6.2 Some reasons for statutory interpretation

6.3.2 A brief overview of the rules of statutory interpretation

There are two approaches

- **The literal approach** – where interpretation relies mainly on the words themselves in isolation.
- **The purposive approach** – has its origins in the mischief rule but is also the approach taken within the EU. This approach is concerned with discovering and giving effect to the purpose for which the legislation was enacted regardless of what the technical meaning of the words may be.

There are three rules (which fit into different approaches above)

The literal rule

Judges using this rule give the words in dispute their 'plain, ordinary literal meaning', 'even though they lead to a manifest absurdity' (Lord Esher in *R v City of London Court* (1892)).

The golden rule

This is a subsidiary of the literal rule.

In its narrow sense it is only used where using the literal rule might lead to an absurd result. In *Adler v George* [1964] 2 QB 7 it was an offence to be 'in the vicinity' of a prohibited place. The defendant was actually found in the prohibited place and the words 'in the vicinity of' were held to include 'in' otherwise the prosecution under the Official Secrets Act would have failed.

In its broad sense it is used to give a different meaning where the plain meaning would be unacceptable for policy reasons. So in *Re Sigsworth* [1935] Ch 89 the word 'issue' was held not to include a person who had killed his parent to prevent a son inheriting from the mother he had murdered.

The mischief rule (purposive approach in modern usage)

This originally derives from *Heydon's case* (1584) 3 Co Rep 7a which identified a four point procedure:

1. examine the common law prior to the Act
2. locate the mischief or defect in the common law
3. identify the remedy Parliament proposed to eliminate the mischief
4. give effect to that remedy.

So in *Corkery v Carpenter* [1951] 1 KB 102 the offence was for being drunk in charge of a 'carriage' but the court held that this included a bicycle because the mischief in the previous law was the absence of protection of road users from those who were drunk and therefore not in control of their actions.

The mischief rule is very similar to the modern purposive approach. The rule specifically examines what was wrong with the law before the Act was introduced, but both are looking for the reasons why Parliament introduced the legislation rather than focusing only on the individual words.

There are also three language rules

- *Noscitur a sociis* – meaning a word is known by the company it keeps. So in *Beswick v Beswick* [1968] AC 58 the words 'other property' were held to refer only to interests in land otherwise known as real property, because that was what the whole statute was about.
- *Expressio unius est exclusio alterius* – meaning that the express mention of one thing impliedly excludes other things not included. So in *Tempest v Kilner* [1846] 3 CB 249 a list in a section of an Act included 'goods wares and merchandise' and so the section was held not to apply to stocks and shares which were not included in the list.

▧ *Ejusdem generis* – meaning of the same type. The rule applies where general words follow lists of specific words. The general words must then correspond to the specific words to fall within the scope of the provision. So in *Powell v Kempton Park Racecourse* [1899] AC 143 the list included 'house, office, room or other place used for betting' so the provision could not apply to an outdoor betting area as all the named places in the list were indoor.

The court makes certain presumptions

Judges presume certain things unless the contrary is demonstrated to their satisfaction. Examples include:

▧ that the common law is not changed by the statute unless it says so
▧ that in Acts defining crimes *mens rea* (or criminal intent) is required to prove the crime unless the Act identifies it as a strict liability crime
▧ that the Crown will not be liable
▧ that the jurisdiction of the courts is not ousted.

There are certain other aids to interpretation: intrinsic (internal to the Act) and extrinsic (external to the Act)

Inside the Act

Long and short titles; margin notes; schedules; headings; preambles; interpretation sections.

Outside the Act

Commonly used aids include dictionaries, other similar statutes, and some academic works. More controversial aids are Royal Commission Reports, Law Commission Reports, *Travaux Preparatoires*, and most controversially *Hansard* (the reports on debate inside the Houses of Parliament) (but see now *Pepper v Hart* (1992) which has now validated the use of *Hansard* if certain conditions are met).

ACTIVITY

Self-test questions

In the right-hand column below in each row identify the rule of statutory interpretation or aid to interpretation indicated in the brief descriptions in the left-hand column.

When you have finished the answers are in the Appendix on page 258 for you to check against. Try to complete the answers without referring to the answers in the Appendix to see if you really do know the different rules and aids.

1.	A schedule at the end of an Act.	
2.	Examining the law prior to the Act, locating the defect in the previous law, identifying the remedy that Parliament proposed to use to eliminate the defect, and giving effect to that remedy.	
3.	Where in lists of words general words follow specific words (e.g. 'and other places') the general words should correspond to the meaning of the specific words (so if all of the places mentioned were indoors the provision could not apply to outdoor places).	
4.	The published report on the debates in Parliament during the passage of a Bill.	
5.	In the case of crimes *mens rea* (the necessary criminal intent) is always required to be proved unless the statute identifies the crime as one of strict liability.	
6.	If the words are ambiguous and applying the literal rule would lead to an absurd result then the alternative meaning of the word should be applied.	

6.3.3 Understanding how statutory interpretation works

You now have a reasonable idea of why judges engage in statutory interpretation and of the basic rules and various rules and other aids that they use. You will in any case learn about these in much more detail in your English legal system course.

It is of course all very well to learn about all of these rules so that you can then write about them and the cases in which they appear in coursework or exams. However, if you are able to understand how to apply them, as the judges have to, you have a much more practical understanding not only of the process itself but also of the sorts of problems that the process throws up.

Below are a couple of exercises where you can put into practice your understanding of the process of statutory interpretation and think about using the rules and aids in the way that judges would have to in a case.

ACTIVITY

Exercise

Trouble at football grounds is something that is regularly in the news, and there has been a big push recently to end racist abuse by football fans. Let us imagine then the following fictitious situation leading to a fictitious EU Directive and a fictitious Act of Parliament.

The European Commission has been put under pressure by MEPs from a number of different EU Member States to deal with unacceptable behaviour. This follows from disturbances at various football matches in European football grounds, in international matches, in European club competitions, and indeed more regularly at ordinary league matches. One thing that MEPs have complained about is abusive, partisan and hostile chants and singing by supporters.

As a result, the Commission has produced draft legislation, under both EU discrimination law and health and safety law, in the form of a Directive which was then passed by the Council following consultation with the European Parliament. The major provisions of this Directive, the Football (Prohibition of Provocative Verbalisation) Directive, are reproduced below. Member States are required to put in place the provisions within the Directive within the time specified. Also reproduced below are the major provisions from the UK's Act passed in response.

Read the extracts from the Directive and the Act, and apply the rules of statutory interpretation to the factual situations that follow. You are provided with the answers to the first two situations to give you an idea. You should then try to complete all of the others on your own. When you have finished, the answers are in the Appendix at the back of the book for you to check against. Try to complete the answers without referring to the answers in the Appendix to see if you really know how to apply the rules and aids.

Remember both pieces of legislation are entirely fictitious.

COUNCIL DIRECTIVE

Council Directive 2016/102 on the approximation of laws, regulations and administrative provisions of the Member States concerning the prohibition of racist and abusive verbal behaviour by football supporters in and in the immediate vicinity of football stadia.

The Council of the European Union, having regard to the Treaty establishing the European Union, having regard to the proposal from the Commission, in cooperation with the European Parliament, has adopted this Directive.

Preamble

Whereas the Council of Ministers considers racist, hostile and provocative verbal abuse by football supporters in and in the immediate vicinity of football grounds to be injurious to the general public, constituting, as it does, harassment of individual groups of people and having the potential for risk to health and safety through public disorder, that the practice of provocative verbalisation by racist, hostile or otherwise abusive singing, chanting or other provocative verbal behaviour by football supporters in and within a 2 kilometre radius of football grounds be prohibited in all Member States ...

Article 1

Scope

This Directive shall apply to all Member States

The date by which the Directive shall be implemented in all Member States is the 1st January 2018.

Continued on next page

Continued

The extract above contains the major provisions of the Directive for your purposes. The UK Parliament, conscious of the past reputation of UK football fans and keen to be seen to be taking a lead, acted quickly, not by introducing regulations through delegated legislation, as would normally be the case, but by passing an Act, the Football Anthems Act 2017. The major provisions of the Act are reproduced below.

THE FOOTBALL ANTHEMS ACT 2017

An Act to prohibit racist, hostile, abusive and provocative singing and chanting at football matches

s 1(1) It shall be an offence for any person to engage in racist, hostile, abusive or otherwise provocative singing or chanting in association with football matches, whether within a football ground or in a public place within reasonable proximity of a football ground.

   (2) A person committing an offence under this Act shall be liable upon conviction to a fine not exceeding five hundred pounds and a ban from attending football matches up to and including a lifetime ban.

s 2(1) In this Act 'public place' shall include any of the following to which the public has access:

    (a) any public thoroughfare within reasonable proximity of a football ground or on the route to a football ground;

    (b) any car park or coach park open to the public within reasonable proximity of a football ground or on the route to a football ground;

    (c) any building licensed for the purposes of eating food or for the consumption of alcoholic beverages within reasonable proximity of a football ground or on the route to a football ground or other similar place;

    (d) any clinic, surgery, hospital or other similar recognised health care facility within reasonable proximity of a football ground or on the route to a football ground where persons injured in connection with a football match may be treated.

s 2(2) In this Act 'thoroughfare' means any road, pavement, precinct or other similar place along, over or through which vehicles or pedestrians pass.

s 4 This Act shall not apply to private residential properties or business premises not open to the general public.

s 5 This Act shall come into effect on 1st August 2017.

You will see instantly that the UK Government has passed the Act within the time limit imposed by the EU. It is more questionable, if you think about it carefully, whether the UK Government has either fully or properly implemented the Directive. First, the Directive covers not only singing and chanting (as specified under the Act), but other forms of abusive verbal behaviour. Secondly, the Directive was limited to the football grounds themselves and the near vicinity, specifically within a 2 kilometre radius. The Act, on the other hand, refers to 'within reasonable proximity', a somewhat loose and ambiguous description. There is also no interpretation section to explain what 'within reasonable proximity' means.

Now that you have read through the extracts from the fictitious Directive and fictitious Act above, try to give answers to the situations below. Remember you are given the answers to the first two straight away so that you have a good idea of how to apply the rules.

All the scenarios that follow occur after the introduction of the Act in 2017.

Scenario 1

Alan, Barry and Chris have been convicted under the Act. They were stopped while walking on a footbridge over a main road about 100 metres from the Rovers stadium where Rovers were due to play Albion. While Albion fans were walking on the pavement underneath the footbridge, Alan, Barry and Chris were singing 'We hate Albion, say, we hate Albion'. Alan, Barry and Chris wish to know whether there is any issue of interpretation of the Act that might allow them to appeal successfully.

Answer to Scenario 1

This is a nice straightforward one to start you off and you should be able to easily answer that Alan, Barry and Chris will have no chance of winning an appeal.

- They are all singing and at the very least the song is provocative to Albion fans – which satisfies s 1(1).
- They are in a public place according to s 2(1)(a) and the definition of thoroughfare in s 2(2) as a footbridge is a similar place to a pavement and pedestrians would commonly use it.
- If the literal rule was applied, Alan, Barry and Chris would be guilty because they satisfy the plain, ordinary, literal meaning of 'public place' and of 'thoroughfare' – there is therefore no need to apply the golden rule.
- If the mischief rule was used, then they would still be guilty because the mischief that was remedied by the Act was the lack of any common law prohibiting provocative and abusive football chants and singing.
- If the purposive approach was used, then they would also be guilty because the whole purpose of the Act was to put in place the provisions of Directive 2016/102, the purpose of which was to prohibit racist, hostile and provocative verbal abuse in and in the vicinity of football grounds because of potential discrimination and health and safety risks through public order disturbances.
- You might also spot that there is an intrinsic aid that even a literalist judge might use here which is s 2(2), an interpretation section.

Scenario 2

Dai, a Welshman, has recently received two convictions under the Act. Both arose following Dai's attendance at an international match between England and Wales. The first conviction relates to Dai singing along when the Welsh national anthem was being played over loudspeakers before the start of the game. The second relates to an incident after the game. Dai was injured in a scuffle with England fans and sang abusive anti-English songs in the ambulance on his way to hospital. Dai is appealing on the basis that neither incident falls within the scope of the Act.

Answer to Scenario 2

This one is a bit more difficult. There are clearly two problem areas that Dai is focusing on. First whether or not singing along to the Welsh national anthem can be classed as 'racist, hostile, abusive or otherwise provocative singing or chanting' for the purposes of s 1(1):

- Dai is inside the ground when he sings the national anthem so both these aspects of s 1(1) are satisfied.
- It would be hard to describe the singing of a national anthem as either hostile or abusive, but the whole point of a national anthem is a demonstration of patriotism and a recognition of different nationality which could therefore be construed as provocative to other nationalities and possibly even racist, if a literal interpretation was used.
- So there is possible ambiguity in the words and the narrow approach of the golden rule might be applied, although it is less certain what the result of this would be.
- For policy reasons the broad approach of the golden rule, the mischief rule or the purposive approach might all be used to determine that this was not the sort of behaviour that the Act intended to prohibit.
- However, there is also an intrinsic aid which complicates things, the title of the Act, since the word 'anthem' is actually used in the title. Of course football anthems are not the same as national anthems so it can be argued that the two, in any case, should be interpreted differently.

Second, whether an ambulance can be classed as '*any clinic, surgery, hospital or other similar recognised health care facility … where persons injured in connection with a football match may be treated*' for the purposes of s 2(1)(d):

- Dai is singing anti-English songs so this aspect of s 1(1) is satisfied whichever rule is used.

Continued on next page

- An ambulance can possibly be classed as a 'health care facility' and obviously people injured in connection with a football match could receive some treatment in an ambulance on the way to hospital, so it is an interpretation of s 2(1)(d) that is needed under any rule of statutory interpretation.
- However, looking at the wording, the specific examples given are all buildings and even using the general words 'other similar recognised health care facility', if *ejusdem generis* was applied, the place would need to be a building so that under the literal rule the conviction would fail.
- 'Facility' might be seen as ambiguous and it is possible that the narrow approach of the golden rule could be used, in the way that it was in *Adler v George,* to uphold the conviction and policy reasons, as in *Sigsworth,* under the broad application of the rule, may also be a factor to achieve the same result.
- Both the mischief rule and the purposive rule, of course, could be used to uphold the conviction since the mischief was the lack of any prior common law prohibiting provocative and abusive football chants and singing, and the clear purpose of the subsection is to prevent health care professionals being subjected to such abusive behaviour and to avoid further trouble.

Now that you feel quite familiar with the application of the different rules and aids, look at the scenarios that follow and see if you can do the same. The answers to these scenarios are in the Appendix on pages 258–261.

Scenario 3

Eric has been convicted under the Act. Eric lives in a house in the same street as the United football ground. On match days Eric regularly leans out of his open upstairs window and sings abusive songs to the away supporters. Eric is appealing.

Scenario 4

Freddie runs a portable fast food stand on a piece of waste land 5 kilometres from the Wanderers' football ground in the north of England. Coaches bringing away fans to the ground regularly pull up in a lay-by near to the wasteland for fans to buy refreshments. Freddie has been convicted after a fight occurred when Freddie told some fans from a London football club that he should not have to serve them because 'all cockneys are animals and you should get your food from the pet shop in town'. Freddie is appealing.

Scenario 5

Gregory, a Town fan, is appealing against his conviction for singing abusive songs about the number of foreign players in the City team. The song includes verses of racial and personal abuse to named members of the City team. He did this while he was on his way to a match at the City ground and was walking on the platform in an underground railway station which (at the surface) is only 200 metres away from the City ground.

Scenario 6

Henry and 17 members of his staff or members of their families have all been convicted under the Act. Henry manages a call centre, which is not open to the public and which is 100 metres from the Borough football ground. Many of the staff, including Henry, are Borough supporters and on match days Henry allows them to park in the company's car park. They were convicted following a recent match against Athletic when they chanted abusive anti-Athletic chants from the company car park at passing Athletic supporters. Henry believes that they should not have been convicted.

If you managed to apply the rules of statutory interpretation in the scenarios in the above exercise successfully then you should now have a pretty good understanding of the way in which judges interpret statutes and the problems they encounter. This will be useful to you not only in your English legal system course but in most areas of substantive law. Even in the law of torts, which is probably the area of law with the least statutory intervention, there are still some important Acts such as the Law Reform (Contributory Negligence) Act 1945 and the Occupiers' Liability Acts 1957 and 1984. Other areas such as criminal law are almost exclusively based on statute, so interpretation is very important.

SUMMARY

▤ Judicial law-making is from two main sources: precedent, from judgments of decided cases, and statutory interpretation.

▤ Precedent can be binding, from courts high enough in the hierarchy, or persuasive, from *obiter dicta*, dissenting judgments, and from courts such as the Privy Council.

▤ There is a fixed hierarchy of courts with Court of Justice of the EU at the top but only on issues concerning EU law; the Supreme Court is the highest domestic court followed by the Court of Appeal and the High Court.

▤ It is possible to avoid precedent by overruling, reversing and distinguishing, and the Supreme Court and the Court of Appeal have individual methods.

▤ The important part of a judgment providing precedent is the *ratio decidendi* – the principle of law that decides the case in the light of the material facts; other judicial pronouncements are *obiter dicta*, or by the way statements.

▤ Statutory interpretation will occur whenever the meaning of words in statutory materials are the subject of dispute.

▤ This can arise for numerous reasons including ambiguity, bad drafting, change of meaning over time etc.

▤ There are two main approaches: literal – taking the literal meaning of the precise words; and purposive – considering what Parliament intended.

▤ There are also three rules: literal, golden (which has a narrow and a broad approach) and the ancient mischief rule.

▤ Judges also have three language rules, can use intrinsic aids (from inside the Act) and extrinsic aids (from outside of the Act), and also make use of certain presumptions.

7

Completing Coursework Assignments 1 – Individual Skills

AIMS AND OBJECTIVES

After reading this chapter you should be able to:
- Identify what the essay title is asking you to do
- Create a structure for your answer
- Identify the key facts in a problem question
- Create a structure for your answer
- Apply the law to the facts of the problem to reach a conclusion
  - Understand how to prepare for an oral presentation
  - Use visual aids appropriately

7.1 Essays

7.1.1 What is an essay question?

An essay question is usually a short statement of law, sometimes contained in a quote, which asks you to answer by way of composition in continuous prose, the query or proposition within it. Essay style questions are designed to test the depth of your understanding, and your ability to analyse and evaluate the law.

7.1.2 Understanding the point of the question

The first thing to do when you receive your essay title is to read it. This may sound rather obvious, but many students file the title away to look at later – often much later – by which time, any opportunity to reflect on what is being asked of you is lost. Now, consider what the subject area of the question is. Start with the widest possible classification – i.e. English legal system or method, criminal law, the law of torts, etc.

Next, break the subject area into a specific topic – if you are in doubt, you may have to use your lecture/tutorial notes as a hint. For example, in English legal system or method (ELS/M), the topic might be juries; in the law of torts, it might be negligence; in the criminal law it might be murder.

To maximise marks, the next stage is vital; *identify the focus in the question within that topic* – so in ELS/M, it could be the right to elect trial by jury; in torts, the scope of the duty of care in the tort of negligence; in criminal law, the meaning of the word 'intent' in the definition of murder. Figure 7.1 indicates how this can be done:

Subject	English legal system or method	Law of torts	Criminal law
Topic	Juries	Negligence	Murder
Focus	Right to elect jury trial	Duty of care	Meaning of the word intent

Figure 7.1 Identify the focus of the question

tutor tip

It is important for you to go through this process so you focus your mind on what is being asked in the question. This will make your research more efficient and you will be able to make the best use of the limited time available to you. It should also mean that your answer is relevant to the title and there are no major omissions.

128

CHAPTER 7 ESSAYS

7.1.3 Instructing words and key words

Have you ever had a comment on a returned essay that says you have not answered the question? If so, it means you have either not followed the instructions (sometimes called the rubric) or you have not identified the key words in the title.

The *instructing words* are the directions that tell you how the marker would like you to tackle the topic. You could be asked to analyse, to compare and contrast, to criticise or to evaluate. If so, you need to do what has been asked of you. The task could involve more than one of the skills below:

Analysis	This consists of breaking the subject matter down into its constituent parts, examining them and providing a result or conclusion according to the question asked.
Contrasting and comparing	This is drawing out the similarities and differences between two things.
Criticise	In law essays, criticising does not mean to concentrate only on the negative aspects of the subject matter, but to provide an objective and balanced argument, examining the positive and negative points, and perhaps offering a solution or recommending a reform.
Evaluation	This is an objective assessment of the subject matter. When you evaluate, you make a judgment about a thing's value, including positive and negative points.

Figure 7.2 Examples of instructing words

A familiar instruction in an essay title would commence 'Critically evaluate …'. In this event, you would provide an objective assessment, structured clearly so the marker or examiner understands the progression of your argument, of the positive and negative points of the subject.

The most commonly used instructing word in law essays is 'discuss'. Many students, especially in the first year of their studies, find this a vague and misleading direction. They say 'Discuss *what*?' or 'Discuss *how*?' The answer to the first question is to discuss the key words – which are dealt with below. The second question is to remember that a discussion is a two-sided (it may be more) debate where one side holds one particular view and the other side(s) disagree(s). The debate is based on the presentation of arguments for and against each particular view. This is what you must present when you 'discuss' in an essay. The arguments used should be based on evidence (cases, statutes or authors; see below).

The *key words* tell you what specifically to tackle on that topic – they answer the question asked by the student 'Discuss *what*?'

For example, underline the key words in the following three sample essay titles. You should be able to do this even if you are not studying the topic areas used as examples:

ACTIVITY

Exercise

Discuss whether the right to elect trial by jury is a fundamental constitutional right or an argument put forward by guilty offenders who think they will be acquitted.

'The decision of the courts to find that a duty of care exists between the claimant and defendant is a matter of policy not legal principle.' Discuss.

'Oblique, or indirect, intent is not based on intention at all. It is based on foresight and foresight is recklessness, not intent.' Discuss.

What you should be able to discern from this activity is that an essay that is just a general (even if accurate) discussion of when a defendant can elect trial by jury will not attain as high marks as an essay that contains the same information, but from the differing points of view that jury trial is and is not a constitutional right. Similarly, a student who merely submits an accurate essay which explains the cases where the judges have and have not found a duty of care to exist will attain a lower mark than the student whose essay explains the same cases, but also includes an analysis of the policy reasons behind the decisions. A strong essay in the criminal law would use the leading cases on the topic of oblique (or indirect) intent and, for each case, would refer the reader back to the key words in the title and comment on whether the case was decided on the basis of intent or foresight alone. This technique is especially important where the title includes a quote. Good essays use the words of the quote in the essay as regularly as possible (do not be afraid of repetition of the key words – it helps the reader identify you are answering the question).

Subdivided questions

Some titles are broken into smaller components: for example (i), (ii) ... or (a), (b) ... The approach here is to answer each sub-question in turn *clearly identifying the two separate parts by a note in the margin*. Unless you are told to the contrary, it would be reasonable for vyou to assume each subdivision carries equal marks.

Even if not specifically subdivided, take a note of those titles which contain more than one issue. As you can see from the essay titles above, the criminal law essay requires a discussion of both recklessness and intent. The marker may not specifically allocate 50 per cent to each, but a discussion of both is obviously necessary.

Where there is an obvious subdivision by (i), (ii) etc. or where there is more than one element to the question, answer in the order asked.

For example, using the ELS/M title above:

- Discuss whether the right to elect trial by jury is – First discuss what the right to trial by jury is, when it arises etc.:
- a fundamental constitutional right – Now consider the validity of this view. What evidence is there in support of this contention?
- or an argument put forward by guilty offenders who think they will be acquitted – Then move on to the validity of this assertion. You will also need to provide a well-reasoned conclusion.

7.1.4 Creating a structure

As with all the best novels, so too with essays: they have a beginning, a middle and an end.

From your essay writing experience so far, you will know that starting the essay is difficult – so do not start writing until you have an idea of what you want to say. If you just cannot seem to get the opening words right, plan the rest of the essay in full, then decide what the start, middle and conclusion should be.

The introduction

Use the contact time with your tutors to ask what sort of basic information would be required, e.g. can you presume the reader will know and understand technical terms such as:

Topic	ELS/M	Tort	Criminal Law
	Indictable, summary and either way offence	Tort Negligence	*Actus reus* and *mens rea*

Figure 7.3 Technical terms

A suggested introduction for each of the essays above might therefore be:

Topic	ELS/M	Tort	Criminal law
	The only defendants in the criminal justice system who have the right to elect trial by jury are those charged with an either way offence where the magistrates have decided the case is suitable for summary trial. In these circumstances a defendant has the option to elect Crown Court trial.	The tests for the existence of a duty of care in the tort of negligence vary according to whether the harm suffered is personal injury or property damage (*Caparo v Dickman* [1990] 2 AC 605); psychiatric harm (*Page v Smith* [1996] AC 155), *Alcock v CC of South Yorkshire* [1992] 1 AC 310) or pure economic loss (*Hedley Byrne v Heller* [1964] AC 465, *Murphy v Brentwood* [1991] 1 AC 398).	Numerous offences are defined so as to require proof of 'intention' to cause specified results. It might be expected that the meaning of such a fundamental term would have been settled long ago but this is not so.[1] [1]Ormerod, Smith and Hogan, *Criminal Law*, 11th edn, OUP, 2005, p 93.

Figure 7.4 Possible ways to start your essay

Never start an essay with the phrase 'In this essay I am going to ...' The marker knows what you need to do – it is in the title; so do not talk about doing it; just do it! The earlier you can start explaining the law, the more marks you will attract and the more focused the answer will be. You may wish to start with a definition of the key terms in the title, but in the following title:

'The decision of the courts to find a duty of care exists between the claimant and defendant is a matter of policy not legal principle.' Discuss.

Do not discuss the meaning of the terms defendant and claimant, but you may wish to explain your understanding of the terms legal principle and policy. Had the assessor wished to know such basic points, he would have asked for them; and the question is clearly focused on the principle/policy point in establishing a duty; not on the meanings of the terms defendant and claimant.

The main debate

The middle of the essay is the bulk of the answer and, on the whole, is where the marks will be awarded. At the planning stage, make sure the middle of your essay progresses logically through the statute or case law explaining the issues that arise in the question. Structure your answer so that each sentence is short and clear. As a rule of thumb, deal with only one issue per paragraph, but do deal with all of that issue within that paragraph – do not make the reader look around for the rest of the point.

In an essay, rather than a problem-style question, an analysis of the development of case law is often required (and it certainly is for the torts and criminal law examples used above); so be logical and deal with the cases in chronological order. Use the word count carefully; you are taking a law degree (of one form or another), so make sure your analysis is of the law, not the facts of the case. There is no hard and fast rule about reciting case facts in law essays but, generally, do not spend too long merely explaining facts. It is often a waste of valuable words to do so and if it does not further your argument; leave it out. Case facts may be helpful, particularly if you wish to use the facts to make a specific point. For example, a paragraph in the torts essay above might be:

'In *Alcock v CC of South Yorkshire* [1992] 1 AC 310, there was held to be no duty of care to the friends and relations of those who died in the Hillsborough disaster who watched the event on television. While a live television transmission of a disaster could be regarded as equivalent to seeing the events in person, there are broadcasting regulations governing what may and may not be shown; and the suffering of recognisable individuals falls into the latter.'

This explanation shows the student knows the facts of the case and they have used the facts to make a point. However, a paragraph that merely explains the facts of the famous case of *Donoghue v Stevenson* [1932] AC 562 is almost certainly wasting words.

As for the end of the essay, see the advice on how to conclude in Section 7 below.

Below is an example of how to structure an essay question.

Discuss the extent to which the rules on involuntary manslaughter are in need of reform.

The subject area is involuntary manslaughter and the critical element focuses on whether the area is in need of reform. The best answers will have that focus throughout, so two tips are:

- Try to make critical comment in relation to each aspect of the legal content.
- Try to refer constantly back to the question reminding the marker that you know what the question is about.

Describe manslaughter:

- Covers all unlawful killings which lack the *mens rea* for murder
- There are three types: unlawful act, gross negligence, and possibly reckless

Comment:

- Covers a broad area from accidental death to murder – so very dependent on sentencing
- Consider also whether it is necessary or advisable to have three different types with different rules – so possibly a case for reform to a more cohesive model

---

Explain unlawful act manslaughter:

- There must be an unlawful act, an omission would not be sufficient for constructive manslaughter (*Lowe*)
- The act itself must be unlawful rather than a lawful act which has been carried out unlawfully (*Andrews v DPP*)
- The unlawful act must be carried out with the appropriate *mens rea* (*Lamb*)
- The unlawful act must be dangerous so there must be a risk of some harm which reasonable and sober people would recognise as a risk (*Church*)
- The act need not be directed at the victim (*Goodfellow*)

Comment:

- Unfair because focus is on the unlawful act not the killing – and the defendant does not have to foresee
- Difficulty of showing the unlawful act e.g. the drugs cases *Cato, Kennedy (No 2)*
- Appropriateness of the objective test for danger – and the role of the jury

Continued on next page

Continued

Explain gross negligence manslaughter:

- Definition – defendant owes a duty of care (*Bateman*) and fell so far below the standard that it goes beyond compensation and amounts to a crime (*Adomako*)
- Decided by jury

Comment:

- Appropriateness of applying civil standards
- The role of the jury and the circularity of the test
- Problem of deciding how far below the standard the defendant must have fallen
- But can use for omissions

Explain reckless manslaughter

- Subjective measure (*Cunningham*)
- Defendant appreciated the risk but carried on to take it
- Appears to have been reintroduced in *Lidar*

Comment:

- Former problems with objective measure (*Lawrence, Seymour*)
- Uncertain use

Conclusions

- Should be based on arguments
- And focus on need for reform – so Law Commission proposals could be included
- One big problem in any case is which to use

Examples like the one above can be found at the end of chapters in all titles in the Unlocking the Law series.

7.2 Problem questions

7.2.1 What is a problem question?

Problem questions are a set of hypothetical facts. They look like a short (and for the parties involved usually an unfortunate) story.

- They look longer than essay titles, which usually ask for an analysis of one area of law for academic discussion, but the areas of law could be similar, as could the length of the answer required.
- The problem question could very well be the sort of problem that clients have when they first go to see a solicitor.
- You may recognise the facts as they might be a mixture of several decided cases in one big question, but more commonly they are similar to decided cases, but different in some important ways we will examine later.

You may feel the facts of the question are entirely unrealistic; do not worry about that. In the world of question-setting, the assessor realises the question is rather fantastical (you will see this from the examples on police powers and the criminal law below: Angela, Robert and Juan are having rather unusual days!) but the lack of realism may be necessary to enable students to get to grips with the legal issues that arise. That's not to say real cases are dull – far from it – just to get you to realise that problem questions are rarely dull either!

Why are so many questions on a law course problem based?

That's the nature of law. That's what lawyers and judges do. They problem solve. To be fair, that's not *all* that lawyers do – they may also be required to comment on and evaluate the law, so essay questions have an important role in a law course too, but most modules will use at least one problem-style question in the assessment regime. This is only common sense as on the one hand it is good preparation for the world of professional legal practice for those that want to enter the profession. Quite apart from that it is an important part of developing the skills of legal reasoning that we covered in Chapter 6. It is vital that you start to develop the special skills required in problem solving as early as possible. We cannot state strongly enough that this reason alone should persuade you that full attendance at seminars is vital; without it, you are going to find answering problem questions tough. It does get easier with regular practice though, we promise.

The most crucial factor to remember from the start is that in answering a problem-based question, *you are the judge*. To illustrate this, read an appeal case: any case at all in any area of the law. Examine the process a judge goes through when delivering a judgment. The judge will identify the material or key facts of the case, will examine the law that governs those issues, will apply the law to the facts and will deliver his or her decision on who wins the case. That is exactly the process you have to go through when answering a problem question.

In fact, if you think about it, all cases are just legal problem questions, aren't they? The difference is that the court cases are real; your problem question will almost certainly be fictitious, but to one extent or another, it will be loosely based on real cases.

The second introductory point is to note that a problem question is not an invitation to write an essay. The facts of the question are important and they are there for a reason: to get you to apply the law.

We will consider the structure of a problem-question answer in more detail below. Let's start at the beginning.

7.2.2 Identifying the area of law

Read the question. Read it again. Do not skim read it. Now do it again.

You should be getting the picture. A failure to grasp all of the issues raised in the question can usually be traced back to a failure to read the facts properly and completely. To give a real example: One student in a problem question kept saying in her answer 'If Bruce had been drunk'. This was amazing; *the question specifically stated Bruce had been drinking alcohol all day and was very inebriated*. Another, when considering a local authority's duty of care, discussed the remoteness of damage *had* his garden flooded; which, on the facts, it had! There is no excuse in coursework – you will be given the question in enough time for you to be able to read the question regularly.

To identify the area of law in the question, you need to know your subject matter well. It comes back to attendance and preparation again. Presuming you have at least some knowledge of either the law of torts (exemplar question 1), police powers (2) or the criminal law (3), we will pick apart some examples.

The torts example

Sample question 1 (torts)
Angela still plays competitively for a woman's hockey team despite being seven months' pregnant. During a match an opposing defender, Becky, trips Angela with her hockey stick while trying to prevent an attacking move. Angela falls heavily, landing on her stomach, and also banging her head as a result of which she loses consciousness.

Continued on next page

Angela is rushed to hospital still unconscious. Doctor Careless carries out an emergency Caesarean section on Angela to save the baby, but the baby is stillborn. During the operation the doctor discovers that Angela also has an infected womb. Although the infection is not life threatening, Doctor Careless performs a hysterectomy (removes Angela's womb).

When Angela is recovering in her hospital bed, Doctor Careless tells her about the hysterectomy. Angela is angry because she wanted to have more children. She shouts at the doctor 'I'll make sure that you never have children either!' Nurse Dowell calms Angela but when she leaves Angela's hospital room she locks the door in case Angela gets angry again and tries to find the doctor.

Fifteen minutes later Doctor Careless goes to Angela's room to give her a sedative but he finds it locked. He then tells Nurse Dowell to unlock the door. Angela is unaware that she has been locked in.

Advise Angela of any actions that she might take.

Figure 7.5 Sample question on torts

Angela is having a very bad day. While she is not real, there are some real legal issues that arise. The next step is for you to get to the detail of the problem. The clues for this will be in the question. Perhaps the most important piece of advice is for you to read every word of the question and read the question several times before you start to write the answer. This will help you identify the specific area of tort law that arises and ensure you do not accidentally omit a key issue. To find out, first use your lecture notes and tutorial questions to see if you recognise the issues. Certain 'flags' or pointers are put in problem questions (usually based on past cases so you can identify them); can you identify the flags above?

- She is playing a sport.
- She is injured by contact with another player's hockey stick.
- She is unconscious when she is taken to hospital.
- The doctor carries out an emergency operation.
- The doctor also carries out an operation that is not an emergency.
- Angela gets angry because of this and threatens the doctor.
- The nurse locks Angela in a hospital room for a short time.
- Angela is unaware that she has been locked in.

What specific topics in torts have you learned that are relevant here? Do you recognise any cases that are similar? You are correct if you identified the question as dealing with the tort of trespass to the person. Within that area of law, however, there is more than one tort (assault, battery, false imprisonment) and it is very common in problem questions to have to deal with a number of issues. The main issues here are whether:

- Becky has committed a battery on Angela
- Becky has a defence of consent
- Doctor Careless has committed a battery on Angela with the emergency Caesarean
- Doctor Careless has a defence
- Doctor Careless has committed a battery on Angela with the hysterectomy
- Doctor Careless has any defence
- the nurse has falsely imprisoned Angela by locking her in
- it matters that Angela is unaware of the false imprisonment.

The police powers example

Some questions are very specific about what the assessor wishes the student to comment on. You will see from the instructing words in the question below that the tutor specifically points out the area of law to be considered:

Sample question 2 (police powers)

Robert, a law student, was walking home from the pub late at night. He desperately needed to go to the toilet and stood behind a tree on the pavement in order to urinate (this is an offence).

Police Constable Woodcock, a uniformed police officer, witnessed this taking place and, when Robert had finished, he approached him and asked him his name and address. Robert replied (truthfully), 'My name's Robert Redford and ha! believe it or not I live in a flat above the Sundance Pub.' (This is the name of a well-known actor who starred in the film *Butch Cassidy and the Sundance Kid*.)

'So you're a comedian are you?' said PC Woodcock. 'Let's see if you think this is funny. You're nicked'.

(a) Advise Robert on the legality of his arrest.

(90 per cent of the marks available for this question)

(b) The police have charged Robert with two offences – urinating in a public place and obstructing a police officer in the execution of his duty. Who will decide whether Robert should face trial for these offences and on what basis is this decision likely to be made?

(10 per cent of the marks available for this question)

Figure 7.6 Sample question on police powers

You will see here that the assessor wants the student to analyse the arrest and the prosecution of Robert, but that the marks for each are clearly specified. If this is the same in your question, relate the word limit to the mark allocation. So in a 1,500-word limited answer, try to spend no more than 150 words on part B (you cannot be given more than 10 per cent of the marks available for that part, however good your answer is).

Just like the tort, we need to identify the flags. Let's focus on the flags in part A. Can you identify the flags in the question?

- It is late at night.
- Robert commits an offence.
- Witnessed by a uniformed police officer.
- The officer asks him for his name and address.
- Robert supplies him with his name and address.
- The police officer does not believe Robert's answer and he arrests him by just stating 'You're nicked'.

The major issue is the question of arrest. You can use the flags as a guide for the answer.

- What are the police powers of arrest?
- What are the procedures to be followed on arrest?
- Can a policeman ask an individual to provide him with his or her name and address?
- Can an arrest be made if a policeman does not believe a name and address that is provided?

The crime example

In criminal law questions more than in any other of law, students tend to be distracted by how the facts of the question could be proved. The answer is that:

- the facts are hypothetical; they are not real
- therefore ignore issues of proof; just accept the facts as stated, and
- you are not concerned with questions of proof, but with questions of criminal liability.

The facts of the question below are sacrosanct – you have to accept what you are told. The assessor has also informed the student which offences the defendants have been charged with; even if you think they have been charged with the wrong offence, or should not have been charged, that is irrelevant.

Sample question 3 (Criminal law)

Juan was shopping in Nottingham City Centre when he was approached by Maria, a campaigner for the 'Save the Trees' charity. Maria was going to ask Juan to sign her petition but Juan thought she was going to attack him and he shoved Maria away. Maria tripped on an uneven cobble stone and fell to the ground, suffering bruising to her hands and elbows.

Ronaldo, who witnessed the incident and who was very intoxicated, shouted at Juan. Juan went to run off, but Ronaldo, because of his drunkenness, thought Juan was going to hit him. Ronaldo punched Juan, causing Juan a concussion from which Juan fully recovered.

Discuss the liability, if any, of Juan who has been charged under section 47 of the Offences Against the Person Act 1861 and Ronaldo, who has been charged under section 18 of the Offences Against the Person Act 1861.

Figure 7.7 Sample question on criminal law

There are two charges. By all means, make sure you do examine whether the elements of these offences are satisfied, but do not spend too many words on that part of the answer because the two offenders have made mistakes about the circumstances – they thought they were acting in self-defence, but they were wrong (this is called mistaken or putative self-defence), and one of them was drunk. These are very important parts of the question to deal with and even though you have not been given a specific instruction to deal with them; the flags are clearly emphasised in the facts.

7.2.3 Sorting out the key facts

These are the 'flags' referred to above. What does this mean?

- No word in a problem question is there without a reason.
- The actions of the parties have been carefully thought out by the assessor to give you hints on the issues and to make sure you deal with the areas of law to be assessed.
- You must make sure you find all of these signposts, or indicators, and deal with the law applicable to each.
- The key facts guide you in identifying which issues of law arise.

As part of your preparation, to find the key facts, you might highlight the different issues in different coloured pens, or underline the flags and put the relevant cases next to the underlined parts. Alternatively, you might find it useful to recite the facts of the question to a person who does not know the law and then you try to explain to them what area of law is involved. This technique can be surprisingly beneficial; sometimes just putting problems into words helps solve them.

So, for instance, if we look at the tort problem again (see Figure 7.5) and do some highlighting of the key facts:

Sample question 1 (torts)

Angela still plays competitively for a woman's hockey team despite being <u>seven months' pregnant</u>. In a match an opposing defender, Becky, <u>trips</u> Angela <u>with her hockey stick</u> while trying to prevent an attacking move. Angela <u>falls heavily landing on her stomach</u> and also banging her head as a result of which she <u>loses consciousness</u>.

Angela is rushed to hospital still unconscious. Doctor Careless carries out an <u>emergency</u> Caesarean section on Angela <u>to save the baby</u> but the baby was stillborn. During the operation the doctor discovers that Angela also has an infected womb. Although the infection is <u>not life threatening</u>, Doctor Careless <u>performs a hysterectomy</u> (removes Angela's womb).

When Angela is recovering in her hospital bed, Doctor Careless tells her about the hysterectomy. Angela is <u>angry</u> because she wanted to have more children. She shouts at the doctor <u>'I'll make sure that you never have children either!'</u> Nurse Dowell calms Angela but when she leaves Angela's hospital room she <u>locks the door</u> in case Angela gets angry again and tries to find the doctor.

Continued on next page

> Fifteen minutes later Doctor Careless tells Nurse Dowell to unlock the door to Angela's room so that he can sedate Angela. <u>Angela is unaware that she has been locked in.</u>
>
> Advise Angela of any actions that she might take.

Figure 7.8 Highlighted sample of question on torts

All of the words that are underlined are critical not just as pointers to what the problem is about but also in identifying the appropriate law that will determine any liability.

One point has already been mentioned above, but is worth repeating: *do not make up facts*. Another point is about *omitted* facts.

In the criminal law question (see Figure 7.7), for example, you have been told that Ronaldo is drunk, but you are not specifically told that Juan is sober. It is acceptable in these circumstances to presume Juan is sober because, if he had not been, you would have been told. (To play it safe, you could add a sentence that you infer that Juan is sober.) On the other hand, you are not told (i.e. the assessor has omitted to tell you) whether the mistakes made by each defendant are honest and/or reasonable. That is because in each scenario, you have to consider these alternatives. In order to assess the depth of your understanding, the assessor will often omit a key fact that in practice a solicitor would ask his client. That said, do not go off onto a flight of fancy. There is no indication that either defendant is insane, so you must not discuss this defence. If the assessor wanted the student to consider the defence of insanity, he would have added a fact (for example, Ronaldo was a diabetic and, having forgotten to take his insulin, upon arrest said that he had not done anything wrong).

You might find it useful to relate this advice to another real example, so what follows (in Figure 7.9) is a full annotation of the criminal law question for you to see how we have identified the key issues.

Sample question 3 (Criminal law)

Juan was shopping in Nottingham City Centre when he was approached by Maria, a campaigner for the 'Save the Trees' charity. Maria was going to ask Juan to sign her petition but Juan thought she was going to attack him

HE MAKES A MISTAKE; THINKS HE IS IN DANGER. ISSUES OF SELF-DEFENCE? CASES: WILLIAMS (GLADSTONE), BECKFORD.

and he shoved Maria away.

ASSAULT/BATTERY? HE HAS ACTED ON HIS MISTAKE – IF ANY DEFENCE, PUTATIVE SELF-DEFENCE. SEEMS SOBER (NOT TOLD HE IS DRUNK).

Maria tripped on an uneven cobble stone and fell to the ground, suffering bruising to her hands and elbows.

CONSIDER SECTION 47 – ASSAULT (HE SHOVED HER), OCCASIONING (CAUSATION), ACTUAL BODILY HARM (BRUISING). CASES: SAVAGE & PARMENTER, ROBERTS, MILLER.

Ronaldo, who witnessed the incident and who is very intoxicated,

WHATEVER HAPPENS, I NEED TO REMEMBER HE IS DRUNK. NEW RULES OF LAW APPLY; MAJEWSKI. NEED TO THINK ABOUT BASIC AND SPECIFIC INTENT ETC.

shouted at Juan.

ASSAULT? DEFINITION? IS THE OFFENCE SATISFIED ON THE FACTS?

Juan went to run off, but Ronaldo, because of his drunkenness,

NOT A MISTAKE HE MIGHT HAVE MADE WHEN SOBER?

thought Juan was going to hit him.

PUTATIVE SELF-DEFENCE EXPLAINED ABOVE – SO NOW I NEED TO ADD DRUNKEN MISTAKEN SELF-DEFENCE – O'GRADY AND O'CONNOR – PERSUASIVE (OBITER).

Continued on next page

Continued

> Ronaldo punched Juan, causing Juan a concussion from which Juan fully recovered.
>
> *SERIOUS INJURY (HE LIVES, SO NOT A HOMICIDE QUESTION); CONSIDER GRIEVOUS BODILY HARM; SMITH.*

Figure 7.9 Annotated sample of question on criminal law

You might wish to adopt a similar method in preparing for tutorials. This will give you plenty of practice for answering problem questions in the coursework and in the exam.

The next stage in your planning is to make a note of precisely what you have been asked to do. Read the instructions. Are you told to discuss, advise one of the parties or examine only one area of law? By the way, if you are asked to advise one of the parties, that does not mean you give one-sided advice, or you bias your answer to suit that side. Imagine you are asked to advise the prosecution. You would be negligent if you did not advise them about the strengths and weaknesses of the defence case too. This is very important because, in court, the lawyers must refer the judges to all of the relevant cases, even if they do not support their argument. Do not forget the first piece of advice we gave you; all problem questions require you to be the judge in the case even if the instructions are phrased in terms of advice. You need to present all arguments (even if you disagree with the law in the area, you need to explain and apply it). A really sophisticated answer would also state which argument wins and why.

Please note you should not give advice in the first or second person (I or you). Use the third person (he, she or it).

Reading the instructions in the question is a crucial activity as the commands in problem questions vary. This can be seen by the instructions in the three questions that are under discussion in this chapter.

TORTS	Advise Angela of any actions that she might take.
POLICE POWERS	Advise Robert on the legality of his arrest.
CRIME	Discuss the liability, if any, of Juan who has been charged under section 47, Offences Against the Person Act 1861 and Ronaldo, who has been charged under section 18, Offences Against the Person Act 1861.

The commands are different. Each question wants a different focus. The police powers scenario requires focus on the legality of arrest. The crime question wants a discussion on liability of two individuals. It is important that you focus exactly on the command given in the scenario. Focus on the following:

- Who are you advising? Is it one individual or is it a number of people?
- Is the advice from a particular viewpoint, e.g. the applicant or respondent?
- Is it offences, defences, liability or a combination?
- Does the question want focus on one area, e.g. arrest, or does it want general advice?

ACTIVITY

Exercise

Think about an area of law with which you are familiar. It may be something you have studied in the past or that you are studying now.

Have you picked a topic? Now think of one aspect of that topic that interested you in particular. It might have been because of a case with funny or peculiar facts, or it could be because the teacher was very critical of the decisions made, or for some other reason.

Got it? If you need to, take a minute and check you are confident that you know the law well. Now write a very short problem question on that topic. What you are trying to do is point to the law through the facts of the question without specifically stating what the law is. For example, if you chose the postal rule, your scenario would include Alf making an offer to sell something and Bert replying by post, but the letter not being received by Alf.

Continued on next page

This activity should get you to think like an assessor does, and if you can *write* problem questions, you can answer them.

7.2.4 Creating a structure

Unlike essays, where a logical and clear introduction is required, some tutors do not miss an introduction to a problem question. At all times, resist any temptation to write a general introduction to the area of law:

- A problem question on breach of contract does not need an introduction explaining offer and acceptance.
- A criminal law answer should not start with a definition of *actus reus* and *mens rea*.
- A problem question on the tort of negligence does not require an introduction to the meaning of the word 'torts'.
- Do not state 'This question involves complex issues relating to public law'. Of course it does. That is why it has been asked.

Second, never start an answer to a problem question with the phrase 'In this answer I am going to ...' The marker knows what you need to do – answer the question set within the fact scenario of the question; so do not talk about doing it; just do it! The earlier you can start explaining and applying the law, the more marks you will attract and the better focused the answer will be.

There is no universal magic formula for writing good problem-question answers. Examiners differ in their preferred practice. What follows is general guidance.

There are three regularly used methods to structuring a problem-question answer and they have a great deal in common as you will see:

- The **IRAC** system
  - State the **I**ssues
  - Explain the legal **R**ules
  - **A**pply the law to the question
  - **C**onclude.
- The **IDEA** System
  - **I**dentify the legal issue
  - **D**efine the legal rule
  - **E**xplain how the rule works
  - **A**pply the rule to the facts.
- In other books in the '*Unlocking*' series the authors use problem questions and refer to:
  - Key facts
  - Key law
  - Applying the law to the facts
  - Reaching conclusions.

Whichever way it is described, the process is effectively the same.

Planning

Once you have identified the key facts (the flags), next list the issues of law that the facts of the question focus on. For example:

TORTS	Becky trips Angela with her hockey stick	Is there a direct and intentional application of force without consent (battery)?
POLICE POWERS	Arrested	Legality of arrest – 'You're nicked' – adequate?
CRIMINAL LAW	Juan thinks Maria is going to attack him	Mistake – self-defence?

Do this for *each* key fact in the question. This is your plan.

tutor tip

You should never recite the facts of the question as your first paragraph of the answer – the marker wants you to get on with explaining and applying the issues of law. The flow chart in Figure 7.10 may help to focus your mind on what the question is all about.

There are certain universally accepted norms:

- in crime questions, never mix in questions of civil law
- in torts questions, never mention the overlap with the criminal law
- in crime questions, never deal with the defences until you have considered the offences.

So, to the plan. This is best done as a flowchart so you can see a pictorial representation of how the answer will progress (logically) from one point to the next. The first few points have been written in full in Figure 7.10 so you can also see how to explain what you want to say as clearly and precisely as possible. Each main arrow in the plan will be its own paragraph. Check:

- each paragraph deals with one issue
- each paragraph deals with that issue in full (including explanation and application; we will come to this below)
- the marker should not get confused from one paragraph to the next; there is a clear flow.

7.2.5 Explaining the law

Once you are satisfied with the plan, you need to start drafting the law. Be aware of the word limit, but do not try to write to the limit; you can always condense and refine your writing later. That said, you cannot afford to waffle so make sure your explanations are as precise and concise as you can as you go along.

QUOTATION

'A bad answer to a problem, even though correct, will not earn many (perhaps not any) marks, because the [marker] cannot tell whether the student has knowledge or is just guessing. Reasons and authorities should, therefore, always be given. Pretend to yourself that the examiner will disagree with your point of view and set yourself to persuade by argument.

One of the most important of a lawyer's accomplishments is the ability to resolve facts into their legal categories. The student should therefore take pains to argue in terms of legal rules and concepts. It is a not uncommon fault, particularly in criminal law, to give the impression that the answer is based wholly upon common sense and a few gleaning from the Sunday papers.'

Smith, Glanville Williams, *Learning the Law*, 12th edn, London, Sweet and Maxwell, 2002, 151.

So the lesson here is that each proposition of law needs to be clearly explained and backed up by authority. Do not spend too long explaining the obvious; the assessor wants you to get to grips with the controversial areas, not spend a quarter of the essay dealing with points of law that are settled and accepted. For example, do not use a number of cases dealing with a single and uncontroversial area of the law such as the definition of the term 'actual bodily harm' in s 47, Offences Against the Person Act 1861. There may be solid criticism of the meaning of the term, but to spend more than 50 words in this answer where there are far meatier issues would be a waste of words.

Uncontroversial issues should be dealt with quickly:

Sample question 1 (torts)
Technically any intrusive treatment by a doctor can be a battery unless it is carried out with the consent of the patient (*Re F (Sterilisation: Mental Patient)* [1990] 2 AC 1). However, in *Leigh v Gladstone* (1909) 26 TLR 139 it was established that consent can be implied in emergency situations where the patient is unconscious because of the doctrine of necessity. As a result the emergency Caesarean section operation on Angela is unlikely to lead to any liability.

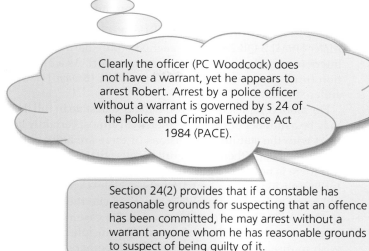

Clearly the officer (PC Woodcock) does not have a warrant, yet he appears to arrest Robert. Arrest by a police officer without a warrant is governed by s 24 of the Police and Criminal Evidence Act 1984 (PACE).

Section 24(2) provides that if a constable has reasonable grounds for suspecting that an offence has been committed, he may arrest without a warrant anyone whom he has reasonable grounds to suspect of being guilty of it.

In addition, the constable must have reasonable grounds for believing that for any of the reasons mentioned in subs (5) it is necessary to arrest the person in question.

Subs (5) must be explained and you must consider whether Robert's name and address could give rise to reasonable grounds for suspecting. Refer to PACE Code G too.

Now move on to the legality of the arrest (what are the rules governing the information to be given under s 28 PACE and are the conditions satisfied?). Has Robert been adequately informed of the arrest? (Is it OK to say 'You're nicked'?)

Figure 7.10 Flow chart on sample question 2 – police powers

Sample question 2 (police powers)

Once you have stated the power to arrest under s 24 (if a constable has reasonable grounds for suspecting that an offence has been committed, he may arrest without a warrant anyone whom he has reasonable grounds to suspect of being guilty of it) all you need to do is explain that PC Woodcock has watched Robert commit an offence and has clear reasonable grounds to believe Robert is guilty of it. You do not need to enter into a debate about the elements of the crime of urinating in a public place. The assessor has told you only to consider arrest and you cannot get credit for anything else.

Sample question 3 (criminal law)

Miller [1954] 2 QB 282 defines actual bodily harm (ABH) as any hurt or injury likely to interfere with the victim's health and comfort. As a bruise clearly falls within this definition (provided it is not trivial or transient (*Brown* [1993] 2 All ER 75, HL), Maria has suffered ABH.

For more complex issues, you will need to state in full the rules of law that apply. There may be a number of rules and there will almost certainly be more than one source of law. Start with the statutory provisions (if there are any), but refer to the relevant section(s) rather than copy them out in full because that is a waste of valuable words.

If there is no statute governing the area of law, or after you have dealt with the statutory provisions, move on to the cases. Unless you are sure they are relevant, do not use old cases to answer a problem question; cite the authorities (the current leading cases) in each area. Do not merely mention the case name nor just the facts. The marks are awarded for explanations of the rule or principle of law established in that case. You may wish to discuss the case in great detail, perhaps arguing that it was wrongly decided, especially if the case directly covers the factual situation but your view is that the decision should not be followed. It is more likely, however, that the facts of the question will fall directly between conflicting authorities. In this event, the marker will be looking for you to analyse which is the better decision.

Sample question 1 (torts)

In the case of Becky tripping Angela with her hockey stick, there are three key issues to discuss:

- Whether the tripping is intentional (which would be necessary for battery – but is not clear here so alternative possibilities would have to be discussed).
- Whether the application of force is in fact direct (again necessary for battery – but you would be able to show through cases such as *Scott v Shepherd* (1773) 2 Bl R 892 that the courts have taken a fairly broad view of the meaning of direct in battery).
- Whether Becky could claim the defence of consent which is common in a sporting context (but for the defence to apply you would need to consider whether Becky is acting within the rules and spirit of the game, which allowed the defence to be used successfully in *Simms v Leigh Rugby Football Club* [1969] 2 All ER 923).

Sample question 3 (Criminal law)

ACTIVITY

Exercise

It is always worth finding the time to practise explaining complex areas of law. The more practice you get, the easier it becomes. If you have studied this area of criminal law, make some notes, citing the leading cases, on the operation of self-defence and the defence of voluntary intoxication. Then compare your explanations with the suggested content below.

The force used must be unlawful force, as is the case with all offences of violence. Thus Ronaldo may have used lawful and reasonable force in self-defence. Academic writers have long debated whether the 'unlawfulness' of the force is an element of the *actus reus* of the offence or is entirely a defence. If it is the latter, the force is a lawful justification (or possibly an excuse) which negates liability despite the commission of the *actus reus* with the requisite *mens rea*. Support for this view comes from *obiter* statements made in the House of Lords in *Brown* [1993] 2 All ER 75. However, contrary case law suggests that lawfulness would negate the *actus reus*, because the force used would not be unlawful force (*Beckford v R* [1988] AC 130, PC; *Williams* (1984) 78 Cr App R 276, CA; *Kimber* [1983] 3 All ER 316, CA; *B v DPP* [2000] 2 AC 428). In terms of criminal liability, whether or not unlawfulness is an element of the *actus reus* or a defence seems to matter only in cases of

tutor tip

Our advice on dealing with conflicting authorities and making critical commentary:

- Be courageous! Make informed arguments.
- Be prepared to argue your point.
- While an important chunk of marks is given for clear and concise and accurate explanations of the law, do not forget that you are also expected to deal with contradictory cases and misleading authorities.

mistaken self-defence or mistaken consent (often called putative self-defence or consent). If the normal rules were applied in this case, Ronaldo would be judged on the circumstances as he saw them rather than as they actually were.

The leading case on the 'defence' of voluntary intoxication is *DPP v Majewski* [1976] 2 All ER 142, HL. This states that voluntary intoxication has no effect on criminal liability unless the accused is charged with a specific intent crime and the intoxication prevented him from forming the specific intent. Accordingly, as Ronaldo has been charged with an offence under s 18, Offences Against the Person Act 1861, since s 18 is a crime of specific intent and since the intoxication prevented Ronaldo having the necessary specific intent, he could not be guilty as charged. Conversely his intoxicated state would not negate liability for a basic intent crime such as s 20 even if it had prevented him from having the *mens rea* normally necessary for that crime. However, two Court of Appeal cases, *O'Grady* [1987] 3 All ER 411 and *O'Connor* [1991] Crim LR 135, asserted *obiter* that a drunken mistake as to self-defence always had to be ignored and could not be a defence to either a specific or basic intent crime. As each case contradicts the established House of Lords' doctrine in *Majewski*, it is suggested that they should be ignored.

The process of application

The second major chunk of marks is for application of the law to the facts. This means you have to relate the law to the facts of the question in turn.

DO NOT

Recite the issues

THEN

Explain all the relevant law in one go

THEN

Apply to the facts in one go – you will either repeat yourself and waste words or will miss something important from this part of the answer

INSTEAD

Identify the first issue

Explain the law relating to that issue

Apply to the facts

THEN

Move on to the next issue

Explain the law relating to that issue

Apply to the facts

AND THEN

Move on to the next issue

Explain the law relating to that issue

Apply to the facts

And so on

AND REMEMBER TO

Conclude

Figure 7.11 Applying the law to the facts

Application does not mean copy out the facts of the question. It means you have to link the law to the question.

Wrong	Right
Intrusive treatment by a doctor can be a battery unless it is carried out with the consent of the patient, *Re F (Sterilisation: Mental Patient)* [1990] 2 AC 1. Doctor Careless has performed a hysterectomy on Angela without her consent.	Although Doctor Careless felt that he was acting in Angela's best interests, it is clear that a doctor must obtain consent before any intrusive medical treatment, *Re F (Sterilisation: Mental Patient)* [1990] 2 AC 1. As a result, the hysterectomy carried out by Doctor Careless may well result in his liability for battery.

Even a correct statement of law followed by a mere repetition of the facts is not application to those facts:

Wrong	Right
The *mens rea* for a battery is intention or recklessness to apply unlawful force to the victim (*Parmenter* [1991] 2 All ER 225). Juan thought Maria was going to attack him and he shoved her away.	The *mens rea* for a battery is intention or recklessness to apply unlawful force to the victim (*Parmenter* [1991] 2 All ER 225). Juan clearly thought Maria was going to attack him and in shoving her away, he acted intentionally. The *mens rea* for battery is therefore satisfied.

Conclude as you progress

Notes:

- In a problem-style question, deal with the issues in chronological order.
- Use the word count carefully and stay within it.
- You are taking a law degree (of one form or another), so make sure your analysis is of the law, not the facts of the question – never repeat the question.
- There is no hard and fast rule about reciting case facts in answer to problem questions but, generally, do not spend too long explaining facts unless you are using them to distinguish the facts of the question itself.

tutor tip

The magic word in all legal arguments, essays and problem questions is 'IF'.

There is no 'right' answer in most problem questions; there are just a range of possible outcomes. You may not have been given enough facts to form a firm conclusion, or you may have a number of conflicting authorities and no clear conclusion can be drawn. That is why IF is such a magic word. You could make it clear that *if* the court followed the case of X, the outcome would be ... but if the court followed the case of Y, the outcome would be different.

Do not say *what* without *why*. Throwing cases names around and then concluding that D is liable or guilty is unlikely to attract a good grade. You need to have stated why first, then conclude. It does not matter if the reader disagrees with your conclusion. You will have achieved most of your marks already anyway and the assessor is not looking for the 'right' answer (remember there is not one in problem questions – that's why we call them problems!) but whether your conclusion is:

- well argued, and
- consistent with the law as explained and applied above, and
- has highlighted areas of law that are inconsistent, and
- has suggested reform to areas of law that are unsatisfactory.

Leave your options open if you have to; don't forget to use *if*.

You may find it useful to use sub-headings if they help. But do not overdo it! If sub-headings assist the structure to your answer, use them. But if you feel that the answer flows logically without them, there is no need to use them. They will almost certainly form part of the word count. However, where there are a number of events that need dealing with, you may find the answer has a clearer focus if sub-headings are used:

Sample question 1 (torts)

Becky tripping Angela

Doctor Careless performing the emergency Caesarean on Angela

Doctor Careless carrying out the hysterectomy on Angela

Angela threatening Doctor Careless

Nurse Dowell locking Angela in the hospital room

Figure 7.12 Sub-headings which may be used for sample question 1 – torts

Alternatively, use sub-headings when planning your answer, but once the answer flows well, delete them.

7.3 Oral presentations

7.3.1 What is an oral presentation?

viva voce

an examination conducted by spoken communication

viva

an oral examination.

tutor tip

We do not ask questions to be awkward; normally we ask a question in order to get you to tell us something which we think you've forgotten, but that you know. Not every question is set out to trick you; in fact we're often trying to help you.

Undergraduate law schools increasingly are using oral presentations, commonly referred to as a *viva voce* or just *viva,* as a form of assessment. As a student this should be something which you see as a positive rather than something to be worried about, as oral presentations can, with proper preparation, allow you to show your understanding and level of knowledge of a particular subject in more depth than you possibly could via a more traditional assessment method.

The idea behind an oral presentation is that a student will be given an allotted time, normally 10 minutes, to present their findings on a particular area of law. The student will then be questioned, normally for another 10 minutes, by the member of staff listening to the presentation. It is hoped that the student will provide a logical, well-articulated, in-depth and relevant presentation in which they demonstrate to the assessor a clear understanding of the subject matter under scrutiny. The assessor is then afforded the opportunity to ask questions in order to draw more information out of the student, and so allow the student to gain higher marks.

It will depend on your particular institution as to whether and where in the course you are required to make an oral presentation for assessment purposes, and the course year and the subject matter may well dictate what is expected of you. However, there will always be a number of common assessment criteria that are referred to by all institutions in assessing a student's performance in a moot. These common assessment criteria will include:

- **Relevance** – how relevant is the presentation content to the subject matter under discussion?
- **Depth of understanding** – does the presentation show a good level of understanding and research?
- **Structure of presentation** – is the presentation logical and easy to follow?
- **Quality of expression** – is the presenter audible, speaking clearly with intonation and at an appropriate speed?
- **Clarity of expression** – is the presenter using appropriate language, sentence construction and grammar?
- **Body language** – does the presenter make eye contact? Are they standing correctly and have no bad fidgeting habits?
- **Use of visual aids** – is the aid selected appropriate for the presentation? Does it include useful material?

7.3.2 Preparing for an oral presentation

Structure

student mentor tip

When working out how to structure things, I was always advised to 'tell them what you're going to tell them, tell them it, then tell them what you've told them'. It works every time.

tutor tip

Signposting is extremely important. If you were out walking and the signpost said 'Pub – two minutes' walk' but the path took you to the duck pond, you wouldn't be happy. If the path took you to the pub in two minutes then you'd be happy. The same goes for presenting. If you tell the tutor where you're taking them and why it's relevant then your presentation will be easier to follow; the tutor will be happy to listen; and you'll get higher marks!

Preparing for an oral presentation requires no extra skills than those required for preparing for a written essay question. It is all about getting the structure right, working out the bare skeleton of what you are going to say, before filling in the skeleton with the flesh of the detail. The advice from Section 7.1.4 'Creating a structure' is just as applicable here as it was there; presentations (like essays) need a beginning, a middle and an end.

The first thing you need to do is work out what the focus of the presentation is. If the presentation subject matter is given to you by your tutor then you would go about this in the same way as you would do for an essay or problem question – consider the main topic area (i.e. criminal law, torts law, English legal method etc.) and then narrow it down further (i.e. murder, psychiatric harm, juries etc.) before focusing on the specifics (i.e. the intention required for murder, secondary victims, disqualification from sitting on a jury etc.). See Figure 7.1 for more help with this. If the presentation subject stems from your own project then it is hoped you will easily be able to identify the topic focus.

Once you have ascertained what the substance of the presentation will focus on then it is time to write out a draft plan. Again the exact method of devising this plan (flowchart, list, graph etc.) will depend entirely on your own personal preferences but to help you with this planning of the structure refer back to Sections 7.1.4 and 7.2.4.

The one thing to keep in mind when you are structuring your presentation is that it should be logical in its development and each separate element of it should be linked so that it flows from beginning to end. You should also provide the audience with prompts, otherwise known as 'signposts', along the way so that they understand what you are going to consider and why.

Timing should also be a crucial element to keep at the front of your mind when planning your presentation structure. All presentations will be time constrained and so you should take this into account when planning what you are going to include. If you have 10 minutes to present then you do not want to spend 5 minutes of that time introducing the topic. Instead, you'd want to spend only a minute or two introducing the subject before going into the substance of the presentation.

The table below provides a brief presentation structure outline with timings and signposting. The presentation title is 'A comparison of prison conditions in the late 19th and late 20th centuries. Has a change in the prison conditions impacted positively upon the reoffending rate?'.

Time	Signpost	Content
1–2 mins	Introduction	What will be covered in the presentation. The project title.
2–4 mins	Prison conditions	Comparison of prison conditions in the late 19th and the late 20th centuries.
4–6 mins	Reoffending rates	Comparison of reoffending rates from the late 19th and the late 20th centuries by way of statistics/other research.
6–9 mins	Critical commentary	Analysis of whether the improved conditions have had a negative or positive impact on the reoffending rate.
9–10 mins	Conclusion	Draw conclusions from the previous discussion and project findings.

Figure 7.13 Outline presentation structure

ACTIVITY

Exercise

Draw up a presentation structure outline including approximate timings and signposts for the following presentation titles. You should be able to do this without any detailed knowledge of the topic areas as it is only a draft plan.

- 'The rules protecting jury room secrecy encourage arbitrary decision making and should therefore be abolished.'
- 'Due to judicial development of the law the five requisite elements of the offence of theft are now too easily satisfied, leaving the law in urgent need of reform.'

7.3.3 The presentation

The purpose of an oral presentation is to disseminate the relevant information to the audience in such a way that it is both comprehensible and engaging. If you read Chapter 10 on mooting then you can utilise a lot of the information given in that chapter for your own presentational purposes, as in essence a moot and an oral presentation are the same thing.

The assessment criteria

One of the best ways to maximise the mark you get for your oral presentation is to ensure that you meet the criteria against which you are being assessed. As we said earlier, most institutions will refer to common assessment criteria when it comes to oral presentations, and you can use these while you are preparing as a guide to what is required of you. However, it is best to obtain a copy of the specific criteria you personally are being judged against, as then you will be able to tailor your presentation to meet each individual criterion.

The assessment criteria may be quite detailed and give, for example, a mark out of 10 for each criterion, or it may be more holistic in setting out the requirements and simply give a grade of a certain classification band for each element. Whatever method of marking your own institution uses, just remember to try and ensure that you meet each criterion during the course of your presentation.

Take a look below at the two different assessment criteria examples for oral presentations so as to get an idea of what might be required of you.

Oral presentation performance criteria	F	3	2:2	2:1	1
Relevance of presentation to the issues raised					
Depth of understanding of the legal (and other) issues					
Depth of research apparent from the presentation					
Quality of explanation and reasoning					
Logical structure of presentation					
Quality of expression					
Ability to answer questions					

Figure 7.14 Example 1: Oral presentation performance criteria

Oral presentation performance criteria	Comments	Mark out of 10
Fluency of expression, without relying on a script. Voice projection, speed, intonation and accurate use of language.		
Clarity of presentation, confidence, persuasiveness and ease of delivery.		
Familiarity with all sources cited.		
Evidence and depth of research apparent from the performance.		
Ability to state the law concisely and accurately.		
The construction of logical, coherent and sustainable argument.		
Analysis of relevant legal/other issues.		
Appreciation of the context within which the law operates.		
Quality of response to questions.		

Figure 7.15 Example 2: Oral presentation performance criteria

Effective advocacy

To help you achieve well against the assessment criteria you need to demonstrate techniques of effective advocacy. This means that you need to speak clearly and slowly, using appropriate intonation and volume. Be concise in what you are saying and ensure that you use appropriate language and speak properly, so no slang or colloquialisms.

Your appearance and body language is just as important as how you orate so ensure that you are dressed properly for the occasion; wear smart clothes, not jeans and a T-shirt. Stand up straight and do not fidget. Don't play with your hair or pick up a pen and fiddle with it. Using your hands as an aid to expression is OK, but only up to a certain point; if it looks like you are working for air traffic control due to you waving your hands around so much then it may be better to stand with them clasped behind your back, or with your fingertips touching the table lightly so as to keep them under control. You want the audience to be concentrating on what you are saying, not on what you are inadvertently doing.

Making eye contact with the audience is also very important. If you make eye contact during the presentation then the audience (or assessor) will feel included in the presentation and you will encourage them to actively engage with what you are saying. If you simply stare at the floor you will not grab and hold their attention. Making eye contact also allows you to gauge the audience reaction to the material you are delivering. If you become aware that the audience have not understood a certain point or have lost the thread of what you are saying then you can tailor your presentation to take account of this. If, however, you just stare at the carpet then you will miss these important visual cues and not allow yourself the chance to rectify matters.

For further advice and information on effective advocacy turn to Chapter 10.

Visual aids

Visual aids can be very helpful when making an oral presentation and there are many different forms which you could use; which one (if any) you choose to use is entirely a matter of personal choice. However, be very careful not to let any visual aid you use overpower your presentation and ensure that you use them appropriately.

The most common types of visual aids are:

■ OHP (overhead projector)
■ computer
■ video
■ flip chart
■ hand-out
■ PowerPoint.

7.3.4 How to use PowerPoint

Many students will choose to prepare a PowerPoint presentation to accompany their oral presentation. PowerPoint is an accessible and easy-to-use product that can allow both student individuality and creativity to be showcased to the audience. This is obviously then a benefit to you and you'd be silly not to use it to the extent of its (and your) abilities, right? Well, it depends. If PowerPoint is used correctly then it can be a very valuable tool in making a good presentation, but if it is used incorrectly then it can distract from the contents of your presentation and actually be more of a hindrance than a help.

The first thing to remember when using PowerPoint as a visual aid in your presentation is that you should prepare the presentation first and then create the PowerPoint slides to complement it, and not *vice versa*; your presentation contents should dictate the contents of the slides, not the contents of the slides dictate the contents of the presentation. You should also bear in mind the phrase 'quality over quantity' when preparing PowerPoint slides. Do not try to use as many slides as possible but rather aim to use the bare minimum instead. For a 10-minute presentation you should aim to have between three and five slides (with five being the absolute maximum). If you have more than five then the audience will not be afforded sufficient time to digest the information on each slide as you speed through them; any less than three slides and the audience will become bored looking at the same slide for the majority of the presentation.

Do not use it as a script

The second thing to remember is that PowerPoint slides should be used as an <u>aid</u> and not as a crutch. It is tempting to put as much detail as possible on to each slide so that you can simply read from the screen when it comes to the actual presentation, but PowerPoint slides should not be used as a script. Take a look at the slide below to appreciate why.

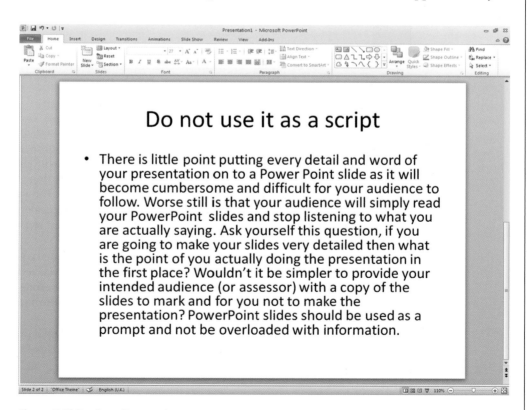

Figure 7.16 Don't use it as a script

PowerPoint slides should therefore only contain the headline points that you want to make. You should then fill in the necessary detail during the delivery of your oral presentation. Use short snappy bullet points on the slides and avoid extended prose at all costs.

Slide presentation

The next thing to be aware of when using PowerPoint is how the slides are presented. You may have included up-to-date pertinent information on the slides but if the audience cannot follow this easily then they will be seen as both redundant in use, and as a distraction to what you are saying.

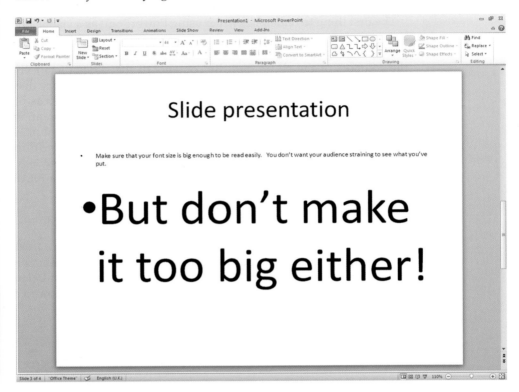

Figure 7.17 Ensure you use the appropriate font size

Ensure that you use an appropriate font size. There is little point using a small font size on PowerPoint slides as you will end up with people either squinting at the slides or not bothering to refer to them; this would be a shame if you have included important information on them that would enhance the audience's understanding of the topic under consideration. Do not use the same font size that you would use for a written document (i.e. 10 to 12) as it will be too small to read comfortably. It is suggested that the smallest font used for PowerPoint should be size 18, with the average font size being between 24 and 32, depending on the typeface used.

However, don't go too far the other way and use a ridiculously large font size as that will be equally as bad (or even worse). If you use a size 50 or above then the audience may feel they are being 'shouted' at via PowerPoint and will therefore be quickly put off reading what you have written, even if it is the most valuable information ever imparted to mankind.

An overuse of capitalisation should also be avoided as it can result in the same 'shouty' effect, and the audience may feel affronted by the unnecessary use of capital letters.

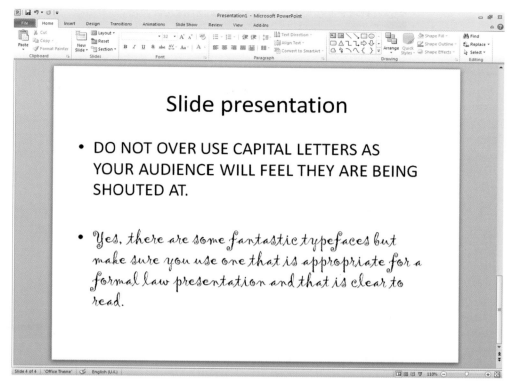

Figure 7.18 Don't use unnecessary capitals and select the right font

The selected typeface can also have a dramatic effect on the effectiveness of the presentation. It is suggested that you stick to the tried, tested and accepted variants such as Times New Roman, Arial, Garamond, Tahoma or Verdana. You need to consider your target audience (law lecturers) and your subject focus (e.g. murder) to decide what is and what is not an appropriate font. If your presentation is on a sensitive subject, such as child murder, then using a font such as Comic Sans MS or Jokerman could be viewed as wholly inappropriate and could even impact negatively upon your assessment mark.

It is also advisable to stick to black lettering wherever possible and to only use colours, such as dark blue or red, which are clearly visible against any background selected. If your audience cannot see the points you are making then they will not be able to read and understand them.

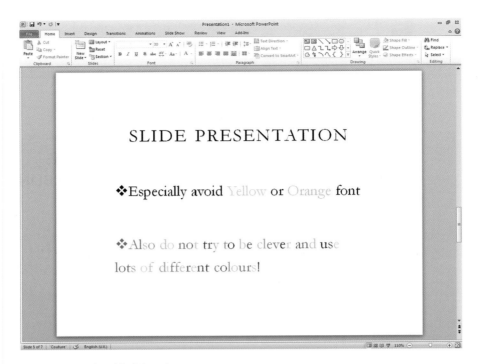

Figure 7.19 Stick to black lettering

Slide background

Your selected slide background also has to match your presentation subject matter. Consider the slide below.

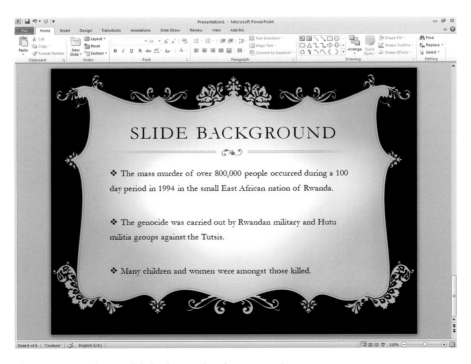

Figure 7.20 Match your slide background to the presentation matter

This slide is paradoxical; the slide background design is very pretty but the content, i.e. genocide, is horrendous. It is often better to keep the slide design as plain as possible, as in that way you can ensure that your audience will not be distracted by the background and instead will keep their attention focused on what you are saying.

The same can be said in respect of slide transitions and special effects. Yes, you can make a slide do 101 fancy things, but do you really need to? To have the word 'negligence' fly in across the screen, or to have a poignant point on euthanasia be made with magically appearing or floating-in letters would again be inappropriate to say the least. Keep it simple and it will be more effective.

Using images

The old adage that 'a picture can say a 1,000 words' does not really apply to Power-Point presentations. Only use a picture if it <u>adds</u> something to the point you are making. Having a perfectly nice but pointless picture will again only distract from the message you are trying to get across, and your audience may spend more time trying to work out why the picture is there rather than listening to what you are saying.

If you want to include a diagram on your slide then consider whether it would be better as a hardcopy hand-out, which you could provide to your audience at the beginning of, or at the relevant point in, your presentation. Complex information will be lost on a PowerPoint slide, and with a hand-out the audience can take it away with them for future reference.

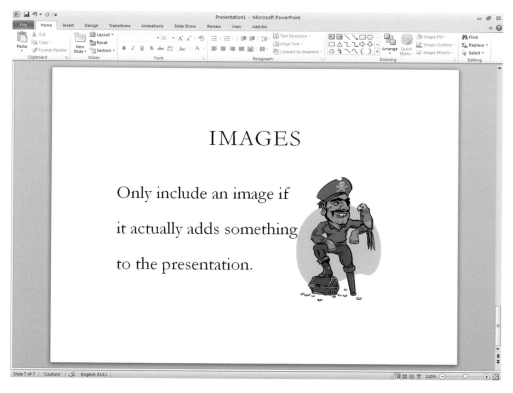

Figure 7.21 Only use a picture if it adds to what you are saying

Referencing

It is just as important to reference correctly in an oral presentation as it is in any other form of assessed work. If you do draw on external sources to bring authority to your presentation then make sure you acknowledge them correctly by adding in a specific reference slide at the end of your presentation listing all of the sources.

Reference in the same way as you would do for any other piece of work. See Section 8.8 for further guidance on how to reference correctly.

SUMMARY

- It is important to know what the question is asking.
- In essays the command words are important – these include analyse, contrast and compare, criticise, and evaluate – and they all require slightly different skills
- A structure is also vital – there should be an introduction, the main argument, and a conclusion.
- In problem questions it is important first to realise that this is simulating the skills necessary to lawyers.
- A different skill is required for problems because first the correct area of law needs to be identified.
- It is important also to sort out the key facts in the scenario.
- Structure is important also – and there are different methods of creating a good structure including IRAC and IDEA.
- Planning is important so that all the issues are covered.
- Explain the law precisely and deal with uncontroversial issues quickly.
- Apply the law to the facts and reach conclusions as you go along.
- Make sure that you structure your oral presentation so that it is logical and easy to follow.
- If you use visual aids ensure that they are easy to follow and do not distract from what you are saying.

Further reading

Smith, Glanville Williams, *Learning the Law*, 13th edn, London: Sweet and Maxwell, 2006, Chapter 9.

Truss, L., *Eats, Shoots & Leaves: The Zero Tolerance Approach to Punctuation*, Profile, 2003.

8
Completing Coursework Assignments 2 – Common Skills

AIMS AND OBJECTIVES

After reading this chapter you should be able to:

- Understand the significance of time management
- Use the assessment criteria to meet the demands of the assignment
- Use relevant material only, and discard irrelevant material
- Quote appropriately from and provide accurate citations to cases, Acts and academic authors

8.1 Time management

How long do you have from the date of receiving the title to the submission date? Between these two dates, how much time (realistically) can you spend on:

- research (hard and electronic copy; textbooks; journals)
- drafting (first and second at least)
- proofreading (at least once; preferably twice or more)
- re-drafting (often a couple of times)
- finalising the essay
- and handing it in (bearing in mind that your computer will crash, the printer will not work and the bus will break down on the way to hand it in)?

In planning the essay or problem, you need to find time for all of these, *and* try to keep full attendance at lectures, full preparation for tutorials and you may have other coursework to write as well. You may also have a job, a family and other commitments (not including excessive socialising; put it on hold until the coursework is done!). To achieve your full potential in this essay or problem question, you need to spend as much time as possible on it, but the term *as much as possible* does not mean you must exclude everything else that has to be done.

First, how much is this essay or problem question worth? It is not a good use of your time to spend 90 hours on an essay worth 10 per cent of one module from three or four in a year, but it might be for an essay worth 50 per cent of a module. Either way, it is certainly not worth missing lectures and tutorials on other key topics to do a coursework – you might miss a topic that comes up in the exam which could be worth far more! The best advice is to plan your time carefully, using a diary, including all stages of the essay-writing process as well as the other commitments you may have. An example follows in Figure 8.1 and Figure 8.2 based on a two-week hand-in date where the student

Week 1	Monday	Tuesday	Wednesday	Thursday	Friday	Saturday	Sunday
9–10	Library – preparation for tutorial subject 1	Library – preparation for tutorial subject 2	Tutorial subject 3	Go to IT room to log on to *Westlaw* and see if there are any recent developments	Have a lie-in until 10.00	Job	Work from home, typing up first draft. Aim for 1,000 words. Make sure case citations etc. are added in footnotes. Back up draft to 2 disks
10–11		Lecture subject 1	Library – preparation for tutorial 4				
11–12	Tutorial subject 1	Tutorial subject 2	Tutorial subject 4	Lecture subject 2	Library – final stage of research including double check against assessment criteria		
12–1	Lunch then library for research for coursework – look in textbooks and photocopy the leading cases to take notes tomorrow	Lunch then library for research for coursework – read the key cases; highlight important quotes. Make notes		Finish reading journals, texts and cases. Have lunch			
1–2			Lunch then library for research for coursework – continue reading cases and also have a look for journals and other texts to expand bibliography	Plan a flowchart – the beginning, middle and end of the essay. Think about which cases and which articles' quotes work best. Roughly estimate word limit per paragraph to stay within 2,000-word limit	Lunch		Lunch
2–3					Lecture subject 3		
3–4	Lecture subject 4	Coffee break then library – preparation for tutorial subject 3 – tomorrow			Write up lecture notes from all 4 lectures this week		Start tutorial preparation for next week
4–5	Library – preparation for tutorial subject 2 – tomorrow						

Figure 8.1 Plan your time carefully using a diary – week 1

Week 2	Monday	Tuesday	Wednesday	Thursday	Friday	Saturday	Sunday
9–10	Library – finish preparation for tutorial subject 1	Library – preparation for tutorial subject 2	Tutorial subject 3	Go to town to buy new printer cartridge	Get into university early to hand in – deadline is midday	Job	Have a lovely long lie-in
10–11		Lecture subject 1	Library – preparation for tutorial 4	Proofread final draft			
11–12	Tutorial subject 1	Tutorial subject 2		Lecture subject 2			
12–1	Lunch then IT room to draft a further 500 words for the coursework	Lunch then IT room to finish draft of coursework in full	Tutorial subject 4	Lunch	Lunch		Lunch
1–2			Lunch then library to read first draft and handwrite changes/spelling mistakes etc.	Final tidy up and double check of word limit			
2–3					Lecture subject 3		Start tutorial preparation for next week
3–4	Lecture subject 4	Coffee break then library – finish prep for tutorial subject 3 – tomorrow		Print two copies of the final coursework	Write-up lecture notes from all 4 lectures this week		
4–5	Library – preparation for tutorial subject 2 – tomorrow		Type-up changes from home – back-up to disk				

Figure 8.2 Plan your time carefully using a diary – week 2

plans to work at their studies from 9.00 am until 5.00 pm but has a part-time job on Saturday.

Obviously, two hours' preparation for each tutorial may not be enough, and under normal circumstances, this student is likely to dedicate more time to this activity; but with careful time management, they will have been able to plan in advance for those weeks where courseworks have to be done to get ahead of themselves. You might also have noticed this student does not work in the evenings. In fact, they approach their studies as a normal full-time job; and it appears to be a very effective and efficient approach.

Some students work best under pressure, within tight deadlines. The student who uses the diary in Figure 8.1 does not, but prefers to work steadily and to include reflection in the drafting process. Either way is fine, but ask yourself whether a last-minute approach will get you the marks you need and/or you think you deserve. You need to answer that question for yourself, but do think about it. The most common discussion tutors have with students who are disappointed with their marks centres around when the essay was started and how much time was put into it. Most students concede: not early enough and not enough time.

Suffice to say here that there is no such thing as a 'spare' five minutes during coursework preparation time. Those five minutes (at the bus stop, waiting for your favourite soap opera to start, whatever) can be spent in thought. As we said above, a tutor can recognise a well thought-out answer. Do not be afraid of having a little thinking time. Look back at the problem questions in Section 7.2.2 and consider: I am Maria and I have been hit. What arguments would I want the prosecution to present? The next time you have five minutes, think about how Robert feels: is having the same name as a famous person reasonable grounds to arrest him? If you can picture yourself as one of the parties you will get a good feel for the issues involved.

8.2 Using the assessment criteria or learning outcomes

Before you start writing the essay, check your plan meets the assessment criteria or learning outcomes. Here are two examples of typical assessment criteria in undergraduate essays:

Example 1

> When marking your coursework, particular regard will be had to the following matters:
>
> - depth of understanding of key legal principles
> - evidence of independent planning and research (including use of a range of information from both primary and secondary sources)
> - ability to apply the law concisely and in good English to the facts
> - knowledge and appropriate use of legal language
> - critical analysis of relevant legal issues
> - ability to construct logical, coherent and sustainable legal arguments.

Example 2

> The student should be able to:
>
> #### Substance
>
> - demonstrate knowledge and understanding of the relevant legal principles
> - demonstrate the ability to apply relevant case law to the question
> - demonstrate research skills to locate paper or electronic versions of the principal cases and/or legislation
> - construct logical, coherent and well-ordered legal arguments
> - provide a conclusion indicating reasoned conclusions on the present state of the law.

Presentation

- present the essay as a neat word-processed or typescript document (min. size 11 font) correctly spelt and punctuated and free from grammatical errors
- provide accurate citations in the proper form for all case references and proper references for all other sources cited or relied on
- provide a bibliography.

When answering problem questions, the assessor will make a specific reference to the demands of answering problem-based scenarios. Common examples are reproduced for you below. Make sure your answer meets those demands *before* you submit your coursework.

Example 1

> When marking your coursework, particular regard will be had to the following matters:
>
> - ability to analyse factual situations and relevant law
> - depth of understanding of key legal principles.

Example 2

> The student should be able to:
>
> - demonstrate knowledge and understanding of the relevant legal principles
> - demonstrate the ability to apply relevant case law to the facts above
> - demonstrate the use of research skills to locate paper or electronic versions of the principal cases and/or legislation.

It is worth double checking that you understand what each means – if not, use your student handbook, or go to see your tutor.

8.3 Grammar, syntax and spelling

Grammar is a branch of language. It is an abstract system of rules which deals with such matters as not saying: 'they was'. Syntax is another branch of language. It deals with the arrangement of words in a sentence. It deals with such matters as not saying: 'Which is why Nottingham Forest lost'.

Why should we care about grammar so much? A good grasp of English is vital for students of law because the law is about words. Words convey and affect meaning. Words produce clearer and more persuasive communication. Well-written answers have more authority. If none of these reasons satisfies you, the final point should: good command of English maximises marks.

You may never have been taught grammar to a high level before; you may think it harsh that you can lose marks for not knowing the rules, but it is the same as not knowing a leading case on an issue. There is no excuse! Spell check can help with spelling BUT avoid American spellings because most programmes accept them and always *always* proofread.

Avoid	Replace with
Isn't	Is not
Don't	Do not
Can't	Cannot
Defendants	Unless you mean more than one defendant in the plural, you almost certainly mean defendant's (e.g. the defendant's right to trial by jury).
Judgement	Judgment

Continued on next page

Continued

Lord Justice Auld	Auld LJ
It's when you mean *Its*	If you are discussing a decision of a court: *its* decision. If you want to write *it is*, then write *it is*; never use *it's*.
I, me or you	Avoid personal terms (*I* is the first person, *you* is the second person). Use the third person – *he*, *she* or *it*.
To justly decide	You should say 'to decide justly'. 'To justly decide' is a split infinitive. Please avoid splitting the 'to' from the active verb. *To* boldly *go* is the epitome of a split infinitive. We appreciate the thrust of the sentence might be lost if it said 'To go boldly', so split infinitives are not banned completely, but use only if unavoidable please.
The issue being duty of care	The issue *IS* the duty of care. The word 'being' is being increasingly used as an active verb in verbal communication. It is not accurate. Have you ever seen a green squiggly line under your work on the computer screen, but you cannot work out what 'Fragment (consider revising)' means? It means the sentence has no active verb; your sentence is not *doing* anything (and it certainly is not scoring you any marks).
Authorize, specialize	Authorise and specialise. The 'z' indicates an Americanism. (We do accept it is also very old English (for those of you who are grammatical pedants) but the 'z' is to be avoided in modern English, please.) Note: your spell check will not assist with this, and it may even tell you the English version is wrong! Ignore it and use an English dictionary.
Would of, could of, should of	This is a wholly inaccurate and inexcusable use of the word 'of' as the past participle of the verb to have. You mean, for example: *The claimant should have known about the clause in the contract because ...*

Figure 8.3 Tips on grammar and syntax

ACTIVITY

Exercise

Now read the brief passage below and rewrite it using correct grammar and spelling to test the understanding that you have gained from this section.

Coursework problem questions aren't as hard as they might look at first site its all to do with sorting out all the possible actions and then working them out individually. The issue being that if you specialize in problems in the exam a lot of the structure of you're answers already worked out for you. You only have to purposefully read the scenario and work out the key facts apply the appropriate law explaining it and not using irrelevant law and reach conclusions. Essay titles tell you what the area of law is but youll probably find that you could of done the problems just as well.

8.4 Using only relevant material

An essay title is never 'Write everything you know about ...', so please do not. Just because you know it and want the reader to know that you do, that does not mean it is relevant. The rule of thumb, as mentioned above, but worth repeating here, is that if it does not further your argument and help you answer the question, leave it out. It does not matter how accurate your answer is. If it contains irrelevancy, you cannot be given credit because to do so would be unfair to those students who did answer the question using relevant material only.

How do you decide what is relevant? First, use your lecture hand-outs to get an idea of the minimum content. If you are in doubt about the best structure to adopt, your lecture hand-outs may also provide you with good hints because your lecturers usually put the hand-outs in a logical order, progressing from the basics to the more complex issues. Remember to make a note of all case citations (doing this as you go along is tedious, but in the long run saves loads of time). Next, refer to a range of textbooks. Do you grasp the point each author is making? Can you express the issues in your own words? (If not, consider whether you need to quote the author, or merely attribute the ideas to the author – see below on referencing.)

Answer the question! This may sound like meaningless advice, but ask any of your tutors and they will all tell you: they mark more formless, 'everything including the kitchen sink' essays, consisting of no more than verbal diarrhoea, than essays where the knowledge has been brought to the question in a thoughtful and informed manner and where the answer clearly makes an effort to relate the content to the question asked.

Never forget that the reader will be looking for evidence to support your arguments. This evidence may be statutes, cases or books of authority.

First, cases. In courseworks, there is no excuse for not citing cases accurately. This means the reference *Donoghue v Stevenson* should *always* be *Donoghue v Stevenson* [1932] AC 562. You need not necessarily spend too long dealing with cases, and you certainly do not need to use an equal amount of words on each. For example, you could say:

'During the 1980s, the test used by the courts to establish a duty of care was very wide, limited only by public policy issues (*Anns v Merton* [1978] AC 728), but this was overruled in *Murphy v Brentwood* [1991] 1 AC 398 and the current test is found in *Caparo v Dickman* [1990] 2 AC 605. The new test is based on three elements, all three of which must be satisfied. The elements are foreseeability, proximity and whether it is fair, just and reasonable to impose a duty of care. It was intended that this test would be applied irrespective of the type of loss suffered.'

Essays must not look like the table of cases from the start of a textbook. Listing cases is an awful habit. Clearly stating the law as decided (the better term is held) in those cases is far better practice.

If one of the sources of law is statutory, make sure you use the correct name for the Act (what is known as the short title) and the correct year. You are generally not required to cite the chapter number (the number given to the Act when it receives Royal Assent); nor do you ever cite the statute book you used to find the Act if you did. Acts are primary sources in themselves. When referring to legislation, try to be specific: if the law you are referring to is in a particular section, refer to that section. As a matter of technique, the word 'Section' is written in full at the start of a sentence. If it arises during a sentence, the abbreviation 's' is used. If more than one section are referred to, sections is abbreviated to 'ss'. Subsections always appear in brackets, e.g., 's 1(3)', rather than 's 1 subsection 3'.

You do not have to reproduce the section in full – it is often a waste of words to do so – but you may wish to extract a few of the key words in the section with which you wish to make a point. For example:

'Section 43 of the Criminal Justice Act 2003 provided for judge-only trial where the judge was satisfied that the "length and complexity" of the case warranted it. However, to come into force, the section required an affirmative resolution of both Houses of Parliament, which the government was unable to obtain. The Fraud (Trials without a Jury) Bill contained a provision to abolish the affirmative resolution procedure, but it was postponed by the House of Lords in March 2007 for six months.'

Everything mentioned in the essay must be relevant to the title to attract marks. For example, in the exemplar essay titles suggested in chapter 7, the following would be irrelevant:

Title	ELS/M	Torts	Crime
Irrelevant	Historical development of the jury trial	Calculating damages for breach of duty of care	The meaning of the word reckless
Why	This has nothing to do with the right of a defendant to elect jury trial	This has nothing to do with the tests used to establish a duty in the first place; damages are assessed only if a duty of care exists	Be careful here: if you were to explain how the definition of intention differs from the definition of the word reckless, this certainly could be relevant; but merely explaining what it is without *making* it relevant to the title will not help you answer the question

Figure 8.4 Irrelevant detail in essays

As you can see from the end column, sometimes the difference between relevant and irrelevant material is how you *use* the information. If you can adapt your explanation to the key words of the title, you can use the material to further your argument. Compare the examples below which might be parts of answers to the ELS/M title:

'Jury trial has existed in the English legal system since the fourteenth century.'
You might say; 'So what?'
All the writer has to do now is add a few words to make the sentence relevant:

'Jury trial has existed in the English legal system since the fourteenth century, which shows it is a tradition, even if not a fundamental constitutional right.'

Rather than wasting the 13 words in the first sentence completely, adding another 13 makes the point and makes it well. Word limits are tight, but it is not always what you say in essays that counts; sometimes it is how you say it. The reader knows you have a word limit and will assess the essay bearing this in mind. Note that word limits are not set randomly – the assessor decides how many words you should need to make the arguments succinctly, accurately and using only relevant information. Remember this: if you find yourself a long way over the word limit on your first draft, ask yourself:

- Are you sure all the information is relevant?
- Have you wasted words reciting unnecessary case facts?
- Have you wasted words in a long quote, when you only really need a few words?
- Have you waffled? Check you have made your points clearly and concisely.
- Have you repeated yourself? Even if you wish to emphasise a point, you do not need to say it more than once; you can presume the reader is intelligent and will follow your argument.

The first draft is never the final draft; and if you have ever submitted the first and only thing you have written on a topic as the final version, you should realise now why you did not do as well as you could have.

Once you have drafted the explanations, you are half way there. However, law essays are not purely explanatory. Most, if not all, titles indicate that some analysis of the state of the law is expected. So, do not just explain what the law *is*; you are also expected to say what is right and wrong with the law, provided your comments are relevant to the title of course. This is the analysis and evaluation element of the essay. You are not, however, expected to provide this analysis from your own personal view. You may do so if you wish (but never state 'I think ...' or 'I believe ...' because such a statement lacks objectivity), but if you cannot think of anything to say, most leading authors will be able to, and you can quote them.

tutor tip

Can you, hand on heart, say 'yes' to the following question? *Would a person who picked up your essay answer, but not the title, be able to make a good guess at what the title is?* If not, you must go back and re-write your response!

In legal problem solving, case facts are not always irrelevant. They may be helpful as illustrations and you will certainly have to refer to them if you are distinguishing.

Sample question 1 (Torts)

For instance in the sample torts problem in Section 7.2.2 you might point out that the soldier in *Murray v Minister of Defence* [1988] 2 All ER 521 was unconscious when he was locked in a room but here Angela is merely unaware of having been locked in her hospital room by Nurse Dowell. In *Meering v Grahame-White Aviation Co Ltd* (1919) 122 LT 44 the claimant was unaware that security police were outside the room and would have prevented him from leaving, although he was obviously being detained for questioning. So the facts in neither of the leading cases that could be applied to Angela here are the same as those in her situation, but you will have to use the facts of the two cases (briefly) to make that point.

Irrelevant material is twice as bad – you cannot get credit for it *and* at the same time you are wasting words you could have used for credit-worthy explanations.

Do not discuss what you have not been asked to discuss. It would be superfluous to consider the legality of the stop and questioning of Robert in Section 7.2.2; you have been asked only to consider the legality of his arrest. Similarly in the tort problem, you are told that Angela has only shouted at Doctor Careless; do not discuss what would have been the case had she jumped out of her hospital bed and hit him.

If it does not further any of your arguments and you feel you cannot apply it to the question, leave it out because it is irrelevant.

An example of how to prepare to use only relevant material is given below. In all *Unlocking* titles there are Key Facts charts in the chapters. These are a useful aid for revision and also as a checklist of relevant law when preparing for coursework problem questions.

Occupiers' liability – general	Case/statute
Occupiers' Liability is covered by two Acts: the Occupiers' Liability Act 1957 in the case of lawful 'visitors', and the Occupiers' Liability Act 1984 in the case of trespassers	
An 'occupier' is anybody in actual control of the land	*Wheat v Lacon*
Premises is widely defined and has included even a ladder	s 1(3) *Wheeler v Copas*
The duty and the standard of care in the 1957 Act	*Case/statute*
A 'common duty of care' is owed to all lawful visitors	s 2(1)
The duty is to ensure that the visitor is safe for the purposes of the visit	s 2(2)
Must take extra care for children, who are less careful than adults, and not put extra danger or 'allurements' in their path	s 2(3)(a) *Taylor v Glasgow Corp*
Applies to any foreseeable danger to the child regardless of what injury is actually caused	*Jolley v London Borough of Sutton*
Although it is assumed that parents should keep control of young children	*Phipps v Rochester Corp*
A person carrying out a trade or calling on the occupier's premises must prepare for the risks associated with the trade	s 2(3)(b) *Roles v Nathan*
The occupier will not be liable for damage which is the result of work done by independent contractors if:	s 2(4)(b)
– it is reasonable to entrust the work;	*Haseldine v Daw*
– a reputable contractor is chosen;	
– the occupier is not obliged to inspect the work.	*Woodward v Mayor of Hastings*

Continued on next page

Continued

Avoiding the duty	Case/statute
Possible to avoid liability where: – adequate warnings are given – exclusion clauses can be relied on – subject to the Unfair Contract Terms Act – defences of consent or contributory negligence apply.	*Rae v Mars*

The scope of the duty under the 1984 Act	Case/statute
The occupier only owes a duty under if (s)he: – is aware of the danger or has reasonable grounds to believe it exists; – knows or believes the other is in the vicinity of the danger; and – the risk is one against which ... he may be expected to offer ... some protection. Compensation is only available in respect of personal injury or death, not personal property The greater the risk the more precautions must be taken	*s 1(3)* *Tomlinson v Congleton Borough Council*

Avoiding the duty	Case/statute
The occupier can defend if he has taken reasonable steps to avoid harm so warnings may succeed – but not against children *Volenti* is also possible if the trespasser is fully aware of the risk	*s 1(5)* *Westwood v The Post Office* *s 1(6)* *Ratcliffe v McConnell*

A typical problem question on occupiers' liability follows. It is a big area so it is unlikely that you will ever have to cover all of the aspects of the topic in one question.

ACTIVITY

Exercise

Chris and Jo have been invited to speak to a conference of undergraduate law students at the Newheantun University and to stay at the Upborough Hotel on the night before the conference. At half past ten in the evening Chris decides to use the hotel gym. A notice on the door of the pool reads 'Danger. No entry permitted between 10.00 pm and 6.00 am Patrons should only use the equipment when there is supervision'. Chris ignores the sign and enters. He uses a treadmill without checking the speed which has been left at fast and he is thrown off breaking his wrist and wrecking his expensive watch.

At the conference on the following day Jo switches on the overhead projector. The machine explodes into flames setting fire to Jo's jacket sleeve and burning her wrist. The explosion is caused by a fault in the wiring which has recently been rewired for Newheantun University by Sparkbright Electrical Contractors.

Advise Chris of any claim that he may make against Upborough Hotel and advise Jo of any claim that she may make against Newheantun University under occupiers' liability.

The Key Facts chart above can be used as a guide to answering the question by only using relevant information, by shading in the unnecessary information as in the revised Key Facts chart below. As you can see there is no need to discuss children or those entering to carry out a trade nor, since Chris is likely to fall under the 1984 Act, the section on warnings under the 1957 Act.

Continued on next page

Occupiers' liability – general	Case/statute
Occupiers' Liability is covered by two Acts: The Occupiers' Liability Act 1957 in the case of lawful 'visitors', and the Occupiers' Liability Act 1984 in the case of trespassers	
An 'occupier' is anybody in actual control of the land	*Wheat v Lacon*
Premises is widely defined and has included even a ladder	*s 1(3) Wheeler v Copas*

The duty and the standard of care in the 1957 Act	Case/statute
A 'common duty of care' is owed to all lawful visitors	*s 2(1)*
The duty is to ensure that the visitor is safe for the purposes of the visit	*s 2(2)*
Must take extra care for children, who are less careful than adults, and not put extra danger or 'allurements' in their path	*s 2(3)(a)*
	Taylor v Glasgow Corp
Applies to any foreseeable danger to the child regardless of what injury is actually caused	*Jolley v London Borough of Sutton*
Although it is assumed that parents should keep control of young children	*Phipps v Rochester Corp*
A person carrying out a trade or calling on the occupier's premises must prepare for the risks associated with the trade	*s 2(3)(b) Roles v Nathan*
The occupier will not be liable for damage which is the result of work done by independent contractors if:	*s 2(4)(b)*
– it is reasonable to entrust the work;	
– a reputable contractor is chosen;	*Haseldine v Daw*
– the occupier is not obliged to inspect the work.	*Woodward v Mayor of Hastings*

Avoiding the duty	Case/statute
Possible to avoid liability where:	
– adequate warnings are given	
– exclusion clauses can be relied on – subject to the Unfair Contract Terms Act	*Rae v Mars*
– defences of consent or contributory negligence apply.	

The scope of the duty under the 1984 Act	Case/statute
The occupier only owes a duty under if (s)he:	*s 1(3)*
– is aware of the danger or has reasonable grounds to believe it exists;	
– knows or believes the other is in the vicinity of the danger; and	
– the risk is one against which ... he may be expected to offer ... some protection.	
Compensation is only available in respect of personal injury or death, not personal property	
The greater the risk the more precautions must be taken	*Tomlinson v Congleton Borough Council*

Avoiding the duty	Case/statute
The occupier can defend if he has taken reasonable steps to avoid harm	*s 1(5)*
so warnings may succeed – but not against children	*Westwood v The Post Office*
Volenti is also possible	*s 1(6)*
if the trespasser is fully aware of the risk	*Ratcliffe v McConnell*

Continued on next page

Continued

To answer the problem:

For both parties you need to explain the rules on occupiers and premises and apply them. They would both appear to be satisfied in both instances.

In the case of Chris:

You need to explain the duty under the 1984 Act, and the possibility of warnings and the defence of *volenti* against adult trespassers, and the damage that can be recovered.

In application you need to:

- Identify that Chris has exceeded his permission by entering an unauthorised place – so falls under 84 Act.
- Discuss whether or not the warning is effective in the case of an adult trespasser.
- Discuss whether Chris will be contributorily negligent and the effect of the Law Reform (Contributory Negligence) Act 1945 on any claim.
- Discuss also whether the risk of injury is willingly undertaken by Chris so that *volenti* applies – which means he must have fully understood the risk and freely accepted it – although a defence of *volenti* seems unlikely in the circumstances.
- Consider that even if Chris can claim he can only recover for his injury not for the watch.

In the case of Jo:

You need to explain the duty under the 1957 Act, and the possibility of Newheantun University avoiding liability if the cause of the damage was the work of an independent contractor, and all three aspects of the rule under s2(4)(b).

In application you need to:

- Identify Jo as a lawful visitor – she has been invited to attend.
- Discuss how Jo suffered damage fulfilling the legitimate purpose of her visit.
- Discuss who is in control of the premises.
- Discuss whether or not Newheantun University can avoid liability if damage is the fault of Sparkbright Electrical Contractors' work. It is reasonable to hire contractors for such a skilled task – the question is whether competent contractors have been hired; checking its public liability insurance would have been one way and whether it was reasonable to inspect their work – Newheantun University officials could at least have switched on the machine beforehand – so may be liable – if not Sparkbright Electrical Contractors will be in negligence.

Problem-solving guides like that above are included as a feature in future editions of titles in the *Unlocking the Law* series.

8.5 Quotations and the avoidance of plagiarism

Never forget to attribute a quote. Put the quote in quotation marks. Put the source information in brackets afterwards or in a footnote. Never pass off an opinion as your own if you have taken it from someone else (even if you happen to agree with it!). Doing so is plagiarism: it is cheating. It is bad academic practice at the very least; it could land you in the middle of an academic irregularity investigation and possibly lead to the Law Society or Bar Council being informed on a reference at worst. It is vital to remember: quoting is not cheating in itself; in fact, quoting well from authoritative sources shows good research skills which will increase your marks, but *failure to state the source (cite it) is plagiarism*. There is no excuse!

ACTIVITY

Quick quiz

Are you sure you know what plagiarism is?

Look in your course/module handbook. Find a definition online if you cannot find what you are looking for (for example, see www.jiscpas.ac.uk or enter 'plagiarism' into a search engine).

Continued on next page

Continued

Answer either true or false to each of the questions below:

- It is not plagiarism if someone else's words are unintentionally reproduced.   T/F
- It is not plagiarism if I only take someone else's ideas but put them in my own words.   T/F
- It is not plagiarism if I copy someone else's diagram, only if I copy text.   T/F
- It is not plagiarism if I change the odd word or phrase from someone else's work.   T/F
- It is not plagiarism if the material I use is available on the internet anyway.   T/F
- Most of my tutors don't recognise plagiarism when it is in front of them and they have no way of finding out that I have copied.   T/F
- It is not plagiarism if I quote a paragraph by placing it in inverted commas with the source cited in a footnote and again in my bibliography.   T/F

All of the above statements are strictly speaking false except for the last one. In fact many universities would not see bullets 1 and 2 as plagiarism and you are likely to be given more leeway in the first year of your degree. In respect of bullet 3, of course diagrams put key points into a visual form and it is difficult to create one that is totally different to another person's. Your tutors are very familiar with the textbooks on the market, and with most of the websites that deal with the subject matter that they teach so bullet 6 is definitely not true.

Each of the authors of this textbook have marked work containing unattributed material copied from their own published works! Even if the copying is not quite as blatant as this, tutors can still identify plagiarised work, and there are websites to which institutions can subscribe to assist tutors in running 'spot checks' on student work. The most well-known is called Turnitin (see http://turnitin.com/static/plagiarism.html). You might find this a useful site too. Students can also subscribe and run their own work through first to check nothing has been unintentionally copied.

Good referencing is a legal skill: poor referencing gets you in trouble, but well-selected quotations enhance your work.

So what to quote? Avoid quoting explanations of the law. Try to express these in your own words so the reader can assess your understanding of the issue. So, for example, the following quote would be better expressed in your own words:

QUOTATION

'Before the plea before venue scheme was introduced, research into defendants' reasons for choosing summary trial and trial by jury (where a choice is permitted) suggested that the major factor was the intended plea ...'

Smith, Bailey and Gunn, *The Modern English Legal System,* 4th edn,
Sweet and Maxwell, 2002, p 919.

On the other hand, the following is more evaluative. It is making a comment on the state of the law, rather than merely stating what the law is, so would make a useful quote:

QUOTATION

'The election for Crown Court trial is arguably a tactic to create further delay, therefore putting pressure on the CPS to accept lower charges, on the prosecution witnesses to drop the case and generally to avoid the "evil day" of trial.'

Smith, Bailey and Gunn, *The Modern English Legal System,* 4th edn,
Sweet and Maxwell, 2002, p 920.

Try to keep other people's comments in your answer to a minimum; it is, after all, your knowledge, understanding and commentary that the reader is assessing; not anyone else's. Remember, too, that however insightful a quote is, unless it helps you to answer the question, do not use it.

Good use of source material is a high-level skill and one that you need to develop. The best answers obviously contain references to other people's work, as long as it only forms part of your overall explanation and argument. The best answer you can write is one that is your own balanced argument reflecting what you have learnt from sources. This is good academic practice.

You can learn how to minimise the amount that you take verbatim from an academic source by looking at the highlighting in Figures 3.4 and 3.5 in Sections 3.4.1 and 3.4.2. Even that amount is more than you need to repeat in quote marks. In those sections you are being shown how to identify key points but you can still reduce them.

Lengthy criticisms are less necessary in problem questions than essays. But a key critique that assists your argument may be persuasive.

8.6 Engaging in a balanced discussion or balancing the arguments

There are at least two sides to every discussion and, in your essay, you need to cover both to maximise marks. You may disagree with one point of view, but do not ignore it. Deal with it and counter the argument as best you can. At undergraduate level, this is rather more sophisticated than presenting a list of the advantages and disadvantages of a particular issue and you should certainly never use bullet points in essays. Write in continuous prose (i.e. full sentences and proper full paragraphs). Never express your personal opinion in the following ways:

✗ I think
✗ In my opinion
✗ It is not fair

There are better ways!
  Try:

✔ There are good grounds for arguing ...
✔ The better opinion is ...
✔ It follows therefore that the law ...

Many law students feel the need to make essays rather grandiose with flowery language. There is absolutely no need to do this. If you were a practising lawyer and spoke like this in court, the judge may wonder what you were talking about and, in a criminal trial, you certainly make no sense to the jury! Instead, keep it simple. You may agree that the law is sufficiently complicated without you adding to the complication of it in the language you use.

One practice that has found its way from the court into law essays is the term 'I submit'. A submission is usually made by counsel, when she is, rather humbly, suggesting to the judge that the law as decided in a previous case was wrongly decided. While this practice has its place in the court room, it is a rather convoluted way to say what you mean. Compare:

✗ I submit that this case was decided wrongly because ...

With

✔ The decision can be criticised on the grounds that ...

The second phrase has the benefit of maintaining a degree of objectivity and as a result it sounds more authoritative.

How to balance the discussion in your essay will depend on what you are being asked to discuss. The ELS/M suggested title above indicates the two views that need to be considered and a list of the advantages and disadvantages of jury trial is not going to answer the question. A reasoned debate, considering (on the one hand) the constitutional right of a defendant to elect jury trial and (on the other) the higher acquittal rate at the Crown Court, will. Say, for example, it is your opinion that jury trial *is* a constitutional right; one technique to consider using is to deal with all of the arguments *against* your view first and then focus the remainder of your answer and your conclusion on what you think are your strongest arguments. In this way, you will persuade the reader that what you say is correct and you will be credited for a clear structure.

For problem questions, also note that you must check that:

■ all the realistic but alternative possibilities have been considered
■ the strongest points in favour of each side have been presented.

8.7 Reaching sensible and reasoned conclusions

Some tutors advise that new information may be given in a conclusion; others say the conclusion should only draw together the arguments already made. Neither is true, however, to the exclusion of the other. Your conclusion should, without doubt, be *based* on arguments made. An essay whose 'middle' part supports the view that oblique intent (the criminal law suggested title in chapter 7) *is* merely a form of recklessness would lose marks if the conclusion stated it was *not*. But your conclusion must not *merely* repeat already-made arguments – this is a waste of words and the marker will not credit the same point twice! The best conclusions are forward looking; this is not as odd as it sounds. Although it is the end of the essay, it is not the end of the matter and the law will continue to evolve and develop, so consider finishing the essay with a brief discussion about any proposals for reform in this area of law and what effect (if any) it might have on the topic discussed. Law Commission proposals are an invaluable source of information in this respect.

Alternatively, you may have a really strong point to make. You may have the winning argument in this discussion and, although it is related to the arguments already raised, you could decide to leave this until the conclusion and go out on the strongest point of controversy you can find. This is a bit more risky; make sure the argument is well explained *and* logical *and* answers the question.

It is not good practice to end with a quote by somebody else because this does not necessarily show your understanding in the best light (the reader wants to know what you know, not what some one else knows) but, if the quote really is the best way to end, go ahead.

Some tutors do not expect conclusions in problem-question answers, but it is important if you have been asked to advise X that you have done so. If you have been asked to consider Y's criminal liability, if any, you should. The problem may be that there are so many variables in the facts it is impossible to conclude firmly one way or another. If that is the case and you are sure you have explained all of the alternatives, it is not imperative to have a vague repetition of this at the end.

8.8 Referencing

Proper referencing in an essay means that the footnotes should be in the correct place, cases always cited correctly and a bibliography (and sometimes a table of cases and statutes) is appended to the coursework.

If you are in doubt about the correct usage and placement of footnotes, refer to a quality textbook and see how they are used and where they are placed (as well as the information they contain). For example, the paragraph below is reproduced from Ormerod, Smith and Hogan, *Criminal Law*, 11th edn, OUP, 2005, p 94 and the case citations in the footnotes have also been shown:

QUOTATION

'In 1979 Lord Diplock said that the matter had been finally settled in this sense by the decision of the House of Lords in *Hyam v DPP*[1]. A majority of the House in *Hyam* was certainly of the opinion that this was the law but the actual decision was that foresight of high probability of serious bodily harm was a sufficient *mens rea* for murder, not that such a state of mind necessarily amounted to an intention to cause serious bodily harm. In *Moloney*[2], however, the House held that the *mens rea* of murder is intention to cause death or serious bodily harm so it was essential to determine the meaning of "intention". *Moloney* must be read in the light of the explanation of it by the House in *Hancock and Shankland*[3], the Court of Appeal in *Nedrick*[4] and by the House in *Woollin*[5].

1. [1975] AC 55, [1974] 2 All ER 41
2. [1985] AC 905, [1985] 1 All ER 1025
3. [1986] AC 455, [1986] 1 All ER 641
4. [1986] 3 All ER 1, [1986] 1 WLR 1025
5. [1999] AC 82, [1998] Crim LR 890'

Most courseworks require a bibliography. It is unusual for a bibliography to be counted in the final word limit, but always refer to your course handbook. There may be an acceptable and required method of providing a bibliography and you do not want to lose marks through ignorance of your institution's rules. Remember, if the inclusion of a bibliography is mentioned in the handbook or the learning outcomes for the coursework, failure to include a bibliography could lose you marks.

A bibliography should include a list of the textbooks referred to in your research (make sure you have included a range of good-quality texts; consider the impression you are making on the reader!), journals, and websites (full web address and the date you accessed the page). A separate list should be given for each.

If you have quoted a judge or an author in the essay, you will have attributed the quote in the essay itself or in a footnote: the information should *also* be provided in the bibliography. Similarly, if you have quoted a judge or author in the essay, merely listing the text or judgment in the bibliography is insufficient. It needs to be in both.

8.9 Reflection and improvement

When you receive your essay back, by all means, first look at the mark, but do not stop there. Your tutors may have spent a lot of time providing detailed feedback and advice – do not ignore it! It has been written to help you to improve in future. The way you respond to the feedback is just as important as the mark you attained. The first thing to do is re-read your essay. If you have kept an electronic copy of the essay, you will find it useful to re-read it the night before it is due to be returned to you. If not, re-read it on its return; but to begin with, do so ignoring the comments made by the tutor. After having spent at least a couple of weeks away from the essay, what are your views on what you wrote? Is the answer clear? Is it well structured? Can you see any obvious errors, irrelevancies, spelling or other grammatical mistakes? Does your essay answer the question that was set? What is accurate in your answer and clearly stated? What mark would you give the essay?

Now re-read looking carefully at the comments made by the marker. Can you see the point of the comment? Examples:

Common comments made	What they mean	What you need to do about it
Spelling	You have spelt something wrong – or perhaps used an Americanism such as 'recognize' instead of the English version 'recognise'. A common mistake in torts essays is to write 'tortuous' instead of 'tortious' because both are English words and spell check does not highlight the mistake (another is statue and statute!). Spelling a case name or short title of a statute incorrectly is a very silly mistake, and one which may cost you marks.	If in doubt, use a dictionary and always proofread your work carefully. Even better, finish the essay a few days before the deadline and ask someone to read it for you looking out for spelling errors.
Sense?	Something in this part of your essay does not make sense. Is this a grammar issue, or have you made an assertion that is wrong in law?	Re-read and, if necessary, say the offending paragraph out loud. If still in doubt, ask your tutor.

Continued on next page

Structure!	Have you jumped from one point to a completely different point half way through a paragraph? This may have caused the reader to get confused. Alternatively, you might have repeated a point already made and the reader is calling your attention to this.	As part of the planning for your next essay, draw a flowchart showing how each point builds upon points already made. Make sure there is a logical progression from one issue to the next.
Citation/Source/ Reference?	The reader has highlighted here that a case has not been cited correctly, or you have not provided the correct reference for a quote or other source of information. This commonly arises where you have said that 'Many people think ...' or 'The Report recommended that ... ' without stating where you obtained the information.	As you research your next coursework, keep a note as you go along of where you found the information *and* case citations. It will save you time in the long run.
Relevance?	You have included material that is either irrelevant or which you have not made relevant to the title.	No student ever submits an essay knowing there is information in it that is irrelevant. But, with hindsight, can you see why you thought an issue was relevant but which in fact is not? You may have to discuss this with your tutor, but do take the time to do so. Once the essay is returned, there is nothing you can do about it, but you can improve for next time.

Figure 8.5 Interpreting the marker's comments

There may be criticisms in the comments – do not take this personally, but learn from them. Now write yourself a checklist for future essays. Keep this handy and before you do another essay, double check you meet the action plan!

SUMMARY

- There are a range of common skills that apply whatever the coursework.
- Time management is critical so that you do not run out of time or hinder your other studies.
- You should become familiar with the assessment criteria – they are a guide to what you have to achieve.
- Good grammar, syntax and spelling are also vital to a good mark – attention will be drawn to errors.
- At all times use only relevant material – you get no marks for extraneous material and this uses up words that could get you marks.
- All quotations must credit the source properly – copying sources verbatim is classed as plagiarism and is academic misconduct.
- The best answers engage in a balanced argument giving consideration to both sides.
- It is vital to finish with a sensible and reasoned conclusion that naturally and logically follows the weight of the discussion.
- In coursework all sources must be correctly referenced.
- You get your coursework back with written feedback – so you should read this and use it as part of your process of improving through reflection on what is said there.

Further reading

Smith, Glanville Williams, *Learning the Law*, 13th edn, London: Sweet and Maxwell, 2006, Chapter 8.

9

Completing Dissertations or Projects

AIMS AND OBJECTIVES

After reading this chapter you should be able to:

- Decide whether, if you have the choice, you would prefer to write a dissertation rather than take a 'taught' module
- Create a structure for your project
- Draft and amend an abstract as you proceed through the dissertation process
- Produce detailed research from a range of sources, noting the relevant citations as you proceed
- Develop advanced time management and organisational skills
- Appreciate fully and take advantage of the support of your project supervisor
- Submit a well-written and well-structured project, on time
- Prepare and perform well in any oral '*viva*' that you may have

9.1 Introduction

Many law schools include a module that is assessed by way of dissertation or project only. In some, this module is compulsory, but in most it is optional. Word limits for the dissertations or projects generally vary from 4,000 to 12,000 words, or possibly even more. If you have to write a dissertation, or if you wish to, we strongly recommend you read this chapter in full before you start, and then refer back to parts of it as and when the need arises.

9.1.1 What is a dissertation?

A dissertation is a long essay written on a single topic, which you research by yourself. Think of it as an independent learning project designed to improve your expertise of the law in a particular area, and to develop your legal research, intellectual and organisational skills.

While projects may vary greatly in scope and topic area, most share a number of key characteristics. First, you determine the subject matter, focus and direction of your work. Second, this work is carried out on an individual, largely independent basis – although usually you will be given support and direction by a tutor. Third, there is a substantial research component to the project, requiring the collection and analysis of legal material. Finally, you will have a more prolonged engagement with the chosen subject than is the case with 'standard' coursework assignments such as essays or reports, with the work consequently expected to be more in depth. This provides you with an opportunity to show your originality and creativity.

In essence, a dissertation requires you to:

- undertake an extensive programme of reading and research
- demonstrate intellectual independence and originality by choosing your own subject of study and defining its nature and scope
- engage in sustained analysis, interpretation and possibly comparison of a substantial body of data
- present the results of your research in a clearly written, cogently argued, logically structured and properly referenced form.

Undertaking a dissertation or a project is excellent preparation for further study and research at postgraduate level. In addition, the skills described above are transferable ones that will equip you, as a law graduate, to work independently and methodically in professional practice.

9.1.2 Choosing a dissertation as an optional module

Working on a dissertation is a different process from following a course. A taught module guides you through the relevant background material in a particular area of study, whereas a dissertation involves finding out yourself what is, and what is not, relevant to your own topic.

If the module is optional (usually in your final year), you are going to have to consider if it is the best use of your time or if you should select a 'taught' module. Complete the following grid, being as honest with yourself as you can be:

Are you ...	Yes	No
Hardworking?		
Self-motivated?		
An independent worker?		
A good time-manager, or able to find the time to complete the project and balance the other modules against it as the year progresses?		
A reasonable, if not yet an expert, researcher?		
Able to stick to a task for an extended period?		

Figure 9.1 Choosing an optional module

If you have said *no* to any of the above, think long and hard about choosing to do a project as an option.

If you have said *no* to any of them, the skills mentioned are the skills that you are going to need; can you develop them? Realistically, do you have the time to develop them before the project starts?

If you have said *no* to any of them, but really want to do a project, ask yourself why. Would a 'taught' module not be able to give you the subject knowledge you want to acquire? If not, then fine. By all means do a project. If it will, think seriously about taking the more traditionally taught course.

We are not trying to put you off doing a project, even if it looks like that. Self-directed study is study in isolation. You will have spells when you cannot face doing work on it. You may lose motivation. You will hit 'writer's block' just as if you were writing a novel (in fact, a project of 12,000 words will feel like it is an epic!).

On the other hand, the keen and eager student may find his time taken over completely by the project. The dissertation must take up only a proportionate amount of your study time and no more (and no less). There is no point writing a good dissertation to the detriment of your other modules as it is likely that the marks from all your modules go

student mentor tip

Don't cheat yourself and say that you'll do it when you know you won't!

towards your final degree classification. See time management in Section 9.6 for further advice on how to organise your project.

9.2 Preparing the title and abstract or understanding the abstract supplied

9.2.1 Choosing a topic area

The first stage in preparing a dissertation is to decide what topic you wish to research in detail and write about. In this process, you should take advantage of the opportunity to pursue a particular personal interest or develop an interest from previous study.

Given the need to develop advanced research skills, it is easier for you to build on modules that you have followed in previous years. However, if a particular topic, which has not been covered, has caught your interest then you are also encouraged to follow your own ideas, if suitable. In certain ways, the dissertation reflects a direct development of the kind of skills that you have acquired through the writing of essays. You will find that your experience of writing undergraduate essays has prepared you for writing a dissertation.

During the first years of your study, your critical insight into the law developed. The dissertation builds on this foundation; it grows out of your own particular interest, both in terms of the material you choose to write about and the topic that provides the focus of your study.

Selecting a topic for your dissertation may not happen right away. You may have to do a great deal of background reading before you arrive at your chosen idea. It may be helpful to talk to a member of academic staff about your ideas and you should also enquire as to whether there is an appropriate staff member who can supervise your project. Many law schools have an academic member of staff who is responsible for overseeing the dissertation or project option and they should be able to advise you as to the likelihood of finding someone willing to supervise your selected topic. From experience we can tell you that it is far easier to find a supervisor for a project based on some of the more common aspects of the law (i.e. criminal or contract law), than it is to try and find a staff member willing to supervise a project on the more obscure aspects of law, such as the Nigerian law system or aviation law, for example.

If the module is an option in your final year, you should really begin the process of considering the subject area during your second year to have made the decision before the end of that year. Then you can spend part of the long summer break identifying and reading around the subject matter, so that you get a good idea of the critical and scholarly material that is relevant to your discussion.

You need to choose an area that:

▪ will hold your interest for the duration of the dissertation (this is often a full academic year)
▪ is not so broad that it prevents you getting into the details of the law and is thus unmanageable
▪ is not so focused on a narrow area that it prevents you from reaching the word limit.

If you cannot decide, we have supervised projects on the following areas, one of which might interest you:

Freedom of contract	Legal professional privilege
Sport law	The defences available to battered spouses who kill
Tax and revenue law	Autonomy
Drugs law	Fair trial rights
Euthanasia	The right to silence

> **tutor tip**
>
> Don't choose an area of law that holds no interest for you just because you think it sounds good or particularly intellectual. If you do then you will get bored quickly and are likely to not do very well overall.

Continued on next page

Continued

Abortion	Regulation of the internet
The admissibility of confessions and unfairly obtained evidence	Crime/criminology
Corporate manslaughter	Crime and mass media
European Union competition law	Employment law
Sexuality and the law	Equal opportunities
Youth justice	Welfare law

Figure 9.2 Some suggested subject areas to choose from

9.2.2 Writing an abstract

Once you have decided on the area of law that interests you, you will need to write a draft working title and an abstract of about 100–200 words. The abstract is a summary or statement of the contents of the project, which pinpoints the essence of your thoughts at this early stage. It is not going to be the one and only version of your abstract that you write out during the course of the project; the question answered in the final dissertation will evolve over the course of your research and so will the abstract, so do not worry too much about your style here. This is your initial starting point, but it is not set in stone. It is important that this is done at the beginning of the project to serve the purpose of keeping you on track in your early research.

In your abstract, try to describe the dissertation's scope, possibly explaining your reasons for investigating your chosen topic. It may be easiest to write this as an action plan of what you aim to achieve. Try not to anticipate the conclusions that you hope to reach in the process of your work as this might lead to confusion. Instead, you might simply say that you have identified certain features or a particular issue in a range of cases, journals or texts. You might also say that your dissertation will examine the relevant materials in order to demonstrate more precisely the relationships between these issues or features, and whether the sources deal with the issues in question appropriately or satisfactorily.

Do not forget that once you have completed the work on the main substance of your dissertation, you will have to return to the abstract and revise it in light of the final title.

> **tutor tip**
>
> If you are having difficulties drafting the abstract then get a friend to write as you talk for about two minutes on what you would like the project to be about.

Example 1

> **Working Title:** Securing a conviction for corporate manslaughter was almost impossible at common law.
>
> **Working Abstract:** Following disasters such as the sinking of the Herald of Free Enterprise, the Hatfield rail crash, and so on, prosecutions against companies were either not brought at all, or the few that were brought quickly collapsed. This project will investigate the apparent failings in the common law to bring defendants to justice, and will also consider whether a conviction in such a case is in any event a desirable outcome. The common law and health and safety legislation will be examined, as will the Law Commission's 1996 proposals for a new offence of corporate killing, which was ultimately enacted by the Corporate Manslaughter and Corporate Homicide Act 2007. The Act is controversial and was subject to extensive ping-pong between the Houses of Parliament during enactment. The contents of the Act will be examined and the sentencing structure under the Act will be evaluated, especially focusing on the nature of community penalties and adverse publicity as a deterrent tool. Analysis as to the success of the 2007 Act in achieving the intended aims will be undertaken and consideration will be made as to how the new law would have changed, if at all, the decisions of the previous case law.

Figure 9.3 Example of a working title and abstract

9.3 Assessment criteria

It is vital that your project meets the learning outcomes and assessment criteria of the module. A couple of examples follow and the first is annotated with what you should be aiming to do to meet each of them.

Example 1

Intellectual skills

The student will be:

❖ able to analyse and synthesise by being able to recognise and distil information in terms of relevance and importance, collect and integrate information from a variety of sources, combine relevant issues in relation to a topic, analyse complex factual information systematically, utilise abstract ideas in an argument and reason logically

> *You need to provide all the relevant primary sources of substantive law (statutes and cases) as well as deselecting irrelevant law and/or academic commentary.*
> *Make sure there is a range of statutes, cases, textbook and journal authors' views.*
> *Also ensure your project has a logical and fluent structure. Clarify conflicting arguments. You may wish to extrapolate (this means hypothesise, in other words to answer the question 'What if?' to expand the arguments).*

❖ able to evaluate by being able to make informed critical and individual judgments and opinions, recognise and justify value judgments, be tolerant towards and handle alternative viewpoints and be perceptive to issues underlying legal principles.

> *Provide a balanced but detailed commentary on both the substantive law and any academic views on the law.*

Key skills

The student will be:

❖ literate in the English language, communicate in writing and orally, précis information, present information in a comprehensible manner and present a clear and logical argument

> *Poor use of grammar, syntax, spelling and legal terminology will lose you marks. Use an English dictionary and a legal dictionary.*

❖ competent in word processing, use the Web and use relevant electronic legal information retrieval systems.

> *Most students have this skill, but make sure you adopt a clear layout for the project and proof read; spell check cannot always be relied on. We have lost count of the number of 'statues' rather than statutes in law projects!*

Continued on next page

Autonomy and ability to learn

The student will be:

❖ able to plan and learn independently, take responsibility for and be committed to his/her own continuous learning, be a reflective learner, be aware of the learning environment and initiate and make use of learning

❖ able to recognise and be receptive to all forms of feedback.

> *Undergraduate law schools have to prepare you for life in the 'real world'. The dissertation is an excellent way for you to show the accumulation of legal knowledge and skills developed throughout the programme. The project will be assessed in light of the final version which is submitted, but some law schools also give a mark for the whole process, including your supervisor's views on your willingness to learn, respond to feedback and open-mindedness. Independence does not mean you cannot ask for help: an independent learner knows when to ask and when to find the answer out for himself.*

Figure 9.4 Annotated example of learning outcomes and assessment criteria

Example 2

A student taking this module will be able to:

• Show development of advanced legal research skills, applying those skills to a project generated on the student's own initiative.

• Show competence in the presentation of a dissertation in an appropriate legal scholarly style.

• Show evidence of virtually autonomous research underpinning self-directed learning, making full use of available resources including those of staff and other students.

• Produce a formal dissertation demonstrating the results of an independent project of autonomous research involving the selection, analysis and comparison of appropriate materials presented in a coherent, logical and perceptive manner.

• Demonstrate the ability to use information technology skills in the preparation and presentation of the work.

• Indicate the acquisition of skills relating to data collection and management and personal organisation including the ability to meet deadlines.

Figure 9.5 Example of learning outcomes and assessment criteria

9.4 Research

You must be willing to put a lot of effort into your research. To build a research trail, start with a textbook (or if your initial thoughts were stimulated by a case or journal article, start with those). That material will make reference to other books, cases and journals. Now read them. That is the start of the trail. From each researched case, extract or article, at least three new avenues should be produced. At some stage, of course, your research will take you off at a tangent. This is where the initial title and abstract come into use; make sure you keep on track and do not be tempted to drift off into new areas that have no bearing on what you want to say.

We cannot over-emphasise the importance of the following point. **Always keep a note of where you have been _and_ how you have searched** – this will help you when you construct your bibliography and also if you need to retrace your steps at any time. It can also help you to avoid duplication of effort.

If you have a helpful librarian, be kind to them. They are going to be invaluable to you because they will have more ideas than you about research, and they will be a good friend to you over the year, especially if the article you are desperate for is only available on an inter-library loan. They may also be able to advise if you are including a comparison with other jurisdictions in your dissertation.

9.4.1 Note-taking

student
mentor tip

Use your Law Librarian! I wouldn't have got the mark I did without mine and she was the first person I thanked in my acknowledgements!

Your notes are going to become the project, so always try to take notes which are precise, concise and accurate. Being precise means making a complete note of where you found the source in the event you have to go back again to edit or correct something. It also means you should be able to reproduce the exact information into the bibliography. Vague notes lead to vague ideas and then to a vague dissertation. However, do not merely reproduce everything you read. Being concise means reducing the key issues in what you have read (paraphrasing) to avoid waffle when you write up the dissertation. Remember to note where you found the sources – you may wish to return to find a good quote (fully attributed of course). Never paraphrase an author inaccurately. In a quote, you must be careful to reproduce the author's exact words, including punctuation. It is likely your supervisor will be aware of the author's views and their published work, so do not get caught out. Be faithful to what the author says and if the ideas you are expressing are not yours (even if you happen to agree with them) state the source.

There will never be enough time for you to read everything. So you are going to have to be selective. On the one hand, the assessor wishes to see evidence of wide reading, but you have neither the time nor the space to reproduce it all. You have to be realistic and you must try to keep your reading within some limits. Challenge yourself without giving yourself an impossible task. For example, if you were to find a reference to an article in an obscure journal that has not been peer reviewed (we call this a non-refereed journal) about how the law you are investigating is dealt with in an island in the Pacific, unless this is what your project is about of course, let it go. On the other hand, failure to cite from the leading textbook will not make a good impression.

tutor tip

If you have a hard time being strict with yourself on how much more to read, remember that marks are available for making a reasoned _independent_ argument – not simply for regurgitating the opinions you have read.

Whatever we say, you will spend too much time reading. Ask every project supervisor and they will tell you that those students who come to their supervisors at the very last minute always say that they have been reading a lot, but need more time to write it up. Such students show poor time management, poor organisational skills and poor independence.

Refer to Chapters 4 and 5 on research and library skills and Chapter 3 on how to read and note-taking.

9.5 Structure

There is an old saying about project writing:
    'Start with a plan.
    Tell them what you're going to tell them,
    tell them it, then tell them what you've told them.'
List the different stages of your argument and then use a flowchart to see in diagrammatic form how you want the final project to look. Select the material that you want to go into your introduction, followed by three or four longer chapters and then a conclusion. This process inevitably involves some de-selecting of material you have researched. As much as you will hate having to leave out material you have spent time and energy discovering, you must not include irrelevant material in your dissertation. Keep re-reading the title and the abstract to keep the focus.

Breaking the project into manageable sections by working to approximate word limits will help you to start. For an 8,000-word project, for example, this is a structure you might like to try:

- Abstract   200 words
- Introductory chapter   800 words
- Chapter 1   2,000 words
- Chapter 2   2,000 words
- Chapter 3   2,000 words
- Conclusion   1,000 words

Dividing the dissertation in this way means that all you have to do is write three 2,000-word essays, add an introduction and a conclusion and you are there. But do not be deceived – a dissertation is not simply four essays fastened together. It is a single argument with a logical progression from one issue to the next.

9.5.1 Drafting the project

The first draft is *never* the only draft. You may have to re-write parts of the dissertation several times, and then delete parts and start all over again. Your time management is vital to the process (see Section 9.6 below).

The introductory chapter

The short abstract sets out what the project is going to investigate. The introductory chapter, which should account for no more than 10 per cent of your dissertation, will build upon this abstract and expand on what your question is asking and why it is important to answer it. This chapter should be written in an explanatory style, telling the reader what each chapter of the **thesis** will cover and the key claims that you will be presenting or defending to justify your arguments.

thesis

another, often more formal, term for a dissertation or degree-level project

The body of the project

This accounts for about 80 per cent of the dissertation. The body is where you develop your argument. It should start with the simplest matters (such as definitions and the clarification of basic concepts) and should then build in clear and yet increasingly more complex stages until you arrive at your answer. This is the main basis on which your work will be judged. What the assessors will be looking for is a clearly expressed and argued thesis based on authority and hypothesis (the 'what if?' question). If you are not sure about the difference between an 'original' piece of work and an 'independent' one, note that 'original' means an idea no one has ever had before. It is very rare to come across an original argument and it is certainly not a requirement at undergraduate level that your arguments are original (although you will, of course, be credited if any of them are). It is sufficient to have an 'independent' idea; that is one where you gather what others have written and you string the ideas together to make a convincing case. Where you find other people have had the same idea already, acknowledge this in a footnote or endnote, pointing out that you thought of it independently.

For any project over 4,000 words, you must divide the body into chapters, each of which deals with a particular stage of your argument. Most dissertations of between 8,000 and 12,000 words should have no fewer than three chapters, and, if necessary, sub-sections too. The exact number of chapters depends on your particular topic. Your supervisor can advise, but each chapter should not be longer than 2,500 words.

You may structure your work so that each chapter or section is devoted to discussion of a particular aspect of your overall topic. The crucial thing is to show the reader that you have a good argument, which means that you must show you have good reasons for arriving at your answer. Cases should be cited correctly with the citation following the case name or in a footnote; do not use endnotes unless specifically directed to by your institution. Quotations should always be attributed to their source. Remember that plagiarism leads to a zero mark, or can even, in worst case scenarios, result in expulsion from your degree.

9.5.2 Suggested structures

Example 1

Title: An investigation of whether the separate torts of negligence and nuisance should be brought under the single tort of negligence		
Abstract	Overlaps in the tests of reasonableness and proximity force us to reconsider whether two separate torts are needed. Should the same tests be used for both and, if so, what is the best test?	200 words
Introductory chapter	Explain the nature of the torts of negligence and nuisance, highlighting areas of overlap. Focus on *Hunter v Canary Wharf* [1997] 2 WLR 684. Summarise contents of Chapters 1, 2 and 3.	1,500 words
Chapter 1	The tort of negligence. From basics to complex. From duty/ breach/damage to the basis of the reasonableness test and the rationale of the tort.	2,000 words
Chapter 2	The tort of private nuisance. From basics to complex. From reasonable user and locality to the *locus standi* of claimants in *Hunter*. Consider the nature of fault and strict liability within this discussion.	2,000 words
Chapter 3	Argue for and against the overlap in the torts. Should there be two separate tests or one that is not limited to type of claimant but purely on a test of reasonableness? Objectively assessed, but not strict liability.	2,000 words
Conclusion	Answer question raised in the abstract.	800 words

Figure 9.6 Suggested dissertation structure 1

Example 2

Title: Women who kill. Does the new law let women get away with murder?		
Abstract	Focus on one or two key cases where the defences on a murder charge against a battered spouse have, under the old law, failed or have been unsatisfactory and consider whether or not the new law under the Coroners and Justice Act 2009 (CJA 2009) addresses the issues raised in relation to these particular defendants.	200 words
Introductory chapter	Basic definition of murder (very brief) followed by a definition of battered spouse syndrome. Indicate that traditionally for this particular type of defendant the only potential defences were either unavailable (self-defence and provocation) or inadequate (diminished responsibility). Explain introduction of new laws under CJA 2009. Summarise contents of Chapters 1, 2, 3 and 4.	1,000 words
Chapter 1 The old defence of provocation	The need for a sudden loss of self control. Define (cases) and argue that battered spouses do not react immediately. Consideration of the 'reasonable person' test and how judicial approaches to the law helped, but did not change the need for the sudden loss. Identification and discussion of the major issues of this defence in relation to battered spouses.	1,500 words
Chapter 2 Other defence options	A consideration of the appropriateness and viability of the two potential defences of diminished responsibility and self-defence. Issues over the stigma caused by diminished responsibility and the breadth of abnormality of mind and 'any inherent cause' limited by the effect of the defence – to name the defendant as abnormal and impaired in their responsibility.	1,500 words

Continued on next page

Continued

	Self-defence. A possible solution to the problems raised by the other defences because leads to an acquittal except for the proportionality element (by their nature, such defendants over react) and/or the 'imminence' of the threat *obiter dicta*. Also consideration of the impact of s 76 Criminal Justice and Immigration Act 2008 in relation to 'reasonable' force.	
Chapter 3 Reform	The Law Commission's Reports. Possible new offences and partial defences. Pros and cons. Political and academic reaction. Analysis of the suitability of the proposals for all defendants charged with murder (could the battering spouses also benefit from any changes?).	1,500 words
Chapter 4 Loss of self-control	Abolition of the defence of provocation and new defence under the Coroners and Justice Act 2009 of loss of self-control. Does it address the problems under the old law? Does it address the issues raised during the reform process? What effect does it have for battered spouses? Would it have changed the outcome of the cases considered in Chapter 1? What issues are anticipated to occur with the new law?	1,500 words
Conclusion	Answer question raised in the abstract.	1,000 words

Figure 9.7 Suggested dissertation structure 2

ACTIVITY

Exercise

Consider the project titles below and suggest an outline structure for them. Remember to include an abstract, introductory chapter and a conclusion.

'Due to the enactment of the Human Rights Act 1998 over 10 years ago it can be said that Parliament is no longer sovereign.'

'Is there still a place for the proverbial reasonable man within the Criminal law?'

Examples of possible structures for these projects are included in the Appendix on page 262.

The conclusion

This should be a 'mirror' of the introductory chapter, in that it restates the question, reviews the key stages of your argument and shows that you have argued logically and convincingly for your thesis. There are no 'right' answers in law, but your mark will reflect whether your thesis is clear, shows a deep understanding of the issues raised by the question and the problems that arise when trying to answer it, as well as making a convincing case.

It is often advisable to leave not only the writing of the conclusion, but also that of the introduction, until you have written the rest.

9.6 Time management

At the outset, devise a timetable for the entire project, from initial research to submission, including interim deadlines as well as meeting the final submission deadline. For example, you should decide for yourself or agree with your supervisor deadlines for:

(i) carrying out your basic research (reading the primary texts, literature survey, and any required data collection)
(ii) producing drafts of chapters
(iii) producing a final draft of the whole dissertation and
(iv) producing the final version.

It is *vital* that you keep to these 'internal' deadlines.

Example project timetable

Year 2 – spring	Decide topic area. Initial draft of a broad title and abstract. Complete module option form. Find/be allocated a supervisor.
Summer	Reading around the subjects. Take notes. Highlight areas for further investigation at start of new term.
Year 3 – September	First meeting with supervisor – agree a working title and discuss areas already researched. Get hints on other areas to investigate. Agree a timetable for the year. Check final submission date. Agree first draft deadline. Meet with the Law Librarian. Ask for support and guidance now and/or in future. Request an update on searching electronic databases. Continue with research.
October	Continue with research. Detailed plan of structure. Write 2,000 words for review by your supervisor.
November	Early in the month – second meeting with supervisor for feedback on first draft and advice on progression. Revise original timetable if necessary. Show detailed plan for review. Agree next deadline. Continue with research.
December	Continue with research and start drafting each chapter. Do relevant bibliography on an ongoing basis. Case citations too. Possibly meet before Christmas break to agree action plan with supervisor.
January	Put all project work on hold: courseworks due in for other modules.
February	Return to project. Re-read all drafts and revise with fresh eyes. Continue with research. Continue to draft.
March	Meeting with supervisor for discussion on content and progress. Continue to draft. Project should be taking shape now.
April	Final re-drafting and refining.
May	Submission.
June	(Possible) oral presentation – see Section 9.9 below.

Figure 9.8 Devise a timetable at the outset

Dissertations *always* take longer to write than students expect. Remember that it is not only writing that you are concerned with, but also with word-processing your text, inserting quotations, producing footnotes, appendices and a bibliography detailing all sources cited. Start early and revise as you progress. Never start writing a 10,000-word project with only a month to go before the submission date. Either you will not finish or you will omit to include something important.

9.7 The supervisor

Almost without exception, law schools will provide a dissertation student with the guidance of a supervisor. The role of your supervisor is very important in the development of your work. It is a different role from that of the lecturer. It is a one-to-one teaching relationship in which you are guided, rather than directed, in your thinking. Meetings between student and supervisor will be more or less regular depending on the nature of the dissertation and the amount of supervision judged necessary by the supervisor. You should, however, aim to meet your supervisor at least three times during the progress of the project.

At your first meeting, be prepared to show your supervisor your initial plan of action and your outline arguments. The supervisor may then set you a deadline for the production of an outline structure and one chapter from the work. If it is possible to do so, record all of the meetings. That way, you do not have to take notes, you can concentrate on what is being said, and you will have a fully accurate record of the advice given to refer back to later.

Your supervisor may agree to read a limited number of drafts of some sections of the dissertation. You should not expect though that the supervisor will read each chapter and certainly not that the supervisor will correct drafts of what you write. All supervisors will be as helpful as possible but can only offer advice as to content. They cannot become too closely involved in what you actually write because this is *your* project. In the end, what remains in and what is left out is your decision. The dissertation is ultimately your own work for which you take responsibility.

Please do not ask, because your supervisor will not be able to answer, what mark you will get. He or she will not be able to suggest a mark for what you have written in the drafts because the mark depends upon what you finally submit (and how you perform in the oral presentation if you have one). Even asking the supervisor to guess at the likely mark is inappropriate, considering the nature of the supervision relationship. After discussion you should make corrections you consider necessary and work on making the final presentation as neat and user-friendly as possible.

9.8 Presentation

The process of preparing your dissertation for final submission starts with a careful final drafting and proofreading of all your chapters. You need to check that your argument clearly and fluently develops from sentence to sentence and from paragraph to paragraph and from chapter to chapter. While you are proofreading, check the accuracy of your spelling and punctuation, and, if in doubt, use a dictionary.

You also need to ensure that your quotations from and references to both primary and secondary materials are clearly and consistently identified according to the conventions of your required referencing system. You will need to read your handbook on the preferred method used at your institution.

Common guidelines for the final presentation of the project might be, for example:

- your dissertation must be typed or word processed on A4 paper
- your own text must be double-spaced in a minimum size 11 font
- indented quotations must be single-spaced
- the pages of the dissertation must be numbered
- it must have a title page
- it should include an acknowledgments page
- it must have a table of statutes (short title and year in alphabetical or chronological order, including secondary legislation if relevant) and a table of cases (in alphabetical order, including citations)

- it must have a bibliography of texts, journals and web pages (include the full address and the date you accessed the site)
- do not consider submitting the project until it has been read and re-read at least four times.

Checklist

1. Are you sure that your introduction states the problem clearly?
2. Does it make clear what the major stages of your argument will involve?
3. Does the structure of your argument reflect what you say in the introduction?
4. Have you divided it into chapters in the best way?
5. Is every sentence necessary? If not, then eliminate the unnecessary waffle.
6. Does each paragraph make only one point?
7. Is your style of writing clear, logical, precise and fluent?
8. Is your use of technical and legal language accurate?
9. Are all of the references and citations complete?
10. Does the conclusion bring your argument together effectively?

tutor tip

If you have to have the project bound before final submission, you will have to leave a few days for that to be done. You may need to book in advance. Do not forget!

viva

an oral examination

9.9 The oral presentation

Sometimes marks are available for an oral presentation based on the dissertation. This is called a *viva*. Not all law schools have the time, staff or facilities to make this part of the assessment, but in the event that you do have to do a presentation (and do please check!) the following advice is for you.

First, find out the structure of the *viva*. How long will it last and for how long do you need to talk? Will you be asked questions? Who will be present? What percentage mark is it worth? And (of course) when and where is it? The date of the presentation will be set so that the supervisor and often a second marker will have read and discussed your project in advance.

9.9.1 The structure of a *viva*

If you have to do an oral presentation, please remember the panel is not trying to catch you out. The questions are being asked to see if you can rise to the challenge of a higher level of evaluation. Many panels ask questions starting with 'What if ...?' This method encourages students to hypothesise in a way they may not have thought of doing in the project. It is a very sophisticated educational technique (it is called synthesis) and if the student can rise to the challenge, he or she will be given a great deal of credit.

Example viva structure

Peter submitted his dissertation on 2 May. His oral presentation is on 1 June, after the date of his last exam. Between the submission date of the project and the date of the *viva*, the Supreme Court decided an appeal contrary to the arguments he made in his dissertation.

The *viva* will last for 20 minutes. He is required to present his findings for no more than 10 minutes, after which the panel (comprising the supervisor and a second marker) may ask questions.

Structure	Minutes	Contents
Peter's presentation	1–2	Peter explains why he chose to do the project on that subject matter and he shares with the panel what he anticipated his findings to be.

Continued on next page

Continued

Structure	Minutes	Contents
Peter's presentation – *contd*	3–6	Peter talks though each chapter of his project, noting the key cases/statutes/academic writings incorporating an evaluation of the material. Peter is far more subjective than he was in his writing; he expresses his personal opinion about the material and why he holds that view.
	7–10	Peter explains the recent decision of the Supreme Court. He has left plenty of time to recite the key facts, the *ratio decidendi* and his views on the decision.
Panel's questions	11–20	First, the panel asks Peter about one of the arguments raised in the project with which they happen to disagree. Peter stands his ground and submits that his view is correct and why. He acknowledges the panel's contrary view has merit, but criticises it nonetheless because of certain weaknesses he discovered.
		The panel then ask whether Peter was surprised by any of his findings. This gives Peter an opportunity to show his open-mindedness and reflective approach to his studies.
		The panel then refers to the recent Supreme Court decision.
		They happen to agree with Peter's opinion on the decision, but in an effort to challenge Peter, they express support for it. Peter is required to go into more detail about why he thinks the decision was wrong (he is happy to do so – he did not have time in the first 10 minutes to say all he wanted to).

Figure 9.9 Example of the structure of a *viva*

For further guidance on making an oral presentation and public speaking see Chapters 7 and 10.

SUMMARY

- A dissertation, also called a thesis or project, is an extended written essay.
- Most law schools offer a dissertation option or module in the final year of study.
- A dissertation is a largely independent piece of work where the student is responsible for determining the subject matter and direction of the project.
- Good planning is essential for a successful dissertation.
- The abstract is a draft summary of the focus of the project. It should be the first written element to be produced as it will provide an invaluable focus throughout the duration of the project. However, an abstract is only a draft and can be changed and amended as the project develops.
- Ensure that you are aware of the assessment criteria and check that your work meets the set learning outcomes.
- Keep a record of all of your research so that you can easily re-find a particular source.
- Do not go off on tangents when researching or writing – keep checking your abstract to make sure you stay on track.
- Before you start writing, draw up a draft plan of each chapter.
- Good time management is an essential skill to learn.

- Your staff supervisor is there to help and guide you so make sure that you use them, and also that you listen to what they say.
- You may be required to make an oral presentation about your dissertation (called a *viva*) after you have submitted the written version.

Further reading

Smith, Glanville Williams, *Learning the Law*, 13th edn, London: Sweet and Maxwell, 2006, Chapter 12.

10

Mooting

AIMS AND OBJECTIVES

After reading this chapter you should be able to:

- Explain what a moot is
- Understand the benefits of mooting
- Decide whether, if you have a choice, you will enjoy and be good at mooting
- Participate with confidence in a moot
- Appreciate the importance of the rules governing mooting

10.1 What is a moot?

QUOTATION

'in some quarters it still remains a moot point whether a whale be a fish.'

1851, Herman Melville, *Moby-Dick*, Chapter 32.

a moot point
a point open to
argument

mooting
to discuss or debate

A modern day example of **a moot point** is 'whether a Jaffa Cake is a cake or a biscuit?'. Canvas this question among your peers and join in with the inevitable debate. Why? Well because if you do and you get a discussion going as to whether it's a cake or a biscuit and in doing so you provide reasoning and justification to substantiate your perspective on this socially important issue then, without possibly even meaning to or even knowing it, you're **mooting**!

In the more specific terms of legal learning a moot is a mock trial, but on an appeal as opposed to a case at first hearing. This means that the fictitious hearing (trial) has already taken place; the witnesses have testified; the parties have adduced their evidence; and the judge (or jury) has deliberated and concluded as to the result. One of the parties to the original case then appeals to the court on a point (or more commonly, two points) of law arising out the case as heard at first instance. This is the basis of a moot. A moot is always set on the facts arising out of a problem-based scenario and can be set on any area of the law, although most moot questions at undergraduate level are founded on one of the seven foundations of legal knowledge, these being: contract law, law of torts, European Union law, public law, criminal law, trusts law, and land law. The moot is argued as if the case was a real appeal and the court that it may be argued in is either a Divisional Court of the High Court, the Court of Appeal or the Supreme Court (formerly the House of Lords).

10.2 Why should I moot?

The benefits to mooting are wide ranging. Partaking in a moot enhances your overall understanding and knowledge of particular areas of law and also enhances overall confidence in public speaking, general research and presentation skills. In particular some of the skills that you will refine through doing a moot are:

Advocacy

advocacy
the act of pleading or arguing in favour of something, such as a cause, idea, or policy

Although the terms '**advocacy**' and being an 'advocate' are normally associated with being a barrister and practising at the Bar it is a skill that is not, and should not be, confined to only one branch of the legal profession. Being a successful advocate means that you are able to present complex information in an impartial, logical and structured format so that it sounds authoritative and persuasive. This is a skill that it is necessary to possess in respect of nearly every profession, regardless of whether you want to be a barrister, solicitor, police officer, schoolteacher or social worker.

Public speaking

For many people the thought of speaking in public is a terrifying concept (unless you are one of the lucky ones who thrive on an audience). Mooting is an experience that allows you to develop confidence in your public-speaking abilities in a safe environment. Initially you may only moot in front of very few people – perhaps a couple of your peers from your course and your tutor. As you grow in confidence you may progress to mooting in front of a small audience (perhaps in an internal mooting competition), and then on to competing in intervarsity and national mooting competitions where there are larger audiences and/or more influential judges involved. There is no secret on how to become a good public speaker; it is something that simply takes time and practice and the more you do it the easier it becomes. Even a very shy and retiring student may find that they are an effective and engaging public speaker once they have developed the confidence to do so.

Eloquence

It matters not how brilliant a mind an individual may have if they cannot communicate their arguments effectively. To be a successful mooter (and public speaker in general) you need to be eloquent in the way that you present your arguments. All lawyers need to develop the skills of fluency of expression and clear enunciation as your aim is to influence your audience and if they cannot understand what you are saying they will not be persuaded by you. This is not to say that regional accents should be discouraged – they should not – but rather mooting will help you to speak clearly, slowly and with intonation so that you are persuasive and engaging to listen to, regardless of geographical origin. Good mooters rarely lose arguments or debates (outside of the moot room at least).

Mental agility

Mooting is not simply about reading out a pre-prepared script and answering a couple of simple judicial questions at the end of your allotted time. A moot is a far more fluid concept and mooters should prepare for the possibility of judicial interruptions at any point during their presentation of the argument. The judge may request that a certain issue be dealt with first, or they may ask questions that you had not anticipated. Mooting requires you to 'think on your feet' and to deal with situations and questions as they arise.

Legal understanding

As a moot question is focused on one or two very specific questions of law you will quickly expand your legal understanding of that particular issue, along with a greater understanding as to the wider area of law in which it operates. The law does not work in a vacuum and lawyers need to appreciate the context of the legal points they deal with. Mooting will help you to be able to quickly identify the issue raised by a question – a skill that will only enhance your overall studies (especially when it comes to exam and other assessment questions).

Research

To be able to present an effective and persuasive legal argument is not something that can be done without preparation. To be able to argue on a particular area of law you will have to undertake a significant amount of research. This will then enable you to substantiate the legal points that you make with relevant authority, and therefore your argument will sound even more persuasive. To be able to research effectively you will need to learn how to access and use the different legal resources and databases available to you, and you will need to develop an appreciation of how much weight a particular type of source (case law, legislation, Law Commission Reports etc.) will carry in the court.

Legal reasoning skills

The overriding aim of a moot is to persuade the audience that the legal argument you are presenting is the correct interpretation of the law. To be able to do this you will be required to justify your argument. By being required to do so you will be honing your legal reasoning skills as not only will you need to be able to create a persuasive legal argument with reference to the law, you will also need to be able to put this into a logical structure that can be understood by all.

Written skills

Mooting is not just about the oral presentation. A written skeleton, and occasionally a more substantial set of written pleadings, is required as part of the moot (see Section 10.6). The written element of a moot is usually subject to strict constraints as to word limit and content and so mooting helps aid you to become concise, succinct and precise in your written word; again this is an essential skill for a lawyer (and other professions) to possess.

Curriculum vitae

Law is an extremely competitive profession, but it is also an immensely popular subject to study at university. To be successful in pursuing a career in law students need to ensure that they stand head and shoulders above their competitors (i.e. other law students). To have mooting on your CV is one way of ensuring that you are a more attractive prospect to potential employers than your peers. In fact, application forms for legal professional courses, solicitors' firms and barristers' chambers often expect that a candidate has, and can provide evidence of, their advocacy or mooting experience while at university (over and above any of the more traditional areas of advocacy, such as debating).

The above is not an exhaustive list of the skills you may acquire through mooting and you might find that undertaking mooting helps you in other areas of your academic (and even personal) life, even those that you did not think it would (or even could) impact on. The one very important thing to bear in mind is that all of these skills are transferable and will benefit you no matter what career path you eventually choose to take.

10.3 Where can I moot?

The opportunities available to moot will depend on the individual institution, but most law schools offer students at least some limited mooting experience. A number of universities have begun to incorporate mooting in the syllabus, even using it as a form of assessment in certain modules. Other law schools may focus more on it being an extracurricular activity outside of the normal course content and structure.

Often law schools will put forward teams of student volunteers to moot externally on behalf of the law school, either in an informal moot with another university, known as a 'friendly', or as part of a national mooting competition such as the English Speaking Union/Essex Court Chambers National Mooting Competition, or even as part of an international mooting competition such as the Jessup or the Telders moots. Alternatively a law school may run internal mooting competitions known as 'exhibitions' where students are pitted against their peers within the law school.

How the mooting activity is run will vary from law school to law school. In some institutions the mooting may be run by a member of the academic staff; in other institutions the mooting may be run by the students themselves, either as part of the student Law Society or Council, or as a separate Mooting Society. If you are considering application to university but have not yet decided where to go then you may want to ask the institutions you have shortlisted about the mooting opportunities they offer or, if you are at university and your law school currently only offers limited mooting opportunities, then why not set up your own mooting society?

10.4 Who is involved in a moot?

It is normal practice for students to take the role of the advocates (the barristers, called 'counsel') in the case. The role of the judge is sometimes taken by other students, but is more commonly taken by law tutors, visiting solicitors, barristers or real judges.

10.4.1 The Master/Mistress of Moots

The person with overall responsibility for organising the moots within a law school is called the Master or Mistress (or occasionally Director) of Moots. A member of academic staff or a student may undertake this role. The Master/Mistress's role is to:

- Organise or write the moot question.
- Find a suitable time and place for the moot.
- Find or act as the judge (and, if the latter, to deliver judgment in the case at the end of the moot).
- Publicise the moot so there is an audience in attendance.
- Organise internal competitions.
- Enter the team(s) for moots against other institutions, or in the national/international mooting competitions.

10.4.2 The judge(s)

Bench
the panel of judges
in a courtroom

The Master/Mistress of Moots will often be the judge in an internal or friendly moot. They will sit on their own or they may ask colleagues or students to sit with them and it is normal for there to be either one or three judges sitting on the **Bench**. If the competition is of a national standard then it is best practice for the judge to be a practising barrister, solicitor or member of the judiciary. It will be the responsibility of the host institution to find the judge, and most moot rules stipulate that the judge cannot have an affiliation with either of the institutions mooting so as to avoid any potential issues of bias.

Every moot judge will ensure that they are familiar with the case and the previous case law in advance of the moot. The role of the judge is not to just sit and listen to the arguments, like in an oral presentation, but rather they are there to test the mooter's understanding of the law and their ability to respond to judicial questioning. As a result the judge will regularly interrupt the mooters so as to ask them complex legal questions.

The questions asked by the judge(s) are not designed to put you off but rather to test your ability in the powers of persuasion and the ability to think on your feet. Questions are also a useful way for the judge to indicate to you as counsel which points of law you should focus on. For example, a judge may ask a question in order to draw out a piece of information which he feels may assist your case, but which you have not yet mentioned. If you have not anticipated this question, take a couple of seconds to allow the question to sink in, take a deep breath and then give a calm answer. The judge is not timing you for a quick response; he will be far happier with a considered and thoughtful answer. Also, what may seem like an eternity of silence for you will actually only be a very short space of time and not long enough to be noticed by others. If you do not understand the question then politely ask the judge to repeat or rephrase it. For example you could say, 'I should be obliged if your Lordship could possibly clarify that question', or 'I am having a little difficulty following your Lordship's meaning'.

In preparation for the moot, try to consider what questions might be asked and have an appropriate answer prepared just in case such a question does arise. Use the skeleton argument of opposing counsel to prompt your thoughts and read any dissenting or minority judgments, or conflicting academic arguments, in an effort to pre-empt the possible line of questioning the judge may take.

10.4.3 Counsel

The standard format of the majority of moots is to have four students acting as the advocates in the case. Two students will be acting for the appellant (the party bringing the appeal) and two for the respondent (the party defending the appeal). In each team there is a lead and a junior. The leading counsel for each side will argue on the first ground(s) of appeal and the junior counsel for each side will argue on the second ground(s) of appeal.

10.5 How do I prepare for a moot?

The secret to a successful moot (as it is to most things in life) is in the preparation; the better prepared you are, the better you will moot. Most students are surprised to learn that the actual advocacy side of the moot is only part of the mooting process, and a minor part at that. The oral presentation is simply the culmination of the extensive groundwork that preceded it. When allocating your preparation time for a moot, it is suggested that you split your time in the following way:

> **skeleton argument**
> a document summarising what an advocate will say during a legal hearing

- 50% on research
- 25% on the written element (**skeleton argument**/pleadings)
- 25% on the advocacy.

As you can see only 25% of the overall preparation time has been allotted to the oral element; the remaining 75% is afforded to the preparation. If your argument has not been well researched and thought out then nothing else will matter; you could be the best advocate in the world but if your content lacks substance then you will not win the argument.

10.5.1 Sample moot question

Below you will find a sample moot question kindly provided by Terence Wong, a former undergraduate student at Nottingham Law School. This has been included as a point of reference and to aid you in your understanding of what needs to be considered when preparing for a moot. It will be referred to later in the chapter when considering issues, such as the contents of a skeleton argument etc.

IN THE COURT OF APPEAL (CRIMINAL DIVISION)

Attorney General's Reference
(No. 5 of 2011)

The deceased, Victor Blend, was attacked by an unknown perpetrator outside his home and received repeated punches to the skull and body. He was found unconscious by paramedics and taken to No-Hope hospital.

Initial diagnosis established that Blend was in a vegetative state caused by traumatic brain injury; sub-arachnoid haemorrhaging caused by a pterion fracture. He also sustained a severe pulmonary contusion.

Continued on next page

Victor was dependent on artificial ventilation and nasogastric feeding due to his injuries. It was agreed by numerous consultants that treatment was not in Victor's best interests.

After four weeks in a vegetative state, Victor was classified as in a persistent vegetative state (PVS). Three days later, an aneurysmal re-bleed occurred further increasing intracranial pressure (ICP) resulting in a herniation of the cerebellar through the occipital bone and compression in the brain stem.

This process is know as coning, prognosis of which is a high probability of respiratory depression and brain-stem death by ischaemia.

The defendant, Dr Gerald Boatman Hades, completed the initial set of tests for brain-stem death alone and (according to other doctors later) surprisingly fast. He claimed that the patient was brain-stem dead and immediately proceeded to remove Victor's artificial ventilator and feeding tubes.

During the few minutes before Victor succumbed to natural death by asphyxiation, Dr Hades used his mobile phone to update his social networking status to '*Feelin' good*' after which he stated '*I win*' and left the room while whistling merrily.

It was discovered afterward that Victor had been having an affair with Dr Hades' wife. Dr Hades himself had known this for several months and desired retribution.

The judge at first instance dismissed the murder charge against Dr Hades on the grounds that on initial diagnosis of brain-stem death the deceased was in law already dead and, even if otherwise, despite the defendant having confirmed to have satisfied the *mens rea* element for murder, the judge was nonetheless bound by precedent from the House of Lords that the withdrawal of treatment from patients in a persistent vegetative state was permissible in law.

The prosecution now appeals, by way of an Attorney General's reference under s 36 of Criminal Justice Act 1972, to the Court of Appeal on the following grounds:

1. Whether death in law occurs upon initial diagnosis of brain-stem death.

2. Whether the withdrawal of treatment from patients in a persistent vegetative state with a direct intention to kill, rather than where it is solely in the patient's best interests, is permissible in law.

Figure 10.1 A sample moot question

ACTIVITY

Quick quiz

Look at the sample moot question above and then identify who needs to argue what point. To help you in this task complete the sentences below by summarising the different point each counsel would need to argue.

• Lead counsel for the appellant is arguing ....
• Lead counsel for the respondent is arguing ....
• Junior counsel for the appellant is arguing ....
• Junior counsel for the respondent is arguing...

Answers to this Activity can be found in the Appendix on page 263.

10.5.2 How to research

The sample moot question above involves two grounds of appeal and the initial concern of a mooter is to determine which ground of appeal is relevant to their role. As stated at Section 10.4.3, leading counsel will argue on the first ground(s) of appeal and junior counsel will argue on the second ground(s) of appeal. You must be clear as to which side of the argument you are to take, as it would be a catastrophic problem if you were to prepare and research the point of law from one side only to find out when it is too late that you should have been arguing the law from the other side.

Once you have established the relevant area of law and the specific issue that your role requires you to consider it is then time to start formulating your argument. The best place to *start* looking for inspiration is in the legal textbooks on that area of law; discover what the leading, pertinent issues and cases are, and what the academic commentary is like in respect of that area of law. Once you have a starting point you can begin to look in further detail at the cases, and other sources, and formulate your tactical game plan.

authorities

legal authority may be found in sources such as legislation, case law, government papers and academic writings etc.

persuasive precedent

a source of law that the courts can consult in deciding a case but are not bound to apply in reaching its conclusion

ratio decidendi

the judicial reasoning for the decision in a case. The *ratio* may be binding on future decisions depending on the court hierarchy

obiter dicta

judicial commentary made in passing which does not form part of the *ratio decidendi*

purposive approach

the interpretation of legislation by reference to the purpose of the legislation

literal approach

the interpretation of legislation by reference to the literal meaning of the words in question

submission(s)

a summary of the legal argument(s)

Ensure that you check the rules carefully in respect of the number of **authorities** that can be cited in the moot. Commonly the number of authorities per ground of appeal is capped at three, or at the very most four; the reason for this being that there is only a limited amount of time for the presentation of the arguments and therefore only a small number of authorities can be properly considered by the court. Sometimes the moot question itself will refer to an authority in the question, in which case this is to be treated as a free authority or court authority, and if you rely upon it then it will not count towards your authority total.

Once you have determined how many authorities you can rely on you then need to decide carefully as to what those authorities are to be. Choose cases with the weightiest powers of persuasion (preferably the Supreme Court or House of Lords, failing that then the Court of Appeal). Consider Privy Council decisions too as they may prove to be extremely persuasive in certain situations. Try to choose unanimous judgments wherever possible; however, this does not mean you cannot rely on minority or dissenting judgments, but be prepared to make strong arguments why the judge should follow a purely **persuasive precedent**. On the whole try and avoid citing textbooks and journals as authority; by all means use them to guide you in your argument preparation but then rely directly on the cases that the author has considered and, if you wish, use the author's arguments in your oral submissions.

You will need to be very familiar with every case that you cite. The judge will ask you questions on the facts of the cases, the *ratio decidendi* of the cases and possibly about any relevant *obiter dicta* in the cases. Your ignorance of any of these key parts of the judgment will quickly become apparent, which will only result in frustrating the judge and causing you acute embarrassment.

A detailed knowledge of the rules governing precedent and statutory interpretation is also vital. You are likely to be submitting that the judge in the moot follows, reverses, distinguishes or overrules previous case law. You will need to be able to tell the judge the circumstances in which each *can* and (in your view) *should* occur. Common mistakes made by novice mooters are to inform a moot judge hearing an appeal in the Court of Appeal that they have the power to overrule a previous House of Lords or Supreme Court decision or, when the case is based in the Supreme Court, that the court is bound by the decisions of the Privy Council, both of which are clearly incorrect. Similarly, you might be trying to persuade a judge to interpret legislation in a particular way. For example, you may wish the judge to adopt the **purposive approach** to interpretation; if so then be prepared to explain what the purpose of the legislation is, why this would be the preferred method to employ and why, for instance, the **literal approach** to interpretation would not be as suitable.

10.6 The written elements

The written elements to a moot are equally as important as the oral presentation. The idea behind the written element is to provide the court (and your opponent) with a summary of the legal argument that you intend to present. The most common method of doing this is by way of a 'skeleton argument', although occasionally a moot may require a more in-depth written summary, known as 'pleadings'.

10.6.1 The skeleton argument

A skeleton argument is a short document outlining the **submissions** that each party intends to adduce, and details the legal authorities they will be relying on. Each side will normally be expected to produce one document, which includes the submissions for both the lead and junior counsel. The individual moot rules will set out the expected format of the skeleton argument but it is normally standard practice that the skeleton will be no longer than one A4 side of paper in total; the production of an effective skeleton argument is an exercise in how to be concise.

The skeleton argument will contain details of the moot parties' and counsels' names. It will also list the grounds of appeal (copied from the moot questions) and the submission(s) on these.

How to formulate a submission

The submission(s) are the argument(s) you are presenting to the court on the ground of appeal. There is no limit to how many submissions you make in respect of an individual ground of appeal but you must bear in mind the time constraints imposed in respect of the presentation of the submissions and it is recommended that a maximum of three submissions are made in respect of a single ground of appeal. You do not, however, have to make three submissions and it may be more prudent to only make one or two submissions instead. It is the quality of the submissions that is the most important factor to take into account and often a single good submission will be more effective than three weak submissions; in fact including too many submissions just for the sake of it can weaken what would otherwise be a good skeleton (and presentation). The rule to follow is one of quality over quantity.

A submission must always include a 'why' or a 'because'. It is no good just making a general statement as to the law. For example:

'It is submitted that the defence of duress should not be available in respect of the offence of conspiracy to murder.'

This is a weak submission as it includes no 'because'. Why should the defence of duress not be available in respect of conspiracy to murder? The submission fails to explain the reasoning on which it is based. A better submission on this point would be:

'It is submitted that the defence of duress should not be available in respect of the offence of conspiracy to murder as the relevant legal principles indicate that to do so would be contrary to public policy.'

Here there is a 'because' included in the submission, this being that to extend the law on duress to the offence of conspiracy to murder would be against public policy. This is then the point that you would explain in detail during the course of your oral submissions, i.e. what the relevant legal principles are and which question of policy is involved.

A crucial point to remember in formulating your submission(s) is that it is not acceptable to simply restate the ground of appeal. The ground of appeal is the question that needs to be resolved by the court; your submission(s) are your suggestion to the court on how that question should be resolved.

Skeleton exchange

There are often strict rules surrounding the exchange of skeleton arguments between opposing teams (again refer to the moot rules to ensure that you are aware of what these are). It is standard practice that the skeleton argument should be sent to opposing counsel, the Master or Mistress of Moots and the judge (if another person) within a certain time frame. This will normally be set out as a number of working days (e.g. three) prior to the moot. Exchange in advance of the moot allows the judge to prepare relevant questions for the individual mooters, and it also allows the mooters time to anticipate these questions based on the contents of their opponents' submissions.

Below is reproduced a skeleton argument in relation to the sample moot question. Again, this skeleton has been kindly provided by Terence Wong, a former undergraduate student of Nottingham Law School, and it shows the high standard that can be achieved.

IN THE COURT OF APPEAL

Attorney General's Reference
(No. 5 of 2011)

SKELETON ARGUMENT ON BEHALF OF COUNSEL FOR THE APPELLANT

First ground of appeal:
Whether death in law occurs upon initial diagnosis of brain-stem death.

Submissions on the first ground of appeal:
The law should not accept the Royal Medical College's equation of brain-stem death as being the death of the individual. The 2008 Code of Practice does not represent the law and the law should accept no less than absolute death; irreversible cessation of heartbeat, breathing, and function of the brain and brain stem.

Continued on next page

Alternatively, if the law is to accord with the current medical definition of death, it must not be applied selectively. Chapter 6.3 of the 2008 Code of Practice demands repetition of brain-stem testing by two separate doctors before the death of the individual is confirmed; death does not occur upon initial diagnosis.

Authorities:
1. Working Party for the Royal College of Anaesthetists on behalf of the Academy of Medical Royal Colleges and Department of Health, *Code of practice for the diagnosis and confirmation of death*, (2008)
2. *Regina v Malcherek, Regina v Steel* [1981] 1 WLR. 690
3. *Could The Right To Die With Dignity Represent A New Right To Die In English Law?* Medical Law Review (2006) 14 (2): 219

Second ground of appeal:
Whether the withdrawal of treatment from patients in a persistent vegetative state with a direct intention to kill, rather than where it is solely in the patient's best interests, is permissible in law.

Submissions on the ground of appeal:
The judgment in *Airedale NHS Trust v Bland*, which permitting the omission of treatment as an exception to murder was *ultra vires*. Lord Lowry in *C (A Minor) v DPP* correctly identified that to invent a new defence to the fundamental legal doctrine of murder is beyond the capacity of judicial legislation; such a change must be made by Parliament.

Alternatively, the principle as created in *Bland* permits only the omission of treatment with indirect intention to kill. Therefore continuing the rationale behind the court's distinction between a positive act or omission, the objective and the legitimate withdrawal of treatment when treatment is futile must be to only satisfy the patient's best interests. The court was incorrect to identify the facilitation of Bland's death as the objective; death was merely coincidental.

Authorities:
1. *Airedale NHS Trust v Bland* [1993] AC 789
2. *C (A Minor) v Director of Public Prosecutions* [1996] AC 1

Figure 10.2 Example of a skeleton argument

10.6.2 Pleadings

Occasionally the moot rules will require the production of a set of written pleadings. These pleadings (or statement of case) are a more comprehensive outline of the submissions that are to be made to the court and will often contain extracts from the authorities relied on in support of the legal arguments, as opposed to simply the citation of the authority. Pleadings can vary in length and word limits, from approximately 1,000 to 6,000 depending on the particular competition.

10.6.3 The bundle

The host institution is often responsible for the production to the moot court of the authorities cited in the skeleton arguments; however it is prudent for each moot team to collate a 'bundle' in respect of the authorities they are to use. In fact best practice is for the moot team to produce three identical bundles: one for the moot judge, one for the opposing team and one for themselves.

The bundle is a tabulated and paginated folder that contains all the relevant sources in a logical and easy-to-access order. The order of the documents should be as follows:

- Copy of the moot question.
- Copy of the skeleton argument.
- Copy of the authorities in the order that they are to be referred to.

case head note

this is a case summary detailing both the outline facts and decision of the case. A head note should never be relied upon as authority

– If referring to case law you should include:
- the **head note** of the case
- the page(s) of the case that you are to quote from (you do not need to include the entire case).

You may highlight the relevant passages of the authorities that you intend to refer to for ease of reference, or alternatively you could highlight down the side of the passage.

10.7 Order of events

Most moots will follow a common prescribed order of events; however be aware that any individual moot may adopt a different format and therefore you should always ensure that you check the moot rules for every competition.

The mooters (and the audience) should take their seats prior to the entrance of the judge(s) and be prepared to moot upon the arrival of the judge(s); the judge(s) will be absent at the start. There is an expected seating order of counsel, as indicated in the diagram below. Counsel will face the judge(s) and (probably to the relief of some) will have their backs to the audience, if in fact there is an audience.

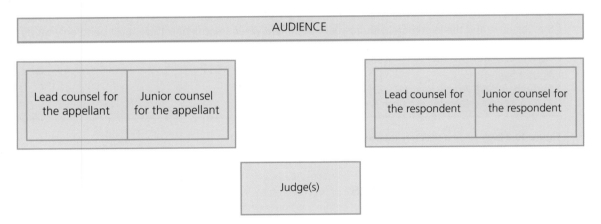

Figure 10.3 Moot court seating arrangements

When the judge(s) enter the court room all counsel and all members of any audience in attendance must be upstanding. Often the court clerk on introducing the judge(s) will knock on the court room door and ask the 'court to rise'. Upon entering the room the judge(s) will walk to the bench, bow and then tell the court to be seated. Unless you have a physical difficulty or disability and cannot stand, it is of the utmost importance that you do stand when the judge(s) enter the court room. When the judge(s) bows to the court you should acknowledge this with your own bow (which in reality is normally little more than an inclination of the head). To do otherwise shows disrespect to both the court and the rule of law.

The judge may then start proceedings by referring to the case in question, or may simply nod at leading counsel for the appellant to indicate that they should commence with their submissions.

Leading counsel for the appellant must first introduce the parties. The standard wording that is often used is:

'May it please your Lordship(s); I [insert name] appear with my learned junior [insert name] for the appellant. My learned friend [insert name] appears for the respondent with his/her learned junior [insert name]. In the instant case before the court today there are two grounds of appeal; I, and my learned friend [insert name] will be dealing with the first ground of appeal, and our learned juniors will be dealing with the second ground of appeal.'

It is also good practice for leading counsel for the appellant, after making the introductions, to ask the judge(s) if a brief statement of the facts of the instant case would be of assistance to them. The judge(s) may or may not agree to such a suggestion, but if the court indicates a brief summary would indeed be helpful, you must ensure that the summary is unbiased and objective. This is not an opportunity for the legal arguments to be asserted; that comes later. Nor should you just read aloud the question facts verbatim; ensure that you summarise the facts succinctly in your own words while encapsulating and explaining all the relevant facts.

ACTIVITY

Exercise

Referring back to the sample moot question of *Attorney General's Reference (No.5 of 2011)* formulate a summary of the pertinent facts. Present this to a friend or family member and ask them to give you feedback on your performance.

After a summary of the facts of the case, or if the judge(s) indicate that no summary is necessary, leading counsel for the appellant will then present the grounds of appeal in the case before moving on to present their own legal arguments to the court; this is often commenced by summarising the points of law made in their skeleton argument. An example of how this may be done is:

'In the instant case before the court today there are two grounds of appeal; I, and my learned friend [insert name] will be dealing with the first ground of appeal, which is [insert first ground of appeal]. Our learned juniors will be dealing with the second ground of appeal [insert second ground of appeal]. In respect of the first ground of appeal I have [insert number] submission(s) to make. These being [insert submissions]. With the court's permission I will commence with my first submission.'

There are two standard moot orders of events that are generally used for most mooting competitions. Which order of events format is adopted will be at the discretion of the institution or individual competition, and it is imperative that you check this out before each moot as the chosen order of events will impact on who speaks when. Below you will find tables detailing these common moot formats.

One further important point to note is the time limits imposed on individual mooters in a competition. Most mooting competitions, be they internal or external to your institution, will be the subject of time limits. This is to ensure that each mooter has sufficient time to present their legal argument but does not have the opportunity to monopolise proceedings, potentially at the detriment of the other mooters. The time limit is normally either 15 or 20 minutes (dependant on your role). It may seem unfair that you are only afforded a short time to present what could be a very complex legal argument, but the proceedings do need to be a reasonable length of time. Also one of the aims of a moot is to enable students to develop the skill of expressing themselves concisely and succinctly.

---

tutor tip

To stay within the time limit and do justice to your argument ensure that you have a clear plan of what you need to say, then say it once and don't repeat it. Repeating points will not make them seem more authoritative, but rather you will come across as being slightly desperate and this will make your argument seem less persuasive as a result.

Lead counsel for the appellant 20 minutes
Lead counsel for the respondent 20 minutes
Junior counsel for the appellant 15 minutes
Junior counsel for the respondent 15 minutes
Appellant's right of reply (not obligatory) 5 minutes

Figure 10.4 Standard order and timing of events

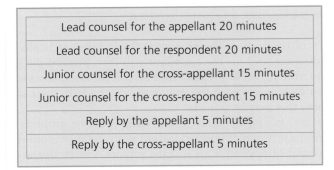

| Lead counsel for the appellant 20 minutes |
| Junior counsel for the appellant 15 minutes |
| Lead counsel for the respondent 20 minutes |
| Junior counsel for the respondent 15 minutes |
| Appellant's right of reply (not obligatory) 5 minutes |

Figure 10.5 Alternative order and timing of events

On an occasion where the moot takes the form of an appeal and cross-appeal, the order of speeches might be as follows:

| Lead counsel for the appellant 20 minutes |
| Lead counsel for the respondent 20 minutes |
| Junior counsel for the cross-appellant 15 minutes |
| Junior counsel for the cross-respondent 15 minutes |
| Reply by the appellant 5 minutes |
| Reply by the cross-appellant 5 minutes |

Figure 10.6 Order and timings of an appeal and cross-appeal

10.8 Notes for the moot

Never read from a script! This is one of the worst ways to present a moot. Having a script may make you *feel* more confident and secure; if it is all written down then you can't forget anything, right? Wrong! A structured script will make you sound wooden and less persuasive. If the judge asks you an unexpected question it will throw you off track; you may lose your place; and consequently you may forget to address an important point. The judge may ask you to start with your second submission first, then you will have to scramble through your notes to find the relevant point. The judge will not have the 'benefit' of having sight of your script and therefore cannot be expected to follow your carefully planned structure. The judge will have their own ideas as to how the issues should be addressed and this is unlikely to match with your own structure. You may think a script is a sure-fire way to ensure you cover every point and sound like you know what you are talking about but in reality it will be more of a hindrance than a help, making you sound at best unsure and at worst incompetent.

The ideal method for preparing your notes is to have a single A4 sheet of paper detailing a flowchart of bullet-pointed issues; each bullet point should be sufficient to remind you about everything you need to say in relation to it. As you address each point you then cross it off so as to ensure you do not repeat yourself. If the judge requests you deal with a point out of turn you can note this on your flowchart (strike it through once dealt with) and you will have clear sight of everything that still needs to be dealt with, ensuring you do not forget anything. However this is a method that requires confidence in your mooting abilities and it may be something that you need to work towards as opposed to it being something which you use in your first ever moot.

A good compromise is the use of note cards. On each note card deal with an individual point or issue. You can include more detail on a card than could be incorporated into a flowchart but you will not have enough space available on a card to include a structured script. As you cover the issues on a card, set it to one side so as to indicate to yourself that the matter has been dealt with. If the judge then asks you a question which is out of turn you can flip through to the relevant card, address the judge on the matter and then continue on with the next relevant card (or return to the card you were originally using prior to the judicial interruption).

The only time in which you can read to the court is when quoting from a case or other source of authority. When referring to such a quote make sure that you read it verbatim (word for word) and do not take the quote out of the context in which it was intended. The judge will be reading not just the quote you refer them to but also the passages preceding and following it on the page in the bundle. This is so as to check that you are not misquoting a judge or attempting to use the judicial commentary out of context in an effort to further your legal argument. The judge will have also read the authorities prior to the moot and so will be familiar with the content and the sentiment of them.

When introducing a quote to the court you must direct the judge's attention to the relevant passage. This can be done by saying something such as:

'If I could turn your Lordship's attention to the judgment of Lord Justice Judge at page 45, paragraph 3, the line beginning "The matter of policy…"'.

or a favourite phrase of mooters when referring to judicial commentary is:

'If I may echo the words of Lord Justice Judge at page 45, paragraph 3, where he states "The matter of policy…"'.

Remember to read any quote slowly and clearly so that the judge can appreciate what is being said, as if you race through the passage so that it is difficult to understand the persuasiveness will be lost.

Also remember to check that the judge is following you while you are delivering the quote and that, after you have presented the quote, you explain to the judge how you suggest it applies to the moot question.

10.9 Practice

Practice makes perfect? Well, yes and no. You should always practice prior to taking part in a moot. You need to check that your timings are correct and that you do not finish speaking within five minutes when you have 15 minutes to fill, or that you do not speak for 30 minutes when you only have 20 minutes in which to present your argument. However over-practising will make you sound scripted and staged, even if you are working from a flowchart. It is a balancing act between practising enough so that you are confident in your abilities and not practising too much so that your presentation still remains fluid. One thing that should be encouraged is practising in front of a mirror. If you watch yourself moot then you will probably be surprised at the unintentional things that you do: gesticulating with your hands, swaying backwards and forwards, constantly touching your hair or your ear or chin etc. All these things can be a distraction and detract from the content of your argument. This is why those studying on courses where advocacy is a key ingredient, such as the Bar Professional Training Course (the course to become a barrister), are video-taped in an effort for them to recognise and rectify their public-speaking idiosyncrasies.

Also, if you can find a willing audience to listen to you present your moot points then this form of practice can be very beneficial. If you present your arguments to someone with a limited (or no) understanding of the specific area of law and they can follow your arguments and find it persuasive then hopefully you are on the right lines and will succeed in convincing the court in the actual moot.

10.10 Court etiquette

The information and advice provided in this section may seem old fashioned, 'stuffy', and even blindingly obvious in places, but it is all equally important and needs to be both remembered and applied. A moot is not just about the legal content of the argument and moots have been won (and lost) due to the court etiquette of the mooters. A court, even a moot court, is a very formal setting and historical traditions are integral to the whole process; for example, referring to your legal opponent as *'learned'* is not only polite, but it is a recognition of the fact that they are learned in the law.

- Always stand up when addressing the court.
- Remain standing when being questioned by the judge.
- If interrupted by your opponent (and **never** interrupt your opponent), sit down while they address the court and then stand again when indicated to continue by the judge.
- If questioned by the judge while your opponent is speaking ensure you stand to respond – even if it is only to give a one-word answer.
- Refer to your team member (co-counsel) as your 'learned leader/junior'.
- Refer to your opposing counsel as either your 'learned friend' or 'lead/junior counsel for…'.
- Make sure you use the appropriate terms of address for your audience:
  – My Lord/My Lady – for when you would normally refer to the judge in the sentence by name.
  – Your Lordship/Your Ladyship – for when you would normally refer to the judge as 'you'.
- Female judges are *always* addressed as 'My Lady' or 'Your Ladyship'; refer to them as 'My Lord' (and vice versa!) at your peril!
- Never confuse 'my' and 'your' – 'My Lordship/Ladyship' or 'Your Lady/Lord' are not recognised terms.
- If you have a mixed Bench (male and female) do not refer to the Bench as 'Your Lordships'. Acknowledge that there is a female judge: 'Your Lordships and Your Ladyship'.
- In a criminal case, refer to the prosecution as 'The Crown', not 'The Queen', and certainly never as 'R' (as in the alphabet letter).
- Never express your own personal views on the matter (e.g. 'In my opinion, the defendant is innocent/the claimant is clearly right'). You are presenting a case on behalf of your lay client and so can only make submissions and, at the most, suggestions to the judge. You should certainly never tell the judge how you think the case should be decided.
- Cases referred to in the course of your submissions must be given with full case citations. This applies equally to both the written skeleton argument (see Section 10.6.1) and when referring to the case in the oral moot.
  – For example, if referring the judge to the case of *R v Brown* [1994] 1 AC 212 you **would** say:
    'The Crown against Brown, reported in the first volume of the Appeal Cases Law Reports for 1994 at page 212';
  – you **would not** say:
    'R (as in the alphabet letter)/The Queen versus Brown, 1994, one (the number) AC (again as in the alphabet letters) 212'.
- If you are not familiar with the citation of a case you intend to use then ensure that you find out what it means and how to say it beforehand. If you do not then you risk the embarrassment of the judge's rude comments.
- When you introduce a case in your arguments, ask if the judge would like to hear a brief summary of the facts of the case. If they would, ensure that you keep it brief and *do not* simply read from the case headnote. If the judge says that it is not necessary, do not go ahead regardless; simply move on to consideration of the relevant legal principle.
- Ensure that you listen to the submissions of counsel who present before you and any judicial responses and questions. For example, you do not want to offer the facts of a case to the court if counsel before you has given a detailed analysis of the same case; if you were to do this then it would appear to the court that you had not been paying attention to the proceedings and this could reflect negatively on the judge's perception of you as a mooter.

- When referring to a judge in a case, ensure you use his or her correct title. For example say 'Lord Justice Judge', not Judge 'LJ'.
- If you are mooting in the Supreme Court or in the Court of Appeal then the court should be referred to as 'The Court'. However, if you are referring to a decision made in the old House of Lords court then you should refer to it as 'The House', i.e. 'The question that was put before the House in the case of…'.
- Never interrupt the judge. If the judge asks you a question wait until he has finished speaking before answering. Do not butt in, be it in an effort to be helpful or in the hope that you will put him off.
- Do not gesticulate wildly while you are speaking. This may look expressive in certain circumstances but in a moot it will simply detract from what you are saying. Stand still; keep your feet and hands still; and do not fiddle with anything, such as a pen or your hair.
- Dress in appropriate court attire, either a suit or other suitable smart clothes. Appearance is important as it indicates the respect with which you regard the proceedings.

10.11 Effective advocacy

So what are the judges looking for?

- **Good technique** – Speak clearly and slowly. If you rush your speech you will lose the power of your argument. Do not rush even if you are quoting from a case and the judge has the extract before them. You are quoting for a reason – to make a point; do not hurry though it as if you do then that point will be lost.
- **Pause regularly** – Use silence to your advantage. If you make a good point then pause for a moment and allow the judge time to absorb what you have just said.
- **Make eye contact with the judge** – By making eye contact with the judge you will be able to gauge whether or not he is following your line of reasoning, and if he is with you or not in respect of it. If he appears not to be persuaded by your arguments then you can spot this and change tack accordingly (if you are simply staring at your papers you will miss this). At the end of one submission you should ask for permission to commence with your next one; the judge may simply nod in acknowledgement and, if you were not watching, you may again miss this which could result in an awkward silence.
- **Be expressive** – Make sure there is intonation in your voice. A judge is not going to be persuaded by counsel who sound bored by their own submissions.
- **Be brief** – Make your submissions as intelligible as possible, avoiding excessive use of legal jargon; the legal equivalent of 'blinding by science' is not an effective advocacy style.
- **Do not refer to authorities for the sake of it** – If you adduce an authority to the court then the judge may question you extensively on it. Be sure that you are prepared to recite a precise proposition as to why any case cited is authority and on what point it is authoritative.
- **Do not worry if you seem to have a weak legal argument** – There are two decisions the judge is required to make when determining a moot: a decision as to the law and a decision as to the moot. Even if you believe that you have a weak legal case it is still entirely possible for you to win the moot. It is how you make your arguments and how convincingly you express your points that wins (or loses) the moot.

SUMMARY

- A moot is a mock trial on a point of appeal.
- The benefits of mooting are great and varied and partaking in mooting at an undergraduate (or graduate) level will instil skills such as advocacy and mental agility, which will be invaluable in your later career.

- Mooting may be run by tutors or by the students, and it may be assessed or purely for fun.
- Mooting is not just about presenting an oral argument on a specific point of law; in fact the speaking element constitutes around only 25% of the activity, with the remaining 75% focusing on the research and written elements.
- The skeleton argument is a concise document detailing a succinct summary of the oral arguments that will be presented to the court; it is a signpost for both the judges and counsel.
- Each submission must have a point or a 'because' to it.
- Never read from a script. You will sound staged and insincere and will not be at all persuasive.
- Remember to abide by the expected court etiquette – some moots have been lost (and won) on this!

Further reading

Snape, J and Watt, G, *How to Moot: A Student Guide to Mooting*, Oxford University Press, May 2010.

11

Preparing for Examinations – Revision

AIMS AND OBJECTIVES

After reading this chapter you should be able to:

▓ Understand the difference between learning and revising
▓ Know when to start revising
▓ Understand the importance of time management
▓ Understand a variety of different revision aids
▓ Understand the importance of practising past exam questions
▓ Manage time effectively during revision
▓ Prepare revision aids that suit you personally
▓ Apply techniques to revise effectively
▓ Feel confident and prepared before exams

Revision is a dreaded time for many students. It is time consuming and stressful. But it is an unavoidable task. Being a law student requires memorising many cases and legal concepts. What makes an excellent law student is the ability to reproduce this information in the required format. It is therefore critical that the revision process goes well.

It also must be remembered that revision is an individual process. What works for one person may be a poor approach for another. It is important to experiment to find the right mix of techniques that work for you. For example, it is important that you are in the right environment. Think about the time of day, noise levels, the materials you need and the timing available. Using a mixture of techniques may be more effective than using just one. Failing to take these issues into account could mean you are wasting your time.

Revision should not be the start of your learning but a way of making what you already know and understand available to you in the exam. Revision can take up a lot of your time and for the best use of that time it should be organised and you must make use of effective techniques.

11.1 When to start

Revision is of course the last stage in the process before you actually sit your exam, although it may actually start a long time before the exam. In fact if you are going to achieve the most you can in the exam then you must prepare for your revision just as the revision itself is a preparation for the exam.

In terms of when to start, very often you will be having lectures right up to a couple of weeks before the exams. You are learning new information at this time but you cannot ignore the need to revise what you learnt earlier in the course. Remember, if you leave everything until the last minute then this gives you little chance of doing your revision effectively. If you suddenly realise how long revision is taking and that you have very little time left to do it all then it will only add to your anxiety.

Revision is to a law student as training is to a sportsman. Sportsmen train regularly to get their bodies in the appropriate physical condition to be able to take part in competitive events. This is really no different to the studying that you do throughout your course. The athlete trains his or her body and you must train your mind. Of course anyone who has been to a football or cricket match or watched an athletics meeting will see the competitors out on the field going through various exercises prior to the start of the contest. This is as vital as all the preparation done before. If the sportsman is not warmed up before the start of the event then he is unlikely to perform well because his muscles will be not be toned for the contest ahead. This is just the same as your preparation for the exam. If you have not exercised your brain sufficiently before the exam it may let you down. Just like with sports people and their training, the earlier you begin your programme the fitter and more finely tuned your mind will be. A span of short sessions spaced over a longer period is much more useful than 'burning the midnight oil' and cramming viciously at the last minute. So begin early.

11.2 Collecting materials

During your course of study you will have learnt a lot of detailed information on the law. It is almost inevitable that your sources of information will not have been broken down into manageable proportions for the purposes of revision. Many if not most textbooks are written mostly in lengthy prose. Until you are very proficient at note-taking your notes also are unlikely to be in a form that is most useful for revision purposes.

Your revision is what helps your memory in the exam to sift through all the detailed knowledge that you have and then to reproduce only the relevant parts from it. You need to be able to focus on the relevant areas of law from the limited information that you are given in the questions.

So before you start your revision you have ensured that you have all of the materials necessary in order to be able revise rather than learn from scratch. Make sure then that before revision you have done the following:

- You have read the necessary sections or chapters of textbooks and have made notes from them to supplement your lecture notes if you need to do so.
- You have checked all of your lecture notes are up to date and in a methodical order, fully amended with any additional information that you needed to supplement them with from other sources.
- If you intend to use in your revision any essays which you have written for your tutors during the course, or any materials that you have prepared for seminars, you have amended them to include any comments made by your tutors, or you have corrected any errors which were identified in them.
- If there are any important hand-outs that you have missed or lost, you have asked your teacher for replacements. Even if this makes you look inefficient it is far better than being without important information that is critical to your effective revision.
- If possible you have some revision aids already prepared such as those identified in Section 11.5 below.

One of the key aspects of your revision is that it is carried out in a methodical rather than a random way. That is one of the great benefits of a revision timetable such as that identified in Section 11.4 below.

You also need to be just as methodical about the materials you are using for revision. If you merely have a collection of books and notes in no particular order then you are less likely to be cohesive in the planning of your revision.

You will be revising more than one area of law. You should therefore have kept your notes in separate folders from the start of your course. Even within the different subjects you should consider your materials as a series of files. If you go on to work in a legal

student mentor tip

The more that you have been to tutorials and seminars the easier it is to organise your revision.

tutor tip

One of your first tasks then at the start of your revision is to go through all of your notes and text books and to prepare condensed versions of the important key points.

student mentor tip

Besides revision aids like key cards, your own notes are the best to revise from, so it is important to keep them organised throughout the course.

office you will certainly have to get used to working with files that are cohesively structured so that you can not only easily put your hand on the appropriate thing that you are working on but also even within the file move smoothly through it to the precise document you need at the time.

You should adopt the same approach to each subject you are studying.

- Treat each topic of the subject as a sub-file within the overall file that represents the subject as a whole.
- If you are keeping your materials for a subject within the same folder then it is a very good idea to use the cards (or dividers) that are provided with ring binders or something similar to separate the different topics.
- Have the name of the topic clearly written on this divider so that you can go straight to the topic you are currently revising.
- Within each sub-file representing a topic area separate your revision aids out into type with the most detailed to start and the more visual and punchier aids towards the end. This is so that you can revise first by reading through the most detailed information and then test yourself against the most abbreviated aids.

11.3 The difference between learning and revision

Learning is the process of gaining knowledge for the first time. Revision is a re-examination of knowledge already learnt to improve that knowledge for an examination. If you know that you have spent too little time preparing for tutorials, contributing in classes and reflecting and refining your knowledge, then you must be prepared for what should be the revision process to be a learning process. Accept that your mark in the exam will inevitably reflect this fact. It will be lower. This is true unless you notice this early enough to remedy the problem.

How can you tell whether you need to learn a topic or revise it?

ACTIVITY

Exercise

Take a piece of paper and choose a topic that you think will come up in the exam. Break it down into elements and list as many as you can. If the sheet is blank, you are going to have to learn it. If the sheet has a few vague comments and many gaps, that indicates a learning process is needed. If there are a few gaps, say of a couple of the elements and a few of the key case names for example, you should be ready to start your revision.

If you have lecture hand-outs or a module pack to hand, use the lecture outline as a starting point and identify which areas are your weakest. Do not fall into the common trap of learning and re-learning topics about which you are already confident. As comforting as it is to spend time reviewing law you already understand, it will do you no good if that topic does not come up in the exam.

Anyone who has ever sat an exam will know that revision is hard work and time consuming. However, as with everything, it is effective use of time that counts. Revision is not the same as learning afresh. It should be the final stage in the process. While you may be realising things during your revision that you had not thought of before, the process should essentially be about fixing in your mind in a methodical way things that you have already learnt.

11.4 Time management

One of the most important aspects of revision is managing your time effectively. Of course this can be said for any aspect of your study, whether it is in making sure that you are punctual for your lectures, organising your time in reading and following up lectures or being aware of the opening times of libraries and resources centres, and it even applies to the day of the exam itself. Time management is a critical factor in any area of your life, not just study.

Time management then is one of the most important aspects of your revision. If you merely sit in front of your book or notes and randomly select topics to read then this is likely to leave you unprepared for the exam, and it is likely that you will have no idea of how well or how poorly prepared you are.

11.4.1 Timing

Revision is often seen by many students as a period of intense cramming of case names and key concepts two to three weeks prior to an examination. This approach has many pitfalls. These include:

- **Lack of understanding of key cases and concepts** – On average a student will forget 80 per cent of information in a lecture within 48 hours.
- **Stress** – Cramming creates pressure as there is only a short space of time to memorise a significant amount of information.
- **A lack of resources** – Leaving revision late leaves little time to prepare revision notes and prepare and review past questions.
- **Focuses heavily on memorisation** – Leaving little time to consider other important examination techniques/factors such as making sure you can answer the question (not the question you want, but the question asked).

In order to make best use of your time you should prepare a revision programme for yourself and you should also make sure that you work to it. If you can start your revision four or six weeks before the exam then you have time to break it down into manageable sessions rather than wearing yourself out at the end. You can begin by identifying what are the harder areas you need to learn because you will need to spend more time on these.

ACTIVITY

Exercise

- On a blank sheet of paper, write out the cases and the concepts that were explained to you in your most recent lecture. Compare your response with your lecture notes.
- Repeat the process above, but now choose a lecture from four weeks ago.

There will be gaps, not only in terms of your ability to remember the cases and concepts, but you may also have found difficulty understanding some issues. It is important to realise that failing to review course material soon after it is delivered will result in the information not being retained. This can mean that in a short space of time you may not be able to recollect the important cases and concepts. The normal cycle of intensive revision prior to an exam will not compensate for this. Can you really memorise six months of lectures in four weeks when you have little familiarity with the subject content?

Revision is therefore an ongoing process. There are three key phases:

- long term
- medium term
- short term.

11.4.2 Long term

Review your lecture notes as soon as possible. Highlight and fill in any gaps within your course notes. Review and research the areas that you do not fully understand – using tutorials and set texts as the basis to seek clarity regarding cases and materials will help with this process. Put your lecture notes in a format that is accessible to you. Collect the necessary case and journal materials and organise them in a logical and accessible order. Then, for each topic produce an overview. See Figure 11.1 overleaf for an example. This will provide you with an accessible overview of the key issues and cases and will be a useful tool for revision.

By doing this you are:

- improving understanding
- improving the retention of information
- preparing revision aids.

11.4.3 Medium term

Your objective is to refresh your mind on prior learning. You therefore need to review the information you prepared in your long-term phase. This process is not time consuming – it should only take 20–30 minutes per topic.

<table>
<tr><td colspan="2" align="center">**Precedent**</td></tr>
<tr><td colspan="2">**Key Terms**
Stare decisis
Ratio decidendi
Obiter dicta
Overruling
Reversing
Distinguishing</td></tr>
<tr><td colspan="2" align="center">Court structure</td></tr>
<tr><td>**Criminal**</td><td>**Civil**</td></tr>
<tr><td>ECJ</td><td>ECJ</td></tr>
<tr><td>Supreme Court</td><td>Supreme Court</td></tr>
<tr><td>Court of Appeal Criminal Division</td><td>Court of Appeal Civil</td></tr>
<tr><td>Queen's Bench Division</td><td>Divisional Courts</td></tr>
<tr><td>Crown Court</td><td>High Court</td></tr>
<tr><td>Magistrates'</td><td>County Court</td></tr>
</table>

System operates by decisions in higher courts having to be followed by lower courts.

Key Concepts

1) Originally Practice Statement 1996 – allows **House of Lords** to move away from past decision when right to so

Cases relevant

London Street Tramways v London County Council
Conway v Rimmer
Herrington v BRB
R v Shivpuri

2) **Court of Appeal's** role
Cases relevant

Young v Bristol Aeroplane
R v Gould
Gallie v Lee
Miliangos v George Frank Textiles

3) **Human Rights Act** section 2(1)(a)
Cases relevant   *Re Medicaments No. 2*

Figure 11.1 Example of an overview sheet

ACTIVITY

Exercise

1. Use the overview sheet and try to explain the issues it mentions. Where there are gaps, revisit the subject content that you have difficulty remembering.
2. Look at past examination questions on the topic and prepare some responses. This may highlight a lack of information in certain areas and prompt the need to revisit the subject content or carry out further research.
3. Produce a concept map on this area. (See Section 11.5.7, page 223 for concept maps.)

This can:

- improve your memory of key cases and concepts
- highlight specific areas of memory loss
- build your confidence in applying these areas of study.

11.4.4 Short term

This is the last process before the exam. In terms of timescale, it normally relates to the two- to three-week period prior to the exam. The aim is to commit the required knowledge to memory. The first task is to produce a revision timetable. This is not a work of art and should not be time consuming. It is important that it is an effective aid. The revision plan should therefore be:

- **Specific** – The revision plan must include not only what you are going to revise but when and for how long.
- **Measurable** – You need to be able to measure the success of the memorisation process. This can be done by getting somebody to test you on the cases and materials you have revised, or by attempting past questions related to your revision topics.
- **Achievable** – There is no point in setting unrealistic targets and goals. Can you really fully understand the whole of EU law within two hours?
- **Realistic** – The plan must focus on how you work. Do not set a start time of 6.30 am if you are not a morning person. You need to take into account a number of factors that will dictate the plan.

Time out

Certain times or days need to be blocked out due to other commitments, for example lectures, playing sport, part-time jobs, etc. This may highlight the need to reduce your commitments or extend the length of the short-term revision phase.

Location

Where are you going to revise? You need to consider access to resources, potential distractions and noise levels.

Ongoing

Your revision plan is a working document; for instance it changes as you progress. Certain topics could take longer than others, while you may find some relatively easy to absorb. It is also important to tick or cross areas you have covered. It will provide a motivational boost through giving a sense of completion.

Time related

There needs to be a time context. Timing relates to two issues:

- the length of time for the short-term revision phase, and
- how long you are spending on individual topics. There is no set time for these two issues.

They are dictated by:

- the success of the long- and medium-term revision process
- individual memorisation skills
- number of exams or topics requiring revision.

It is important not to underestimate the time needed in this phase as you could find yourself in the unfortunate position of not completing the required revision before the exam. It is necessary to leave free space at the end of the cycle as a contingency.

Revision timetable example

Time	9–10	10–11	11–12	Lunch	1–2	2–3	3–4	4–5
Day 1	Omissions	Omissions	Causation		Causation	Lecture	Lecture	Seminar
Day 2	Seminar	Lecture	Murder		Murder	Plan answers to causation, omission and murder	Watch TV	Meet friends
Day 3 sport	Review prior topics for gaps	Loss of control	Loss of control		Play sport	Play sport	Play sport	Play sport
Day 4	Loss of control	Lecture	Seminar		Diminished responsibility	Diminished responsibility	Work	Work
Day 5	Lecture	Lecture	Work	Work	Work	Work	Work	Work
Day 19	Contingency							
Day 20	Contingency							

Figure 11.2 A section of a sample revision plan

ACTIVITY

Exercise

- Make a list of the modules on which you will be examined.
- For each module make a list of the examinable topics.
- Estimate how long it will take to memorise and apply these topics and record this on the table.
- Work out the number of days available for revision.
- Select your start and finish times.
- Make a list of the times and activities that prevent revision in those slots.
- Place all the information into the plan. This may call for an adjustment by either increasing the days or removing certain leisure activities.
- Leave two days at the end of the plan blank to give flexibility in case certain topics cause delay.

You should in any case prepare your revision programme a long time in advance of your actual revision. Then you will be able to make a note as you go along how much time you need to give individual areas.

11.5 Preparing revision aids

The key to good revision is to bring your existing knowledge and understanding into a form that can stay in your mind and be easily remembered during the exam itself. Reading your textbooks over and over again is very time consuming. In any case, you can only read to remember in short bursts and chapters of most law textbooks take a long time to read. Besides this you are unlikely to remember large and detailed bodies of information effectively. The proper time to read your textbooks is during the course.

This is also the time when you should be extracting key points of information as we have already seen in Chapter 3.

As the exam gets closer it will be very time consuming continuously to read over your lecture notes time after time. Once you have the essential knowledge you need to reduce the time you spend looking at each individual area. For this you need to prepare revision aids that will have sufficient information to jog your memory and to focus your attention on things that you do not so easily remember so that you can go back to these in your books or lecture notes. However, they do not need to be extensive. Students do this 'reducing' in many forms and there are even books on the market that do the same very effectively, such as the *Key Facts* series published by Hodder Education. However, even those may be quite detailed and be more lengthy to read through than you may want or need.

Revision aids are the means of unlocking your knowledge. They are a system of mapping knowledge. If you were to go into any office, legal or otherwise, and look at the filing cabinets you would find little cards on the front of each drawer. If they are only arranged 'A–C', 'D–G', 'H–L' etc. you would know to look in the file 'H–L' if you wanted for instance to look for the file on Mrs Huxley-Binns. Within that file you would then be able to find all the information you have on that particular client.

A good textbook will operate in exactly the same way. You can look in the contents list and see for instance that the chapter on occupier's liability in tort is Chapter 8. Even within that contents list you can find more particular information because a good textbook will have sub-headings as well as chapter headings. So you might find for instance that liability to lawful visitors under the Occupiers' Liability Act 1957 is in Chapter 8, Section 8.2. A good textbook will go even further so that you can find that Section 8.2 has sub-sections also. You might be able to find: Section 8.2.1 Potential claimants; Section 8.2.2 The scope of the Act – the common duty of care; Section 8.2.3 Liability to children; Section 8.2.4 Liability to persons entering exercising a calling; Section 8.2.5 Liability for the torts of independent contractors; and Section 8.2.6 Avoiding the duty. If your question in the exam involves some children injured on premises and also that this has resulted from some faulty work done on the premises by some independent contractors, then you would very quickly realise that what you need to know is in Sections 8.2.3. and 8.2.5.

You should be able to operate this methodically in the exam, getting right to specific aspects of your knowledge that relate to the questions in front of you. Revision aids can help this process. They act as the list of letters on the front of the filing cabinet or the contents list of the textbook. For this reason they all involve reducing the information that you already have to a manageable amount. They should contain the essential pointers but never be overloaded with information.

It may be helpful to develop the skill of producing your own example of the art. This can be done in different ways as long as you end up with something that has a brief reference to all the relevant and necessary information and it is an effective memory jogger for you personally.

There are numerous examples of revision aids that can be used and you should always aim to choose a type of aid that suits the way that you remember. Below are a number of different examples. This is by no means an exhaustive list. There are as many ways of producing revision aids as there are students who have to revise.

11.5.1 Repetition and review

On the face of it this is one of the simplest ways of revising and it certainly involves the least preparation. This involves the reading of notes constantly. Periodic reviews are undertaken to test the absorption of information into the memory. Variations on this method involve rewriting notes. The merits and defects of this method of revision are outlined below.

Merits

- simple
- needs no resources other than the notes or books that you already have.

Defects

- lack of focus on certain skills, e.g. exam timing
- takes a significant amount of time
- it is passive method and some learners may become easily bored
- it is not systematic.

11.5.2 Revision aids: making key cards

Perhaps the most common example that we see students produce is in the form of a key card, reducing the information to its barest form. In fact listening to students and learning from the ways that students choose to revise is at the heart of the *Key Facts* revision books. Key cards are a very personal thing. You should practise getting just the right amount of information into these aids with just the amount of detail that you think is necessary. Different students will want to include different amounts of detail but you should never include too much detail so that it becomes like reading your notes or reading your textbook.

Criminal law is a classic example of where you have to remember sections of Acts as well as the appropriate cases, as well as having a clear understanding of how the law applies. In the exam you will need to remember all of this. Below is an example of a key card on the area of duress by threats, which can be quite a difficult area but can still be reduced to some essential elements. Try practising the same for all of the offences and defences but remember to include the appropriate cases and sections as this does. You should use the key cards as a constant means of memorising the area on the card. Try to use them as we have looked at already, not just to memorise the specific details on the card but as a way of remembering other detail not contained. If you cannot remember specific details when you are testing yourself or being tested go back to your notes on that detail and look at them again.

Duress by threats

Definition
The defendant escapes liability as a result of a successful defence having provided an acceptable excuse for his behaviour.

The defence is thus a 'concession to human frailty'.

Test for whether the defence applies
The two-part test in *Graham*:

- That the defendant's will was overborne by threat of imminent violence to self or close family – so that the defendant was impelled to act as he did.

- That the court is satisfied that a sober person of reasonable firmness would have been similarly affected by the threats and would have reacted in the same way.

Role of jury
To apply the test to the facts of the case.

Availability

- Generally available.
- But not available to murder or secondary participation in murder – *Howe*.
- Nor to attempted murder – *Gotts*.
- But is available to a charge of s 18 GBH.

Continued on next page

Continued

Limitations created by the courts
- Not available if there is no nexus between the threat and the offence committed by the defendant – *Cole*.
- Rarely available if self-induced (*Shepherd*) unless the defendant is unaware of the violent tendencies of his associates.
- So not available where the defendant voluntarily associates with persons of known violent tendencies – *Sharp, Hasan*.
- Not available if a safe means of escape exists – *Hudson & Taylor*.
- Not available if the threat is not imminent – *Abdul Hussain*.
- Not available where the threat is not one of violence – *Valderrama-Vega*.

Figure 11.3 Example of a key card for duress by threats

11.5.3 Cue cards

This is a more specific type of key card and can be used for instance as a memory jogger for individual cases. It involves putting cases and their important issues on cards. Cards are normally placed in date order or information order. Learners then memorise by continuously reviewing the cards. This allows you to memorise the law as it progressed or is logically explained.

Take the example below. Both the brief facts of the case are indicated as well as the key issues arising from the case. A brief recitation of the facts of the case is important for being able to apply the law in problem questions.

R v Cunningham
Facts
D broke into a gas meter to steal the money. Gas leaked out of the damaged meter and seeped into the house next door. The next door neighbour became seriously ill. D was charged with maliciously administering a noxious substance so as to endanger life.

Key issues – relevance to revision
- is the leading case for recklessness
- made recklessness a subjective test
- there have been tests different to this but this was seen as the most acceptable.

Figure 11.4 Example of a cue card for *R v Cunningham*

Key cards and cue cards are really just different names for the same type of aid, although as they are presented here they are achieving slightly different ends. It is an entirely personal decision how you use them and what amount of detail you include. The merits and defects of both of the above aids are as follows:

Merits

- quick to prepare
- portable so you can test yourself on the move
- easy to use
- can involve others to test you.

Defects

- lack of focus on certain skills, e.g. how to use the information to answer the question within the time restraints of the exam
- it is passive and certain learners may become bored
- it is easy for the cards to become muddled. You will need strong organisational skills to ensure different topics are categorised appropriately.

11.5.4 Revision aids: reducing statute law to key elements

Again textbooks rarely reduce law to its essential elements. Criminal law is a classic example of where the law can be quite hard to remember simply in the form in which you usually find it. You will have to know all of the various aspects of many sections of different Acts and this can be quite frightening if you are simply trying to remember the sections off by heart as was traditionally demanded of law students. A better way is to reduce the lengthy wording of the sections to simple key elements. You must of course understand the wording of the sections before you can do this. Putting a statute in a simplified form may prove to be a much quicker and easier way to revise than trying to learn all of the various sections from the Acts themselves.

Essential elements of crimes

The following are the essential ingredients of many of the major areas of crime studied on most degree courses.

Offences against the person

Murder

1. A sane person over the age of 10
2. Unlawfully cause the death of
3. A living human being
4. Within the jurisdiction of the English courts
5. With intent:
   a) to kill; or
   b) to commit GBH

Constructive manslaughter

1. A sane person over 10
2. Intentionally or recklessly
3. Does an unlawful and dangerous act
4. Which causes the death of
5. A living human being
6. Within the jurisdiction of the courts

Gross negligence manslaughter

1. A sane person over the age of 10
2. Acting under a duty
3. Does an act or omission which is so negligent that it goes beyond mere compensation and amounts to a crime
4. That causes the death of
5. A living human being
6. Within the jurisdiction of the courts

Wounding with intent – contrary to s 18, Offences Against the Person Act 1861

1. Unlawfully and
2. [Maliciously]
3. a) wounds; or
   b) causes GBH
4. To any person
5. With intent to
   a) cause GBH
   b) resist lawful arrest

Continued on next page

Unlawful wounding – contrary to s 20, OAPA 1861

1. Unlawfully and
2. Maliciously
3. a) wounds, or
   b) inflicts GBH
4. On any person

Assault occasioning actual bodily harm – contrary to s 47, OAPA 1861

1. Does an act (assault or battery)
2. That causes another
3. Actual bodily harm
4. a) intending to cause apprehension/inflict violence
   b) reckless as to whether apprehension/violence is caused

Common Assault – s 39, Criminal Justice Act 1988

1. Does an act
2. a) causing another apprehension of immediate and unlawful violence
   b) inflicting violence on another
3. a) intending to cause apprehension/inflict violence
   b) reckless as to whether apprehension/violence is caused

Offences against property

Theft – contrary to s 1 Theft Act 1968

1. Dishonestly
2. Appropriates
3. Property
4. Belonging to another
5. With the intention to permanently deprive the other of it

Robbery – contrary to s 8, Theft Act 1968

1. Steals (*actus reus* and *mens rea* of theft)
2. Immediately before or at the time of the theft
3. Uses force or puts in fear of force
4. For the purpose of stealing

Burglary with intent – contrary to s 9(1)(a), Theft Act 1968

1. Enters
2. A building or part of a building
3. As a trespasser
4. With intent to
   a) steal
   b) inflict GBH on a person therein
   c) cause criminal damage

Burglary – contrary to s 9(1)(b), Theft Act 1968

1. Having entered
2. A building or part of a building
3. As a trespasser
4. a) steals
   b) inflicts GBH
   c) attempts either

Continued on next page

Making off without payment – contrary to s 3, Theft Act 1978

1. A person knowing payment on the spot is required
2. Dishonestly
3. Makes off without having paid as required or expected
4. Intending to avoid payment

Criminal damage – contrary to s 1(1), Criminal Damage Act 1971

1. Without lawful excuse
2. Destroys or damages
3. Property
4. Belonging to another
5. a) intentionally
   b) recklessly

Recklessly endangering life – contrary to s 1(2), Criminal Damage Act 1977

1. Without lawful excuse
2. Destroys or damages
3. Property
4. Belonging to himself or another
5. a) intentionally, or
   b) recklessly
6. a) intending to endanger life, or
   b) reckless as to whether life is endangered

Inchoate offences

Attempt – contrary to s 1, Criminal Attempts Act 1981

1. With intent to commit an offence
2. Does an act
3. More than merely preparatory to the commission of the offence

Conspiracy – contrary to s 1, Criminal Law Act 1977

1. Agrees
2. With another person or persons
3. To pursue a course of conduct
4. Amounting to or involving an offence
5. Intending to play a part

Incitement

1. Communicates encouragement or persuades
2. Another person
3. To commit an offence
4. Intending an offence is committed

Figure 11.5 Example of the key elements of an area of law

Although the defences are mostly creations of the common law rather than Parliament, they are still difficult to remember if you are trying to do so from the chapters of textbooks. Just as we have created a simpler version of the elements of the offences themselves, we can do the same for the important elements of the various defences.

The following are the essential elements of the major defences studied on all courses. In their simplified form they should prove to be a quicker revision aid than learning the definitions supplied in the judgments of cases or even sometimes than the rather lengthy explanations given in some textbooks.

Essential elements of defences

Incapacity through age (infancy)

1. Based on irrefutable presumption
2. That a child under the age of ten
3. Is incapable of forming criminal intent – so no *mens rea*

Insanity

1. Available to all crimes
2. Can mean defendant:
   a) is incapable of pleading; or
   b) was incapable of forming *mens rea* at time of crime
3. Based on a legal rather than a medical definition
4. Defendant is:
   a) labouring under a defect of reasoning
   b) caused by a disease of the mind (internal factor)
   c) and does not know the quality of his act
   d) or if he does, he does not know that what he did was wrong

Non-insane automatism

1. Defendant
   a) has no voluntary actions – so is not responsible for the *actus reus*; and
   b) is unconscious of his deeds – so has no *mens rea* either
2. So based on
   a) an act done without any conscious control
   b) such as a reflex, spasm, convulsion
3. Will be caused by an external factor, e.g.
   - concussion
   - attack by a swarm of bees
   - anaesthetic
   - but not sleepwalking

Intoxication

1. Covers alcohol and drugs
2. Voluntary intoxication is not a complete defence
   a) but can be a defence to specific intent offences, e.g. murder if *mens rea* not formed
   b) but not in basic intent offences where voluntary intoxication will be recklessness
3. Involuntary intoxication
   a) is no defence if D had necessary *mens rea* when committing the offence
   b) but can be a defence where D does not have the necessary *mens rea*

Consent

1. In some ways not really a defence since if the victim consents there is no offence
2. In theft consent to appropriation does not necessarily remove liability
3. In assault the consent means the action is not unlawful – so is common, in e.g. contact sports
4. Not generally available to wounding or GBH on public policy grounds
5. But consent to assault in a domestic context may be accepted
6. A genuinely mistaken belief in consent may be accepted

Continued on next page

Continued

Duress

1. A 'concession to human frailty'
2. D has a defence when he committed the crime under threat of violence to himself or his family and a person of reasonable firmness would have done the same
3. But there must be a connection between the threat and the crime
4. Not available as a defence to murder, attempted murder, being an accomplice to a murder
5. Not available if D
   - could have escaped but did not
   - voluntarily associated with the maker of the threats knowing of his violent character

Duress of circumstances

1. Available as a defence if from an objective view the accused acted reasonably and proportionately to avoid the threats
2. Available to all crimes except murder, attempted murder, being an accomplice to a murder
3. There must be
   - imminent peril of death or serious injury to death or others within D's responsibility
   - the jury must be satisfied that the threat overbore D's will at the time of committing the offence
   - execution of the threat need not be immediate

Necessity

1. Traditionally not considered to be available for any offence
2. And this could work unfairly
3. Now linked to duress of circumstances
4. Possible now in rare cases – but only if
   - the act is needed to avoid inevitable and irreparable evil
   - no more is done than is reasonably necessary for the purpose to be achieved
   - the evil inflicted is not out of proportion to the evil avoided

Mistake

1. To be a successful defence the mistake must be one of fact not law
2. So that if the facts were as D believed
   - there would be no *mens rea*; or
   - D would have been able to rely on another defence
3. The mistake need only be an honest mistake – it does not have to be reasonable
4. A drunken mistake may negate the *mens rea* of the offence

Self-defence

1. Available as a complete defence on the basis of justification
2. Can use self-defence to protect self, others or property
3. But only possible where the defendant has used reasonable force

Where murder is charged there are also some partial defences that have been identified in the Homicide Act 1957. They are not complete defences because they merely reduce the charge to one of manslaughter and remove the mandatory life sentence. They also can be represented in a simple form.

Diminished responsibility

1. Section 52 Coroners and Justices Act 2009
2. Defendant suffered from
   - an abnormality of mental functioning
   - arose from a recognised medical condition
3. This substantially impaired his ability to
   - understand the nature of this act
   - form a rational judgment
   - exercise self control

Continued on next page

Defendant lost control – which need not be sudden

Because of a qualifying trigger:

- Fear of serious violence from the victim or another; or
- Things said and/or done; or
- A combination of the above

A person of the defendant's sex and age with a normal degree of tolerance and self-restraint in the same circumstances would have reacted in the same way.

Failed suicide pacts

1. Section 4, Homicide Act 1957
2. Defendant
   - agreed with one or more people
   - to carry out a course of action that would result in their deaths
   - and the other person(s) died
   - but the defendant did not
3. The defence can satisfy the court that there was in fact a suicide pact

---

Figure 11.6 Example of the key elements of defences

The merits and defects of the above aids are as follows:

Merits

- more portable than textbooks or even your notes so you can test yourself on the move
- quite easy to use and to memorise in this form
- less bulky than key cards and reasonably easy to organise
- other people can test you.

Defects

- lack important detail that you still need, i.e. the case law
- you must understand the sections well to be able to complete such a list so it may be time consuming to create
- lack of focus on certain skills, e.g. exam timing.

11.5.5 Revision aids: diagrams and charts

Most complex information can be reduced into diagram form and there is no end to the types of diagram that you might use. Diagrams are visual so they are a good stimulus for memory.

The following is a very basic diagram from tort illustrating the essential elements required for proving an action in negligence:

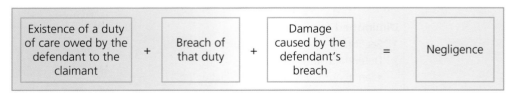

Figure 11.7 The basic elements of an action for negligence

The following is another simple diagram from contract law illustrating the difference between the past consideration in operation and its exception from the rule in *Lampleigh v Braithwaite*:

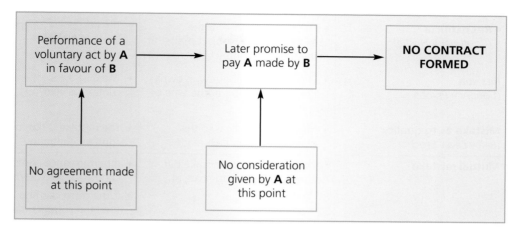

Figure 11.8 The operation of the past consideration rule

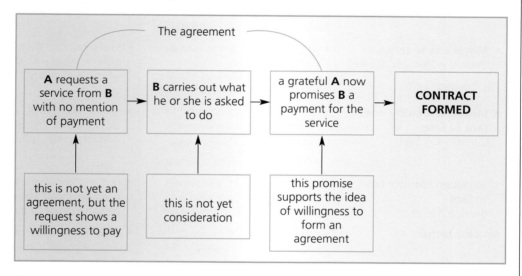

Figure 11.9 The exception in *Lampleigh v Braithwaite* in operation

Of course the diagrams above are only illustrating fairly narrow areas even of topics within a single subject. Consideration is an important area in contract law but it includes many more significant aspects than the past consideration rule.

You can of course use diagrams and charts to cover a whole area of law. Then inevitably you have to think carefully about the amount of information that you include or the diagram will become too big or too cumbersome for you to revise from effectively.

Below is a chart that in effect covers the whole of a large and quite complex area in contract law, the law of mistake. It gives a full understanding of all the different types of mistake and how they differ in their essential elements. What are missing from it of course are many of the cases that you would also need to learn, although some have been included as an illustration.

The class of mistake	The character of the mistake	The legal consequences of the mistake
Common mistake	The same mistake is made by both parties:	
• *Res extincta* (*Couturier v Hastie*)	• The mistake concerns the existence of the subject matter at the time the contract is made	• The mistake is 'operative' and the contract is void
Res sua (*Cooper v Phibbs*)	• The mistake is about who owns the subject matter at the time of contracting	• The mistake is 'operative' and the contract is void
Mistake as to quality (*Bell v Lever Bros*)	• Mistake is merely as to the quality of the bargain made	• The mistake is not 'operative' – contract continues
Mutual mistake	Both parties make a mistake but not the same one – they are at cross purposes	• If performance is impossible then the contract is void (*Raffles v Wichelhaus*) • If the court can find a common intent then the contract may continue (*Smith v Hughes*)
Unilateral mistake	Only one party is mistaken – the other party knows and takes advantage of the first party's mistake:	
• Mistake as to terms (*Hartog v Colin and Shields*)	• (i) One party mistaken over a material detail; (ii) Other party knew of mistake; (iii) Mistaken party not at fault.	• If all three mistake is 'operative' and contract void – if not then may be voidable in equity
• Mistaken identity not face to face (*Cundy v Lindsay*)	• (i) Mistaken party intended to contract with someone else; (ii) Mistake material to contract; (iii) Mistake known to other party.	• If all three mistake is 'operative' and contract void – if not then may be voidable in equity
• Mistaken identity face to face (*Lewis v Avery*)	• Party contracts in person with someone who claims to be someone else	• Not an 'operative' mistake – mistaken party deemed to be contracting with person in front of him
Non est factum	• Mistake concerns nature of the document being signed • The document is (i) Materially different to what it was represented to be; (ii) There is no negligence by the person signing it.	If both are present then there is an 'operative mistake' – the contract is void – but if not then there is no effect on contract (*Saunders v Anglian Building Society*)

Figure 11.10 The different types of mistake and their legal consequences

Another way in which a diagram can be useful as a revision aid is when you need to understand the differences or connections between different areas of law. This may be appropriate because you could be called on to make a comparative analysis in the exam. It may even be useful for you in understanding problem questions on areas that seem fairly similar. You may then more easily work to the correct area, as the diagram has helped your basic recognition in reading the scenario.

Below is an example of a chart of that type on the basic differences between the various torts concerning land.

	Trespass to land	Private nuisance	Public nuisance	*Rylands v Fletcher*
Claimants	A person in possession of land	A person with a proprietary interest in land	A member of a class of Her Majesty's citizens	A person harmed by the escape of the dangerous thing
Defendants	Any person carrying out the trespass	A landowner, or a person creating or adopting nuisance	A person creating nuisance	A person in control of land from which thing escapes
Duration of interference	A single trespass is enough	Must be continuous	A single interference is enough	A single escape is enough
Directness	Must be direct	Must be indirect	Could be direct or indirect	Could be direct or indirect
Need to prove fault	Actionable *per se* – so no need to prove fault	Requires unreasonable use of land – which is similar	Fault need not be proved	*Cambridge Water* says foreseeability is required – so suggests fault
Locality of interference	Not relevant	Relevant unless damage is caused	Could be relevant, e.g. to losing client connection	Could be relevant in deciding what is non-natural
Availability of damages	Any damage related to the trespass – and no need to show damage	Physical harm, personal injury to proprietor, economic loss	Physical harm, personal injury, economic loss	Physical loss and personal injury
Defences	Customary right to enter, common law right, statutory right, consent, necessity, licence	Statutory authority, prescription, consent, act of stranger, public policy, over sensitivity of claimant	General defences	Consent, common benefit, act of a stranger, or God, statutory authority, contributory negligence
Whether also a crime	Yes – possible under some Statutes	No – unless statutory	Yes – can be	No

Figure 11.11 The similarities and differences between the torts relating to land

11.5.6 Revision aids: using flow charts

Particularly in the case of problem questions in an exam where you have to apply the law, often in sequence, flow charts can be a very useful way of preparing yourself. A good flow chart is one that asks and then answers the type of questions that you would need to ask yourself in the exam in order to tackle the problem.

If you understand the major elements of the particular area of law then they are reasonably easy to prepare and you can find examples in a number of student-focused textbooks.

In the exam if you apply the type of checklist that comes from a good flow chart then you should be able to go methodically through the question and answer all parts of the problem effectively.

The first example below is a very simple flow chart still explaining the difference between an offer and an invitation to treat, something you will learn very early on in your contract law course.

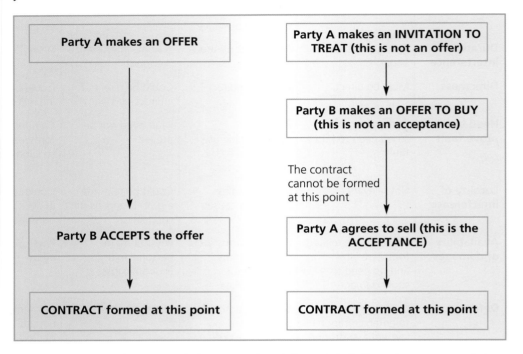

Figure 11.12 Showing the point at which a contract is made in a standard offer and acceptance, and where there is firstly an invitation to treat

You can develop flow charts for information that involves one relatively simple aspect of a topic as above. You can also use them to cover a whole topic. The example on the next page from tort on occupiers' liability under the Occupiers' Liability Act 1957 is an example of that.

One of the things that is missing from the above is the cases that you need to use to illustrate your answer, but you can use your key cards to include that information. The above flow chart is still relatively simple because the information is not that complex. But you can use a flow chart for even very complex information as in the example below on registering land charges in land with unregistered title. This is an area of land law that students often find very daunting.

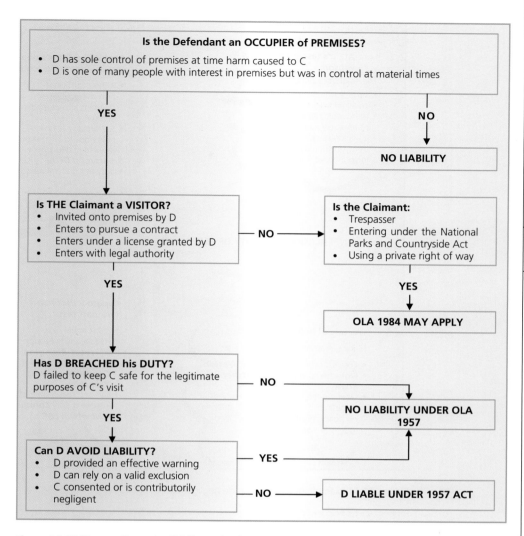

Figure 11.13 Diagram illustrating liability under the Occupiers' Liability Act 1957

student mentor tip

The mind maps in the front of the *Key Facts* books can save you time making your own.

11.5.7 Concept/mind maps

This involves producing a graphic overview of a subject. It is not about recording every detail within a set topic. It is a summary chart showing the logical links. This can be done freehand or by computer. The use of various colours can improve the memorisation process and words can be substituted for pictures to give memory links.

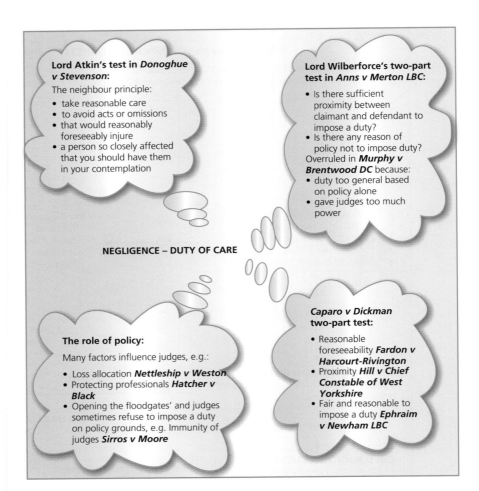

Figure 11.14 Example of a mind map on negligence

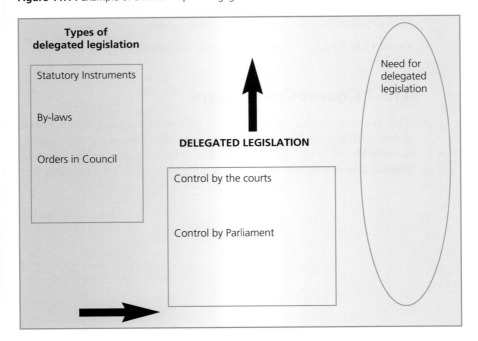

Figure 11.15 Negative factors of delegated legislation

The above are two examples of mind maps both produced in different but very visual forms. They also allow you to incorporate different levels of detail. The first (Figure 11.14) is a simple map detailing some of the significant aspects of the duty of care in negligence and a useful pointer for a number of different essay titles. The second (Figure 11.15) is more specific and deals with some of the more contentious aspects of delegated legislation from your English legal system course.

The various merits and defects of using mind maps are indicated below:

Merits

- allows you to see the topic as a connected whole
- easy to produce
- can be individualised making them specific to your needs
- it is an active process and particularly effective for visual learners.

Defects

- lack of focus on certain skills, e.g. exam timing
- gets more complex with the more detail that needs to be included.

11.5.8 Storyboarding

student mentor tip

You do not have to be an artist; stick men work just as well.

This involves putting a topic into a set of visual images, which represent the key issues involved. This can be a quite broad storyboard running through a subject (as in Figure 11.16 below) which may give you a thread through a large topic. It could also be a fairly narrow area. Some people are very talented and can draw really beautiful little pictures or cartoons, but they do not need to be masterpieces. Simple stick men will do as long as the visual imagery is sufficient to stimulate your learning process and activate your memory in the exam.

Figure 11.16 below shows a fairly simple storyboard explaining the basis of the duty of care principle in negligence.

Negligence developed from Lord Atkin's 'narrow principle', in *Donoghue v Stevenson* – a manufacturer owes a duty of care not to harm users or consumers of his products.

But Lord Atkin also identified a 'broad principle' (the neighbour principle) – you owe a duty of care to anyone who might foreseeably be affected by your acts or omissions.

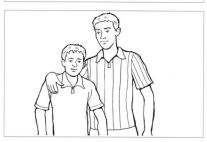

Now, following *Caparo v Dickman*, a duty will be imposed by a three-part test:
- is damage foreseeable?
- are the parties legally proximate to each other?
- is it fair, just and reasonable to impose a duty?

Continued on next page

Continued

And duty of care has developed incrementally, situation by situation. So it has been applied to fellow road users as in *Froom v Butcher*.

And it has been applied to doctors in relation to their patients, for instance to examine them as in *Barnett v Chelsea and Kensington Hospital Management Committee*, but in many other aspects of their work too, including diagnosis, treatment, advice, etc.

Figure 11.16 An example of a storyboard

The relative merits and defects of this type of revision aid are indicated below:

Merits

- a good technique for those who have a visual learning style
- student illustrations can be replaced with magazine images for those learners who have weak artistic skills.
- it is an active process and should negate boredom.

Defects

- drawing images can deter some individuals
- lack of focus on certain exam skills, e.g. timing
- difficult to cover technical issues.

11.5.9 Remembering the 'buzz words' for problem questions

Many students think that problem questions are more difficult than essay questions. This is actually understandable because one of the first things that you have to do with a problem question is to identify the area of law that the problem is concerned with. Learning to recognise areas of law from the factual circumstances in a problem is indeed a skill that you need to master and it can be quite baffling to start with.

Doing this confidently is a skill that only develops with time. The more confident you are with the law the more that it will become second nature for you. However, practising the art of examining the wording of problems for the key words or 'buzz words' is also a useful means of developing the skill. The more examples of problem questions on past papers that you see and tackle, the more familiar you will get with the skill.

Below are just some examples of key wording in tort problems on various key areas of any tort syllabus that you might study.

Occupiers' Liability Act

- A key feature here will be someone visiting the premises of another person, for example *Gemma has been staying at the Crest Hotel*.

- Remember though that premises can be a variety of things, for example *Richard was taking Valerie for a cruise down the river in his motor launch.*
- The occupier is the person in control of premises so there may also be clues as to who the potential defendant is, for example *Gareth has fallen and cut himself on broken glass in the Victoria Precinct. Westchester Corporation is responsible for cleaning the precinct.*
- Since children are treated differently under the Act there will usually be some reference to a child also, for example *Terry, aged seven, went to fetch his ball from Gordon's garden and fell in a trench which Gordon had dug, injuring himself.*
- And remember also that trespassers are protected under the 1984 Act so somebody being on premises unlawfully is a straightforward clue, for example *Rod was stealing lettuces from George's allotment one night when he tripped over a barrow left unattended and injured himself.*

Nuisance

- Here the obvious clue is that nuisance is indirect interference so it will involve things like smells, noises, vibrations, etc., for example *Des is building an extension. He drills and hammers often into the early hours of the morning. As a result Derek and Mavis, his neighbours regularly lose sleep.*
- It also involves an unreasonable use of land which is measured by things such as location, but what is a nuisance in one location may not be in another, for example *Stan is annoyed because his car is always dirty from the dust which drifts from the quarry.*
- Continuity is also a factor, so a one-off will not usually be a nuisance, for example *Sid and Ada had no sleep on the Friday night when the rock festival was held in the field behind their house.*
- Malice is also a factor which can affect the outcome of an action and therefore is commonly included in a problem, for example *Hattie became so annoyed by the constant crying of the baby next door that whenever it did cry she turned her stereo and her television up to full volume.*

Vicarious liability

- Here the immediate clue is that the tortfeasor is doing work for someone else, for example *Ralph is repairing Sam's guttering. He leans too far on the ladder and falls onto a passerby, Andrew, injuring him.*
- One point which will usually be in a question is whether the tortfeasor is an employee or an independent contractor, so a problem will include, for example *Horace makes his own tax and NI contributions, but is not allowed to accept work from anyone but Bodgitts Co.*
- The other key issue will be whether the employee commits the tort in the course of the employment or not, for example *Fred was injured when Dave gave him a lift home in the works van. Dave was taking an unofficial lunch break to go to see his wife.*

Nervous shock

- Here the obvious clue is the type of injury suffered by the plaintiff, for example *since the car crash Gail has suffered a complete personality change, has regular flashbacks of the accident and is too afraid to go out.*
- Another common feature of such problems is distinguishing between primary victims and secondary victims so a question would include, for example *Harriet suffered shock when the racing car bounced off the barrier, flew into the air and came over the fence towards her* – compared with – *Raj was shocked when he was rushed to the hospital to find his daughter dead and still covered in blood.*
- Rescuers are a class of claimant who are also commonly referred to in a problem, for example *Eric, a fireman, had struggled hard to release trapped people but had been forced to jump clear when the petrol tank exploded, and had suffered shock when the passengers burnt to death in front of him.*

Some other negligence issues

- Standard of care – look for phrases indicating factors such as practicability of precautions, for example *despite the golf club erecting a thirty-foot high fence, Cyril was still injured by a sliced ball.*
- Causation – look for the possibility of *novus actus interveniens*, for example *when Tania arrived at the hospital her injury was not immediately diagnosed, but she was left waiting on a trolley for two hours.*
- Remoteness – look for damage which is not foreseeable, for example *Ali, who was trapped in his car after the crash, was actually killed when another driver, Colin, collided with the wreckage.*

ACTIVITY

Exercise

The box below is the basis of a very simple chapter on a quite easy area from contract law – the intention to create legal relations. Read through the extract and then try to create a revision aid from the examples you have seen in the sections above. Remember it can be in any form as long as you abbreviate it sufficiently while keeping the essential knowledge.

Intention to create legal relations

Introduction

We all regularly make arrangements with each other, and we may even be doing things in return for something, and this seems as though there is consideration too.

However, we do not always intend that if we fail to keep to an agreement the other party should be able to sue us. Nor would it be sensible for the courts to be filled with actions on all of the broken promises that are ever made. My children may expect their pocket money regularly but would you want them to be able to sue if I forget to give it to them one week?

The law makes a sensible compromise by assuming that in certain situations we would usually not intend the agreement to be legally binding, while in others we usually would. The first covers social or domestic arrangements where it is presumed there is no intention to be legally bound. The second concerns commercial or business agreements where an intention to be legally bound is presumed. In either case the facts can show that the presumption should not apply. So intention is very much decided on the facts in individual cases.

Social and domestic agreements

Arrangements between family members are usually left to them to sort out themselves and are not legally binding.

Balfour v Balfour [1919] 2 KB 571

A husband worked abroad without his wife who had to stay in England due to illness and promised an income of £30 per month. When the wife later petitioned for divorce her claim to this income failed. It had been made at an amicable point in their relationship, not in contemplation of divorce. It was a purely domestic arrangement beyond the scope of the court.

Where husband and wife are estranged an agreement between them may be taken as intended to be legally binding.

Merritt v Merritt [1970] 1 WLR 1211

Here the husband had deserted his wife for another woman. An agreement that he would pay her an income if she paid the outstanding mortgage was held by the court to be intended to create legally binding obligations.

Sometimes of course families make arrangements that appear to be business arrangements because of their character. In such cases the court will need to examine what the real purpose of the arrangement was.

Jones v Padavatton [1969] 1 WLR 328

A mother provided an allowance for her daughter under an agreement for the daughter to give up her high-paid job in New York, study for the bar in England and then return to practise in Trinidad where the mother lived. When the daughter was finding it difficult to manage on the allowance the mother then bought a house for her to live in, and part of which the daughter could let and supplement her income. They later quarrelled and the mother sought

Continued on next page

repossession of the house. The daughter's argument that the second agreement was contractual failed. The court could find no intent.

If money has passed hands then it will not matter that the arrangement is made socially. It will be held as intended to be legally binding.

Simpkins v Pays [1955] 1 WLR 975

A lodger and two members of the household entered competitions in the lodger's name but paying equal shares of the entry money and on the understanding that they would share any winnings.

If parties put their financial security at risk for an agreement, then it must have been intended that the agreement should be legally binding.

Parker v Clarke [1960] 1 WLR 286

A young couple were persuaded by an older couple to sell their house to move in with them, with the promise also that they would inherit property on the death of the old couple. When the two couples eventually fell out and the young couple was asked to leave their action for damages succeeded. Giving up their security was an indication that the arrangement was intended to be legally binding.

Commercial and business agreements

An arrangement made within a business context is presumed to be intended to be legally binding unless evidence can show a different intent.

Edwards v Skyways Ltd [1964] 1 WLR 349

An attempt to avoid making an agreed *ex gratia* payment in a redundancy failed. Although *ex gratia* indicates no pre-existing liability to make the payment, the agreement to pay it once made was binding.

The offer of free gifts where this is to promote the business can still be held to be legally binding.

Esso Petroleum Co Ltd v Commissioners of Customs and Excise [1976] 1 WLR 1

Esso gave free World Cup coins with every four gallons of petrol purchased. The customs and excise wanted to claim purchase tax from the transaction. Since Esso were clearly trying to gain more business from the promotion there was held to be intention to be bound by the arrangement.

The principle has also been developed to cover situations where prizes are offered in competitions. The purpose of such events is generally to promote the body offering the prize so there is intention to create a legal relationship which is binding and can be relied on by members of the public who enter the competition.

McGowan v Radio Buxton [2001]

The claimant entered a radio competition for which the prize had been stated to be a Renault Clio car. She was told that she had won the competition but was given a four-inch scale model of a Clio. The defendants argued that there was no legally binding contract. The judge held that was intention to create legal relations. The claimant entered the competition as a member of the public and that 'looking at the transcript of the broadcast, there was not even a hint that the car would be a toy'.

However, it is possible for the agreement to contain no intention to be legally binding where that is specifically stated in the agreement itself.

Jones v Vernons' Pools Ltd [1938] 2 All ER 626

The pools company inserted a clause on all coupons stating that '... the transaction should not give rise to any legal relationship ... but be binding in honour only ...'. When a punter claimed that the company had lost his winning coupon and sought payment he failed. The clause prevented any legal claim.

The same type of principle applies with so-called comfort letters. Although such letters are worded so that they appear almost to amount to a guarantee, they do not and will not give rise to legal obligations.

Kleinwort Benson Ltd v Malaysian Mining Corporation [1989] 1 WLR 379

Kleinwort lent £10 million to Metals Ltd, a subsidiary of MMC. The parent company would not guarantee this loan but issued a comfort letter stating their intention to ensure Metals had sufficient funds for repayment. When Metals went out of business without repaying Kleinwort the latter's action based on the comfort letter failed. If they had wanted a guarantee they should have insisted on one.

Figure 11.17 Extract on intention to create legal relations

11.5.10 Online self-assessment

Even as recently as the 1990s there was little source material on law that you would be able to find online. There were online databases of the type that you have read about and been instructed how to access in Chapters 4 and 5. However most of these involved were under licence and involved paying a fee.

Now there is a vast amount of information online that you can access. This includes the databases that your university subscribes to but there also free sites. Many universities will also operate a virtual learning environment and staff in the law department often post self-assessment materials on them.

Legal publishers also offer online services and many books are now offered in e-format. Some of them also offer online self-assessment. Hodder Education is no exception. The *Unlocking* series has its own specialist website at www.hodderplus.co.uk/law. On this site you will find a lot of useful help with assessment, problem-solving techniques, multiple-choice questions and other features for each title in the series.

11.6 Practising past papers

The revision process is not complete until you have practised an examination question on that topic from a past paper or from one of the books on the market (for example Blackstone's/Oxford University Press publish a series called *Q&A*). Two of the unavoidable problems with the published books are that:

- students may skip over practising the question and jump straight into reading the suggested answer which means they do not learn as much as they could from the process
- the cases used as illustrations of legal issues may differ in the text from that followed on a programme, causing the student to become confused or undermining their confidence.

The best way to practise is to complete as much revision on a topic as you can and then find the time (make the time) to complete a question under exam conditions. We always found parents and housemates to be very supportive of this process ('Please do not disturb me for 45 minutes: I'm doing an exam question').

Do not try to assess your answer straightaway. Leave it for at least an hour and preferably longer if you have time and then, using your revision notes as a marking scheme, read your work and assess:

- what was well expressed?
- what was well structured?
- how well were the case/statutes incorporated?
- what was omitted (why, did you think it was not relevant and on reflection you have changed your mind, or did you forget it)?
- what was waffle?
- what mark would you give the answer?

Now consider if you are unhappy with the answer what you could do in the future to rectify the situation.

Think about this: is there any other activity you do only on an annual basis? For me, that is skiing. I know for a fact that the first run is always pretty dreadful. I seem to have forgotten how to turn, stop, bend my knees and it always takes me a few runs to get back into the swing of things. So many students seem, however, to think that sitting an exam is something that does not have to be practised from one June to the next. It is common sense that practice makes perfect.

So what can you get out of timed past-paper practice?

- It can highlight areas of weakness that need to be revisited
- It can highlight areas of strength that do not have to be revisited, producing more efficient revision

■ It can indicate where there are time-management issues (for example, on reflection you spent too long explaining very basic information and ran out of time before you could get onto the complex areas which attract higher marks)

■ It is a safe opportunity to make mistakes (you learn from the mistakes and you are unlikely ever to do the same mistake in the exam)

■ It can build confidence (there is nothing as confidence-building as knowing when you walk into the exam that you can write for 45 minutes on each topic that can come up on the paper).

There are many different models of assessment in any subject and law is no exception. While essay-style analysis and legal problem solving are common models, the use of multiple-choice questions, objective questioning, reports, presentations and a variety of other models are used by different institutions.

Even within standard models, such as essays and legal problem solving, the style of questioning can vary from institution to institution. For this reason it is always the best suitable advice for students who use past questions as a revision aid to use ones from their own institutions. You can usually find these on the university VLE or on the website. Alternatively you could seek advice from:

■ Students in the years above you – who may have kept past exam papers and course-work questions.

■ Module leaders – who will usually have saved an electronic copy of the questions that they have devised.

■ Resource centres – which may also have hard copies of past assessments.

SUMMARY

■ Revision is a process of consolidating information already learnt in preparation for examinations – it should not involve learning the material for the first time.

■ It depends on having first collected and collated all necessary materials including lecture notes, notes from specific textbooks or other primary and secondary sources, hand-outs given by lecturing staff and any formative essay writing.

■ It is important to remember that there is a difference between learning and revision.

■ Time management is critical to success.

■ Preparation is of three types: long term, reviewing materials during the course to ensure they are fit for purpose; medium term, ensuring that materials to be used are appropriate to revise from; and short term, the two or three weeks before the exam committing knowledge to memory.

■ It is important to produce a revision timetable to ensure that balanced amounts of time are used for each topic and also to include leisure time for winding down and limiting stress.

■ Revision aids reduce a large volume of information into key points that are memory joggers.

■ There are numerous possible revision aids; the exact type used depends on the type of learning style – they include: repetition and review, key cards, cue cards, reducing lengthy statutory materials to essential elements, diagrams, charts, flow charts, concept or mind maps, story boards, use of buzz words for problem questions, as well as practising past papers – it is important to choose a style of revision aid that suits your learning style.

12

Sitting Examinations

AIMS AND OBJECTIVES

After reading this chapter you should be able to:

- Understand the importance of final preparations
- Understand the importance of reading the question
- Understand how to select the right questions to answer
- Understand how to plan answers
- Understand the importance of answering the actual question set
- Understand the importance of time management during the exam
- Plan answers effectively
- Answer the questions effectively
- Manage time effectively
- Secure the best mark possible appropriate to your ability and the work you have put in

In many cases you will have completed assessment through coursework. While coursework may seem quite comforting because you do it at home and usually have many weeks to do it, it can still be quite demanding trying to complete lots of coursework assignments with the same deadline.

It is unlikely, however, that you will be able to complete a whole degree course in law without taking some exams. Most students seem to think that exams are pretty horrible things and yet, if you think about what an exam is, you should not really be scared of it as an exam is simply the culmination of a particular part of your course. Like all assessments, it is nothing more than the means of you showing the people who have taught you the level of understanding that you have gained from the course and demonstrating some of the skills required by the subject.

It is a way of showing that you are competent in the subject. If you are competent and if you are prepared then the exam should not be a frightening experience. In fact you should see it as your opportunity to show how good you are.

There are three important aspects to sitting exams successfully:

- being properly prepared for the exam
- knowing how to respond to the paper (which means reading the questions properly, selecting appropriate questions, and planning your answers)
- using your time effectively.

12.1 Preparing for the exam

12.1.1 Final preparations

It is surprising how quickly the exam period comes round but there is no reason to get into a panic if you are fully prepared for it.

Chapter 11 looked at what you can do to make sure that you are properly prepared for your examinations. If you have tried your best to understand the information covered during the course and you have revised effectively then you should have done enough to cope with the questions on the exam paper, whatever they are.

However, it is important to remember that there are others things besides revision that you can do to increase your chances of success in your exams.

Being organised

All of your hard work so far will be wasted if you are faced with the unexpected on the day of the exam so to avoid any nasty surprises you should make sure that you are fully organised before the exam day. There are a number of things that you can do to ensure that the day goes smoothly:

- Make sure you know the correct time of the exam – sometimes exam schedules change. Just because one of your exams starts at 2.00 pm it does not mean that all of them will. There is nothing worse for your nerves than finding out that you are late!
- Make sure that you know the correct exam room and are familiar with where it is – again exam rooms may change from the original schedule. Your exam may be scheduled in a room that you have never been taught in. If the exam timetable shows that the exam is in an unfamiliar room, take the time to find it before the exam so that on the day you can go straight to it.
- Prepare a checklist of all the things that you need to take into the exam room – in law exams this is unlikely to be more than a pen, a highlighter and possibly a statute book. However, always take a spare pen or two in with you.
- Give yourself plenty of time to get to the exam – public transport is not always reliable and, even if you have your own transport, allow plenty of time just in case you break down.
- There is no merit in revising right up to the exam door. If you do not know it by then you are unlikely to suddenly learn and remember it and this last-minute cramming can drive other things out of your memory.

Being healthy

To perform at your best it is vital that you are in good physical and mental health. You are unlikely to perform well if you are feeling unwell or under the weather. To help you achieve your best there are certain things you can do to try to keep healthy for the exam:

- Get plenty of exercise in the days before the exam – this needn't be a full-on physical training programme; regular brisk walks are as good as anything and you get the benefit of fresh air to balance out the times you spend cooped up in your room revising.
- Eat well and eat properly – try to avoid junk food; eat plenty of fresh food, vegetables and salads. Eat sensibly and ensure you drink plenty of water.
- Avoid artificial stimulants such as coffee – these make it much more difficult for you to relax and in fact caffeine actually increases rather than reduces nervous tension, which you are trying to avoid in the exam.
- Try to get enough sleep – when we sleep we are not consciously focusing on the stress of the exams. Adequate sleep allows the brain to digest and order what we have learnt.
- Take some time out for relaxation – as we have said in Chapter 11 on revision, you will do yourself more harm than good if you spend all of your time working. Work should be broken up with periods of relaxation. On the night before the exam avoid last-minute cramming. Instead take the night off and enjoy yourself so that you are fresh and relaxed going into the exam.

....
tutor tip
....

Do not bring your revision notes to the exam room – leave them at home. If you bring them with you and are caught with them then even if you have an innocent explanation your university might think you were trying to cheat.
....

- On the morning of the exam try to eat some breakfast as this will maintain your energy levels during the exam.
- If you are allowed to, take a drink and perhaps some sweets into the exam. Tension makes your mouth go dry so water is good for you; you can trick your mind into a calmer state by ensuring that you are properly hydrated. Sucking a sweet may also help you to concentrate but be considerate to everyone else in the room and don't choose sweets with wrappers that rustle.

12.1.2 Dealing with exam nerves

As senior examiners of many years, we appreciate that an exam is a nerve-racking experience. This is inevitable because your skills, knowledge and understanding are all being tested. Whenever we test ourselves, in whatever context, the adrenaline begins to flow. This is both normal and healthy.

The nervous tension that exams create is often compared to the way an athlete feels building up to a competitive event. Athletes prepare their minds as well as their bodies for the competition. They will have done all of the necessary training in advance to make them perform to the best of their abilities on the day. That physical training programme can be compared to the learning that you have done during the course of your studies with the revision honing your mental faculties. If you are prepared, just as the athlete is prepared, then you have the means to succeed. An athlete will suffer from nerves as the contest is about to start, just as you may before the start of the exam. However, remember that these nerves are productive and healthy; they are your body's way of helping you rise to the challenge of doing well, rather than simply being due to the fear of taking part. This is the mental mind-set that you should have when you go into the exam and you should be able to use it to your advantage if you are properly prepared.

You can prepare for these nerves in advance of the exam and you can learn how to control the apparently uncontrollable impulses to panic. We have already identified the importance of leisure and relaxation during your revision. If you are in a reasonably relaxed state going into the exams you are more likely to be able to think clearly, recall what you need and perform well.

Panic and anxiety, the so-called 'flight or fight' syndrome is the body's natural biological reaction to uncomfortable situations. However, you need not 'fly' from the exam nor 'fight it'. What you really want to do is to take part in it successfully. Relaxation is the body's natural way of combating anxiety. It is a simple fact that the body cannot be both anxious and relaxed at the same time; different chemical reactions are involved. What you need to be able to do is to be capable of forcing yourself into a relaxed state.

There are several methods of relaxation and you can buy tapes that help you to relax, not just through peaceful music, but through repeated positive affirmations. Quite simply if you lie relaxed, let your body go limp and tell yourself that you are relaxed, you will be.

Although it seems strange to think of it as something to learn, learning to relax is certainly a lot easier than learning one of your legal subjects. The important point is that once you have mastered the practice of relaxing yourself you can use it in any stressful situation, so not just in the exams but also before interviews, when you are playing sport, or even in those awkward social situations.

12.1.3 Remembering what the exam is all about

Remember that an examination is simply a test of your knowledge, understanding and skills. The key to a successful exam is the preparation prior to it. However, the work done before the exam can be undone by poor examination technique. It is important that you are as calm as possible and refreshed before and during the exam.

You must approach the exam in a methodical manner in order to avoid mistakes and you must ensure that you attempt the most appropriate questions for you. A vital part of choosing the appropriate questions is to read the exam paper thoroughly and to be certain of what the questions are. You should never assume that because you recognise

---

student mentor tip

In the days leading up to an exam I often take a few minutes to shut my eyes and imagine being in the exam room, sitting at the desk, listening to the instructions from the invigilator and then turning over the exam paper. I then practise my relaxation techniques, telling myself to be calm and relaxed. This helps me feel more relaxed and less stressed when I go into the real exam and helps me perform well.

a subject from a quick read of the paper you are really aware what the question is about. You must always read the question paper properly.

12.2 The examination paper

12.2.1 The instructions

Note what instructions you are given. In particular, check the time allocated for the paper and the number and combinations of questions to be attempted. The time allocated to the examination paper will allow you to work out the time needed per question. To work out the average time per question, simply divide the total time by the number of questions.

For example, a three-hour exam with four questions means that you have 45 minutes of planning and writing time. This, therefore, indicates an extensive piece of writing is required per question.

However, note this assumes that all questions carry the same mark total. If you have questions with different numbers of marks allocated, you need to calculate how long is needed per question. To do this, divide the number of minutes allocated by the maximum mark of the paper. This will give you the number of marks per minute. Then, for each question, multiply the mark per question by the marks per minute. It is also important to note the number – and any potential combination of – questions that are requested. It is disheartening to see a number of exam candidates each year who do not read the instructions and, consequently, make mistakes. Some papers require all questions to be answered. Others require the candidate to answer a set number of questions from one section and a set number of questions from another.

For example, you must answer one question from part A (which attracts 30 marks) and one from part B (which attracts 70 marks) in two hours. You should aim to spend 36 minutes on part A and the remainder of the time on part B.

ACTIVITY

Exercise

The examination is two hours long. Work out how much time you should spend on each question.

Question 1 carries 25% of the marks
Question 2 carries 20% of the marks
Question 3 carries 5% of the marks
Question 4 carries 3% of the marks
Question 5 carries 12% of the marks
Question 6 carries 15% of the marks
Question 7 carries 20% of the marks

Answers can found on page 264 of the Appendix.

12.2.2 The questions

First scan the paper, reading the question or selection of questions fully. This allows you to become familiar with the areas under examination. It is then important to re-read the paper. Your objective is to identify what each question wants you to discuss. Take each question in turn. This will allow you quickly to identify the key concepts and to ensure that the subject content matches what you originally thought was being asked. In exam conditions, it is easy to confuse what is being asked.

This is the point at which you are beginning to be selective about what you are going to write. You must make sure that you do not just assume what the title demands. For instance, in an exam question a few years ago on offer in contract law the question was 'Critically examine the circumstances in which an offer terminates'. The question was not asking for all of the rules on offer. In fact it was asking for an in-depth answer on a fairly narrow area of the topic. Many candidates, used to seeing offer and acceptance as a single area, not only wrote a lot of unnecessary detail on offer, but also wrote extensively on acceptance, which was not called for at all. The candidates did not lose marks for writing about unnecessary material. However, they did in effect cost themselves marks by writing about something not called for when they could have spent the same time writing about things that would have earned them marks.

ACTIVITY

Exercise

What are the following exam questions asking you to consider?

1. 'Individuals should be able to inflict physical harm upon one another for sexual pleasure. Although the current legal principles are still far too restrictive the decision in *Dica* (2004) is to be welcomed.'
   Discuss with reference to authority.
2. 'The judiciary is too white, too middle class and too old for modern day societal requirements.'
   Critically analyse the above statement.

Answers can be found in the Appendix, page 264.

Answers can be found in the Appendix, page 264.

12.3 Answering the paper

12.3.1 Selecting the questions

> **tutor tip**
>
> Reading the questions accurately and establishing what they call for without assumptions is vital – even in selecting questions.

For examinations that involve a choice of questions you will need to select the ones which you feel will offer the chance of most success. In an ideal world you should be able to complete every question. If this is the case then put the questions in order of preference. Start with the questions you believe are the easiest. This allows you to build confidence and puts you at ease.

Some or all of the questions might not be possible for you to tackle. This could be due to:

- a lack of revision
- a lack of focus on certain aspects of a topic
- failure to understand the question.

If you cannot complete the number of questions required by the exam (e.g. it may be that the examination is asking for three responses, but you believe that you can only attempt two), again; start with the questions which you feel are the easiest. This will give you confidence because you are completing part of the exam. The remaining time can be dedicated towards the questions that you are having difficulty with in the time you have remaining.

For the question(s) that you have perceived a difficulty with, it is important to approach them in a methodical manner. You may be misconstruing the question or stress may be causing a memory block; not understanding a question doesn't necessarily mean that you don't know the subject matter. If this lack of comprehension occurs:

> **tutor tip**
>
> Even if you don't think you can write a full answer to a question then make notes or write a bullet-pointed outline answer, including as much detail as possible, i.e. case names etc. Something is better than nothing and we are really looking to give you as many marks as we possibly can.

- reread all the questions
- make a note next to each question of the subject content, for example Parliamentary sovereignty, offer and acceptance, etc.
- try to remember the cases that are relevant and the points of law and write them down
- compare your knowledge per question and select the question(s) that show(s) you have the greatest awareness.

Although this process will not result in a fully developed response that is capable of a first-class standard, it will result in you achieving marks. This could make the difference between pass and fail or improving your overall mark. This process may also remove the mind block or stimulate the mind regarding the issues that you are having difficulty with.

12.3.2 Understanding the questions

Law exam questions tend to be one of two types: the essay question, or the problem or scenario-related question. They each need a different approach, but there are common issues to both: understanding the focus of the question and identifying the relevant subject content (see Figure 12.1 below). An indication of the question's focus is given by its command words. These are the descriptors that dictate how you should focus on the subject content. See Chapters 7 and 8 for common command words.

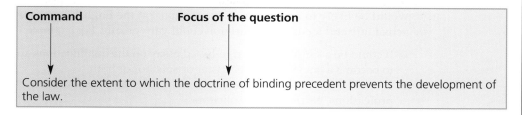

Figure 12.1 Identify the command and focus of the question

Many students look at the subject content of the question and write everything they have memorised about that topic. In effect, what they are writing is an answer to a completely different question as such a wide answer cannot address the main issue the question is asking. In reality this generalised 'include everything' answer is answering a 'what is' question (for example, 'What is the free movement of workers?'), and a 'what is' question is rarely found on an undergraduate degree-level exam paper.

How the question is phrased is critical because it dictates how the question will be marked. A failure to identify the emphasis of the question will result in a significant loss in marks.

It is important to identify the question's subject content. From there you need to use the skills discussed in Chapters 7 and 8 to produce relevant answers to the set questions.

12.4 Planning your answers

12.4.1 Planning

In exams always prepare a plan. A plan has a number of key benefits:

- it gives you an indication on how well you can answer the question
- it acts as a guide
- it creates an order
- it stimulates the mind into thinking how to answer the question
- it is useful when a memory block occurs because it acts as a reference.

Drafting a plan will normally use up about five per cent of the time allocated to that question. However, it should be noted that it takes longer to plan a problem-style question than an essay.

The key steps of an effective plan are as follows:

- identify the question's main issues
- jot down the key cases and concepts related to the issues identified
- work out an order to present the information.

There is no fixed way of producing a good plan. It is an entirely personal thing. Some students will plan in the form of a list while others use spider charts and others use more elaborate diagrams. The key point is that you should produce a plan that enables you to organise your thoughts best and gives you sufficient points of reference for you to get everything down that you want to in answering the question.

If you write a list it should also be done in a way that represents the order in which you are going to write. This is important because a good structure to an answer makes it more readable, more accessible and therefore more easily understood for the reader. Since this is the examiner who is giving you marks it is vital that he is able to pick up the points very easily and also follow the thread of your discussion with ease.

12.4.2 Essay question plans

Let us take the example of a simple essay title on the legal professions. Such an essay would be likely to appear on an exam paper on the English legal system; however, the actual title and focus of the question could vary greatly. For example:

▪ It could be a simple knowledge-based essay on the qualifications and training needed to become a lawyer, either barrister or solicitor or both.
▪ It could be an essay on the contrasting roles and organisation of the two leading professions, barristers and solicitors.
▪ It could involve critical comment on the ways in which the two professions are disciplined, or on the ways in which a disgruntled client may take action against or resolve a dispute with a lawyer of whichever profession.
▪ It could also be an essay calling for a discussion of the various reforms that have occurred over recent years and asking for speculation on the future of the professions.

Of course the approach to each would be different and this should be reflected in the planning so that you do not engage in time wasting by discussing aspects of the legal professions that are not called for in the question.

Below is a fairly full checklist on the legal professions in a diagram form of the type that we have already used in Chapter 11. The benefit of having a revision aid in this form is its visual impact and in writing the plan you can selectively remove from your mind all but the relevant information. So you would know that if the question referred only to solicitors, you could ignore the references to barristers. It is a good way of focusing your mind in the exam to have the material you will use broken down in a systematic way in your mind.

Then you can plan your answer in the exam by reference only to the material that is relevant.

	Barristers	Solicitors
Training and qualification	*Three stages of education and training:* 1. **Academic stage** – law degree OR any degree and Common Professional Examination (CPE), a conversion degree in core areas of law. *Must then join an Inn of Court (and dine a number of times or go to weekend schools before call)* 2. **Vocational stage** – Bar Professional Training Course (BPTC), formerly only at Inns of Court School of Law in London now available in some regional centres – skills based, e.g. advocacy, drafting *Students can be called to the Bar after this* 3. **Professional stage** – Pupillage – shadowing a practising barrister (Pupil Master) for two periods of six months. *May accept a fee after first six months' pupillage*	*Three stages of education and training:* 1. **Academic stage** – again a law degree OR any degree plus (CPE) OR non-graduate route is possible through qualification as a Legal Executive 2. **Vocational stage** – Legal Practice Course (LPC), again a skills-based course including, e.g. client counselling, account management, etc. 3. **Professional stage** – two-year training contract working in a solicitors' office and paid at minimum rates *Not enrolled on Solicitors' Roll and entitled to practise until third stage complete*
Organisation and role	*More than 15,000 practising:* • self-employed, sole practitioners • work from Chambers and share services and costs of a clerk • members of an Inn of Court (Gray's Inn, Lincoln's Inn, Middle Temple or Inner Temple)	*More than 115,000 in private practice:* • usually work in partnerships as partners or associates • solicitors have the first contact with clients

Continued on next page

Continued

	Barristers	Solicitors
	Work is of three types: • advocacy (presenting cases in court) • writing 'counsel's opinion' on cases for solicitors • drafting legal documents *Some barristers are employed and others (about 2,000) are 'non-practising'*	Work is very varied: advocacy, particularly in lower courts though with an Advocacy Certificate they may now appear in higher courts; conveyancing; wills and probate, registering companies, general advice and litigation; contract *About 20 per cent are employed solicitors working for companies, for local authorities, Crown Prosecution Service and as Magistrates' Clerks*
Discipline and complaints	Senate of Inns disciplines as does General Council of the Bar. Complaints can be made to either and there is also a Complaints Commissioner and the Legal Services Ombudsman	Law Society controls and disciplines solicitors. Complaints are to Office for the Supervision of Solicitors, run by the Law Society, or to Legal Services

Critical comment – The future of the professions

'Fusion' of the professions was formerly an issue – due to problems caused by restrictive practices of professions.

Courts and Legal Services Act 1990, Access to Justice Act 1999, and other provisions have removed Bar's monopoly on higher court advocacy and the solicitors' monopoly on conveyancing. Training and continuing professional development is also required in both cases. The Bar is most under threat with extended rights of audience to solicitors and employed lawyers, e.g. CPS. Solicitors have lost work to licensed conveyancers, and are under threat from increased use of 'paralegals'. The Legal Services Act 2007 introduced the concept of Alternative Business Structures, which are now becoming a reality and will change the face of the legal profession.

Figure 12.2 The legal professions: checklist

Plans in list form

Looking at the area of the first point in Figure 12.2, let us imagine a very simple question (probably a part question) *'Discuss the qualifications and training needed to practise at the Bar'*. In picturing your checklist you only need to repeat the top box on the left-hand side of the chart. So your plan would simply be as follows:

Three stages of education and training:

1. **Academic** – law degree OR any degree + CPE (seven core areas)
2. **Vocational** – BPTC (skills based, e.g. advocacy, drafting)
3. **Professional** – Pupillage (2 × 6 months shadowing practising barrister)

Must join one of four Inns of Court (Inner Temple, Middle Temple, Lincoln's Inn, Gray's Inn) + keep term (dine 12 times) before being called

May accept a fee after first six months' pupillage

Difficulties – cost, number of places, competition, limited tenancies, etc.

Figure 12.3 Planning your answer in list form

Of course so long as you know your own form of abbreviation the plan could be made even shorter and will take very little time to jot down if it is in your memory.

Plans in a chart or diagram form

Many students like a more visual reference to get everything they need down and tie it all together. Charts are popular where there is a contrast called for. A common plan in a diagram form is a 'spider chart'. This is useful because you put the main theme in a box at the centre and have the various sub-themes radiating around that box like the legs of a spider.

So let us take the example of the theme in the second bullet above: this being the contrasting roles and organisation of the two leading professions, barristers and solicitors. This essay question calls for a comparison between the roles and organisation of the two professions. A simple way of identifying the contrast is to merely repeat the part of your revision chart that is appropriate, that is the section for both barristers and solicitors. So it would look like the following.

More than 15,000 practising: • self-employed, sole practitioners • work from Chambers – share services and costs of clerk • members of Inns of Court (Gray's, Lincoln's, Middle Temple, Inner Temple) Work = • advocacy • writing 'counsel's opinion' • drafting legal documents. Some are employed directly by organisations.	More than 115,000 in private practice: • work in partnerships as partners or associates • first point of contact for clients Varied work Advocacy (in lower courts or with Advocacy Certificate in higher courts); conveyancing; wills and probate, registering companies, general advice and litigation; contract; About 20 per cent employed by companies, for local authorities, Crown Prosecution Service and as Magistrates' Clerks etc.

Figure 12.4 Planning your answer in chart form

We can also reproduce the same information in the spider chart which would look something like the following:

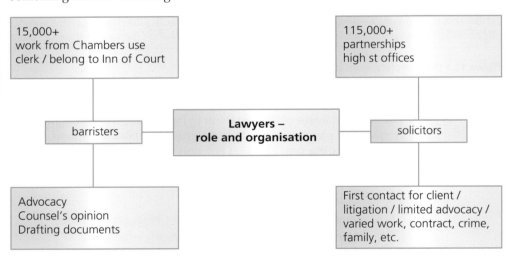

Figure 12.5 Planning your answer in a spider chart

Remember the above examples are essay titles that call for little more than factual information. In reality, most essays require you to write critically. You should plan your critical comments in exactly the same way. It may be that you can write a brief reference to a critical comment next to each piece of information in your plan. It may be preferable to make a bullet list of comments, and refer to it as you go along.

12.4.3 Problem-question plans

Producing a plan for a problem question is slightly more complex because it is not just a case of jotting down information. You need first to look carefully at the facts in the scenario and sort out in your mind what law they are leading you to examine. Then you sort through your knowledge to make a plan with the appropriate law so that you can apply it.

Consider the following fairly simple problem on offer and acceptance in contract law:

Problem

On 11 May Andy wrote to his friend Brian offering to sell Brian his Cup Final ticket for £150. Brian posted a letter on 12 May which said:

> 'Dear Andy,
>
> About the Cup Final tickets. £150 seems a bit on the steep side. I don't mind paying a bit over the odds but I'd be happier paying £100. Or could I pay you £100 now and the other £50 when I'm paid again at the end of the month?
>
> Yours Brian'

Later in the day Brian wrote again to Andy:

> 'Dear Andy,
>
> I've thought again about that ticket. I really want to go and it's cutting it a bit fine to get one from anywhere else. I'll pay you the £150.
>
> Yours Brian'

He posted the letter the same night.

Andy received Brian's first letter on the morning of 13 May and sold the ticket to another friend Chris at work that day.

When Andy returned home that evening Brian's second letter had been delivered in the later post.

Brian missed the Cup Final and now seeks your advice.

Figure 12.6 Example of a problem question in contract law

In planning your answer there are obviously two things that you would have to do:

- First, you would need to have a clear idea of the critical facts on which the resolution of the problem depends. (This may mean that you have to organise them in your mind, particularly where there are a number of issues or a number of different people involved. You can do this in a number of ways – you can highlight key points on the paper, or you could put arrows next to key points so that you can then list the law next to the arrows, or you could make a brief list of key factual points.)
- Second, you will need to think what the law is that you need to introduce. That should then be applied to those facts – this is where your ability to think as a law student comes in.

The two boxes below represent a brief plan identifying the key facts and the appropriate law needed for answering this question.

The facts

1. Andy made an offer to Brian on 11 May of a Cup Final ticket for £150.
2. On 12 May Brian replied that he would prefer to pay £100 to £150, and alternatively asked if he might pay £150 in two instalments.
3. Later on 12 May Brian sent a straightforward letter of acceptance.
4. Andy sold the ticket to Chris on 13 May after receiving Brian's first letter.
5. Andy received the second letter later the same day.
6. All of these communications were carried out by post.

The law

We know that the problem concerns formation of contracts because the facts are all about whether Andy is obliged to sell the tickets to Brian or not. In particular, the rules governing offer and acceptance are required (indeed the word offer is used in the situation).

The appropriate law would appear to be:

- a contract can only be formed if there is an agreement, which is a valid offer followed by a valid acceptance

- an offer must be communicated – *Taylor v Laird*
- an offer can be withdrawn any time before acceptance – *Routledge v Grant*
- but this must be communicated to the offeree – *Byrne v Van Tienhoven*
- a contract is formed once the offer is accepted
- the acceptance must be communicated to the offeree – *Felthouse v Brindley*
- where the post is the normal, anticipated method of accepting then the contract is formed when the letter is posted not when it is received – *Adams v Lindsell*
- a counter-offer is a rejection of the offer that is longer open to acceptance – *Hyde v Wrench*
- but a mere enquiry has no such effect – *Stevenson v McLean*.

Whatever way you choose to make a plan it should be methodical and contain the appropriate amount of detail for you to remember to write everything you want to write. It should not be a reproduction of the essay or the problem itself.

'Answer the question set' is a statement that students everywhere no doubt get very bored with since it is one that teachers constantly remind students of before exams. However, it is worth repeating because it is absolutely true to say that the best exam answers are the ones that actually answer the question that was asked. Another way of saying this is to say that one of the biggest failings of students sitting exams is not answering the question set.

Students often look at past question papers in preparing for exams. Indeed teachers often use them as exercises or even give students prepared answers to past questions. This is perfectly legitimate. It is a good way of getting a feel for what questions are like in the exam and it is also good to be able to see how you would go about answering a particular question.

However, you MUST read the question and answer the specific question asked in that particular exam and not simply regurgitate what you know about the area in general. To help you in answering the question set remember the following:

- **Do not** – assume that it is sufficient to give all your knowledge on the particular area of law identified in the question. Essay questions will demand that you show critical awareness so you have to pass **comment** on the law. Problems demand that you **apply** the law effectively so you have to be able to use the law to deal with the factual scenario in front of you.
- **Do not** – just trot out all the law you know on the particular area. You have to be selective. It may well be that an essay on negligence, for instance, is only demanding that you discuss the development of the idea of 'duty of care'. There is little point in this instance in discussing either breach or causation, although you might briefly mention them as elements of negligence.
- **Do not** – assume that because a question has been asked in one way on previous exam papers that it is going to be asked the same way on the paper you are sitting. (This can also mean that you must not assume that a particular area will always come up as a problem or another area as an essay.)
- **Do not** – learn only the main aspects of a particular topic. Sometimes examiners will ask you about the fringe areas of the subject – so know those too.
- **Do** – always read the question carefully. You can only really know precisely what you need to write about if you have read the question thoroughly and established exactly what aspects you have to write on.
- **Do** – always plan before you write. You can eliminate at this stage knowledge that you have brought into the exam room but that is not called for in the question. It will not gain you marks if you write about it.
- **Do** – always maintain a clear focus on the question itself when you write. One way of doing this is to keep referring back to the question in what you write. But remember to do this only if you have made a point that justifies your assertion that you are answering the question. We sometimes see candidates who keep repeating the question but are actually doing so only after giving some factual information rather than some critical comment.

....
tutor tip
....
Do not write a 'kitchen sink' answer where everything is thrown in together in the hope that some of what you write is correct. If you do this then the irrelevant points will distract from any good points that you make.
....

12.5 Time management

One of the most significant things about an exam as a means of assessing your knowledge, understanding and skills is that it is a time-constrained affair. In coursework assignments you may look ahead over the weeks or months until the coursework is due and think that you have plenty of time for both the research and the writing. Although, in fact, this is rarely the case when you analyse the time you have to spend at university, the number of other assignments that you probably have to complete at the same time and the fact that you need some time for relaxation and other pursuits.

12.5.1 Following the rubric

As a student on a law course at university, it is most probable that you will have already experienced both coursework and exams. You will already know then that however long you are given to complete an exam (three hours is usually the longest in exams such as A-Levels or GCSEs) the time goes very quickly in the exam room and most candidates will be struggling to get down everything that they want to say within the time allowed.

Accordingly, organising your time in an exam is crucial. In this respect one of the first rules to follow is to know the rubric and if you are not aware of the structure of the exam before you get into the exam room you must at that point make sure that you read the rubric.

12.5.2 Key features of the rubric

The rubric is the instructions on the front of an exam paper that tells you exactly what you should be doing during the exam. There are three critical points that you must know in order to make maximum use of your time in the exam room:

The length of the exam	You should also take note of any reading time available. This is not uncommon in certain exams.
The number of questions that you are required to answer from those on the paper	In certain exams you will have to answer all of the questions. In others you get a choice from a larger number. This is very useful because it has given you the opportunity in advance to focus on certain areas and in the exam room it means that you get the opportunity to select the questions that you think you will perform best on.
The number of marks available for each question	Very often the marks for each question are the same. Sometimes, however, different questions attach different marks and this is useful in making choices on which questions to start with and also if you are running out of time where to get the most marks from.

Figure 12.7 Key features of the rubric explained

You may have a subject that you are bursting to write about, that you know absolutely everything about and could spend the whole exam writing about, but it is very bad exam strategy if you do so. If you have to answer three questions and you only provide an answer to one then you have lost two-thirds of your marks. This is an extreme example of bad management, but it can happen!

Even if you answer all three questions, if you spend (let's say) half the time available on that one question, you are still losing valuable time on the other two. This might prevent you from getting the marks that may otherwise have given you the grade of which you were capable, or at worst the pass of which you were capable.

It is a simple truth about exam questions that it is easier to get the first 50 per cent of the available marks than it is to get the next 50 per cent. Many, if not most, pass marks in exams are set at 40 per cent. In this way, making sure that you answer all the questions that you must and ensuring that you give equal time to answering them is the surest way of achieving the pass mark.

A simple understanding and rigid adherence to the three points above give you the best chance of doing as well as you can.

12.5.3 Keeping to a schedule

Let us take the example of an exam lasting 2 hours and 15 minutes where you have to complete three questions out of five. This is a fairly standard timescale. The mathematics is easy: 3 into 135 minutes (2 hours and 15 minutes) = 45 minutes for each question.

Forty-five minutes is also a fairly standard time for both essays and problem questions. Remember the examiner has devised the questions so that they can be answered accurately and effectively within that timescale. In other words allocate yourself 45 minutes to each question and try not to exceed it.

Take a watch into the exam with you (although this is not absolutely vital because there is normally a clock in the exam room which you can refer to).

If your 2 hour 15 minute exam starts at 9.00 am and finishes at 11.15 am then you can set yourself, right from the start of the exam, a schedule.

A simple schedule might be as follows:

- 9.00 am–9.45 am   question 3
- 9.45 am–10.30 am   question 5
- 10.30 am–11.15 am   question 1

Of course it may be possible for you to work to this type of schedule but it in fact hides the reality of working in an exam. There are a number of things to consider:

- First, before you can answer any questions effectively you must know which questions are the ones that are appropriate for you to answer. This means reading all the questions and this takes time – probably at least five minutes.
- Second, before you start writing your answers you should prepare properly for them (see Sections 12.3. and 12.4. above). Your plan for the answer can take a variety of forms as you have already seen but, whichever type of approach you use, this is going to take time – probably about five minutes each, or 15 minutes in total.
- Third, you should leave some time aside to read through your answers to check that you have not made any silly mistakes that would cost you marks, or that you have not missed some important points that could be added, or even to add in the names of cases that you have now remembered – again this is probably going to take another 15 minutes.

This means that of your 135 minutes you are likely to use about 35 minutes of that in reading and selecting questions, planning your answers and reviewing what you have done. You are left with 100 minutes or about 33 minutes for each answer for the actual writing.

Your new schedule, taking all this into account then could look something like the following:

- 9.00 am–9.05 am   reading questions and selecting
- 9.05 am–9.10 am   writing plan for question 3
- 9.10 am–9.43 am   answering question 3
- 9.43 am–9.48 am   writing plan for question 5
- 9.48 am–10.21 am   answering question 5
- 10.21 am–10.26 am   writing plan for question 1
- 10.26 am–10.59 am   answering question 1
- 10.59 am–11.15 am   reading through answers

Alternatively, you may write all three plans at the start when your mind is fresh and you are full of energy and adrenalin.

- 9.00 am–9.05 am   reading questions and selecting
- 9.05 am–9.10 am   writing plan for question 3
- 9.10 am–9.15 am   writing plan for question 5
- 9.15 am–9.20 am   writing plan for question 1

- 9.20 am–9.53 am   answering question 3
- 9.53 am–10.28 am   answering question 5
- 10.28 am–10.59 am   answering question 1
- 10.59 am–11.15 am   reading through answers

Of course it is unnecessary to write down your schedule in such detailed terms since this is taking up more of your precious time. Nevertheless, it is possible to make a quick checklist of the times that you need to finish each stage by so that you can stick to it during the exam.

It is almost inevitable that you will start with the question that you feel most confident about. This is a good strategy. The quicker you can get writing the more relaxed you will feel since you are busy and do not have time to worry about any nerves you are feeling. It is also good strategy because if you feel confident about the question you are likely to make a reasonable job of the answer and this will give you confidence as you go through the rest of the paper.

However, the temptation may be for you to carry on writing the answer to this question no matter how long it takes. This is not good strategy. Remember the point above that the first 50 per cent of available marks are earned much more quickly and much more easily than the final 50 per cent. The chances are that by the time your 33 minutes is up, you have already earned some pretty reasonable marks. It certainly is going to be the case that if you carry on writing for too long after that the time that you spend is going to be picking you up fewer and fewer marks per minute.

The sensible strategy is to finish where you are at the 33 minutes and move on to the next question. If you still have things to say then you can always come back to it later. Remember you have already accounted for a review time in your calculations. It may also be that when you answer another question, perhaps your final answer, you have more time than you need because you have less to say. Again, you can pick up where you left off in the first question. You are far more likely to fail to gain marks by not answering a question through running out of time, than by failing to drag every last morsel out of what you could have written on one.

Remember the golden rule: the examiner has set the question in such a way that it is possible to give a good answer in the time given. If you find that you have masses more to say than you can get down in the time then you are probably straying off the point and not really answering the question set. A common fault here is to try to write down everything you know about the area, when in fact you are being called on to be selective within that topic.

Of course, it is also possible that you sit an exam where the weighting of the different questions is not equal. You can still make effective use of your time by following the same formula.

Let us say for instance that the examination has within it a compulsory question worth 50 per cent of the marks and that the exam is three hours long with you having a choice of questions from a second section of which you have to complete two.

Again you are looking at two questions which you have 45 minutes each to complete, as in the example above, but this time you also have one question which you must devote half of your time to, or 90 minutes (one and a half hours).

Taking the formula above you would still use at least five minutes of your time reading the questions and five minutes on each of the two questions from the second section for preparing a plan. However, because the compulsory question is so much bigger the chances are that you would need extra time for preparing your plan, say ten minutes. If you add 15 minutes for final reviewing, you will use up 40 minutes of your time on reading the questions, making plans and reading over your answers. This leaves you 2 hours and 20 minutes for writing, or 140 minutes. Half of this should be used for the compulsory question, or 70 minutes. This leaves you 70 minutes for the other two, or 35 minutes each. This is an example of how longer exams actually work in the students' favour. It may seem to you as though you are under more pressure because of the longer question, but in fact you are under less. It is usually sensible to complete the larger, compulsory question first, as it is clearly more demanding.

If the exam started at 9.00 am and finished at 12.00 noon, the schedule this time would be as follows:

- 9.00 am–9.05 am — reading questions and selecting
- 9.05 am–9.15 am — writing plan for question 1 (compulsory)
- 9.15 am–10.25 am — answering question 1 (compulsory)
- 10.25 am–10.30 am — writing plan for question 5
- 10.30 am–11.05 am — answering question 5
- 11.05 am–11.10 am — writing plan for question 3
- 11.10 am–11.45 am — answering question 3
- 11.45 am–12.00 pm — reading through answers

Another possibility is that you have a first section where you have to complete, say, ten small questions each worth five per cent of the marks rather than one big compulsory question. Again you would need to follow the same rules and leave yourself half the time for the compulsory section and divide the other half between the two larger questions. A schedule for this type of exam would be as follows:

- 9.00 am–9.05 am — reading questions and selecting
- 9.05 am–9.15 am — planning for ten compulsory questions
- 9.15 am–10.25 am — answering compulsory questions
  - 9.15 am–9.22 am — Question 1
  - 9.22 am–9.29 am — Question 2
  - 9.29 am–9.36 am — Question 3
  - 9.36 am–9.43 am — Question 4
  - 9.43 am–9.50 am — Question 5
  - 9.50 am–9.57 am — Question 6
  - 9.57 am–10.04 am — Question 7
  - 10.04 am–10.11 am — Question 8
  - 10.11 am–10.18 am — Question 9
  - 10.18 am–10.25 am — Question 10
- 10.25 am–10.30 am — writing plan for question 5
- 10.30 am–11.05 am — answering question 5
- 11.05 am–11.10 am — writing plan for question 1
- 11.10 am–11.45 am — answering question 1
- 11.45 am–12.00 pm — reading through answers

The basic point is that whatever the character and structure of the exam it is easy enough, if you are prepared for that structure beforehand, to create a disciplined schedule to work to in the exam.

Remember the schedules indicated above are nothing more than a guide to how you can organise your time in the exam. You do not need to write down anything as elaborate. Something as simple as follows will suffice, as long as you remember in your mind to include time for reading the questions, planning each question, and a bit of checking through after.

So in an exam of three hours with four questions to do with equal weighting you might just jot down:

- 9.00 –9.45
- 9.45–10.30
- 10.30–11.15
- 11.15–11.00

The important thing is to not overrun.

12.5.4 Avoiding time-wasting during the exam

Remember exams are assessments where you are bound by a time constraint. You cannot perform at your own leisure in an exam; you have to get on and work productively all the way through it.

You should also remember though that the people writing the exams do not just dream up any old questions without giving them careful consideration. The whole idea of producing a successful exam is that the answer can be given in the time set. An obvious example of how examiners have to think within time limits is where you have compulsory questions worth half the marks and then two or three other questions. In producing the paper the examiner is obviously including different demands for the different questions so that the compulsory question is designed to take you two or three times the amount of time of the other questions.

Students inevitably want to give the examiner the benefit of all their knowledge. This is clearly a good thing, but do not let this eagerness to show off cause you problems. A classic example is not being able to remember the name of a particular case that you want to use and no matter how hard you try it will just not come to you. We have all been there (yes, we sat law exams once). The problem is that you can become obsessed by one tiny bit of information that is going to be worth actually very few marks to you. As invigilators we have seen it many times: students scratching their heads and becoming very distressed. Their pens go down; they look around them for inspiration; and they go to their scrap paper writing down little lists trying to take them to the case they want. More importantly two things happen:

- First, they are not writing. It is a simple truth in an exam that you do not get any marks for not writing and you could be taking up time for writing other things that you could be getting marks for.
- Second, and much worse, you are distracted from your overall purpose and the clear danger is that trying to concentrate too hard on one little piece of information can drive other more important things out of your mind. You are also just making yourself more nervous.

The proper thing to do in the circumstances is to move on. You can always come back and write the case name in afterwards if you remember it. Besides you can always write 'In a case in which ... happened' and make the point that you want to make. The examiner will know that you know what you are talking about. You may not get all the marks available but you are only missing a tiny proportion of the marks by not getting the case name.

We have already said in Section 12.1.1 in 'Final preparations' that you should make sure that you are prepared in advance so that you can be in the room on time and with all the equipment you need. You do not want to waste time by arriving late when you could be gaining marks by writing. Neither do you want to waste time in the exam sharpening pencils or filling fountain pens when you could be writing.

Sometimes things happen during an exam that could be distracting. This is unfortunate for you but it can often not be avoided. People coming into the exam room late is an obvious distraction, as is people who are not so well prepared as you and leave early; both of which can be annoying. A person may be taken ill during the exam and sometimes this can be quite dramatic; you may feel very sympathetic for the stricken person. Whatever the distraction is remember it does not concern you and you should not concern yourself with it either. There are other people, the invigilators, available to deal with the disturbance. Your complete focus must be on what you are doing yourself, not on what is happening to others around you.

Particularly with well-prepared students, it is possible that you may need more pages than you are given in the answer booklet in order to complete your answers. You should not wait until you have finished writing on the last page before you put your hand up to ask the invigilator for more paper. You then have to wait for him to get to you and you might be in a big hall. He may not see your hand straightaway and you may be unlucky and he comes to see what you want and then goes back to get you more paper. This is all time wasted when you could be writing.

One final point is also worth noting. It applies particularly while you still have other exams to sit, but applies also even when you have sat your last exam. Once you have

tutor tip

Never take too long over one question at the expense of what you could be writing and getting marks for on another.

tutor tip

Never allow yourself to get over distracted by a missing piece of information; move on and come back to it later if you can.

tutor tip

Do not waste time in the exam room doing things that you could have prepared for beforehand.

tutor tip

Do not waste time in the exam by getting distracted by anything happening in the exam room.

tutor tip

When you turn onto the last page of blank paper put your non-writing hand up straightaway to get more paper and keep writing while you wait.

finished the exam and left the exam room you have done everything that you can to complete that exam successfully. After that you simply have to wait for it to be marked and to get the results. Students often engage in post mortems after the exam either with their friends or by trying to extract from their teachers whether they said the right thing in the exam or not. This is wasteful of your emotional energy and can create even more stress than you would suffer already. It is a practice that is best avoided. Relax after the exams and forget about them until you get the results.

Good luck!

SUMMARY

- Be organised.
- Be healthy.
- Learn how to combat exam nerves with relaxation techniques.
- Follow the instructions on the exam paper fully and properly.
- Read all questions and make brief notes as to their focus before selecting which questions you are going to answer. Ensure that you understand what the question is asking you.
- Create an answer plan to guide you in writing out your full answer. Use the plan then as a reference point to keep you on track.
- Ensure you are doing as the question asks you. If it requires critical analysis then make sure you provide sufficient relevant commentary; if it is a problem question ensure you identify and then apply the relevant law.
- Manage your time effectively in the exam. Work out how long you need to spend on each question and then **stick to your timings.** Answering all questions, with one being a mediocre answer, will attain you a higher overall mark than simply answering one or two questions very well.
- Do not waste time in the exam. You need to spend every minute concentrating on doing well; don't pay attention to what everyone else is (not) doing.
- Do not carry out an exam paper post mortem – it will not change what you wrote and will only cause you worry you until you get your results.

Further reading

Foster, S, *How to Write Better Law Essays*, Pearson Longman, 2007.

Appendix

Chapter 1

Answers to Activity on page 7:

1. A prosecutor.
2. Magistrates' Court, High Court, Court of Appeal, House of Lords.
3. The claimant must prove his claim on a balance of probabilities.
4. He or she is acquitted.
5. The defendant.
6. Damages usually, or equitable remedies such as injunctions.
7. To keep order in society and to punish wrong doing.

Answers to Activity on pages 12–13:

1. (c)
2. (b)
3. (c)
4. (b)
5. Beyond all reasonable doubt is **criminal**   Liable for a claim is **civil**
   Prosecutor is **criminal**   Balance of probabilities is **civil**
   Theft is **criminal**   Damages is **civil**
6. (d)

Chapter 2

Examples
Summary Sheet

Lecture: Precedent – Practice Statement House of Lords change law when right to do — Supreme Court	Date: 20/10/07
Key cases: *London Street Tramways v London County Council* *DPP v Smith* *Conway v Rimmer* *Herrington v BRB* *Pepper v Hart* *R v Shivpuri*	Key comment and analysis: • Needed to stop rigidity. • House of Lords reluctant to use it. • Reluctant to use it. Note date of *Pepper v Hart*.
Links to tutorial activities: Refer to tutorial manual to compare	Academic references: See reading list

	House of Lords
What is the role of the Supreme Court?	This is the most senior domestic court. When matters do not involve Europe it has the final decision on the case. This court binds all courts below it.
Why was the House of Lords bound by its own decisions?	*House of Lords & the Practice Statement* Originally the House of Lords had flexibility and could change its mind about its own past decisions but in 1898 the court decided that certainty in the law was more important than flexibility, so in *London Street Tramways v London County Council* the court decided that the House of Lords was bound by its own previous decisions.
What problems did this create?	*This created a rigid system, as seen in DPP v Smith* A man murdered a police officer. The House of Lords made a mistake by giving a poor definition as to the mental test for murder. Due to this mistake, Parliament passed the Criminal Justice Act 1967 to replace the mistake.
What was the criterion of the Practice Statement?	1966 Lord Gardiner issues a Practice Statement. This allows the judges in the House of Lords to depart from past decisions when it is right to do so.
What case illustrates its first use?	It was first used in *Conway v Rimmer*. This was not seen as a major use as it only involved a technical matter.
	Examples Civil
What civil examples highlight the Practice Statement?	*Herrington v British Railways Board overruled Addie v Dumbreck* These cases concerned what duty of care was owed to a child trespasser. In *Addie* it was decided that there was only a duty when injuries to a child were caused deliberately or recklessly. *Herrington* overruled this due to the changes in social conditions and made the duty owed stronger. *Herrington* was the first major use of the Practice Statement.
	Pepper v Hart overruled Davis v Johnson These cases concerned the use of *Hansard*. In *Davis* the use of Hansard by a judge as an aid to statutory interpretation was not allowed. *Pepper v Hart* removed this limit.
	Examples Criminal
What criminal examples highlight the Practice Statement? What problems can be seen with the use of the Practice Statement?	*R v Shivpuri overruled Anderton v Ryan* These cases concerned the criminal nature of attempting the impossible. *Anderton* decided that you could not have criminal liability if what you were doing was impossible. This was contrary to an Act of Parliament. *Shivpuri* therefore overruled *Anderton*. It can now be a crime if you attempt the impossible. This was the first criminal case to use the Practice Statement.

251

APPENDIX

Spider diagram

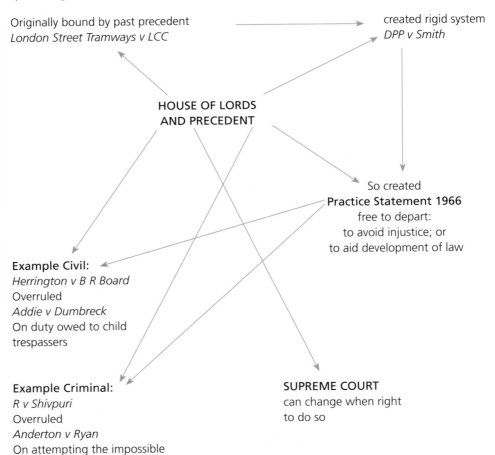

Originally bound by past precedent
London Street Tramways v LCC

created rigid system
DPP v Smith

**HOUSE OF LORDS
AND PRECEDENT**

So created
Practice Statement 1966
free to depart:
to avoid injustice; or
to aid development of law

Example Civil:
Herrington v B R Board
Overruled
Addie v Dumbreck
On duty owed to child
trespassers

Example Criminal:
R v Shivpuri
Overruled
Anderton v Ryan
On attempting the impossible

SUPREME COURT
can change when right
to do so

Chapter 3

<table>
<tr>
<td>

Hyde v Wrench

Rolls Court [1840] 3 Beav 334; Jur 1106; 49 ER 132

June 6. The defendant wrote to the plaintiff offering to sell his farm for £1,000. The plaintiff's agent immediately called on the defendant and made an offer of £950, which the defendant wished to have a few days to consider.

June 27. The defendant wrote to say that he would not accept this offer.

June 29. The plaintiff wrote accepting the offer of June 6.

The plaintiff brought an action for specific performance.

The defendant filed a general demurrer.

THE MASTER OF THE ROLLS (LORD LANGDALE): Under the circumstances stated in this bill, I think there exists no valid binding contract between the parties for the purchase of the property. The defendant offered to sell it for £1,000, and if that had at once been unconditionally accepted, there would undoubtedly have been a perfect binding contract; instead of that, the plaintiff made an offer of his own, to purchase the property for £950, and he thereby rejected the offer previously made by the defendant. I think that it was not afterwards competent for him to revive the proposal of the defendant, by tendering an acceptance of it; and that, therefore, there exists no obligation of any sort between the parties; the demurrer must be allowed.

</td>
<td>

Material facts

*Outcome – no contract
Original law – agreement = offer followed by unconditional acceptance*

A counter offer = a rejection of the offer

So the offer is no longer open to acceptance

</td>
</tr>
</table>

KEY FACTS

Hyde v Wrench

- An acceptance must be unconditional.
- A counter offer amounts to a rejection of the offer.
- The offer is no longer open to acceptance.

Chapter 4

Grobbelaar v News Group Newspapers Ltd

House of Lords

You should cite the Weekly Law Reports version as this appears above the other versions in the hierarchy

[2002] 4 All ER 732 – All England Law Reports

[2002] 1 WLR 3024 – Weekly Law Reports

[2003] EMLR 1 – Entertainment and Media Law Report

Rees v Darlington Memorial Hospital NHS Trust

House of Lords

You should cite the Law Reports Appeal Cases version as this appears above the other versions in the hierarchy

[2004] 1 FLR 234 – Family Law Reports

[2003] 3 WLR 1091 – Weekly Law Reports

[2004] 1 AC 309 – Law Reports Appeal Cases

MCC Proceeds Inc v Lehman

Court of Appeal

You should cite the All England Law Reports version as this appears above the other versions in the hierarchy

[1998] 4 All ER 675 – All England Law Reports

[1998] 2 BCLC 659 – Butterworths Company Law Cases

(1998) 142 SJLB 40 – Solicitor's Journal Law Brief

What does EMLR stand for?	**Entertainment and Media Law Reports**
What does BWCC stand for?	**Butterworths Workmen's Compensation Cases**
What is the correct abbreviation for the Criminal Appeal Reports (Sentencing)?	**Cr App R (S)**
What is the correct abbreviation for the Criminal Law Review?	**Crim LR**

Chapter 5

What is the chapter number of the Access to Justice Act 1999?	**Chapter 22**
What is the title of the act with the official citation 1995 Chapter 50?	**Disability Discrimination Act 1995**
On what date did the Education Act 2002 receive Royal Assent?	**24 July 2002**

1. What is the title of the 5th Act to receive Royal Assent in 2011?

Postal Services Act 2011.

2. What is the title of Section 13 of the Human Rights Act 1998? Which source did you use to find out?

Continued on next page

Continued

Section 13: Freedom of thought, conscience and religion

Source used: You could use any of these sources: *Westlaw, LexisLibrary, Lawtel, JustCite, BAILII*, HMSO website, Public General Acts, *Halsbury's Statutes of England and Wales*, Current Law Statutes Annotated.
HMSO

What is the title of the 99th Statutory Instrument to be made in 2011?

The Electronic Money Regulations 2011.

Look up the case '*Whiston v Whiston*, Court of Appeal, Civil Division, 23 March 1995'. What is this case about? Which database or printed source did you use to find out?

About: Bigamy and financial provision.

Source used: You could use any of these sources: *Westlaw, LexisLibrary, Lawtel, JustCite.*

Using *Halsbury's Laws* (either in print or online via *LexisLibrary*), find out what the punishment is for possessing a live badger.

Punishable on summary conviction with a fine not exceeding level 5 on the standard scale.

Using the *Legal Journals Index* (either in print or online via *Westlaw*), find out how many articles have been written about the case *Savage v Fairclough*.

Six (at October 2011)

Chapter 6

Exercise 2

1. **Jittery J in his judgment indicates that he is bound by the decision of Rough-Justice J in *Berry v Branch*. Consider what you think Jittery J believes to be the *ratio decidendi* of *Berry v Branch*. (Remember that it is only the *ratio decidendi* of a previous decision which can bind a judge in a later case.)**
   Answer:
   Here we have yet another situation where the judge, Jittery J, has not really made it clear in his judgment either what he believes the *ratio* in *Berry v Branch* to be, or indeed what the *ratio* is in the case of *Bunny v Browning*.

   All that we can do is to eliminate those principles which appear to be too tightly tied to the facts of either case to be a *ratio* in both of them.

   If we do this then we must eliminate the statement in *Berry v Branch* '... *if someone plants a poisonous tree, they must be liable for the damage it does* ...' because there is no poisonous vegetation in *Bunny v Browning*. This principle then can obviously not be applied. Similarly the statement about firing a gun into a neighbour's garden from *Berry v Branch* cannot be applied. There are no facts in *Bunny v Browning* that would support this as the *ratio* of that case.

   What is left then from *Berry v Branch* is the statement about the duty of neighbours living cheek by jowl in cramped suburbia; and also the statement about the obligation imposed on anyone who undertakes a dangerous activity. If we study these two carefully, then the statement about the duty of city-dwelling neighbours towards each other seems to be the most likely that Jittery J has applied. It is the narrowest of the two possibilities; and in Justice Jittery's view there is an underlying similarity between all modes of urban life as compared to life in the country.

2. **Consider whether in his judgment Jittery J has in fact widened the application of the principle from _Berry v Branch_.**
   Answer:
   Yes. We are able to suggest that he has. By saying that he considers _Berry v Branch_ to be a precedent, he is, at a minimum, widening its authority into situations which do not involve poisonous plants. However, we must also remember that how far he has widened it depends on what we decide is the _ratio_ in his own case, _Bunny v Browning_.

3. **Identify the _ratio decidendi_ of _Bunny v Browning_.**
   Answer:
   Again there are several possibilities:

- If someone fires a gun into his neighbour's garden, the neighbour is entirely innocent and should not suffer a loss. (We can identify this from our answers to Exercise 1 as one of the _obiter_ from _Berry v Branch_. Remember that an _obiter dictum_ from one case can serve only as a _persuasive_ precedent in a later case.)
- People who live cheek by jowl in cramped suburbia must pay due regard to those who live next to them.
- If someone embarks on any activity which is dangerous, then they should take the consequences.

Jittery J does not make it very clear which of these he considers to be decisive in the case. Therefore, it will once again be left to another judge, dealing with a later case, to define the legal principle on which _Bunny v Browning_ was decided.

4. **Assuming that _Berry v Branch_ is sufficiently analogous to _Bunny v Browning_ to serve as a precedent in the case, consider whether it is a persuasive precedent or a binding precedent.**
   Answer:
   Both cases were heard in the QBD and therefore, following the principle that respect should be shown for same level precedents, the decision in _Berry v Branch_ is very persuasive and probably would be followed by a later judge in the same court who found the situation to be analogous.

Exercise 3

1. **Consider what you think could be said in favour of using _Berry v Branch_ as precedent to be followed in this case.**
   Answer:
   Looking at the facts of _Bunny v Browning_ three of Rough-Justice J's propositions in _Berry v Branch_ might have some application:

- In cases 'where a man throws acid into his neighbour's property or fires a shotgun over his fence ... the neighbour is entirely innocent and should not suffer a loss' and if he does 'the miscreant takes the risk, not the neighbour' (clearly here damage has resulted from Dove firing a shotgun).
- 'People who live cheek by jowl with others in cramped suburbia must pay due regard to those who live next to them' (again the claimant and defendant are near neighbours).
- 'if someone embarks on any activity which is dangerous, then they should take the consequences' (even in very controlled circumstances the use of firearms must be seen as intrinsically dangerous).

On this basis, it is reasonable that Mr Dove's counsel should have sought to rely on _Berry v Branch_ as a precedent.

2. **Consider the reasons that might be used in the case to distinguish it from Berry v Branch.**
   Answer:

Here we might look back to the reasons given by Miss Trigger, the counsel for the defendant in *Bunny v Browning*, for distinguishing that case from *Berry v Branch*:

- She suggested there that the material facts of the two cases were too different for the one to follow the principle in the other (that could equally be said of *Dove v Digger*. Damage to carnations in a greenhouse caused by a missed clay falling through a green-house seems to be quite different to a dog being killed by eating poisonous leaves).
- She also suggested that there was no inherent hazard in *Bunny v Browning* which there certainly was in *Berry v Branch* (the yew leaves). Here also we are not looking at a natural hazard.
- She also said that the damage suffered by the claimant was not foreseeable in the way that the death of the dog was in *Berry v Branch*. Again the damage to the carnations may seem a more remote possibility than the death of the dog.

It is therefore also possible for Careless J to distinguish from *Berry v Branch*.

Exercise 4

1. **Identify the *ratio decidendi* of the Court of Appeal in *Blaster v Burns*.**
   Answer:
   In the Court of Appeal in *Blaster v Burns* it is plain from Highman LJ's judgment that he is approving of the proposition of Rough-Justice J's which he refers to in the case that 'if someone embarks on any activity which is dangerous then they should take the consequences'. It is also plain, since he also refers to it in his judgment, that he approves of Rough-Justice J's proposition that neighbours 'living together cheek by jowl in cramped suburbia' should have 'due regard' to one another. Nevertheless, the judgment is insufficiently precise for us to say with absolute certainty which of these propositions he is using to decide the outcome of the case. The one real clue we have that he actually favours the first of the two, and therefore the much broader principle, is that he states that, even if the experiments had been carried out in open countryside, he would still have found Mr Blaster liable.

2. **On the basis of Highman LJ's judgment what do you consider the *ratio* in *Berry v Branch* now to be?**
   Answer:
   Following on from 1. above this is still not absolutely certain. One thing can be said, however, from Highman LJ's judgment. He is not seeing the decision in *Berry v Branch* being based on the narrowest principle – that of planting poisonous trees leading to duty. So he clearly prefers a broader *ratio* with wider application for further cases. The key feature of the case in fact is that the *ratio* in *Berry v Branch*, whatever it is, is no longer of great significance. This is because we now have a precedent from a higher court which must include any of the possible *ratio* from *Berry v Branch*. The precedent to be carried into further cases is now that in *Blaster v Burns* in the Court of Appeal.

3. **Identify anything in Highman LJ's judgment that you consider to be *obiter dicta*.**
   Answer:
   This is not so obvious but there is in fact an *obiter* statement. Highman LJ refers to what the possible outcome of the case would be if the facts had occurred in open country rather than in a built-up town. Since the facts of the case concern town dwellers, this point has no bearing on the outcome of the case and must be *obiter*.

4. **Assuming that the essential facts of the cases are sufficiently similar, consider whether Highman LJ is in fact bound to follow the decision in *Berry v Branch*.**
   Answer:
   The answer here is clearly no. Whatever the similarities in the facts of the two cases they are decided by two different courts at different points in the hierarchy. The Court of Appeal is the higher of the two courts so, even though *Berry v Branch* may have been very persuasive, as a High Court case it could never have been binding on the superior court.

Exercise 5

1. Identify the *ratio decidendi* of the case.
Answer:
This is now quite easy to identify: 'if a person undertakes a dangerous activity, whether in the context of urban confines or in the countryside, he or she must bear responsibility for the consequences.'

2. Is the law on responsibility of neighbours now settled and in what way could it be developed or changed?
Answer:
The principle is now a clear precedent for all courts to follow. Since the House of Lords approved of the principle stated by Highman LJ in *Blaster v Burns* when the case reached them, this principle is now binding on all lower courts in cases involving neighbours' liability. This will be the case until either:

■ the law is amended by a subsequent House of Lords decision or
■ Statute changes or develops the law since Parliament is the supreme legislator.

3. Consider whether any of Clearly J's comments in the case amount to *obiter dicta*.
Answer:
There is an indication of a legal proposition that has no bearing on the case itself and this can therefore be classed as *obiter dictum*: that liability is possible for the 'storage of explosives or volatile substances'.

4. Consider in what way the case is a development from the decision in *Berry v Branch*.
Answer:
We were originally uncertain what the precise *ratio* in *Berry v Branch* was. All we could say for certain was that there was liability for the planting of poisonous trees – a fairly narrow principle of law. *Porker v Fly*, applying the principle accepted by the higher courts, confirms that there is a broad principle imposing liability on anyone in either town or country for the consequences of dangerous activities for which they are responsible.

Answers to self-test questions on page 121

1. This would be an intrinsic (or internal) aid to interpretation.
2. This is the mischief rule from *Heydon's case* (1584).
3. This is the *ejusdem generis* rule – one of the three language rules.
4. This is *Hansard* – which is an extrinsic (or external) aid to interpretation.
5. This is a presumption – which will be followed by judges unless a contrary intent is shown by Parliament.
6. This is the narrow approach to the golden rule (which is said to be an extension of the literal rule).

Answers to the exercise on page 122

Scenario 3

Eric has been convicted under the Act. Eric lives in a house in the same street as the United football ground. On match days Eric regularly leans out of his open upstairs window and sings abusive songs to the away supporters. Eric is appealing.

Answer:

Again this one is not necessarily as straightforward as it may look at first sight. The clear problem is that Eric is singing inside his house and according to s 4 'The Act shall not apply to private residential properties'.

Continued on next page

- He is singing abusive songs so he certainly falls within s 1(1).

- He also lives near to the ground so he is also *'within reasonable vicinity of a football ground'* for s 1(1).

- Using the literal rule technically he cannot be said to fall within the Act because of s 4 – he is in a private residence, not a public place.

- The only category of public place under s 2(1) that might apply is (a) 'any public thoroughfare'.

- Public thoroughfare is defined in s 2(2) (an interpretation section and therefore an intrinsic aid) as 'any road, pavement, precinct or other similar place along, over or through which vehicles or pedestrians pass'.

- Using a strict literal interpretation, Eric could not be convicted because he is in his residence and does not conform to the definition in s 2(2).

- The words in s 2(2) are not ambiguous so again the golden rule would not be used in its narrow sense (although again public policy may mean that the broad application of the rule is used to add the circumstances into the definition).

- However, if the mischief rule was used then we can see the similarity with the case of *Smith v Hughes* (prostitutes soliciting from a first floor balcony) – Eric's conviction is likely to stand under this rule – he is technically in his house but in effect by leaning out of the window he could be said to be in the 'thoroughfare'.

- Similarly use of the purposive approach would mean the conviction would be upheld because the purpose of the Act was to prohibit 'racist, hostile, abusive and provocative singing and chanting' and Eric's behaviour is certainly provocative.

- The conviction would also satisfy the purposes of the EU Directive which the Act was introduced to comply with.

Scenario 4

Freddie runs a portable fast food stand on a piece of waste land 5 kilometres from the Wanderers' football ground in the north of England. Coaches bringing away fans to the ground regularly pull up in a lay-by near to the wasteland for them to buy refreshments. Freddie has been convicted after a fight occurred when Freddie told some fans from a London football club that he should not have to serve them because 'all cockneys are animals and you should get your food from the pet shop in town'. Freddie is appealing.

Answer:

This one has lots of complicating factors. The key difficulties are that: first, Freddie is speaking to the fans rather than singing or chanting as identified as illegal under the Act, although it would be illegal under the Directive, and secondly he is doing so outside of the 2 kilometre limit identified in the Directive, although the Act is less specific. He is also on a piece of waste land when the offence occurs and it is questionable whether this can be classed as a public place in the terms in which the Act is drafted.

- Freddie has not been singing or chanting therefore technically this does not fall under s 1(1). If the literal rule is applied on this point then the conviction will be quashed on appeal.

- This is a point on which the Act fails to give full effect to the Directive. Public policy may dictate that the judges include Freddie's spoken abuse as 'other provocative verbal behaviour' under the broad application of the golden rule, thus conforming with the Directive.

- In any case a judge applying the mischief rule or the purposive approach may look to the Commission reports (extrinsic aid) leading to the Directive and decide that the purpose of the legislation is fulfilled by covering spoken abuse or provocative speech, as well as singing and chanting.

Continued on next page

Continued

- It would obviously be useful here to have another extrinsic aid available, *Hansard*, to see why Parliament chose to legislate only on singing and chanting, and maybe the fact that the Act is this restrictive is down to a drafting error. Obviously this could only apply if the criteria in *Pepper v Hart* are met.

- There is still the problem of fitting Freddie into the definition in s 2(1)(a) which is unlikely as he is not on a 'road, pavement or precinct', and even though a language rule, *ejusdem generis,* might be used here it is unlikely that other similar places would include wasteland which does not appear to conform to the specific words in the list.

- If the literal rule is used his appeal is likely to succeed on this basis.

- However, the *Smith v Hughes* principle may allow the conviction to be upheld under either the mischief rule or the purposive approach.

- The other obvious possibility is (b) 'any building licensed for the purposes of eating food or for the consumption of alcoholic beverages'.

- The problem is whether a portable hot dog stand could satisfy the definition of building.

- It is generally accepted that a building is a permanent structure so under the literal rule the conviction could not stand.

- Also since the word is relatively unambiguous it is unlikely that the golden rule could be applied, unless it was the broad approach for policy reasons.

- However, once more the mischief rule or the purposive approach might allow the conviction to stand, allowing that the judges take the line in the second bullet above on Freddie speaking provocatively rather than singing or chanting.

- The final problem is obviously that the words 'within reasonable proximity of a football ground or on the route to a football ground' are potentially very wide and ambiguous.

- Within the Act it would seem that, using the literal rule, a conviction might succeed where the offence occurred hundreds of miles from the football ground because of the words 'on the route to a football ground'.

- Judges applying the purposive approach may see that this goes well beyond the very strict wording of the Directive and cannot be what Parliament intended.

Scenario 5

Gregory, a Town fan, is appealing against his conviction for singing abusive songs about the number of foreign players in the City team. The song includes verses of racial and personal abuse to named members of the City team. He did this while he was on his way to a match at the City ground and was walking on the platform in an underground railway station which (at the surface) is only 200 metres away from the City ground.

Answer:

Again the situation is not absolutely straightforward. Gregory seems to satisfy s 1(1) in general and is certainly engaging in exactly the behaviour the legislation is seeking to prevent. However he is on the platform in an underground train station so the question is whether he satisfies the definition of public place in s 2(1)(a) and s 2(2).

- In relation to what Gregory is doing, the conviction would clearly stand whatever rule of interpretation is used.

- If the literal rule is used, then Gregory is singing racist and abusive songs – exactly what the Act prohibits.

- There is no need for the golden rule to be applied as there is no ambiguity and using the literal rule would not lead to an absurd result.

Continued on next page

Continued

- Both the mischief rule and the purposive approach would also lead to a conviction since what Gregory is doing is the 'mischief' that the Act was intended to remedy and prohibiting such behaviour is the clear purpose of the Act.

- The key question then is to decide whether or not Gregory is in a public place as defined in s 2(1).

- Again the most likely is 2(1)(a) 'any public thoroughfare'.

- Again we have to examine the definition of 'public thoroughfare' given in s 4, the interpretation section – 'any road, pavement, precinct or other similar place along, over or through which vehicles or pedestrians pass'.

- We can apply the same principles as we did in Eric's situation in Scenario 3 and Freddie's in Scenario 4.

- If a strict literal interpretation of s 2(2) is used then there can be no conviction – Gregory is not in a public thoroughfare as defined in s 2(2).

- However, if we apply either the broad application of the golden rule for public policy reasons, or the mischief rule or the purposive approach, then upholding the conviction should be possible.

- Clearly once again we have to look to the EU legislation to see that the simple definition given there is much broader than that drafted into the Act.

Scenario 6

Henry and 17 members of his staff or members of their families have all been convicted under the Act. Henry manages a call centre, which is not open to the public and which is 100 metres from the Borough football ground. Many of the staff, including Henry, are Borough supporters and on match days Henry allows them to park in the company's car park. They were convicted following a recent match against Athletic when they chanted abusive anti-Athletic chants from the company car park at passing Athletic supporters. Henry believes that they should not have been convicted.

Answers:

Henry seems to have a point. While what they were clearly doing was prohibited under s 1(1), s 2(1)(b) and s 4 need to be examined carefully. Nevertheless, this is a reasonably simple and straightforward one to finish with:

- Subject to the definition of public place, s 1(1) appears to be satisfied under any of the rules.

- The question then is whether Henry and the others who were convicted engaged in abusive chanting in a public place.

- A very strict literal application of the words of s 2(1)(b), 'car park or coach park open to the public' indicates that the company car park is not a place that the public has access to and is therefore not a public place. Such an interpretation would not be unlike that in *Whiteley v Chappel* so there is precedent for such strict but apparently unrealistic application of the rule.

- Moreover, s 4 states that the Act does not apply to 'business premises not open to the general public' so again applying the literal rule, there is no way that the convictions could stand.

- The words 'open to the public' and 'not open to the general public' are plain and clear with no ambiguity so the narrow approach of the golden rule could not be used.

- However, Henry and his colleagues are doing exactly what the EU and UK legislation were seeking to prevent – antagonising the Athletic supporters – so to apply the literal rule would lead to an absurd result and so a purposive approach is far more acceptable in the circumstances.

- Taking a policy stance under the broad approach to the golden rule, applying the mischief rule or the purposive approach are all likely to ensure that the convictions stand.

Chapter 9

Answers to Activity on page 181:

Example of a structure for the project 'Due to the enactment of the Human Rights Act 1998 over 10 years ago it can be said that Parliament is no longer sovereign.'

Abstract – 200 words

Consideration of the impact of the HRA 1998 on domestic law with a focus on how Parliamentary sovereignty has been affected, if at all. Will look at why the HRA 1998 was introduced; consider the primary provisions, s 3, 4 and 6 and their effects and the courts' interpretation of them. Consideration of relevant areas of law (e.g. evidence) and conclude.

Introductory Chapter – 1000 words

Explanation of what is to be discussed in the project. The state of the law pre-HRA 1998 and how Parliamentary sovereignty works. The effect of the enactment of the HRA on Parliamentary sovereignty. Consideration of cases pre- and post- and concluding on how, if at all, the will of Parliament has been affected.

Chapter 1 Why do we have the HRA 1998? – 1500 words

Why was the HRA 1998 enacted by Parliament? Discussion of the historical development of the HRA 1998 with reference to the ratification of the ECHR in 1950 by the UK and the fact that cases with human rights issues couldn't be dealt with in the domestic courts. Prohibitive time and cost of a referral to the ECtHR.

Chapter 2 How the HRA 1998 works – 1500 words

Consideration of the s 3 provisions and requiring legislation to be compatible 'so far as it is possible to do so' with the ECHR. With particular focus on the meaning of the words in the quotes. Does this mean that the courts (s 6) are required to misapply Acts of Parliament if they are deemed as not compatible? Consideration of s 4 and how often and when used.

Chapter 3 How the HRA 1998 works in practice – 1500 words

A detailed evaluation of the cases pre-HRA and post-HRA and how the courts use the law in practice. Look at cases such as *Mendoza*, *Sheldrake* and *Kebilene* etc.

Chapter 4 Should we get rid of the HRA 1998? – 1500 words

If the will of Parliament is no longer supreme should the HRA 1998 be repealed? Discussion of what alternatives there would be to achieve the aims of the HRA but ensuring that the will of Parliament is not diluted. Would this be an acceptable and desirable route to take? Look at academic commentary.

Conclusion – 1000 words

Conclude as to whether or not Parliament is still sovereign and whether or not the previous assessment has lead to the finding that the HRA 1998 should be replaced. If so, with what? How should the law then be reformed? Answer the question raised in the Abstract.

Example of a structure for the project "Is there still a place for the proverbial reasonable man within the criminal law?'

Abstract – 200 words

Who is the reasonable man? By what standards is he 'reasonable'? Is he the same person throughout the criminal law? A consideration of the different reasonable 'men' who appear in different areas of the criminal law.

Introductory Chapter – 1000 words

An overview of the project. Why do we have the reasonable man? Who is he? Why 'the man on the Clapham omnibus'? A consideration of the different reasonable men found within the criminal law and with a conclusion as to whether he should be retired or retained.

Chapter 1 Where can we find the Reasonable Man? – 1500 words

An evaluation of the different areas of law which feature the concept of the reasonable man such as theft, criminal damage, murder, involuntary manslaughter, duress etc. Consideration if the man is the same man throughout these areas and if there are differences what are these? He tends to make an appearance in the more serious offences – is this right?

Chapter 2 The Objective Young Female Man – 1500 words

Discussion as how the courts have adapted the reasonable man with a consideration of different cases and the inclusion of certain characteristics individual to the defendant. *Camplin, Smith Morgan, Alhuwahlia, Thornton, Elliott v C, G, Church, Howe, Hegarty, Horne, Bowen, Ghosh* etc.

Chapter 3 The Robin Hood phenomenon – 1500 words

A more in-depth look at the problems with requiring a jury to decide on who the reasonable man is and the fact that this will depend on the individual jurors in a case. Different jurors could result in different results on the same fact. Consideration of ECHR implications.

Conclusion – 1000 words

Conclude on whether the reasonable man is or is not appropriate in the modern day criminal law. Should there be one standard or not? If he needs retiring comments on how he should be replaced.

Chapter 10

Answers to the Activity on page 192:

Each counsel would argue as follows:

- Lead counsel for the appellant is arguing that death in law does not occur upon initial diagnosis of brain stem death.
- Lead counsel for the respondent is arguing that death in law does occur upon initial diagnosis of brain stem death.
- Junior counsel for the appellant is arguing that the withdrawal of treatment from patients in a persistent vegetative state with a direct intention to kill and not solely in the patient's best interests is not permissible in law.
- Junior counsel for the respondent is arguing that the withdrawal of treatment from patients in a persistent vegetative state with a direct intention to kill and not solely in the patient's best interests is permissible in law.

Chapter 12

Answers to the Activity on page 235:

Question 1 – 30 minutes

Question 2 – 24 minutes

Question 3 – 6 minutes

Question 4 – 4 minutes

Question 5 – 14 minutes

Question 6 – 18 minutes

Question 7 – 24 minutes.

Answers to the Activity on page 236:

1. The question requires a consideration of the law relating to non-fatal offences and the issue of consent. The answer should consider the leading authority in this area, *Brown*, and explain what principle this case provides – that a person cannot consent where actual bodily harm is intended and/or caused. Discussion should then focus on how appropriate this principle is in modern society with reference to the exceptions set out to this rule in *Brown*. Evaluation of cases such as *Emmett*, *Wilson*, *Slingsby* etc. would be expected before then considering the case of *Dica* and providing evaluation as to where this case now leaves things.

2. The question requires an analytical evaluation of the composition of the judiciary and so answers should consider who the judiciary is primarily comprised of. Consideration of relevant statistical information could be used to show the average composition of the judiciary, with particular focus on age and ethnic background. Reference to academic commentary would also be expected. Students would then need to consider whether a judiciary so composed is fit for purpose and what issues could arise with a judiciary that is predominately too white, middle class and old. Discussion of the role of the Judicial Appointments Commission and its aim to readdress the imbalance in the judiciary should also be present.

Glossary

Abstract
a summary of the contents in a dissertation

Academic journals
published journals including articles based on research and developing academic debate on specific areas

Adjectival law
refers to the processes and procedures governing the trial of legal disputes in court

Adjudication
the decision-making process of a system of courts

Adversarial
a legal contest between two parties in dispute where a judge (or in criminal law a jury) independently decides the outcome

Advocacy
the act of pleading or arguing in favour of something, such as a cause, idea, or policy

Arbitration
a non-court legal process for deciding the outcome of certain disputes – will involve an arbitrator, usually decided on by both sides prior to the action, and reach decisions by which both sides are bound

Assessment criteria
a hierarchical structure of performance descriptions which determine marks in a piece of assessment

Authorities
legal authority may be found in sources such as legislation, case law, government papers and academic writings etc.

Bail
the process whereby a person charged with a criminal offence is released pending trial possibly with conditions attached – can be granted by police and by magistrates

Bar
the strand or organisation of the legal profession to which barristers belong

Bench
the panel of judges in a courtroom

Bills
prospective legislation under consideration by Parliament which, if passed, will become Acts

Brief
the legal documents or case file relating to a particular case

Burden of proof
the rule identifying the person who has to prove the case i.e. the usual rule is 'he who accuses must prove' – so would be the prosecution in criminal law and the claimant in a civil action

By-laws
a type of delegated legislation usually introduced by local authorities, but sometimes by corporate or other statutory bodies – given to those bodies to introduce because they have specialist knowledge

Case books
published resources incorporating abridged or sometimes adapted extracts from decided judgments from the law reports

Case citations
shorthand references to locate full text versions of case judgments. Case citations usually include the year of reporting, volume number, abbreviation for the law report series and the page number

Case head note
this is a case summary detailing both the outline facts and decision of the case. A head note should never be relied upon as authority.

Case law
broadly defined as law made from the published decisions of judges in courts of law

Civil liability
the law regulating disputes between individuals either about their behaviour or agreements made between them

Codification
a system of law based on a single written document or series of inter-linked documents

Conciliation
a non-court legal process where an independent conciliator advises both parties how to resolve their dispute but cannot make a decision that is binding on them

Contents pages
the list at the start of a textbook which includes the chapter headings, sub-headings and possibly sub-sub-headings

Delegated legislation
statutory rules other than Acts of Parliament – enforceable because the body

introducing them has been given authority by Parliament to introduce them

Dissertation

a form of assessment which is based on individual research by the student

Equity

a system of rules which is supplementary but usually superior to other rules and which is aimed at producing fairness between the parties – the rules have become formalised over the centuries

Essay

a form of assessment which requires the student to analyse or evaluate through discussion in extended writing

Grammar

a system of rules for the creation of structured writing

Index

a table at the back of a book which divides alphabetically key words or phrases that can be found in the book and which identifies the pages on which they can be found

Injunctions

orders made by courts which usually are aimed at preventing a party from doing something which would interfere with the other party's rights

Inquisitorial

a legal action where the judge can ask questions of the parties

Judgment

what a judge has written about a case – includes the decision; the principles deciding the case (*ratio decidendi*); and other comment (*obiter dicta*)

Jurisdiction

the area or country covered by a particular body of rules

Law reports

recognised and authorised transcripts of the judgments of decided cases – the main ones are The Law Reports (AC, QBD, Fam and Ch); the Weekly Law Reports (WLR); and the All England Reports (All ER)

Lecture

an educational activity with a lecturer providing information in a formal setting

Legislation

broadly defined as law made by Parliament

Literal approach

the interpretation of legislation by reference to the literal meaning of the words in question

Mediation

a non-court legal process where an independent mediator helps both parties to reach a solution to their dispute but cannot make suggestions to them and does not reach any binding decisions about the dispute

Mind maps

a revision aid incorporating key words into a visual chart

Moot

a mock appeal where students research and then argue the application of relevant law in the appeal

Mooting

to discuss or debate

Moot point

a point open to argument

Obiter dicta

judicial commentary made in passing which does not form part of the *ratio decidendi*

Orders in Council

a form of delegated legislation made by the Privy Council usually in times of emergency

Paginate

to organise notes or other resources into a sequenced system of page numbers

Persuasive precedent

a source of law that the courts can consult in deciding a case but are not bound to apply in reaching its conclusion

Precedent

a process whereby in a present case a court is bound by the principles created in judgments of decided cases in higher courts in a strict hierarchy of courts (or are sometimes bound by courts equal in status or by themselves)

Primary legislation

law made directly by Parliament, and published as Acts of Parliament

Primary sources

in law these are authorised copies of statutory materials such as Acts and delegated legislation; decided judgments of cases in the law reports, and also EU Treaties and subordinate legislation

Problem

a form of assessment which requires the student to apply legal principles to factual situations to reach reasoned conclusions

Public law

those areas of law where the state is a party to the dispute e.g. criminal law, administrative law

Purposive approach

the interpretation of legislation by reference to the purpose of the legislation

Ratio decidendi

the judicial reasoning for the decision in a case. The *ratio* may be binding on future decisions depending on the court hierarchy

Rescission

an order made by a court which puts both parties back to a previous position – usually used in contracts where the order puts the parties back to the position that they were in before the contract was made

Research

the process of independent study and learning through examination of primary and secondary sources

Revision

the process of consolidating knowledge already learnt in preparation for assessment, usually examinations

Revision aids

prepared resources collected or made by the student that help to consolidate knowledge already learnt

Scan reading

reading quickly through pages of a written document or resource looking for useful key words or phrases

Secondary legislation

law made by organisations to whom Parliament has delegated authority, and published as Statutory Instruments. May also be referred to as subordinate or delegated legislation

Secondary sources

academic writing about legal issues in journals, textbooks, and other materials

Seminar

a form of educational activity where students have been given a series of questions or activities in advance to prepare and which are then discussed in a formal setting

Skeleton argument

a document summarising what an advocate will say during a legal hearing

Specific performance

an order of the court which makes a party carry out some obligation – usually in contract law

Standard of proof

the level of proof required – beyond a reasonable doubt in a criminal action, on a balance of probabilities in a civil action

Statutory interpretation

a process whereby a judge decides on the meaning of words or phrases in a statutory provision such as an Act or a piece of delegated legislation – occurs when the meaning of the words is in dispute

Study buddy

a system of study with a trusted fellow student sharing tasks of learning

Submission(s)

a summary of the legal argument(s)

Substantive law

actual areas of legal rights and obligations, e.g. contract, torts, criminal etc.

Syntax

the grammatical structure of words to form proper sentences

Thesis

a more formal term for a dissertation or degree-level project

Viva

an oral examination usually connected with a dissertation

Viva Voce

an examination connected by spoken communication

Index